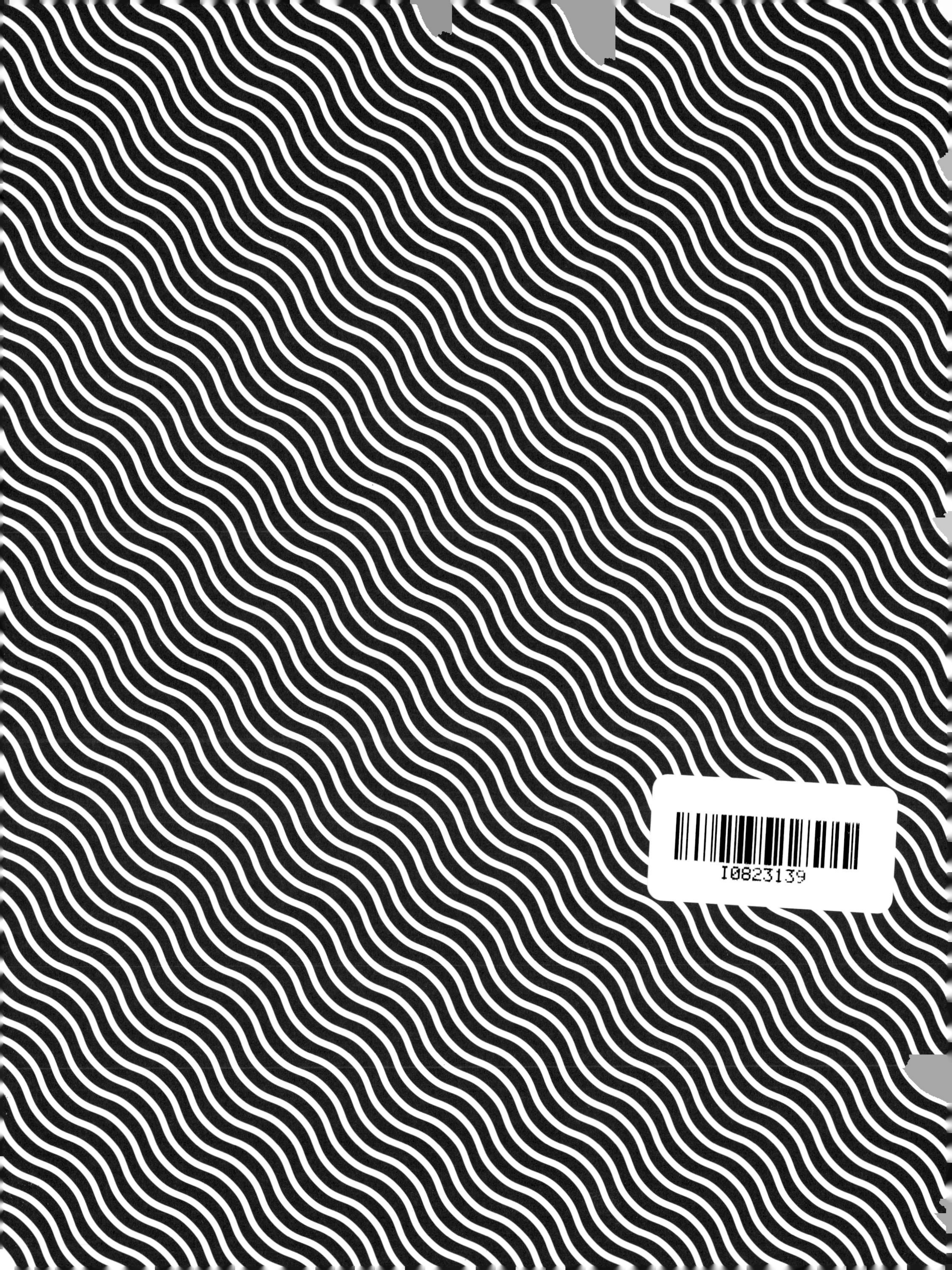
I0823139

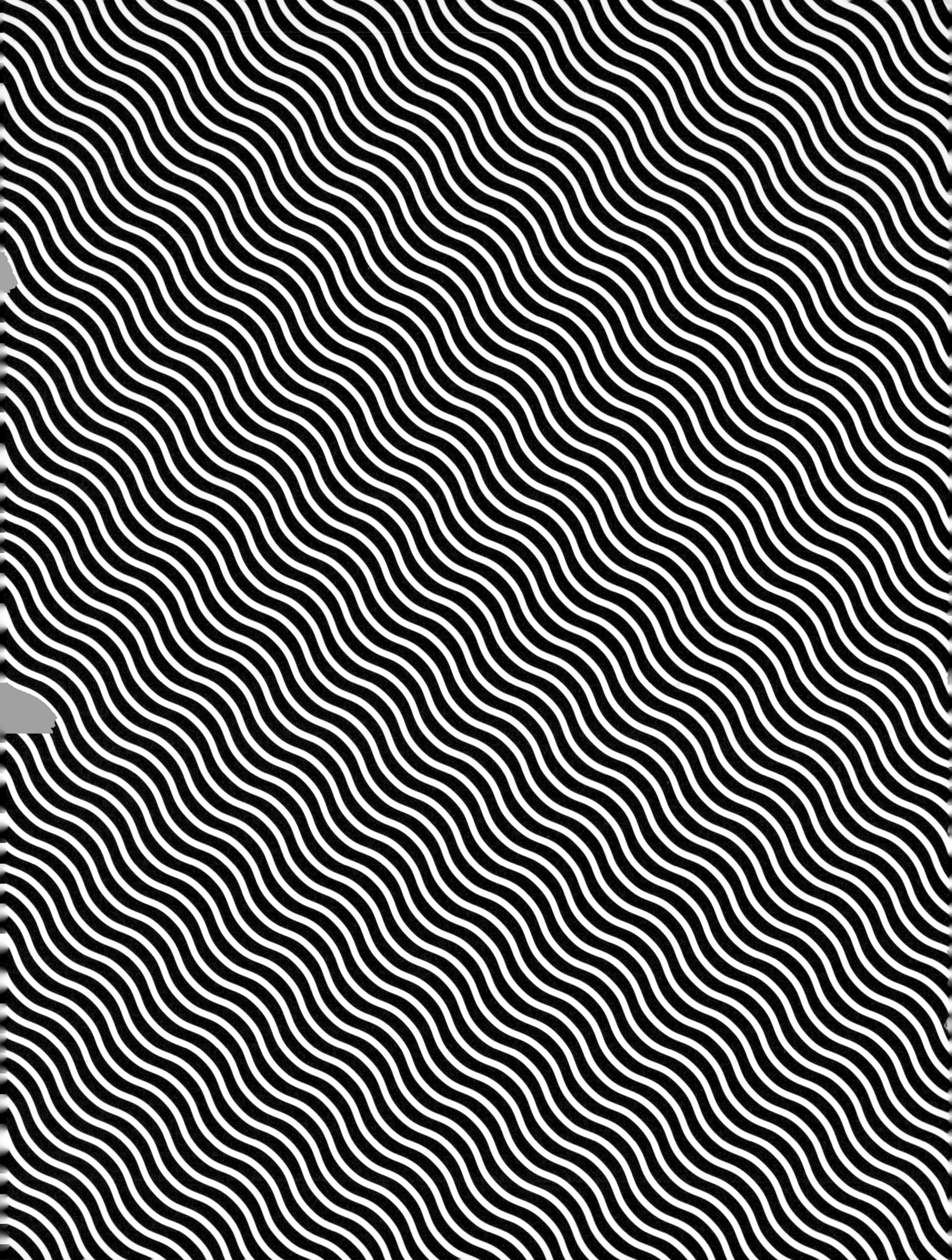

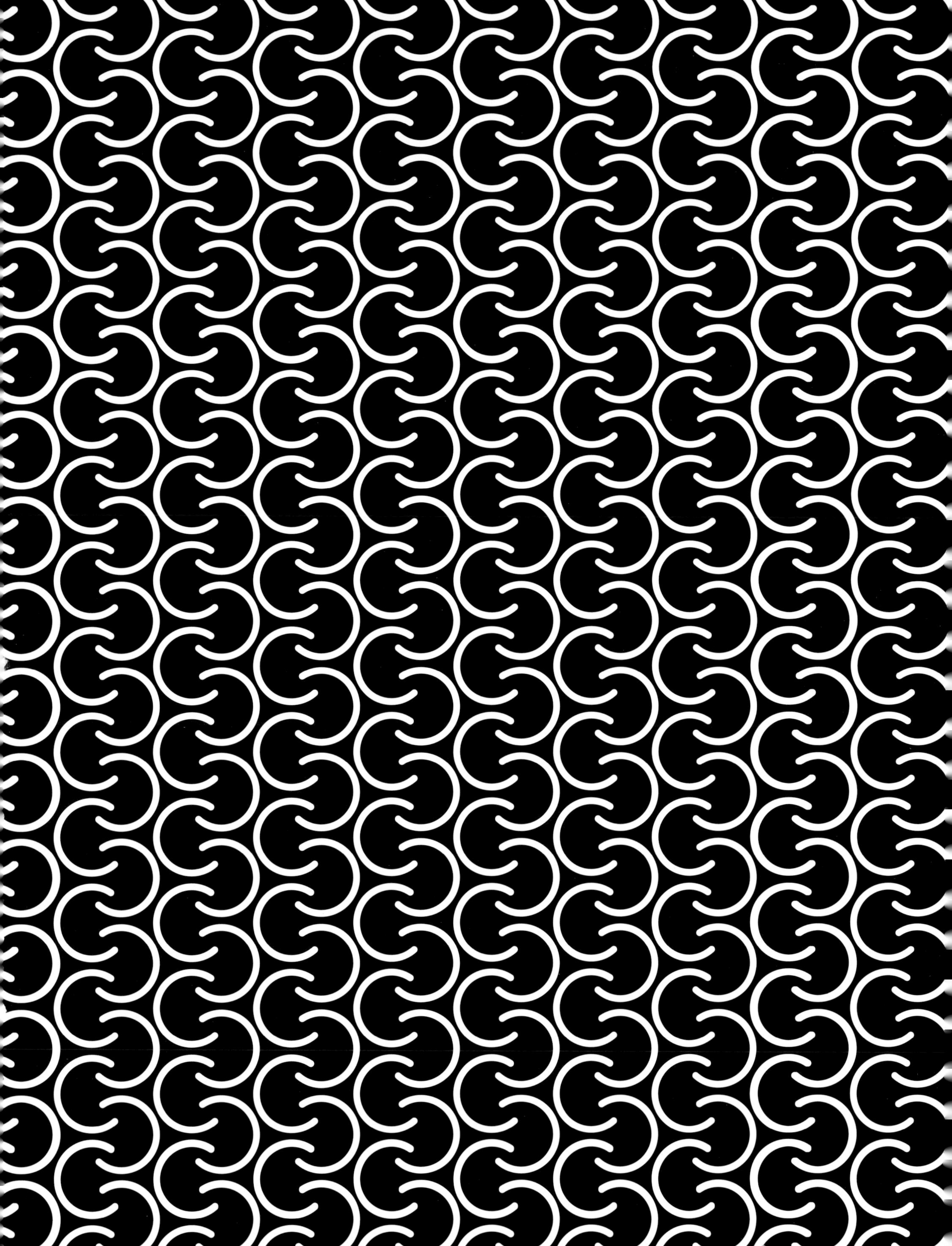

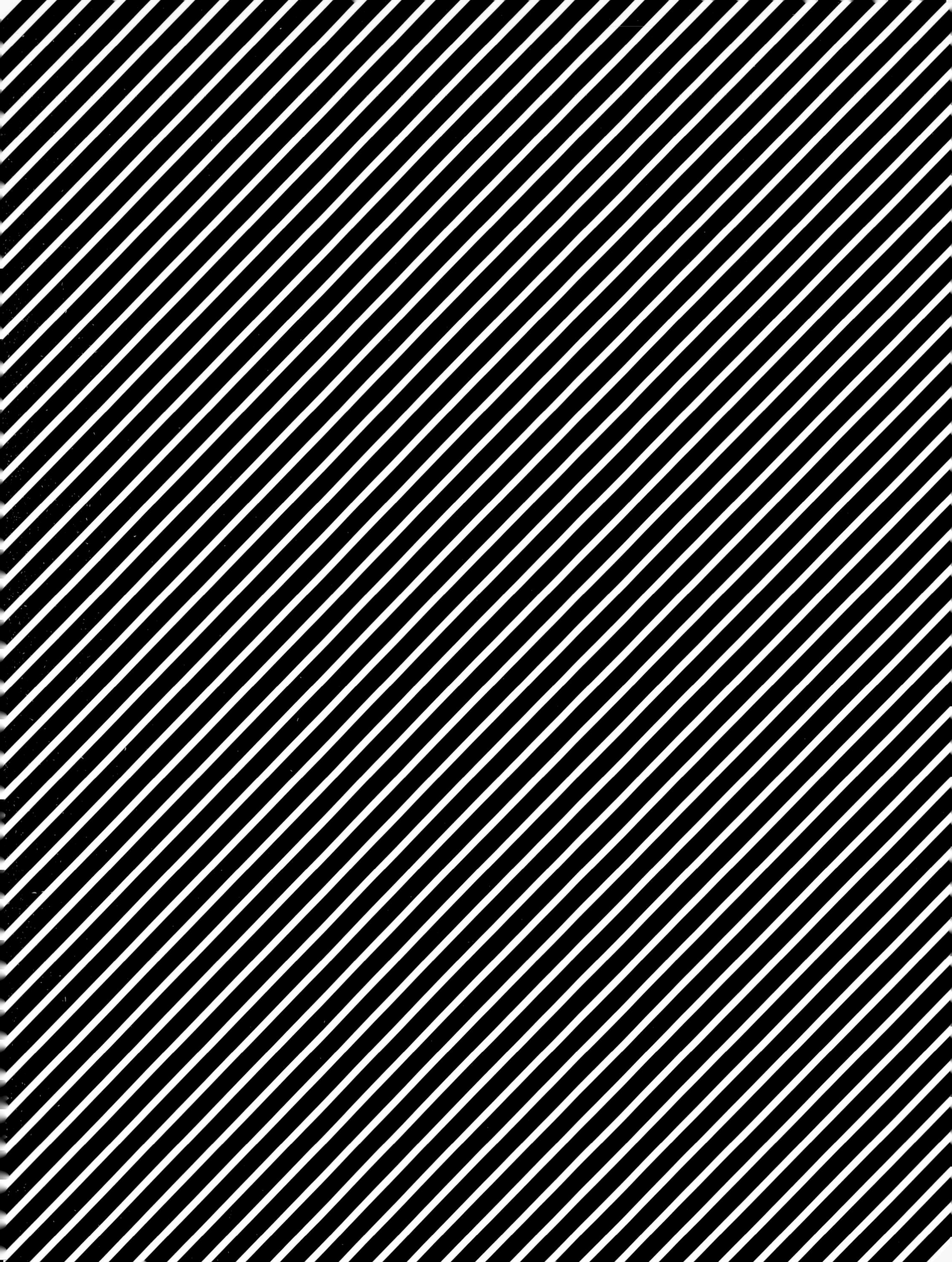

TEXTURES

THE HISTORY AND ART OF BLACK HAIR

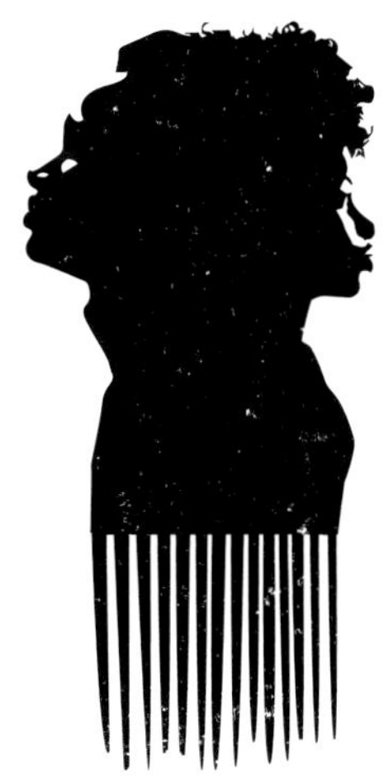

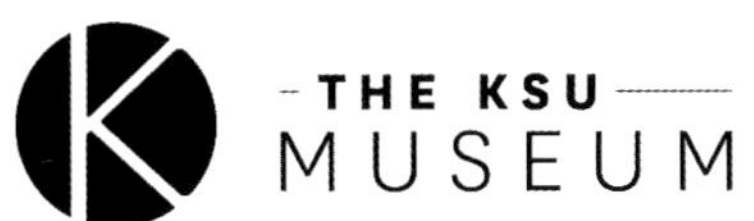

HIRMER

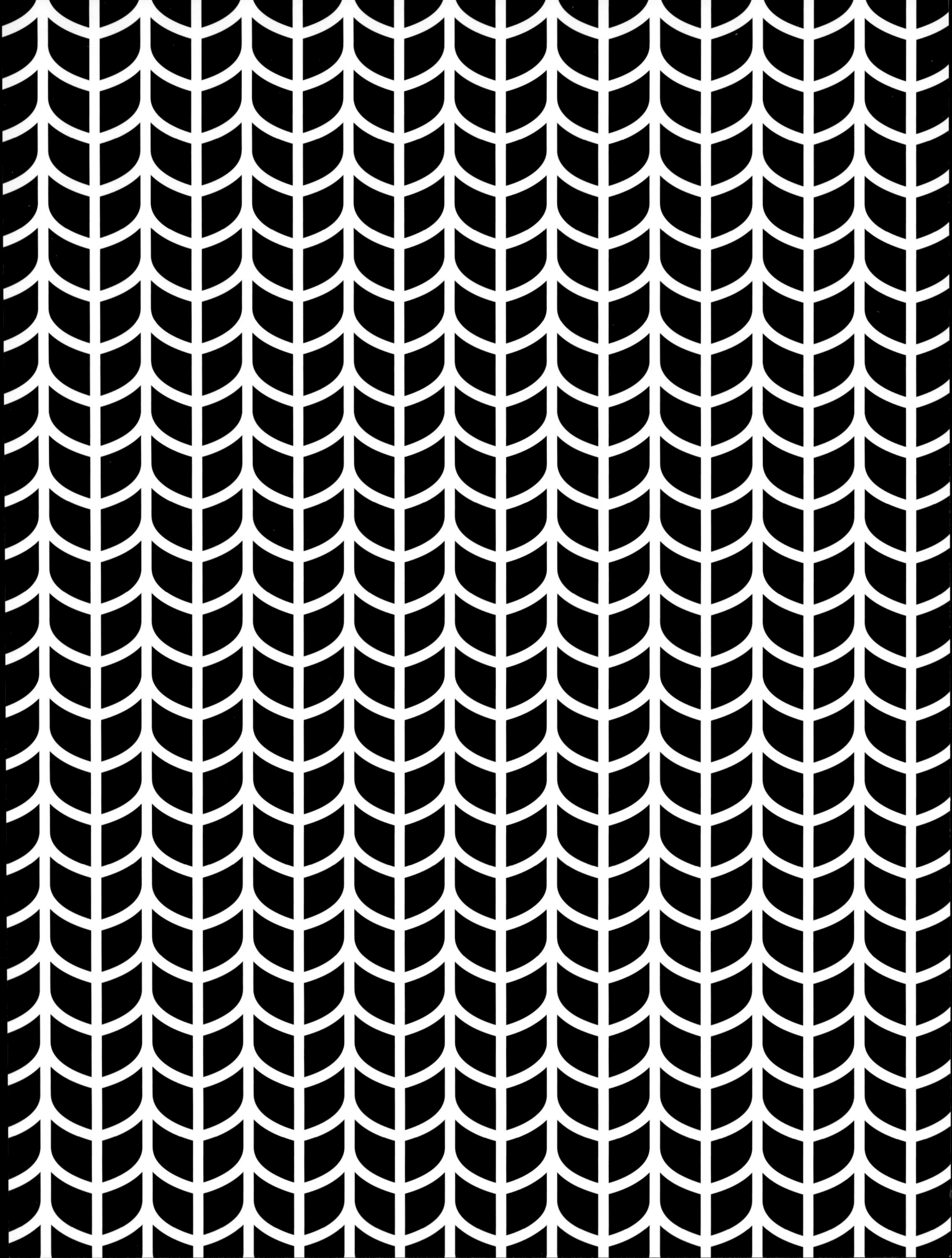

SPONSORS

We are grateful for the support of many who have made this exhibition and publication possible. These include Lead Sponsor Procter & Gamble and Presenting Sponsor L'Oréal. Additional support from the National Endowment for the Arts, the Ohio Arts Council, the Kent State University (KSU) School of Fashion, KSU Divison of Research and Sponsored Programs, KSU College of the Arts, KSU Pan-African Studies, and the KSU Global Understanding Research Initiative (GURI).

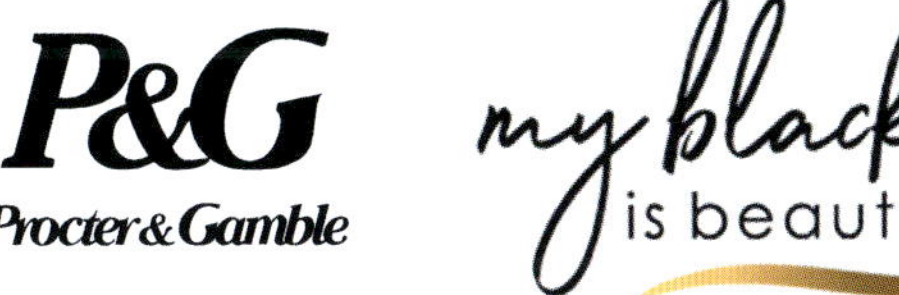

L'ORÉAL

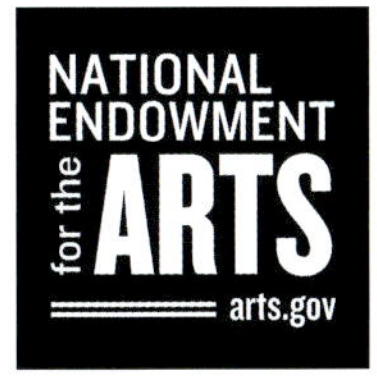

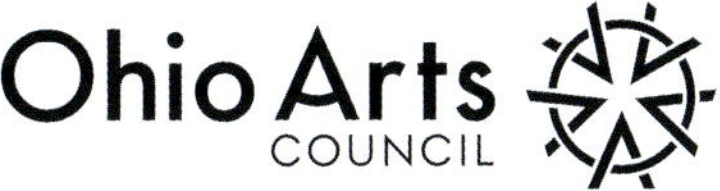

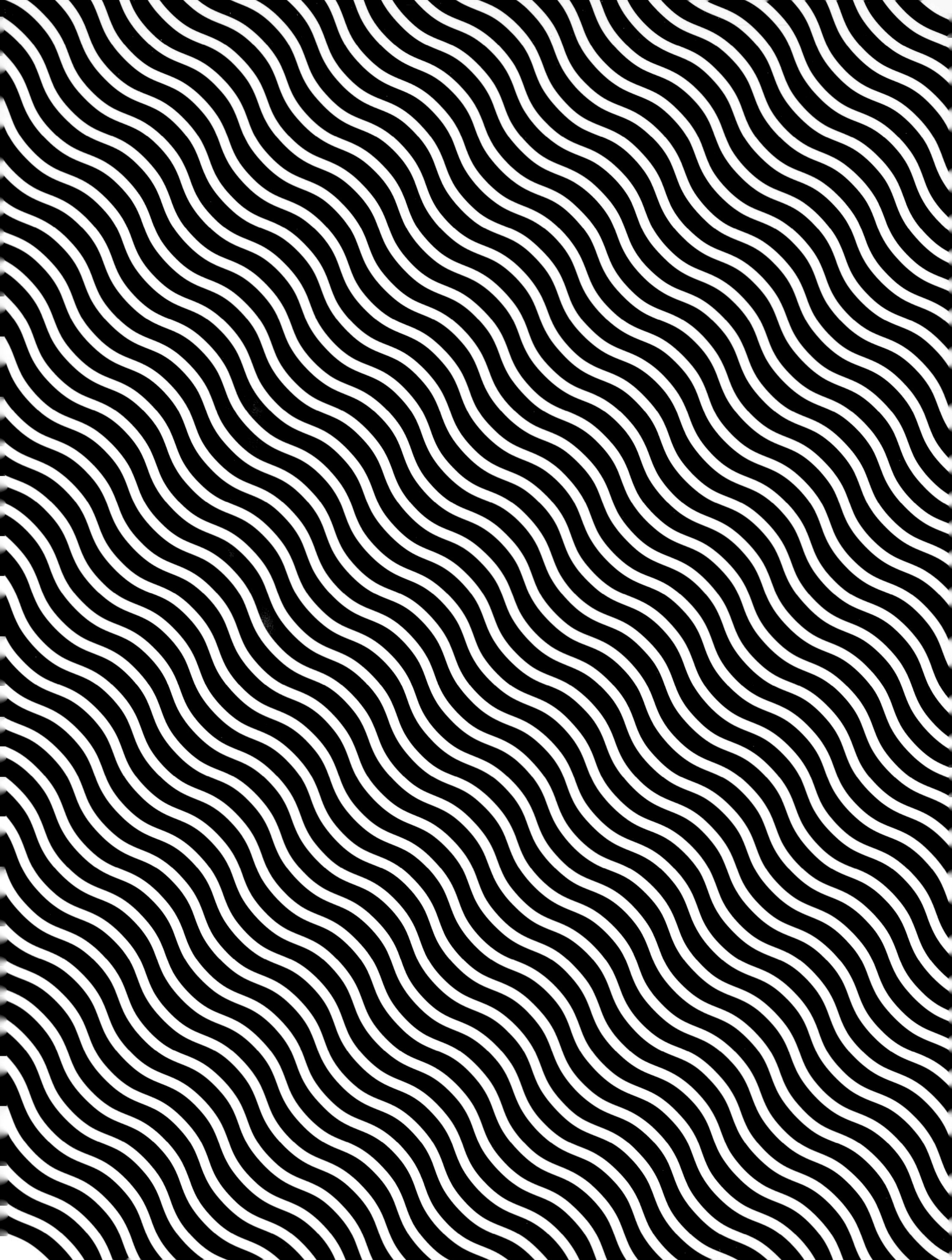

CONTENT

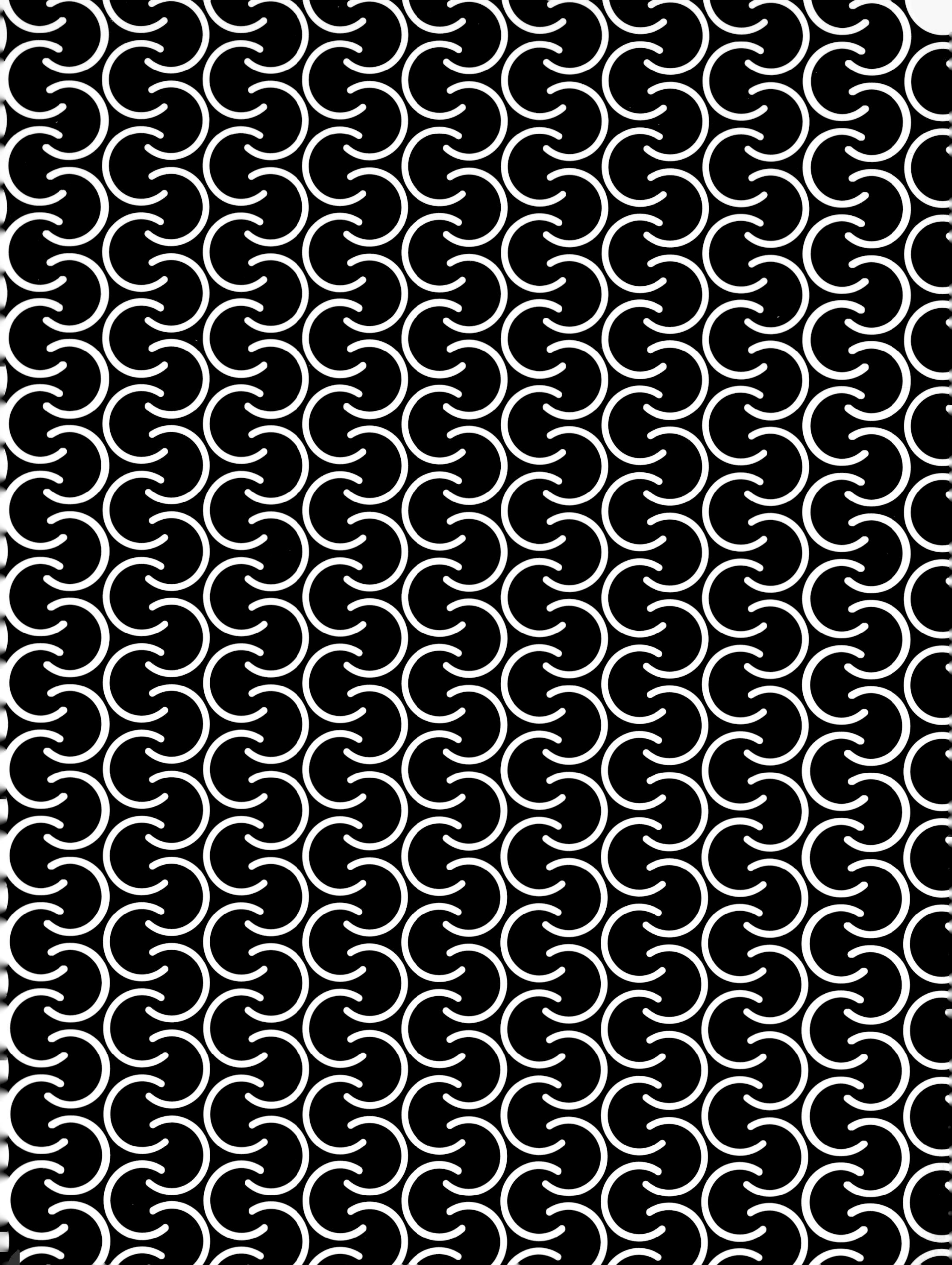

FOREWORD / ACKNOWLEDGEMENTS

The Negro Motorist Green Book, also known as the *Green Book*, was published from 1936 to 1966 as a guide to safe spaces for African Americans as they traveled through segregated America. What began as a directory of hotels and restaurants soon expanded to include local stores and barber shops. The *Green Book* was the vision of Victor Green, a United States postal worker in Harlem, and its first edition focused on New York City and environs. Eventually the guides covered every state. With the Civil Rights Act of 1964, it was expected that the need for such guides would disappear. Fifty-six years later there have been many changes, but racial tensions, inequality, and cultural divides continue. The Black Lives Matter movement is a testament to the need for ongoing discourse and change.

I think of this extraordinary exhibition and publication, *TEXTURES: the history and art of Black hair,* as carrying forward the legacy and the spirit of the *Green Book*, by providing a place to share information and connect around a very basic human fact: hair. Black hair is a source of joy and pride, but also of ruthless stereotypes and racism. It can be a complex, provocative, and contentious issue across communities of color and beyond. *TEXTURES* is an innovative platform for all to better understand the history and currency of Black hair and thus larger issues of race and cultural assumptions as we navigate our journey towards a more equitable future.

Like most great projects, *TEXTURES* grew from long research, scholarly thinking, and dialogues around shared interests, approached from different perspectives. Dr. Tameka Ellington's research during the past decade has focused on issues of what she calls "texturism," or the cultural capital of "good hair" as it intersects with the social hierarchies of colorism. Dr. Joseph Underwood is an art historian of modern and contemporary art whose scholarship focuses on artists of the African continent and the Diaspora. Together, Ellington and Underwood constructed the framework of *TEXTURES* and populated it with the work of contemporary artists, historic items from museums, and the tools of barbers and hair stylists. Both are faculty at Kent State University: Dr. Ellington is Associate Professor in the Fashion School and Interim Assistant Dean in the College of the Arts and Dr.

Underwood is Assistant Professor of Art History in the School of Art. The Kent State University Museum (KSU Museum) is honored to collaborate with these talented co-curators and bring this compelling and timely exhibition to life. Drs. Ellington and Underwood have expertly conceived an innovative platform for meaningful and relevant dialogue. They are to be congratulated for their outstanding work.
TEXTURES is the most ambitious loan exhibition ever organized by the KSU Museum and its small, but mighty, staff. The project required a tremendous level of dedication to manage the infinite details with the artists and lenders over the past year. None of this would have been possible without the meticulous focus of Joanne Fenn, KSU Museum Collections Manager, supported by the student curatorial assistants from the School of Art, Sarah Hagglund, Maria Kuhn, Mark Libbey, Brianna Robinson, Christina Timmons, and Marissa Tiroly. James Williams, KSU Museum Exhibitions Designer, worked closely with the curators to create a stunning installation design that supports their vision. David Hassler, Director of the KSU Wick Poetry Center, Nate Mucha and the team of Each + Every, generously shared their expertise and partnered on the interactive experiences in the exhibition. Additional support from KSU Museum Staff Administrative Assistant, Bianka Hausknecht, and Museum Curator, Sara Hume, was also invaluable. Marshall Shorts of Soulo Theory Creative designed the perfect logo for the project. We were fortunate that Dr. Ellington brought in our community advisors, Ladosha Wright, owner of Wright About Hair in Cleveland, and Carmine Robinson, owner of Transformations Barber & Beauty in Akron, at the beginning of the process to advise and help build relevant programs. Their partnership led to an interview series with other local barbers and cosmetologists which will be featured in interactive story walls. This publication is the KSU Museum's first partnership with Hirmer Verlag and we are grateful to Elisabeth Rochau-Shalem, Rainer Arnold, and designer Sophie Friederich for their care in translating the curatorial vision into this publication.

As always, John Crawford-Spinelli, Dean of KSU's College of the Arts, was an early and enthusiastic supporter of the project as were Marie Bukowski, Director of the School of Art, and Dr. Louise Valentine, Director of the Fashion School. Such ambitious projects depend on the great generosity of many donors and sponsors, including the College of the Arts. Thanks to the efforts of Terry Robertson, KSU's Corporate Relations Officer, and Effie Tsengas, Communications and Marketing Director for the KSU College of the Arts, we were able to engage Lead Sponsor, Procter & Gamble, and Presenting Sponsor, L'Oréal. I am especially grateful to Lela Coffey, P & G's Brand Director, Multicultural Beauty, and to Angela Guy, L'Oréal's Senior Vice President Diversity & Inclusion. Both leaders immediately and enthusiastically embraced the importance of *TEXTURES*.

The exhibition is also made possible with a grant from the Art Works program of the National Endowment for the Arts and ongoing support of the Ohio Arts Council.

The curators created meaning through the vision and voices of many artists past and present who are represented in the exhibition, as well the talented writers who have contributed to this volume. Thank you, Dr. Ingrid Banks, Dr. Afiya Mbilishaka, Zoé Samudzi, and Lori L. Tharps, for your thoughtful words and insights that serve as guideposts along the path. To all the artists and lenders who have graciously agreed to part with their objects for the year-long exhibition, we are most grateful.

Actress CCH Pounder-Koné is an avid collector of work by African and Diasporic artists. We are honored that she collaborated in sharing these artists and their work within the context of global Blackness.

Among the very special objects that tell the *TEXTURES* story are over ninety objects from the collection of Dr. Willie Morrow, an inventor, activist, author, and pioneer in the care of African American hair. Today, at eighty years young, Dr. Morrow continues to remind us that hair, Black hair, is about more than just a style, but is entangled with politics, cultural identity, and self-image. And that is why sharing these Black hair stories matters.

"Hair, in other words, is the basic, natural symbol of the things people are or want to become. The social-cultural significance of hair styles should not be underestimated."
Dr. Willie Morrow, *400 Years Without a Comb*

SARAH J. ROGERS, Director of the Kent State University Museum, has over twenty-five years of curatorial and museum management experience in the visual arts, performing arts, and science center arenas. Her curatorial work focuses on contemporary artists, while her management skills have included strategic planning, capital campaigns, and community partnerships.

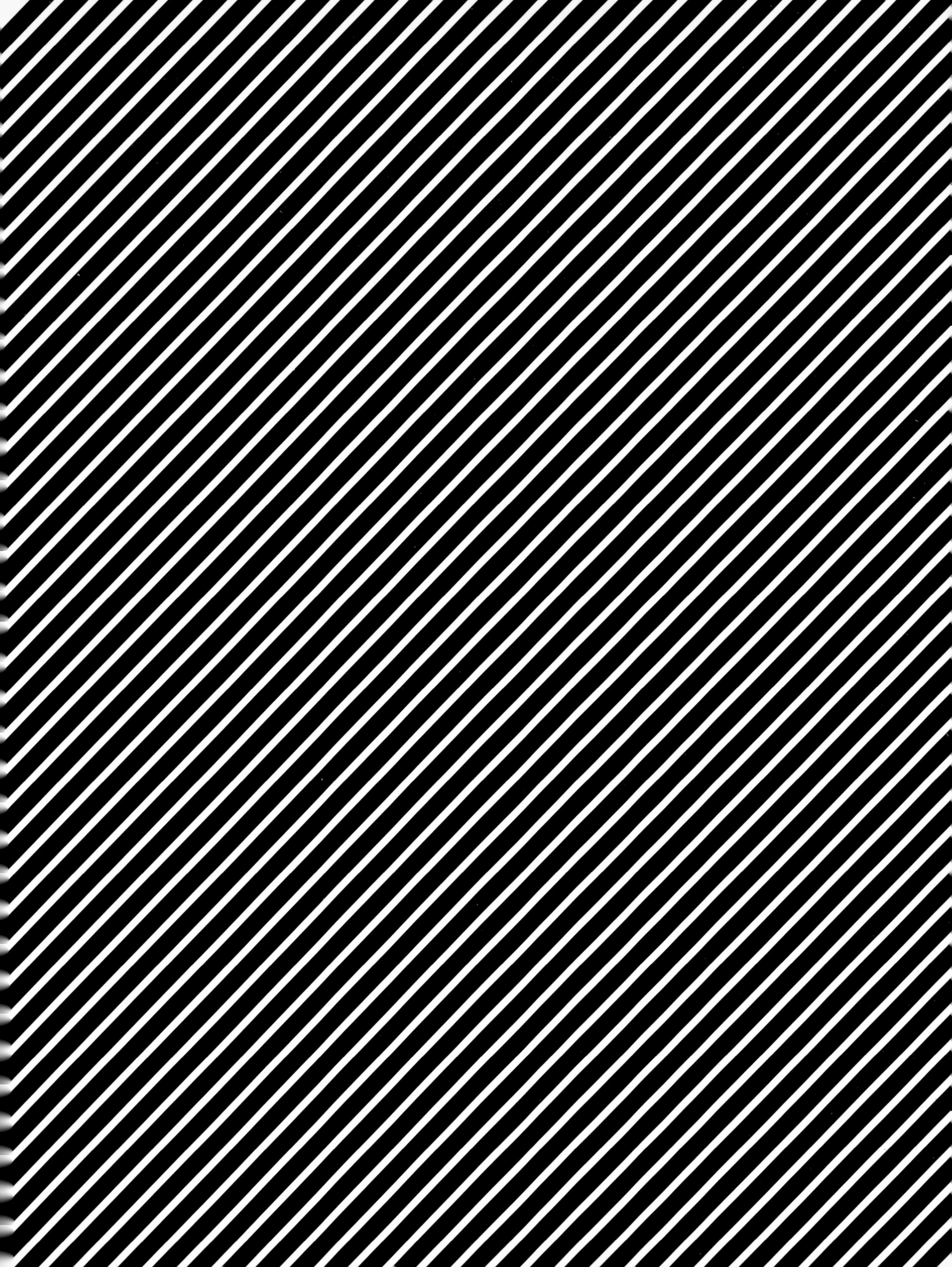

THE CONCEPTION OF TEXTURES: THE HISTORY AND ART OF BLACK HAIR

BY TAMEKA N. ELLINGTON

I woke up startled from a night of restful sleep when I heard my mother standing over my five-year-old body screaming, "My baby's hair!" Only the day before I had been enjoying one of the most fun times in my short little life. After previous days of me and my brother begging and pleading, my mother had finally agreed to take us to the neighborhood swimming pool. The pool was located on DuPont Hill in the inner city of Cleveland and was about a mile away, but the back-way shortcuts shortened the walk by about a quarter mile. And our excitement, running halfway there while our mother hurriedly walked behind, made the trip seem even shorter. That day was my first ever experience of being in a swimming pool.

Most Black people I knew (especially women and girls) did not know how to swim. This fact was due to the long legacy of Jim Crow which prohibited Blacks from visiting public spaces such as local pools and beaches. The actress Dorothy Dandridge was the first known African American to step her foot into a Whites-only pool at a fancy hotel in Las Vegas, Nevada. Management later had the pool drained and scrubbed. More frightful consequences for daring to enter the Whites-only public pool included getting bleach, acid, or nails thrown into the water.[1] So there were good reasons why Black people at that time rarely knew how to swim.

My brother and I played for what seemed like hours at the DuPont Hill pool. Totally exhausted, we walked the mile back home, ate our dinner, and went straight to bed. Unbeknownst to my mother, she had overlooked a crucial step that evening. Since she was never a swimmer, she had no idea that the chemicals in a pool are harmful to your body and hair (particularly hair that had been chemically straightened) and that a bath and good hair washing were required after coming in contact with chlorine. And so that morning I woke up in horror, because all my shoulder-length hair was lying on my pillow in piles, leaving me with hair that was only three or four inches long. For my return to kindergarten the following day, my mom did the best she could to dress my hair in pretty bows and barrettes, so as to obscure the reality that the hair I had on Friday after school was no longer a part of my body on Monday morning. I did not experience a pool again until I was eighteen years of age. I am still a non-swimmer. Hair trauma #1.

As I stood in line to exit my fifth-grade classroom with the rest of my classmates, up walked the cutest boy in the entire grade. All the girls in our class had a crush on him, including me. As he gingerly walked by, I could not help but stare. He must have felt me watching him because he whipped his head around and said, "What are you looking at, Napparoni?" Then he belted out in song, "Napparoni, the San Francisco treat!" lyrics he adapted from the popular television advertisement for Rice-A-Roni. I was mortified, heartbroken, and embarrassed as the rest of my classmates stood there sneering and pointing. That was the first experience when I understood that my level of beauty was not up to par. It was the first time that I was told I had ugly hair. Until then, I only knew that my mom would make comparative references while styling my hair, saying it was not as soft as my sister's, and that she was spending extra time on my "kitchen" (the curliest part of the hair at the nape of the neck). Although she made these comments, never once did she say I was not pretty. Well, this boy took care of that! That incident in fifth grade was the day when I began to develop a complex about my hair. As I got older, that complex grew because I began to realize that girls with certain types of "good" hair (usually long and straight) had privileges I did not. Those girls got to date any boy they wanted and could wear their hair in almost any style they wanted, while I (along with other kinky hair girls), was limited in my choices for boys and hairstyles. Hair trauma #2.

From the late 1980s through the early 1990s I wore a "Leisure Curl," which was just a jazzed-up, less greasy version of the "Jheri Curl" which was popularized in the 1980s. By the early 1990s those wet, curly hairstyles began to slowly fade out of trend. All the girls were switching over from the drippy curl to a straight processed hairstyle: the perm. Some girls had a difficult time with that transition because of hair damage, and even hair loss, as a result of the abrupt change in the chemicals used to manipulate their hair. I was under the naïve impression that my hair could survive because ever since the chlorine incident in kindergarten, it had been pretty healthy. I thought for sure I would not have to experience the trauma of losing hair, but I was wrong. Just like those of other people, my ends started splitting terribly which forced me to cut off half of my hair. Thank God the asymmetrical stacked mushroom haircut had been popularized by the rap duo Salt-N-Pepa, because I was able to save the one side of my hair that was not as badly brittled. Hair trauma #3.

When I was in college in the late 1990s, Black female celebrities like Lauryn Hill and Erykah Badu began wearing their hair in its natural state. I admired these women and their confidence to wear their God-given textures. I explored the idea of wearing my own hair natural as well. I could only make that decision just then because I was no longer under my mother's roof.

In the summer of 1996, I began experimenting with more natural hairstyles—nothing chemically straightened. My go-to hairstyle became a cute curly Afro that I created with tiny perm rod rollers and setting lotion. I loved rocking my Afro, and many others complimented me on how cute I looked in it! Having had so much fun living on my own at school, I extended my independence by getting a job at the amusement park an hour from my house. As a merchandiser in their stores, I lived in the dormitories that the amusement park built for student employees.

The new college recruits went through an intensive all-day training session. Management described all the policies, rules, and regulations about staying on the grounds and working at the amusement park. When they got to the dress code, they brought in samples of the uniforms and discussed expectations for the overall "look" of the employees. They explained that employees were not allowed to wear extensive body piercings, tattoos, or unnatural colored hair dye. Further, employees could not wear Afros, braids, or dreadlocks–the natural hairstyles typically worn by Black people. As this policy was divulged, I was taken aback because, as I sat in that meeting, I was wearing my cute, curly Afro. Their last words were "Employees must look All-American." From that instant, I knew I was not going to endure an entire summer at that amusement park! After one month of employment, I went back home. Hair trauma # 4.

This fourth instance of hair trauma ignited my curiosity for understanding why Black beauty, and more particularly Black hair, was such a point of contention in so many minds and life situations. In 2002, as a graduate student at Michigan State University, I knew there was no other thesis topic that would suit me except studying Black hair. It was the one and only component of my life that had such an impact on the way that I lived, on who I dated, and what employment I decided to take. By the time I enrolled at Michigan State, I had been on my natural hair journey for three and a half years.

The main component of my interview-based research centered on the self-esteem and self-acceptance levels of the participants. The overarching theme in the data was that in order to wear natural hair, a person had to have a heightened level of self-esteem because of the societal stigma regarding Black hair. Many participants talked about friends and family not approving of their natural hair. Women confessed that many of their spouses did not find their natural hair attractive. Participants also revealed that they believed they had been passed over for jobs or promotions because of their choice to wear natural hair. Even after completing my thesis, I still had so many questions about Black hair. Among these was one similar to a question posed by Chris Rock in his documentary, *Good Hair* (2009)–"Why do Black women straighten their hair and wear weaves?"

Many Black women had mixed feelings about Chris Rock's movie, because it exposed too much of the story behind the pain of Black hair.[2] There is a continual gut-punch women feel when asked the controversial question of why they straighten their hair. It has been said that Blacks who do so are not "real" Blacks.[3] As research shows, hair straightening started before the end of slavery as a means of assimilating into White society in order to be considered employable. After slavery was abolished in 1865, Black people did everything they could to survive and better their families. Using harsh lye chemicals to straighten their hair was at the top of the list. Throughout history, Blacks were brainwashed to believe their hair was unacceptable and that the only way to gain acceptance was through assimilation into White culture. Today, straightening our hair is optional so… why continue the tradition of assimilation? April Bey's *Creamy Chris* (p. 125) was created from a photo of Chris Rock which she painted as a clown and finished with a shellacking of creamy hair-straightening mixture over the top. This work was a way to express the artist's disdain for how

Chris Rock ridiculed Black women by making light of a very sensitive subject, and for the way he failed to explain the deep history behind why Black women straighten their hair and wear weaves. Unfortunately, the effects of that brainwashing and pressure to assimilate are still prevalent.

In 2012, I began my trek on the tenure track as an Assistant Professor at Kent State University. As I developed my research inquiry, the topic of Black hair crept back up, along with all the unanswered questions about Black women's sense of beauty and self-worth. I started collecting data through a framework that was much improved from my methods a decade earlier. I really wanted to find out how Black women's perceptions about their hair had changed, as well as their thoughts on society's progressive (or lack thereof) views on Black hair.

Comparative analysis showed that not much had altered besides an increase in the number of Black women who wore their natural hair, and a greater variety in the types of hairstyles (the 2002 group mostly wore dreadlocks). Women still believed that heightened self-esteem was a prerequisite to proudly wearing their natural hair texture. They still talked about the men in their lives taking issue with their hair, although those numbers had somewhat decreased as well. One of the themes that came from this research was the emphasis on quality of life. Black women discussed the fact that their lifestyle was better overall when they wore natural hair. Not having to sacrifice the time and money that it took to create straightened hair was one aspect of this heightened quality of life. Another was the fact that the women felt "free" to move about this world without constantly worrying about their hair. Keturah Ariel's painting *Internal Battle* (p. 115) being recreated into a Pinterest social media meme[4] with an arrow pointing to the straightened side of the girl's hair exclaiming "Before the gym" and then an arrow pointing to the curly side of her hair with "After the gym" is a perfect example of the tension Black women feel about wanting to be more healthy but having to face the aftermath of their straightened hair "going back". This phenomenon is another reason why the majority of Black women do not swim or workout.

Further in my work, I coined the term *texturism*, a sister to the term *colorism* that was first proposed by Alice Walker.[5] Colorism is the ideology that light-skin Blacks are more beautiful, more intelligent, and more civilized. The same goes for texturism in that Black hair was once dehumanized to being called wool[6] instead of hair, thus the straighter (less wool-like) the hair, the more beautiful society claimed it to be. *Battleship 3* (p. 122) by Charly Palmer represents the deprogramming that all Black people must go through in order to learn who they are and the value of their lives. Black women are facing this war internally and externally while trying to maintain a sense of self-worth in their African ancestry and self-acceptance of their own beauty. *Battleship 3* speaks to the juxtaposition of war and love that dominates the Black female essence.

As the years continued on, my desire to more creatively educate others on the topic of Black hair increased. From research to writing, I shed light on issues around Black people's hair and ways of dress. My interview-based research took a turn to content analysis because social media became a safe space for Black women to discuss their hair journeys, to educate and support one another. I published works on social networking sites as a means of support for Black women wearing natural hair.

After several publications, I began envisioning what an exhibition encompassing artwork and artifacts focusing on Black hair could be. Through divine intervention, Dr. Joseph Underwood joined the Art History team at Kent State University. I knew from the moment I met him that he was going to be the perfect partner to help get this concept from my head to paper, and then from paper to real time. He and I began fleshing out the conceptualization of *TEXTURES: the history and art of Black hair* in the fall of 2017. After many ups and downs, grant rejections and sponsorship acceptances, 100+ team conversations and 100+ emails, this exhibition is finally here for ALL to enjoy. Our goal is that our audience walks away with a newfound respect for the humanity of Black people, a clearer understanding of the complicated history of Black hair, and a sense of the deep, deep pride many Black people feel for their African roots. With open minds, we can HEAL as one people.

1 Victoria W. Wolcott, "The Forgotten History of Segregated Swimming Pools and Amusement Parks," *The Conversation*, (July 9, 2019), https://theconversation.com/the-forgotten-history-of-segregated-swimming-pools-and-amusement-parks-119586.
2 Alynda Wheat, "Good 'Hair?' Hardly. How Chris Rock gets it Wrong," *Entertainment Weekly*, https://ew.com/article/2009/10/12/good-hair-hardly-how-chris-rock-gets-it-wrong/.
3 Margo Okazawa-Rey, Tracy Robinson, and Janie Victoria Ward, "Black Women and the Politics of Skin Color and Hair," *Women & Therapy* 6, no. 1 (1987): 89-102.
4 Joanna Mapondera, "How You Can Exercise without Sweating out Your Edges" *Cosmopolitan of South Africa*, https://www.cosmopolitan.co.za/beauty/how-you-can-exercise-without-sweating-out-your-edges/.
5 Alice Walker, "If the Present Looks Like the Past, What Does the Future Look Like?", in *In Search of Our Mothers' Gardens*, ed. Alice Walker, (New York: Houghton Mifflin Harcourt Publishing Company, 1983), 290–312.
6 Shane White and Graham White, "Slave Hair and African American Culture in the Eighteenth and Nineteenth Centuries," *The Journal of Southern History* 61, no. 1 (1995): 45–76.

DR. TAMEKA N. ELLINGTON is an Associate Professor at the Kent State University Fashion School and Interim Assistant Dean for the College of the Arts. Her African-inspired creative scholarship and her publications on the social-psychological aspects of Black hair and dress are internationally awarded and recognized.

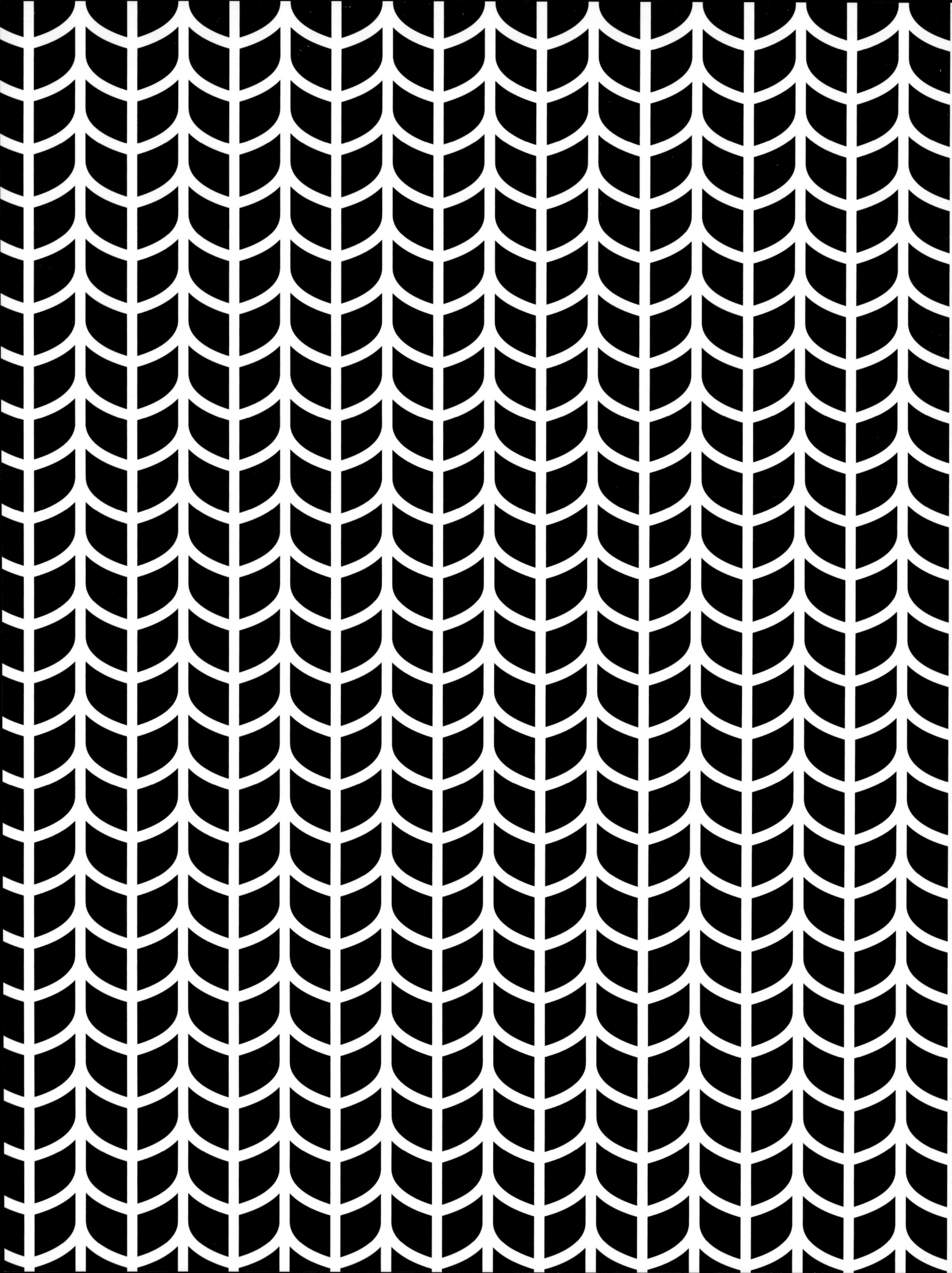

BLACK HAIR IS ...

BY LORI L. THARPS

It is hard to believe that the follicles growing out of the heads of Black people could mean so many things to so many people. But Black hair is complicated. Actually, that's not true. Black hair is not inherently complicated; it became so in the process of removing it from its original birthplace and placing it in hostile territory where people were unable and unwilling to appreciate its greatness.

In fifteenth-century Africa, before the onslaught of European colonization, we know that Africans deeply revered and lovingly cared for their hair, as they believed it was imbued with an untold number of positive attributes. The hair was a source of pride, power, and identity. A general rule across Africa's diverse people groups was that the more status a person had in society, the more elaborate the hairstyle, for both men and women. Intricate, gravity-defying styles would take days to create and would be carefully protected by the wearer with special tools and furnishings meant to keep the head elevated at all times, even in sleep. Hairstyles were chosen based on a person's family, ethnic group, and station in life, therefore providing a visual marker of belonging for every person in the community. In Hector Acebes' photographs (p. 94–95) of a Fulani woman in Guinea and a Maasai man in Tanzania, we can see examples of these unique styles. Though the photographs were taken in 1953, these traditional styles harken back to those worn in previous centuries.

Because the hair rested on the highest elevation of the human body, people believed that it was the vessel where messages from the divine would be received, therefore making the hair all the more sacred, precious, and potent. Records show that in Cameroon the hair was considered so powerful that medicine men would cover their medicinal containers with human hair to add "potency and protection" to their healing potions.[1] In some cultures, a single strand of hair could be used to cast a spell on or bring harm to another person. As an example, in Wolof traditions, women could make men fall in love with them by "calling on the power of the genies and spirits in the hair."[2] Some of these ideas about the hair's connection to a person's spirit, and its perceived magical powers, continue to fuel Black hair superstitions and beliefs today. One common superstition stipulates that a person should always burn the hair in their brush or after a haircut (rather than just throw it away), because someone could use it to put a hex on that person.[3]

So from the beginning of African civilizations the hair wasn't complicated; it was complex. It served several purposes, but above all the hair was a visual marker of a person's identity. Whether chief or servant, warrior or widow, hairstyles conveyed an unspoken message about a person's status in the community and beyond.

And then, brutally, the hairstyles were destroyed. Hacked off. Shaved by slave traders preparing their cargo for travel to the "New World." And *that's* when Black hair became complicated.

BLACK HAIR IS DEMONIZED

From the time Africans were brought to the United States to be enslaved, their hair has stood in the way of assimilation, obedience, and submission. African hair refused to be tamed or subdued, despite the best attempts by Africans themselves to force it into some semblance of European standards of acceptability. The rules regarding the hair of the enslaved Africans were varied. There was no standard across the country. Some slave owners demanded that the women keep their hair covered. Others wanted heads shaved. What was common practice, however, was the ubiquitous demonizing of African hair by the White majority.

Indeed, one of the ways White slave masters justified the violent treatment of their slaves was by classifying them as subhuman, something closer to an animal than a "superior White man." In many written descriptions of Black people made by White people in antebellum America, Black hair was referred to as "wool" or "fur." Slave owners leaned on scientific racism to prove that the features that distinguished Africans from Europeans—their darker skin, their kinky hair, their wider noses—were the things that made them uncivilized and animalistic.[4] They theorized that if Black people felt themselves to be inferior, then they would be less likely to fight for their freedom. Instead, they would learn to hate themselves for not being like their masters.

This brainwashing worked on many Black people, but not all. But more importantly, it didn't work on the hair. Through multiple generations—even mixing with White and Native American—Black hair refused to give up its distinctive kinks and coils. The hair on Black heads refused to submit to the pomades, potions, lye, and heat forced upon it in a desperate attempt to straighten it into an approximation of Whiteness.

Of course, not every enslaved Black person wanted their hair to look like Master's. And the more likely scenario is that most Black people captured in the nightmare of slavery were too busy trying to stay alive or escape to freedom to focus much time on their hair. It was not a constant preoccupation. Nor was the hair universally hated or scorned. Many Black men and women continued to wear braided styles that harkened back to their homelands. In addition, while there are no official records to prove it, oral histories throughout the Americas suggest that some braided styles, like cornrows (or canerows in the Caribbean where slaves were used to plant sugar cane), were used to embed secret codes and maps for those fleeing slavery. The hair was also used to hide and/or transport seeds that were then grown in the slaves' own gardens.[5] So, even in the face of unfathomable odds, Black hair continued to be a useful tool and cultural touchstone that allowed Black people to survive this darkest period of our past.

BLACK HAIR IS A SOURCE OF ECONOMIC EMPOWERMENT

After the American Civil War, Black people collectively had to find new ways to make a living. Hair provided an expansive opportunity. Initially, Black men and women found financial success cutting and styling the hair of White people. This made sense as White people had the disposable income that allowed them to pay others for these types of treatments.

But by the turn of the twentieth century when a Black middle class started to emerge, industries began to cater for them. The beauty and barbering industries were leaders amongst them. The legend of Madam C. J. Walker is well known. Walker, the daughter of former slaves, founded her own hair care products empire that included beauty schools and salons. Black women could sell Madam Walker's products door-to-door to other Black women and/or become a licensed stylist in one of Walker's salons. Walker provided economic freedom to thousands of Black women in the United States and the Caribbean. She instilled a sense of pride in Black women regarding their hair, something that had been missing for some three hundred years. Walker preached a message of liberation from the past. She sold her products by telling Black women they deserved to look and feel beautiful.

Walker wasn't alone. There were dozens of other Black-owned companies at this time, catering to the beauty and tonsorial needs of Black Americans. Thanks to the impressive financial success of people like Madam Walker, Annie Turnbo Malone, and Sarah Spencer Washington, the Black hair care business was an example of an industry that did not require the participation of White America in order to flourish. Moreover, the success of these businesses led to the success of the Black community, because the hair care entrepreneurs would funnel a portion of their profits directly back into the community, building schools, colleges, theaters, and community centers. It was a precedent that would carry on well into the twenty-first century.

But the enormous success of the Black hair care business indicated an underlying trauma in the Black community. A legacy of slavery and the Middle Passage, Black hair in its natural state continued to be demonized. Respectability politics was the name of the game, and a head full of shiny, straight hair was about more than aspirational beauty ideals; it was an entry ticket into mainstream society. Without it, doors were closed and tightly locked. What's more, without straightened hair one might be deemed uncivilized, uncouth, or ignorant by one's own family and friends. Sadly, these hair rules were upheld not only by White America, but by Black America as well, if not more so. Black employers, social groups, educational institutions, and even churches, all had spoken and unspoken requirements for the hair.

BLACK HAIR IS POLITICIZED

Despite the fact that the early twentieth century saw a proliferation of hair straightening for both men and women in the Black community, there were always outliers who argued that straightening the hair and lightening the skin were just some of the many ways White people had taught Black people to hate themselves and therefore keep them too preoccupied to fight for real equality and justice. However, by the time the Civil Rights movement was in full swing there were many more Black people who felt the same way. It was time to stop straightening the hair in order to assimilate. It was time to stop pretending that respectability politics worked. It was time to acknowledge that even with the straightest hair possible, a Black woman still couldn't walk into a restaurant and expect to be served. A Black man still couldn't walk down the street and not fear he would be attacked by the police for a crime he didn't commit.

So in large numbers Black people stopped straightening their hair. Of course not every Black person in America embraced the Afro, but enough did to create a movement. And that Afro said a lot in its bountiful, haloed grace. The Afro, like ancestral African hairstyles, was a visual marker that provided an unspoken message of defiance, rebellion, and, in some ways, surrender. Black people were surrendering to the truth. The truth that said Black hair in its natural state grew up and out and did not need to be attacked with heat and chemicals on a regular basis in order for the wearer to be deemed acceptable in polite society. The Afro told White America that Black people were done, literally and figuratively, making themselves smaller in order to claim their seat at the proverbial table. The Afro, therefore, became a clear symbol of the Civil Rights movement and of radical Black behavior. Indeed, because of her impressive, gravity-defying Afro, Angela Davis is often invoked as the poster child for the movement. Witness the *FBI Wanted Poster for Angela Davis* (p. 121) to see a popular image that, intentionally or not, played a part in linking the Afro to criminal behavior.

Even today, almost sixty years after the height of the Civil Rights movement, the Afro is still deemed a rebellious hairstyle. It still conveys unspoken messages of defiance. But defiance of what? And who is interpreting the messages? Black hair became overtly politicized in the 1950s and 1960s (although some would argue it has been politicized since 1619) and it has remained as such, despite attempts to challenge the idea that an Afro in the twenty-first century does not carry the same meaning as it did in the 1960s. Despite the fact that Afros—and by extension braids, dreadlocks, twists, and other natural styles—have gone so mainstream that White and Asian people have co-opted the styles. Despite the fact that Afros and other natural styles have origins and cultural context that can mean something other than defiance, like a spiritual connection to the Creator, or a desire to have a chemical-free hairstyle that connects with one's green lifestyle. Black hair is still political today and probably will be for years to come as long as the hair on Black people's heads continues to be misread by persons in power and utilized to restrict their freedoms.

BLACK HAIR IS RESILIENT

Watching a Black high-school wrestler have his dreadlocks hacked off by a White woman was hard to stomach in 2018.[6] Reading a story in 2019 about a TV news broadcaster losing her job because she decided to stop straightening her hair was maddening.[7] One has to wonder why America hasn't been able to reconcile its relationship with Black hair in the four hundred years that we've been here. With our hair! Yes, the natural hair movement of the first decades of the twenty-first century has increased the visibility and acceptability of Black natural hairstyles in the workplace, schools, and everyday society. And yes, the introduction of the CROWN Act—state and city-based legislation that makes discrimination against Black hairstyles illegal in public schools and workplaces—has given Black people some recourse if they are the victims of a hair-based attack.[8] But the news headlines still show that Black men, women, and children continue to be assaulted, attacked, or isolated because they choose to wear their hair in styles that don't conform to a Eurocentric aesthetic.

But Black hair is resilient and Black people even more so. Despite the constant onslaught of negative attention to our hair, Black people continue to innovate and iterate new ways of styling and loving on their crowning glory. From extravagant hair shows to wellness-based hair conferences, the community protects and promotes the beauty of Black hair. What's more, thanks to the democratization of the internet, Black people can counter the negative news and lack of support promulgated by mainstream society about Black hair with their own supportive and inclusive imagery and narratives.

Black hair survived the Middle Passage, slavery, and the terrorism known as Jim Crow's America. Black hair thrives despite America's best attempts to subdue her. Black hair has been our crowning glory, our economic emancipator, and our freedom song. Black hair continues to be our link to Africa, our greatest cultural creation, and a physical reminder of our amazing strength and resilience. Black hair is not complicated. Black hair is everything.

1 Ayana Byrd and Lori Tharps, *Hair Story: Untangling the Roots of Black Hair in America* (New York: St. Martin's, 2014), 5.
2 Byrd and Tharps, *Hair Story*, 4-5.
3 Byrd and Tharps, *Hair Story*, 23.
4 Byrd and Tharps, *Hair Story*, 13-14.
5 Judith Carney, "Seeds of Memory: Botanical Legacies of the African Diaspora," in *African Ethnobotany in the Americas*, eds. John Rashford and Robert Voeks (New York: Springer, 2013), 27-29.
6 Michael Gold and Jeffrey Mays, "Civil Rights Investigation Opened After Black Wrestler Had to Cut His Dreadlocks," *The New York Times*, December 21, 2018, https://www.nytimes.com/2018/12/21/nyregion/andrew-johnson-wrestler-dreadlocks.html
7 Chrissy Callahan, "Brittany Noble Jones was told her Natural Hair was 'unprofessional' and fired," *The Today Show.com*, January 17, 2019, https://www.today.com/style/brittany-noble-was-told-her-natural-hair-was-unprofessional-fired-t146857
8 Mariel Padilla, "New Jersey is Third State to Ban Discrimination Based on Hair," *The New York Times*, December 20, 2019, https://www.nytimes.com/2019/12/20/us/nj-hair-discrimination.html

LORI L. THARPS is a journalist and author. In addition to *Hair Story*, she is the author of the book, *Same Family, Different Colors: Confronting Colorism in America's Diverse Families* (Beacon). She is also the founder and host of the podcast and blog, My American Meltingpot.

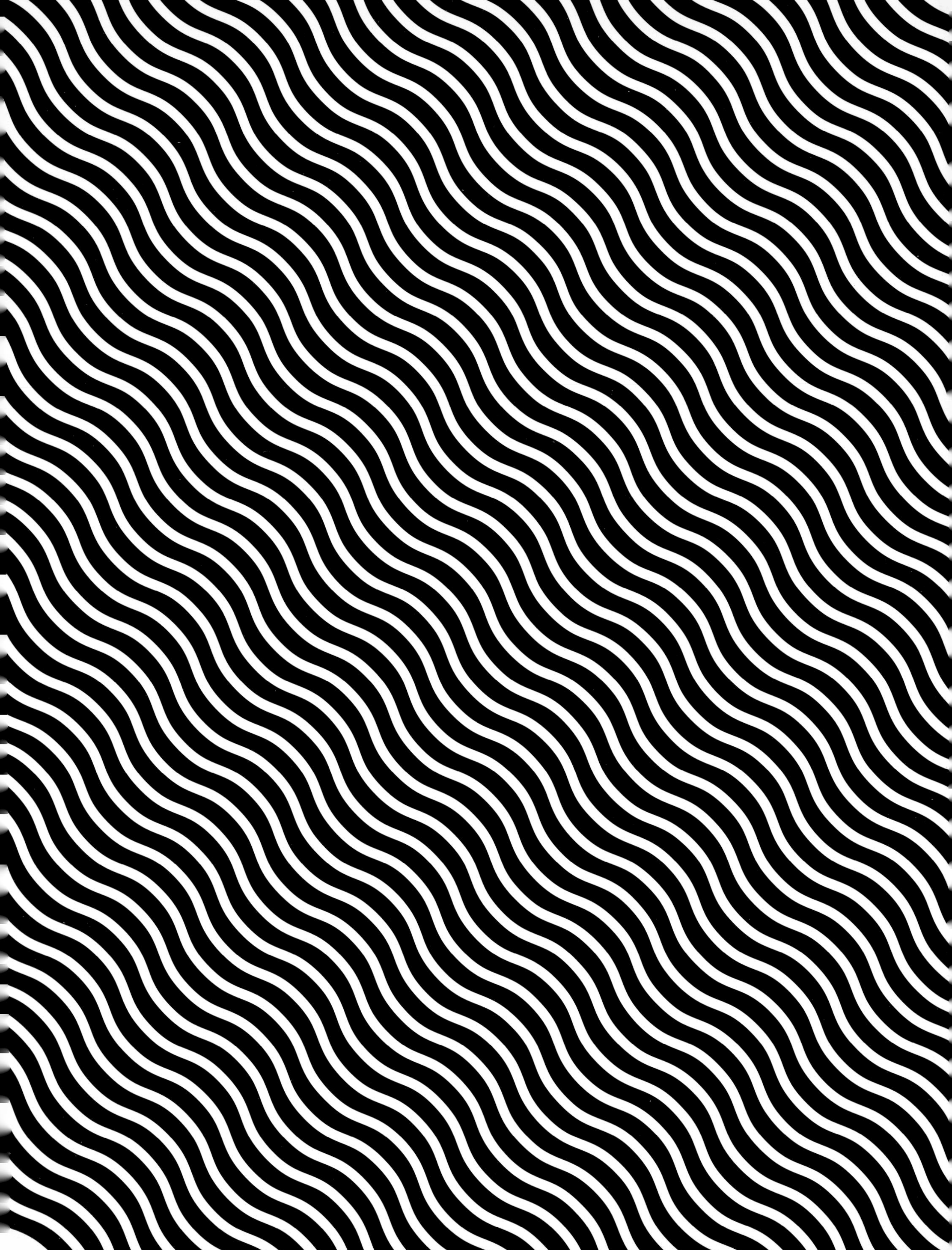

WHOSE STORY IS IT ANYWAY? CONSIDERING KETURAH ARIEL'S *INTERNAL BATTLE* AND BLACK HAIR

BY INGRID BANKS

Keturah Ariel's painting *Internal Battle* might be read as the Black hair equivalent to W. E. B. DuBois's notion of double-consciousness. In his groundbreaking text at the turn of the twentieth century, *The Souls of Black Folk*, DuBois argued: "It is a peculiar sensation, this double-consciousness, this sense of always looking at one's self through the eyes of others, of measuring one's soul by the tape of a world that looks on in amused contempt and pity. One ever feels his two-ness, an American, a Negro; two souls, two thoughts, two unreconciled strivings; two warring ideals in one dark body, whose dogged strength alone keeps it from being torn asunder." DuBois's male-centered rendering of the Black body notwithstanding, the "two warring souls" imaged in Ariel's *Internal Battle* (p. 115) are presented through the lens of a straight vs. natural narrative "in one dark (female) body." *Internal Battle* might also be read as an expression of Black women's free will in choosing to go straight or natural in spite of interracial and intra-racial constructions of beauty that attempt to restrict Black women's choices.[2] Quintessentially, the heart of the struggle lies in how we read *Internal Battle*. To borrow from Kimberlé Williams Crenshaw's query, "whose story is it anyway?" in her brilliant discussion of feminist and antiracist appropriations of Professor Anita Hill's story as a struggle to combat racial *or* gender injustice, the question is whether *Internal Battle* presents a story of double-consciousness *or* free will?[3] Given the weight of Black hair's past and present, the answer is both at once.

Willie Morrow's text, *400 Years Without a Comb*[4], and the Willie Morrow Collection in the exhibition *TEXTURES: the history and art of Black hair* detail the centrality of hair grooming practices among people of African descent across centuries. Hairstyling practices were central in identifying ethnic affiliation, social status, age, gender, etc., within various pre-colonial African societies. Morrow appreciated the cultural, ritual, and aesthetic value and meaning of hair for Africans prior to the transatlantic slave trade. When African bodies were transported across the Atlantic, their enslaved status denied the passage of material items used to groom and adorn hair. However, enslaved Africans carried the memory of their grooming practices across the Atlantic. Being left without the tools and therefore the ability to properly groom hair was yet another manifestation of the oppressive system of slavery denying people of African descent the right to bodily integrity. The Morrow Collection highlights the importance of this history in artistic renderings of picks and combs with carvings of African women, men, and cultural symbols. Curling irons, hand clippers, hair dryers, crimpers, and stoves are descendants of the combs that Morrow understood as central to the adornment and cultural well-being of enslaved Blacks. The *TEXTURES* exhibition places the past squarely in the path of the present. The *Internal Battle* imaged on Ariel's oil and wood is at once part of Morrow's historical narrative and a contemporary tale of Black hair's diasporan struggles, specifically one centering Black women.

Presenting Black hair and hairstyling practices within a "battle" narrative is quite apropos here. Whether during the early part of the twentieth century when Black leaders like Nannie Helen Burroughs chastised beauty culturalists (for example, Madam C. J. Walker) for selling out the race by producing Black hair care products that sent the message to Black women that they needed to straighten their hair to mimic White standards of beauty to be deemed beautiful, or in the battle to reject a Negro (straight) and embrace a Black (Afro) identity in the late 1960s / early 1970s, or in the moment in the 1980s when Black women employees at American Airlines and Hyatt Hotels went to court to demand their right to wear braids, the metaphor of "battle" offers an insightful approach in grappling with the cultural and political significance of hair in Black communities.[5] More recently, Black people have faced repressive actions against their right to wear natural hairstyles at work and school.[6] The groundswell of anti-Black policy targeted at natural hairstyles has led to important anti-discrimination legislation that reinforces Black people's right to retain sovereignty over their hair and hairstyling practices. Once unimaginable, the legislation is quite remarkable, part of an enduring struggle to ban discrimination against Black people, regardless of hairstyle. In February 2019, the New York City Commission on Human Rights passed legislation outlining new legal enforcement that defines discrimination on the basis of natural hair and hairstyles, which disproportionately affect Black people, as unlawful under the New York City Human Rights Law. The protections and enforcement target discrimination in employment, education, and public accommodations.[7] In July 2019, California became the first state to ban discrimination based on natural hairstyles. California State Senator Holly Mitchell introduced the CROWN Act (Senate Bill

No. 188), associating hair as an extension of one's race, and therefore a legally protected category against discrimination. These battles speak to DuBois's "two warring souls," where Black adults are expected to adhere to acceptable hair grooming and hairstyling practices within a mainstream work context, while Black children are held to similar restrictions at school or face punishment. These restrictions invariably embrace Eurocentric beauty ideals that aim to police Black people's appearance to serve White mainstream comfort. Black people may integrate, but the terms of the said integration must adhere to preventing the "Negro" side of double-consciousness from crossing the boundary to the "American" (i.e., White) side. When the boundary demarcating DuBois's "two-ness" is blurred, given the emergence of a post-civil rights early twenty-first century integration in which Black people feel entitled to bring their Blackness to work and school, it is mainstream society that must reconcile the determination by Blacks to reject double-consciousness. Instead of Black people having to reconcile a double-consciousness that emanated from a legally sanctioned segregated society, mainstream White society must face looking at Black people through Blackness—and the qualities of Black hair and hairstyling practices are ground zero in the battle today. Ariel's *Internal Battle* can then be read as representing a centuries long battle that has literally been played out on Black people's heads.

Given these struggles, reading Ariel's *Internal Battle* as also a story of choice becomes even more imperative as a social justice narrative through art. The NYC Commission on Human Rights and the California CROWN Act illustrate that Black people, and Black women in particular, have been denied the right to exercise the fullest extent of free will with regard to hairstyling practices within mainstream contexts. The battle is not simply within the individual as imaged in Ariel's artistic rendering, but within a complex societal matrix that embraces the belief that Black lives do not matter. In addition, the struggle is not simply about natural hairstyles. It is about a Black person's right to wear their hair as they desire, whether to make a statement about identity or simply to embrace style. To read Ariel's image as presenting choice centers an agency that pivots on the various ways that Blackness is presented in hairstyling, whether straight, natural, in between, or on the margins. Even the perplexed expression on the young woman's face reiterates the same double-consciousness that DuBois theorized. We might imagine her look as a battle over making a decision because of the existence of *choice*. Individuals face such decisions every day: what should I wear, what should I eat, where should I go? Having the right to exercise free will is what matters. As such, Ariel's *Internal Battle* may also be read as a story that centers the empowerment that comes with having options and the right to make decisions based on those options. Black people have not always enjoyed bodily sovereignty as both a human and individual right. The right to wear one's hair natural, straight, or in between illustrates the progress that has been made more recently in fighting anti-Black policies that attempt to deny Black people choice. *Internal Battle*, then, is a story about Black people having a positive right, in which the state intervenes through legislation (for example, the CROWN Act) by granting access to the literal and figurative comb once denied with the emergence of the transatlantic slave trade that Morrow chronicles in *400 Years Without a Comb*. Still, state intervention has come as a reaction to Black people exercising a choice to wear natural hairstyles in spite of punitive repercussions. Thus, even when Black people have been systematically denied choice, acts of protest have prevailed in going against the status quo. To be sure, Black people have found ways to exercise free will in the face of repressive policies that threaten Black life, Black liberty, and the pursuit of Black happiness.

In *Internal Battle*, Keturah Ariel magnificently presents a complex story that pivots on both DuBois's double-consciousness and free will. To read the work as simply a story of double-consciousness denies the existence and insurgent nature of Black agency. To read the work as simply a story of free will denies the very real existence of anti-Black practices that New York City and California now deem illegal. The importance and timely aspects of the *TEXTURES* exhibition illuminate how the cultural production of art intersects with the long arc of social justice labor (cue the *FBI Wanted Poster for Angela Davis*, p. 121) that Black people have engaged in for centuries. Black people's hair and hairstyling practices remain key sites for institutionalizing anti-Blackness, as well as Black people's right to embrace the diverse beauties and identities that make Blackness so rich. Whose story is it anyway? Regarding Black people's relationship to hair and hairstyling practices, the answer lies in a story that resists a reductionist narrative.

DR. INGRID BANKS is Associate Professor and Chair in the Department of Black Studies at the University of California, Santa Barbara. Her research areas include race, gender, culture, beauty, Black popular culture, black feminist theory, politics of the body, critical race theory, and ethnographic methods. She is the author of *Hair Matters: Beauty, Power, and Black Women's Consciousness* (New York University Press, 2000).

1 W. E. Burghardt Du Bois, *The Souls of Black Folks: Essays and Sketches* (Chicago: A. C. McClurg & Co Publishing, 1903).
2 See Maxine Craig, "The Decline and Fall of the Conk; or, How to Read a Process." *Fashion Theory: The Journal of Dress, Body & Culture* 1 no. 4 (1997): 339-420, and Robin D. G. Kelley "Nap Time: Historicizing the Afro." *Fashion Theory: The Journal of Dress, Body & Culture* 1 no. 4 (1997): 339-351.
3 Kimberlé Williams Crenshaw, "Whose Story is it, Anyway? Feminist and Antiracist Appropriations of Anita Hill." In Toni Morrison, ed., *Race-ing Justice, En-gendering Power: Essays on Anita Hill, Clarence Thomas and the Construction of Social Reality* (New York: Pantheon Books, 1992), 402-440.
4 Willie Morrow, *400 Years Without a Comb* (Black Publishers of San Diego, 1973).
5 See Noliwe Rooks, *Hair Raising: Beauty, Culture, and African American Women*. (New Brunswick, NJ: Rutgers University Press, 1996) and Ingrid Banks, *Hair Matters: Beauty, Power, and Black Women's Consciousness* (New York, New York University Press, 2000); Craig, 1997; Kelley, 1997.
6 The news is riddled with stories like these: "When Black Hair Violates the Dress Code," *NPR.com*, 7/17/17; "US school faces backlash after Black student's 'unnatural hair' criticized," *BBC News*, 8/23/18; "Why Are Black People Still Punished for Their Hair?" *The New York Times*, 8/29/18; "H.S. wrestler forced to cut dreadlocks; viral video stirs questions of whether race was factor," *ESPN.com*, 12/21/18; "When hair breaks rules: Some Black children are getting in trouble for natural hairstyles, 2/23/19; "Black Texas teen told to cut his dreadlocks to walk at graduation," *NBC News*, 1/23/20.
7 Official Press Release, New York City Commission on Civil Rights.

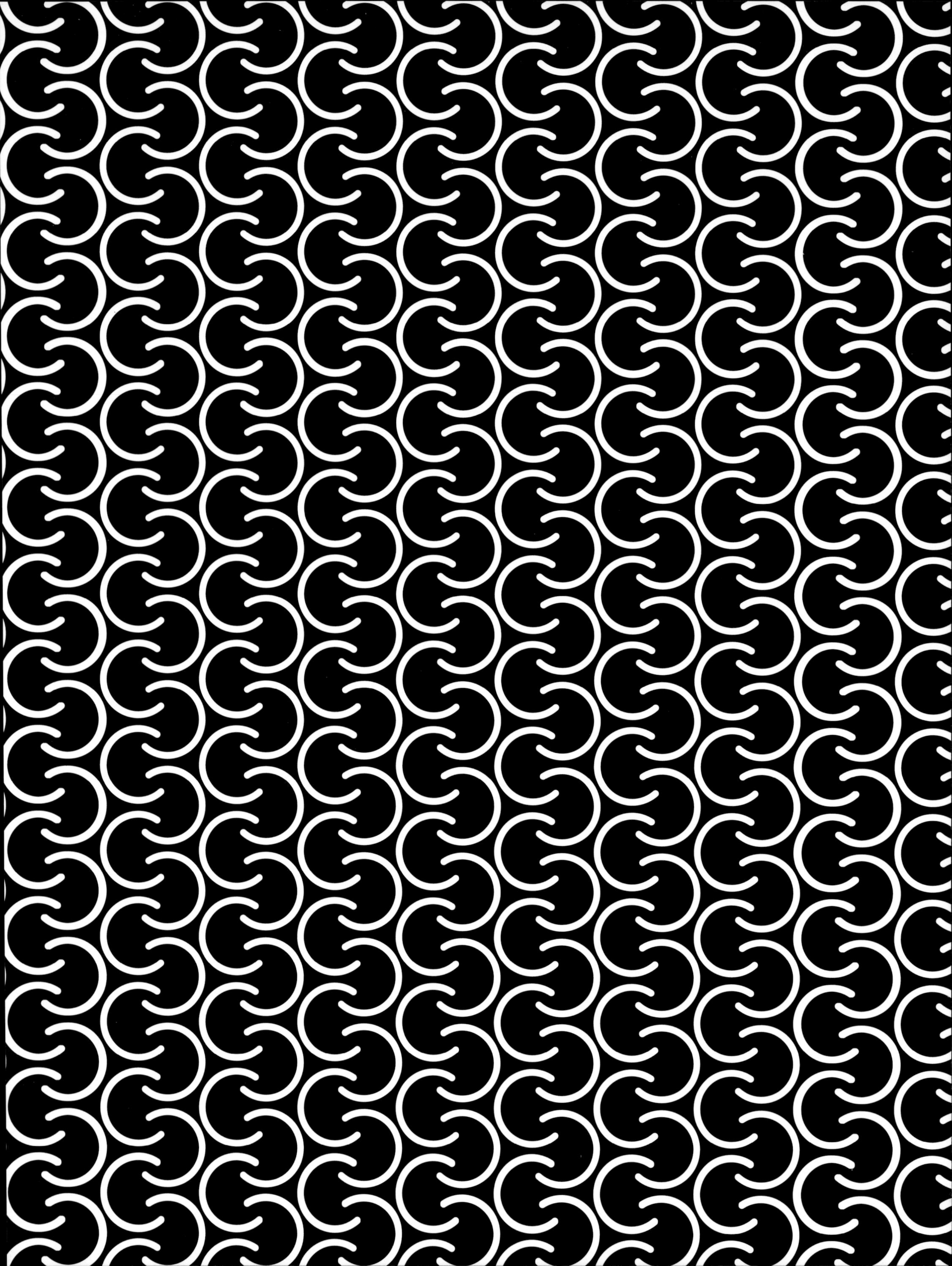

COMBS AND CURLING IRONS: THE PSYCHO-EMOTIONAL TOOLS FOR SHAPING BLACK HAIR TEXTURES AND CULTURAL CONSCIOUSNESS

BY AFIYA MBILISHAKA

The year 2020 is witnessing the second coming of a Natural Hair Movement in America, a movement that emboldens people of African descent to care for their natural hair textures. This movement trails the Black is Beautiful Movement in the 1960s and 1970s, fueled by the Black Power Movement. With a relocation of a cultural identity from "Negro" and "Colored," to "Black" and "African," cohorts of people of African descent repositioned aesthetic preferences away from stretching out hair follicles to letting hair coil. The current Natural Hair Movement surfaced in the late 2000s as a collective attempt to disrupt White beauty ideals of long straight hair and detox hairstyling techniques by removing chemicals to alter Black hair textures. No longer is hair straightening the default grooming technique in mainstream spaces or in the digital world.

Black hair textures range from silky straight to tightly coiled. However, technologies have been developed over millennia to carefully craft coiffures embedded within a cultural consciousness.[5] The focus of curating an exhibition entitled *TEXTURES: the history and art of Black hair* must be grounded in understanding why there is hair texture variation. Hair exists to regulate the temperature of the brain and body. This adaptive system of hair for mammals is what distinguishes our ability to regulate body temperature and maintain a specific temperature in the body system to operate optimally. Humans have a range of hair textures as a response to environmental factors of extreme cold and high heat.[6] In temperate climates, the humans that survived had hair that covered not only the scalp but also the full neck and back. But in arid climates, hair served as a means of protection from the blazing heat of the sun. Thus short coils to ventilate the heat of the head and skull make the hair a useful mechanism in many African regions.[7] These anthropological and phenotypic outcomes are filtered through a cultural lens and meaning making is produced from negotiating hair texture.

Hair texture is psychologically significant and emotionally layered for people across the African Diaspora.[8] It is also a topic that takes up space within Black communities, as evidenced by conversations within hair care spaces, on YouTube tutorials, and in classrooms[9]—a phenomenon reflected in April Bey's *Creamy Chris* (p. 125), a painting covered in hair relaxer that riffs on the fact that Chris Rock's 2009 documentary *Good Hair* largely co-opted styles and techniques that were made popular by Black women on the internet. From the physical to the digital, and from the celebrity to the civilian, there are a multitude of opinions regarding proper treatment of hair textures. Nearly all Black people can recall early childhood memories of hair grooming with their primary caregivers and extended family; memories filled with feelings of rejection or acceptance based on whether their hair texture and length were considered "good" or "bad".[10] So too, romantic relationships are sites of negotiations for Black hair texture and satisfaction.[11] The novice and professional alike need to understand the physical tools that can shape the meaning of Black hair textures.

COMBING THROUGH CULTURE

In traditional African societies, hair texture was utilized to create shared understanding. Hair offered an opportunity to express identity, ethnic group membership, relationship status, fertility, wealth, religion, age, and career.[12] From birth through death, hair was utilized for the purpose of ritual to establish communication between the spiritual and physical world.[13] For example, creating height in hair—like Masa Zodros' *Femme Totem Blue* (p. 158)—offered a closer connection to the heavens and the gods. Specifically, in many West and East African ethnic groups, like the Yoruba and Maasai, new parents shave the hair of their newborn children during the naming ceremony to make a spiritual offering of renewal to the family and ancestors.[14] Upon the start of menses, in many West and North African societies, including the Tuareg and Shai peoples, girls are instructed on how to groom their hair texture in certain styles to communicate that they are now ready for marriage and childbirth.[15]

Our ancestors discovered that highly textured hair can be manipulated like clay. Hair like this can be stretched through pulling, separating, and wrapping. Highly textured hair can actually defy gravity. Therefore combs serve as a critical tool in shaping the texture of Black hair. Combs could create ornate hairstyles that formed art, but they also created art forms of their own. Carved wooden combs had the power to bless someone and heal their illnesses. Combs were powerful tools, using the energy of the stylist or the barber to address spiritual needs.[16] For the Yoruba, every girl is taught how to braid hair, and any girl that is skillful in detangling the hair and making precise parts with the tips of carved wooden combs becomes responsible for the entire community's braids.[17] For the Mende, opening up a conversation about hair combing is an invitation for a deep friendship, because it is understood that properly combing hair is a significant investment of time and emotional energy.[18] For the Akan tradition, Adinkra symbols are carved into the combs, such as the Sankofa bird, which means "to go back and fetch it," implying that descents of Africa can return to their "roots."

SOME LIKE IT HOT: BRIEF HISTORY OF THERMAL HAIR MANIPULATION THROUGH CURLING IRONS

Within the integration of White supremacist thinking forced upon colonized and enslaved Africans, hair straightening became a means of survival during the eighteenth and nineteenth centuries. Scholars have noticed that enslaved Africans particularly benefited from practices of hair straightening, as it afforded them reprieve from the harsh heat of the sun when doing manual labor and offered indoor tasks such as cooking, cleaning, and childcare.[19] Those who naturally had straighter hair texture, or could easily straighten their hair, could acquire the relative social benefits of being a domestic, which resulted in eating higher quality foods and dressing in fairly fashionable clothing.[20] Thermal straightening techniques were developed during plantation life, which could require women to lay their hair flat on an ironing board and have it ironed just like fine cotton or linen clothing.[21] (p. 72) The temperatures far exceeded healthy practices, resulting in burns of the hair, scalp, and skin, permanently damaging hair, causing scars, and even hair loss. Refined techniques in the 1800s included the extension of smaller handles that could be easily gripped and required sectioning of the hair in order to concentrate and regulate the amount of heat on the hair (for example, the steam curling iron [p. 126] from the Willie Morrow Collection). The standard comb was modified in metal form to further isolate hair follicles for the short and highly coiled hair textures (stove with hot comb and three-barrel Marcel curling iron, p. 110). After straightening the hair thermally, further techniques were implemented to offer uniformity or definition (electric wave crimpers and crimpers used on a hot stove, p. 59, 116). With shifts in the use of higher voltage in electric sockets, miniature stoves were developed just for maintaining the heat of the curling iron tool (electric stove with removable irons, p. 117).

PSYCHOLOGICAL OUTCOMES OF TEXTURE OVERMANIPULATION

Psychology, often conceptualized as the scientific study of behavior and mental processes, can be used to interpret the manipulation of Black textures. Simply understood, behaviors that are reinforced/affirmed will recur, and texture manipulation is on high repeat because of direct reinforcement of texture bias. Tight braids and laid edges earn likes on social media and compliments in social settings. When Black hair textures are over-manipulated through combs and curling irons, people may experience hair stress. Hair stress is the result of "harmful physical and psychological effects of hairstyling methods used to transform the hair from its natural state to achieve and maintain an unnatural texture and appearance."[22] Low self-esteem and shame coincide with the emotional and physical labor of overly pulling and stretching Black hair textures.[23]

We need systematic exposure and unpacking of this psychological phenomenon of hair stress. We all need to be texture positive. Exposure to a counter-narrative with evocative imagery has been utilized by the leaders of the Black is Beautiful Movement, current #TeamNatural social media influencers, and

Black parents engaged in protective racial socialization. For example, Ngozi Schommer's self-portrait (p. 167) directs our attention to the positive psychological qualities of self-agency in practicing regular hair care. Psychologists and hair care providers should collaborate to create healthy hair care spaces for Black communities struggling to value their birthright of highly textured hair, offering additional healthy hair care techniques that support the retention of natural Black hair textures and coping strategies that honor the lived experiences of being Black.[24] With psychological interventions to unpack aesthetic trauma, positive images of natural Black hair textures matter.

DR. AFIYA MBILISHAKA is a Hairstylist, Therapist and Assistant Professor of Psychology at the University of the District of Columbia. Her research focuses on traditional African cultural rituals for contemporary holistic mental health practices. Through her work she has developed "PsychoHairapy," where she uses hair as an entry point for mental health services in beauty salons and barbershops, as well as through social media.

1 Ayana Byrd and Lori Tharps, *Hair Story: Untangling the Roots of Black Hair in America* (New York: St. Martin's Press, 2014).
2 Latisha Neil and Afiya M. Mbilishaka, "'Hey Curlfriends!': Hair Care and Self-Care Messaging on YouTube by Black Women Natural Hair Vloggers," *Journal of Black Studies* 50, no. 2 (March 2019): 156-177.
3 Nikki Walton and Ernessa T. Carter, *Better Than Good Hair: The Curly Girl Guide to Healthy, Gorgeous Natural Hair* (New York: Harper Collins, 2013).
4 Daniel Davis, Afiya M. Mbilishaka, and Terrisia Templeton, "From 'About Me' to 'About We': Therapeutic Intentions of Black American Women's Natural Hair Blogs." *Journal of Social Media in Society* 8, no. 1 (2019): 105-123.
5 Willie Morrow, *400 Years Without a Comb: The Untold Story* (San Diego: Black Publishers of San Diego, 1973); Byrd and Tharps.
6 Nina G. Jablonski and George Chaplin, "The Evolution of Skin Pigmentation and Hair Texture in People of African Ancestry." *Dermatologic Clinic* 32, no. 2 (2014): 11-321.
7 Ibid.
8 Afiya M. Mbilishaka, Wilson I.-P., Ray M., Hall J., Hall J. "'No toques mi pelo' (don't touch my hair): decoding Afro-Cuban identity politics through hair," *African and Black Diaspora* 13, no. 1 (2020): 114-126.
9 Afiya M. Mbilishaka and Danielle Apugo. "Brushed aside: African American women's narratives of hair bias in school," *Race Ethnicity and Education* (2020): 1-20.
10 Ingrid-Penelope Wilson, Afiya M. Mbilishaka, and Marva L. Lewis, "'White Folks Ain't Got Hair like Us': African American Mother-Daughter Hair Stories and Racial Socialization," *Women, Gender, and Families of Color* 6, no. 2 (2018): 226-48.
11 Afiya M. Mbilishaka, "Strands of Intimacy: Black Women's Narratives of Hair and Intimate Relationships with Men," *Journal of Black Sexuality and Relationships* 5, no. 1 (2018): 43-61.
12 Byrd and Tharps.
13 Victoria Sherrow, *Encyclopedia of Hair: A Cultural History* (Westport: Greenwood Press, 2006).
14 Ibid.
15 Carol Beckwith and Angela Fisher, *African Ceremonies* (Ann Arbor, MI: Harry Abrams, 1999).
16 Ibid.
17 Byrd and Tharps.
18 Ibid.
19 Morrow.
20 Byrd and Tharps.
21 Morrow.
22 Evelyn B. Winfield-Thomas and Arthur L. Whaley. "Hair Stress: Physical and Mental Health Correlates of African American Women's Hair Care Practices." In *Women and Inequality in the 21st Century*, eds. Brittany C. Slatton and Carla D. Brailey (New York: Routledge, 2019), 159-176. p.162.
23 Winfield-Thomas and Whaley.
24 Mbilishaka, "PsychoHairapy".

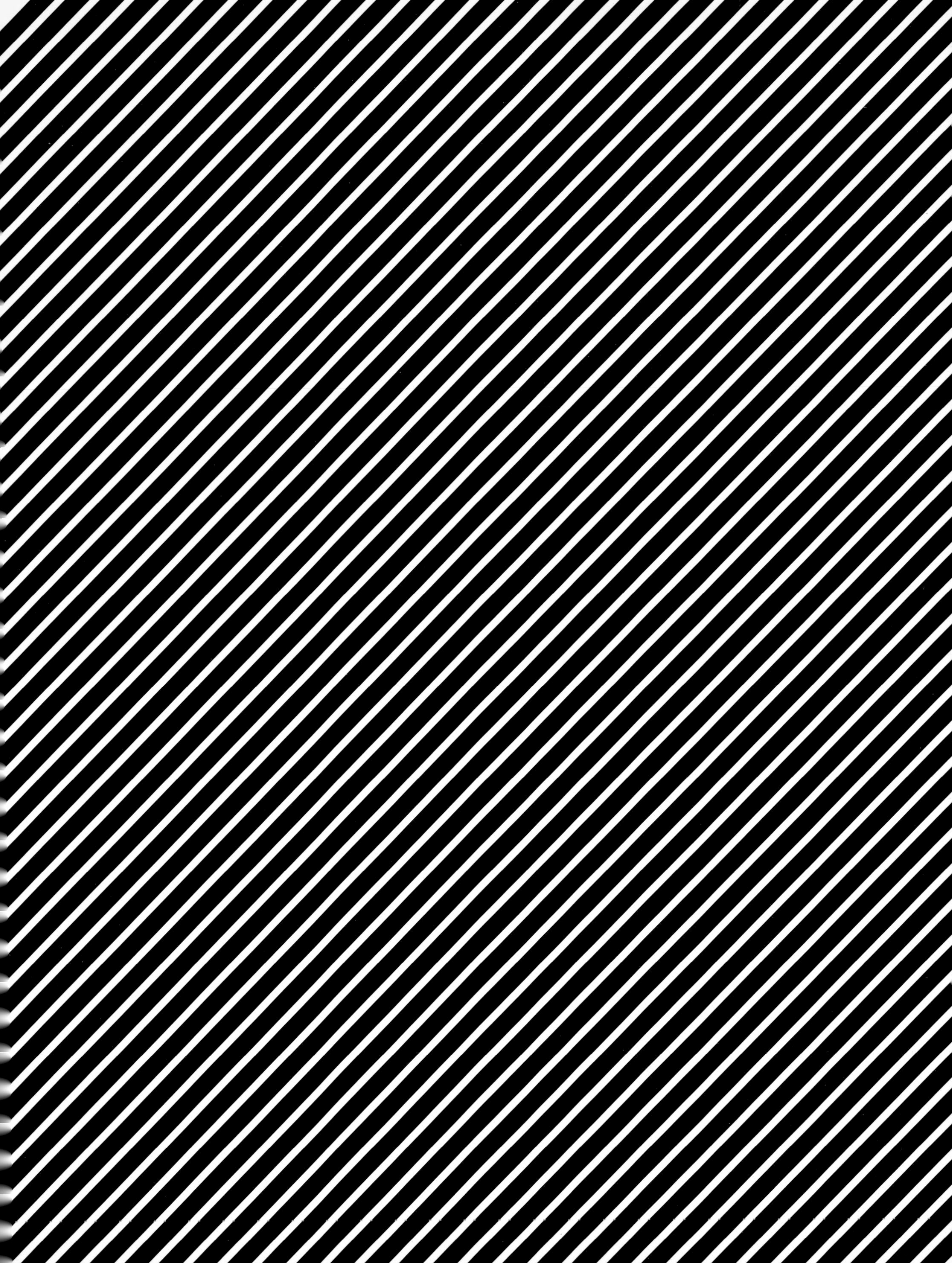

[THE] DEAD MATTER

BY ZOÉ SAMUDZI

I was standing on one side of Independence Avenue in Windhoek, Namibia's Central Business District, waiting for the pedestrian light to change so that I could cross the busy street. While mustering my courage and waiting for an opening in the flow of afternoon traffic in anticipation of the inevitable need to jaywalk, I saw a reddish-tinted woman walking across the street. Her rust-colored, clay-covered locks made her instantly recognizable to me as a Himba. The Himba people are an indigenous pastoralist group from the Kunene Region of northern Namibia and the other side of the Kunene River in southern Angola. It's hot and dry in Windhoek and in so many other parts of Namibia, including the Kunene Region.[1] To protect their skin from the combination of harsh, direct sunlight and a scarce supply of water, the Himba famously cleanse and protect their skin and hair with a pigmented mix of milkfat and red ochre (a naturally occurring earth material composed of ferric oxide, sand, and clay) called *otjize*, which is sometimes mixed with omuzumba (a flowering plant related to frankincense and myrrh) for a rich aromatic quality. Otjize paste is as aesthetic as it is functional. It's evocative of the highest cultural cosmetic standard—the rich hues adorning the skin symbolize life-giving and community-sustaining soil and blood—and it encases the different kinds of decorative plaits that signal a woman's station in life, a beautiful code. (p. 93)

In the introduction to his comprehensive aesthetic survey *On Ugliness* (its twin, conveniently, being *On Beauty*), Umberto Eco laments the fact that although we have cultural artifacts from "archaic civilizations" and "primitive peoples", "we have no theoretical texts to tell us if these were intended to cause aesthetic delight, holy fear, or hilarity."[2] The western canon has an almost incalculable number of primary and secondary instructive sources that direct our understandings of beauty, including beautiful hair, throughout the ages. Eco continues: "To a westerner an African ritual mask might seem hair-raising—while for a native it might represent a benevolent divinity. Conversely, believers in some non-European religion might be disgusted by the image of Christ scourged, bleeding, and humiliated, while this apparent corporeal ugliness might arouse sympathy and emotion in a Christian." He offers a Hegelian approach to beauty, a positing of a mutual illegibility and incomprehensibility, to simultaneously justify this Eurocentricity and circumvent the responsibility to answer exactly how European accounts of beauty and ugliness (and follicular management) became adopted as global truths (largely by force). But in the posthumously published *Lectures on the Philosophy*

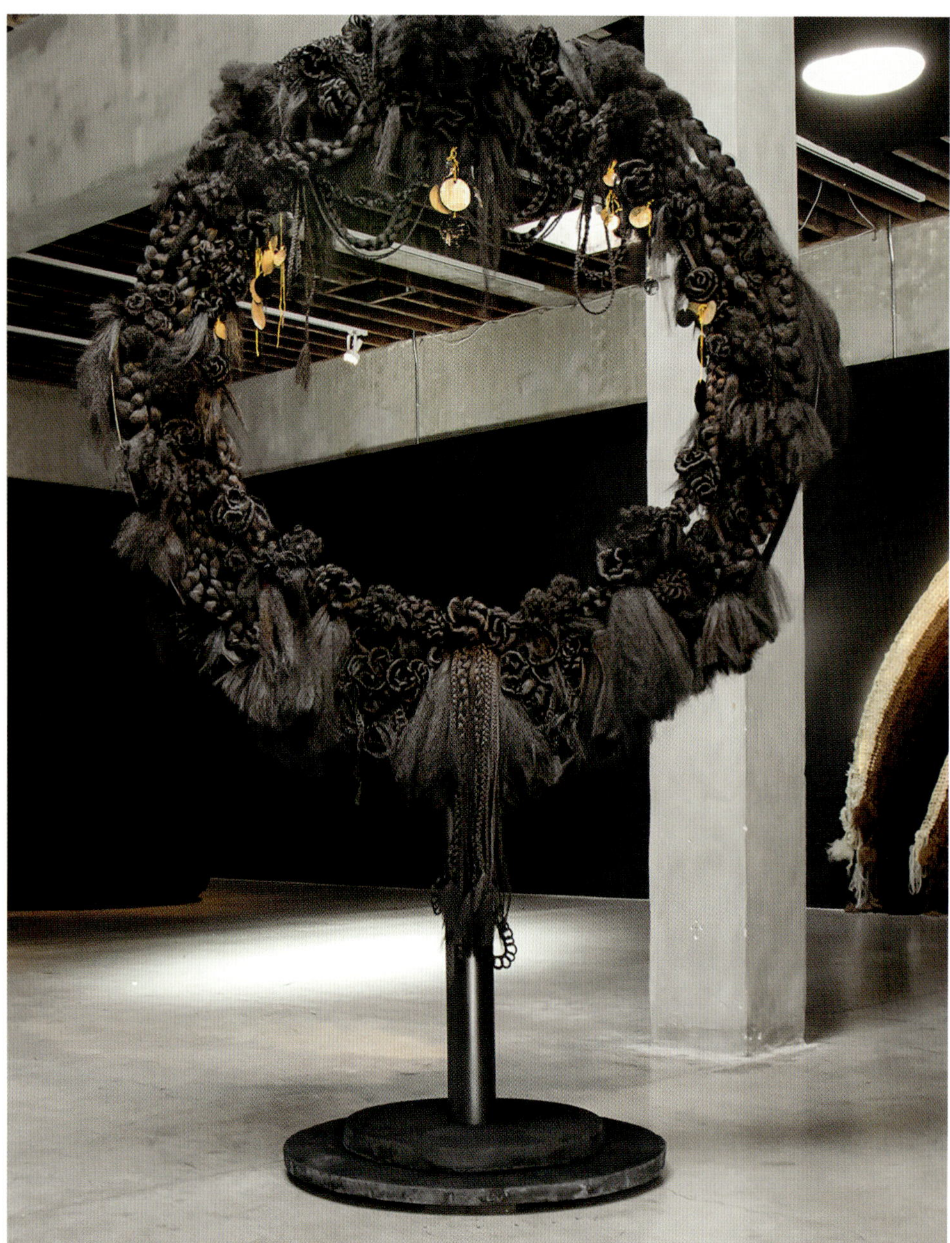

Angela Hennessy,
Installation view of
When and where I enter,
Southern Exposure, 2017.

of History, Hegel himself offers an unequivocal answer: he claims that the "Negro ... exhibits the natural man in his completely wild and untamed state" and that Africa "is no historical part of the World; it has no movement or development to exhibit."[3]

To understand the multifaceted nature of the Himba's use of otjize and, in fact, diasporic and continental Black hair politics more generally, is to commit to an act/process/praxis of historical and aesthetic recovery.[4] In the United States, Black relationship with hair can be incredibly fraught, in no small part because of what Michel Foucault describes as the political anatomy[5] of chattel slavery. The mechanics of racial power of the plantation

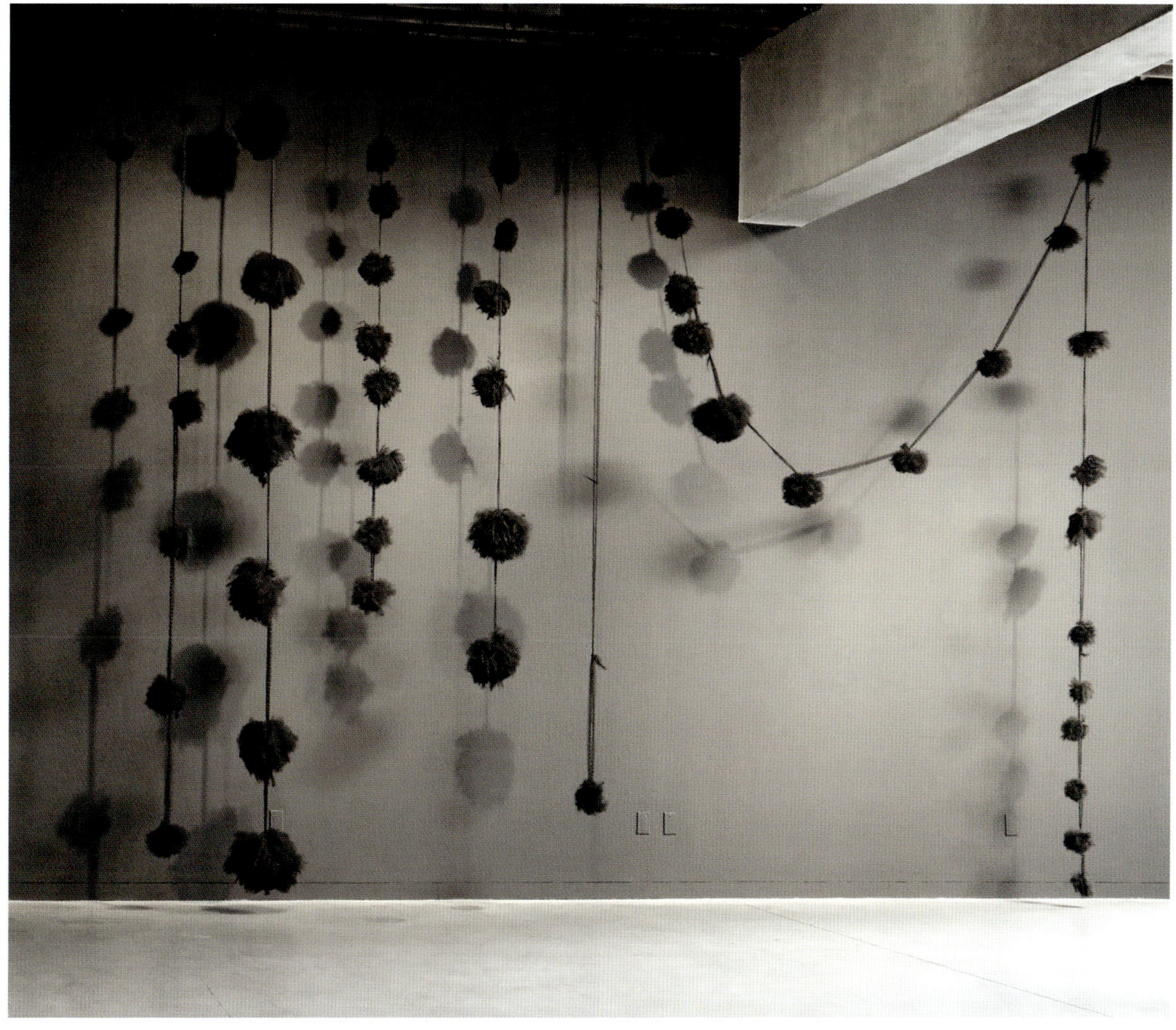

Angela Hennessy, *Unidentified Grieving Objects*, 2017,
Synthetic and human hair, artist's hair, dimensions variable.

demanded total control over the bodies of the enslaved, from structures of forced labor to the presentation and markings of the slaves themselves. With the criminalization of natural hair, the demands for its management in the name of "neatness" and "professionalism" reveal the endurance of these anti-Black, slavery, logics in the present. "Of all the parts of the body, hair has the most mystical associations," writes Orlando Patterson, "on the private or individual level, there is hardly a culture in which hair is not, for males, a symbol of power, manliness, freedom, and even rebellion; and for women, the crowning expression of feminine beauty."[6] The slave had no self and no community beyond that which was created for him by his master; the forced removal of his hair is an even further divorce from the elaborate ecosystem of cultural decoration to which they are indigenous (as well as a sense of cultural belonging more generally). Let us consider a

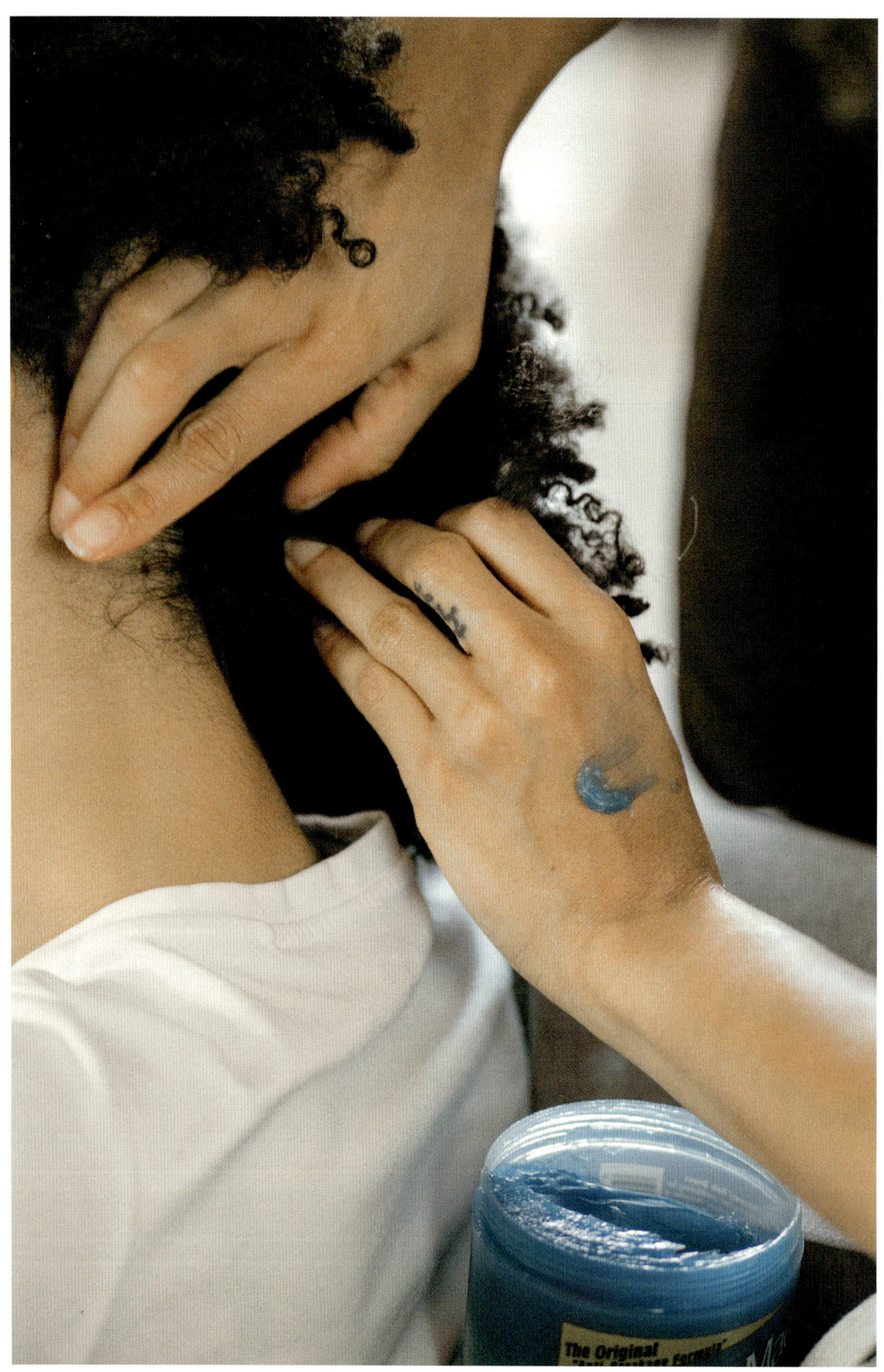

Kierra Johnson, *And Then What II*, 2018,
Photograph, 20 × 22 in. (50.8 × 55.9 cm).

mobilization of what Ariella Aïsha Azoulay has named "potential history."[7] It is a new historiography that is not simply a refusal of the strictures of power-knowledge and canonical production or an aspiring alternative to hegemony, which still reifies hegemonic truths (rather, Truth). It is a development of a "non-imperial grammar" that serves as "a form of being with others, both living and dead, across time, against the separation of the past from the present, colonized people from their worlds and possessions, and history from politics."[8]

The negotiation of this history is not simply an attempt to integrate hair politics into an exclusionary canon of western beauty as narrativized by Eco, but rather a reckoning with how treatments of hair materiality must also capture the literal treatments and punishments of hair that is "unruly." Black people were forced to be ruled and governed by regimes of racialized aesthetics—Hegel's aforementioned description of a "wild and untamed state," an ungovernability that must be broken and brought to heel. In her solo exhibition, *When and Where I Enter* (2017), Angela Hennessy's treatment of hair as a eulogy sources synthetic and human hair for sculptural material from Oakland wig and beauty supply shops. Some of the hair is used for fashioning into wreaths—described as "a response to cross-cultural rituals of offering hair as a sign of respect and grief for the dead"—and other death-evoking motifs as is characteristic of her work. (p. 38) "Hair," she says "has long served as a material exchanged between the living and the dead. As a symbol of one's identity, it is a potent tactile reminder of the separation caused by death." Her piece *Unidentified Grieving Objects* (p. 39) appropriates language used to describe non-human aliens (i.e. "unidentified flying objects"), a piece created by suspending a net-like tapestry of woven together pom-poms from a beam. Here, she evokes the all too familiar strange southern fruit and juxtaposes that imagery alongside "a pervasive but sometimes vague feeling of grief in the air that often ornaments Blackness" and that is "so familiar that it has a decorative effect."[9] As per longstanding continental and Afro-diasporic tradition, death—ancestralization—is to be celebrated and embraced in this collective articulation of new grammars. "Fear not death," says poet Aja Monet, "we visit kinfolk there."[10]

The only actually living part of hair is found within the hair follicle. The visible and ornamented part, the hair shaft, is considered to be dead because there is no real biochemical activity within it. The multi-billion dollar industry[11] created for the styling and maintaining of Black hair is, in a way, dedicated to the culturally (and personally valuable) aestheticization and beautification of dead matter. But this scientific reality makes the practices and communal engagements with hair no less important: beautification is a time and space-transcendent method of organizing identity.

I will speak for myself in saying that managing my hair is not something for which I have ever been particularly well-suited. I remember nostalgically the weekend afternoons spent between my mother's knees having my scalp greased and my thick hair twisted, a haptic and olfactory memory evoked effortlessly by Kierra Johnson's *And Then What* series (2018) (p. 40). I wanted hair like a White girl. I wanted hair that would swish around me and then return to its place, not hair that would hold fast in whatever position it was molded into. My first relaxer came at age fourteen or so, and to the chagrin of my mother who had spent the prior years dutifully attending to my hair as someone would to a beloved garden, I proceeded to cut it into different shapes. When I was nineteen I became honey blonde, the same color as my mother when she had locs; when I was twenty-two, I dyed my hair purple and then red and then a number of other colors. The constant dying and re-bleaching made my hair brittle and unhealthy. I detested the tedium of washing and conditioning and twisting and wrapping; I felt like I was choking on it (à la Nakeya Brown's *Hair Portrait #3*, p. 124). So I shaved it.

A personal review of hair as dead matter reframes my relationship to "the big chop," the colloquial description of cutting off a large amount of hair. It felt, paradoxically (considering the meaning Patterson ascribed to the hair shaving of the enslaved), like a release: a turning away from the routine laboriousness of hair care, a shedding of dead weight in the most literal way, an act of gendered agency when Black women's hair (like our bodies) are still treated like community property. Ruth Sutoyé's *"Bald Black Girls"* appraises and celebrates the beauty of baldness in her project's considerations of the masculinizing nature of short hair, the politics of desirability, and the gendered dynamics of the barbershop and hair salon—her short poetic film, *Reign*, synonymizes baldness and tenderness.

What do I have in common with that Himba woman, and why—beyond the stark contrast of her indigenous expression in downtown Windhoek—was her appearance so striking on that completely ordinary afternoon? Her hair is long, my hair is closely cropped, and yet after many rounds of local and diasporic practical, political, and social considerations, I think we both understand our respective presentations as the pinnacle of feminine beauty to different degrees. The beauty of Black hair is in its structural ability to be transformed and to hold such a vast diversity of shapes and styles, its ability to hold the past and evolve alongside presenthood and projected futurity.

ZOÉ SAMUDZI is a writer, photographer, and doctoral candidate in Medical Sociology at the University of California, San Francisco. Her work concerns genocide, African colonialism, identity-making and ancestry, biomedicine, visual ethnography, memory, and the politics of seeing and witnessing (and surveilling).

1 The region was formerly known as Kaokaland, the administrative unit that was meant to be a self-governing *bantustan* while Namibia, then South West Africa, was a part of apartheid South Africa—a government was never established.
2 Umberto Eco, *On Ugliness*, trans. Alastair McEwen (London: Harvill Secker, 2007): 10.
3 Babacar Camara, "The Falsity of Hegel's Thesis on Africa," *Journal of Black* Studies 31, no. 1 (September 2005): 82-96.
4 The notion of "recovery" is inspired by "The Question of Recovery: An Introduction" from Helton et al.'s 2015 introduction to *Social Text* 33 (4). It is inspired by the diversity of attempts to read Blackness into an exclusionary canon-archive and against a backdrop of transatlantic African slavery, and troubled by the fact that "the social death of slavery renders dispossession a defining feature of Black history." It is not synonymous with reclamation.
5 Michel Foucault, *Discipline and Punish: The Birth of the Prison*, trans. Alan Sheridan (New York: Vintage Books, 1995): 136.
6 Orlando Patterson, *Slavery and Social Death: A Comparative Study*, Cambridge: Harvard University Press, 2018: 154.
7 Ariella Aïsha Azoulay, *Potential History: Unlearning Imperialism*, London: Verso, 2019.
8 Ibid, 71.
9 Quotes taken from Nehat Yohannes' review of Hennessy's show, "Angela Hennessy's Solo Show Offers Up Hair As Eulogy" in *KQED Arts,* published on October 26, 2017: https://www.kqed.org/arts/13812673/angela-hennessy-southern-exposure-when-and-where-i-enter.
10 *Aja Monet: Where the Land is Free*, featuring Aja Monet, Saul Williams, and SCRAAATCH, Red Bay Coffee, Oakland, CA, September 28, 2019.
11 See "Black Impact: Consumer Categories Where African Americans Move Markets," *Nielsen. February 15, 2018.* <https://www.nielsen.com/us/en/insights/article/2018/black-impact-consumer-categories-where-african-americans-move-markets/> for more on the impact of Black spending: "Black shoppers spent $473 million in total hair care (a $4.2 billion industry)."

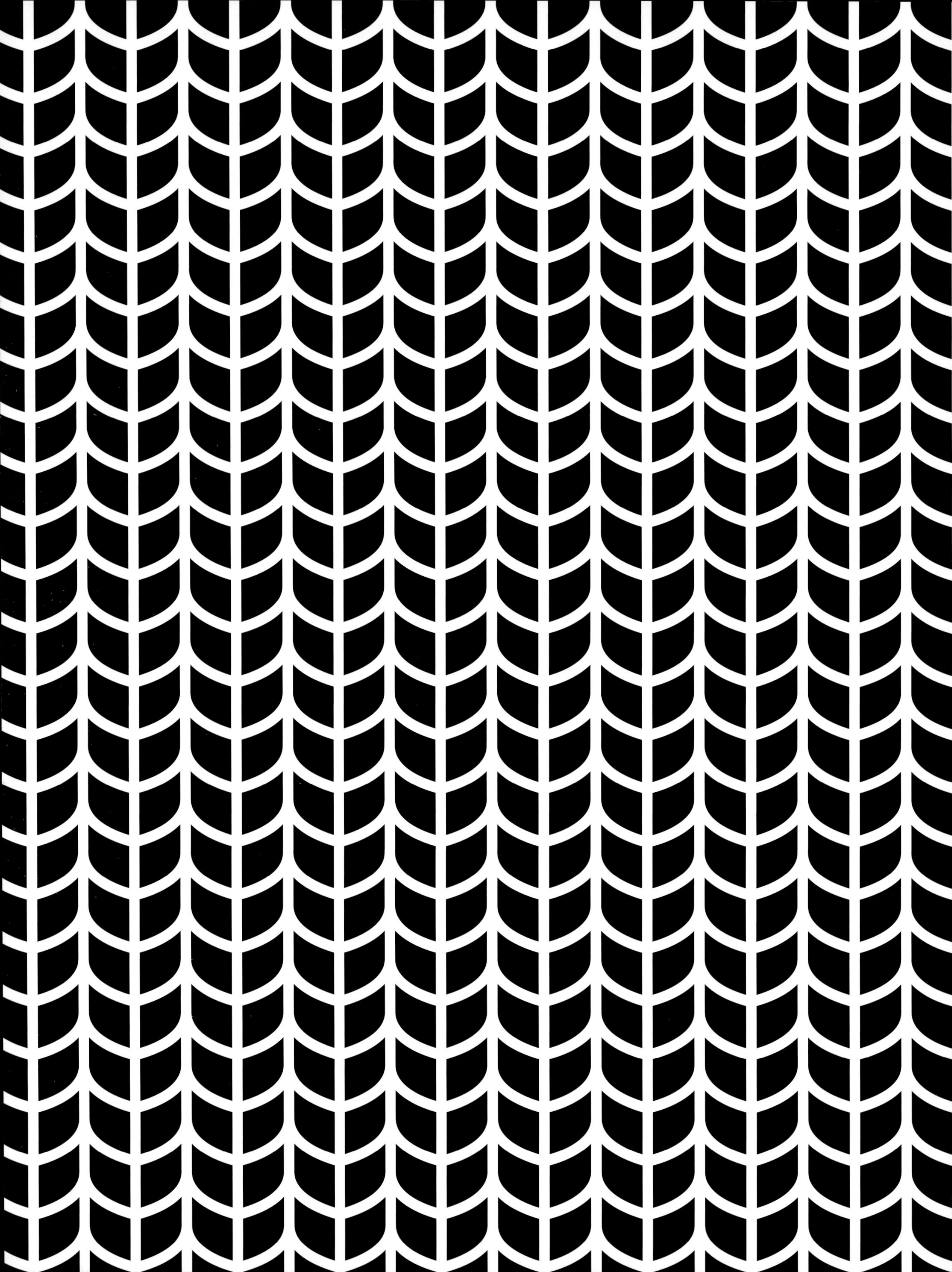

UNDER THE LENS: PHOTOGRAPHY AND BLACK HAIR

BY JOSEPH L. UNDERWOOD

There are few things as universal as hair. A biological phenomenon with endless social implications, hair is both alive in the root and dead in the strand—a banal material with endless potential for metaphor, symbolism, and significance. In curating an exhibition on the history and significance of Black hair, there are thousands of hair-centric artworks to consider for their ability to convey socio-cultural nuances from that artist's world . . . but there are also an infinite number of images in which Black hair is not the focus, but nevertheless signals the status, agency, and milieu of its wearer. Though we ultimately decided to categorize the exhibition into three overarching themes, the implications of Black hair span so many historical periods and geographic regions that the nuances are as numerous as the hairs on your head. To that end, this curatorial essay offers a narrowed analysis on the role of the camera, asking us to consider how photography by artists from Africa and the African Diaspora challenge the misconceptions and violence wrought by non-African photographers during the colonial and postcolonial eras.

In his influential essay for the landmark *In/Sight* exhibition on African photography, art historian and artist Olu Oguibe unpacks how the "voyeuristic camera" of Europeans doubled as "an instrument of war."[1]

As a point of departure, let us consider the rise of documentary photography in the United States through the lens of White Missouri native Walker Evans to assess how the effects of colonial photography linger into the twentieth century. In this image (p. 47), Evans shows one scene of everyday life as the Great Depression wreaked havoc across communities in the South. Only two years later, in 1938, Evans was honored with an exhibition at the Museum of Modern Art, codifying him as a photographer of the American vernacular, an artist who brought the sights and denizens of small towns to the national eye. Focusing on the African-American presence in Vicksburg, Mississippi, this photograph shows three men of modest dress gathered outside the local barbershop. Given that it was a street scene, Evans likely did not ask permission of the subjects before shooting. Instead of meeting them in their space—i.e. the barbershop which they frequented, which was probably owned and operated by a fellow African-American—the photographer took their likeness from a public space for later exhibition elsewhere in the States. This tendency to arrive from afar, capture a so-called "authentic" or "native"' perspective on Black life, and distribute the image in alternative contexts is a ghostly echo of colonial photography, and remains problematic in travel and documentary photography even today. Did Evans know the particular history of Black citizens in Vicksburg, Mississippi? Was he aware that the town had elected African-American Peter Crosby as their sheriff in 1874, only for him to later be held captive and exiled by White protesters—a riotous group who would go on to kill three hundred Black citizens in Vicksburg and the adjacent counties?[2] Instead of a photograph that roots the Black bodies of Vicksburg in their history or their contemporary context, Evans favored aesthetics of decay, foregrounding the dilapidated, rattletrap building only brightened by posters for Camel cigarettes, cold remedies, and the new film *Rose Marie*.

Fortunately, as photography approaches its two hundredth birthday, generations of African and Diasporic artists have also wielded the camera as a tool of self-fashioning, offering a corrective lens to the Eurocentric (mis)perceptions that enjoyed more visibility, dissemination, and canonization. Contemporary practitioners, like British-Liberian artist Lina Iris Viktor, consciously combat this overwhelming archive of images: "I'm taking on various tropes of ethnographic photography and turning them on their head ... rendering the figures powerful and regal, rather than vulnerable objects of fantasy or degradation."[3] This, then, is the first of three photo-based strategies evidenced by artists in this exhibition: embodying the colonial trope to claim agency of the disempowered Black body.

In photographing her nude body, rendering the image onto canvas, and painting with a palette of matte black and 24-karat gold sourced from Ghana, this image (p. 119) from Viktor's *The Dark Continent* series reclaims a century of disempowered women whose bodies were photographed, dissected, and labeled by ethnologists. The series' title refers to the racist mystique that homogenized a diverse continent into one mass of unknowable, primitive Black people. As the blackness of her body reverberates against the shadows of the night scene, it is her hair that catches the golden, celestial light. The fullness of the buns parallels the abundance of the full moon. Similarly, both forms evoke sculptural qualities as the length of Viktor's hair spirals in diverging directions, with stray strands winding away from the coil, and the craters and crevices of the moon are signaled by the impasto brushstrokes. The energy that emanates from these golden forms is palpable, electrifying what would otherwise be a still, black night. Viktor takes full authorial control of colonial stereotypes and builds a series that simultaneously undermines historic photographs of African bodies and asserts the agency of the woman to present her body, her hair, and her dynamic with the natural and celestial realms.

The practice of Senegalese artist Ibrahima Thiam is similarly rooted in archival images of African bodies, but his strategy focuses on the work and legacy of African photographers working in the region since the

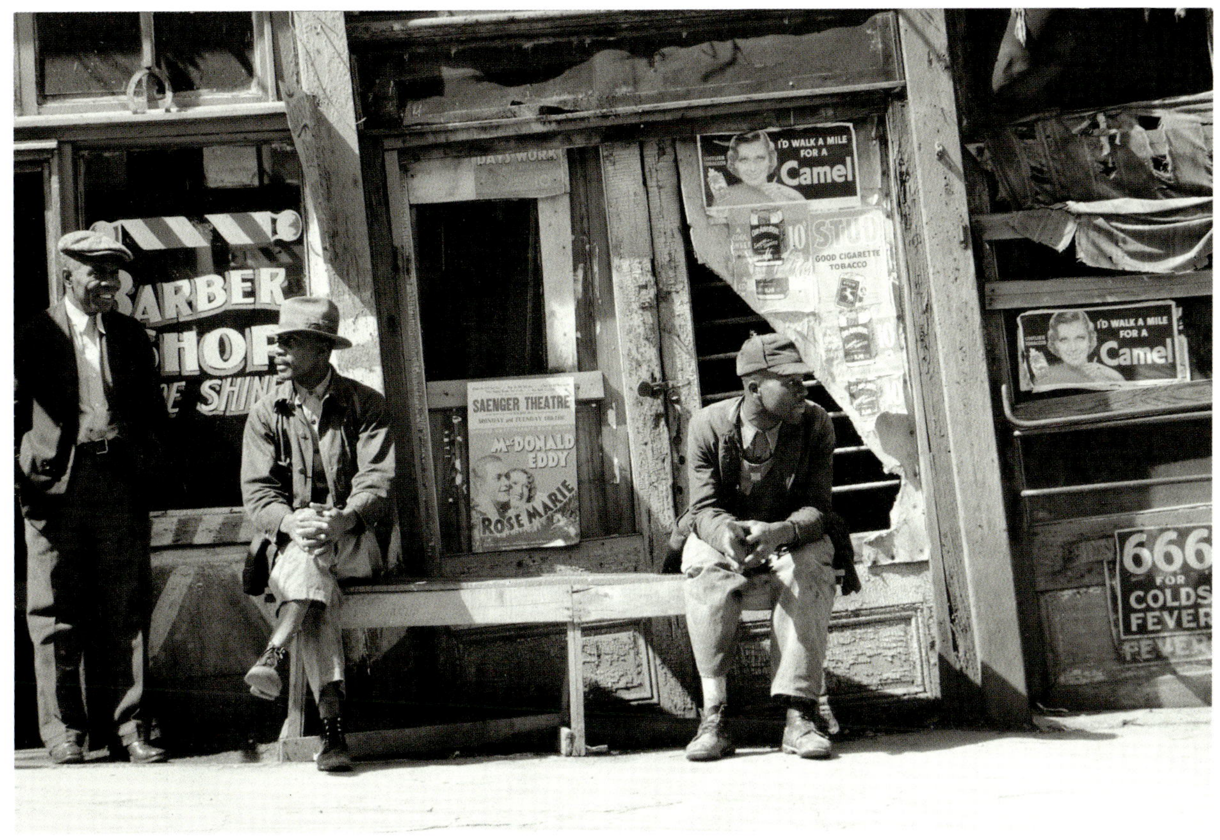

Walker Evans, *Street Scene, Vicksburg, Mississippi*, 1936, Gelatin silver print, 4.75 × 7.1 in. (12.1 × 18 cm). Collection of the J. Paul Getty Museum.

late nineteenth century. Besides the well-known studio photographers like Seydou Keïta and Malick Sidibé, there were dozens of pioneering West African photographers who built careers by photographing their contemporaries. Jonathan Adagogo Green, the Lisk-Carew Brothers, and George A. G. Lutterodt were some of the earliest practitioners who carved out a niche for Africans to claim a sense of agency and self-determination in the studio—even in the midst of formal colonization. A native of Saint-Louis, Senegal, Thiam is particularly inspired by Mama and Salla Casset, brothers from a middle-class family who operated between their shared hometown and Senegal's capital, Dakar. Working primarily with young female subjects, the Casset brothers' lenses are one of the few historical records that recount the sartorial tastes of the time—a unique blend of local traditions and styles taken from the newspapers and magazines that had begun to flow more freely between Europe, Africa, and the Americas.

African photography has only entered the art historical canon and the global consciousness in the last two decades. Prior to that, even images from now-famous artists were exhibited in museums with an "unknown artist" label.[4] Most of the original negatives and seminal prints from these landmark photographers have been lost, with remnants found across informal familial collections and in the personal archives of photo enthusiasts who were concerned about the visual legacies of the Black Africans who defined generations of portraits, street scenes, and social events across the colonial and independence eras. Ibrahima Thiam is one of these self-appointed archivists and his collection is regularly activated in his own practice that seeks to re-stage and valorize the significance of these early African photographers. This is the second strategy evinced by a photographer in this exhibition: using contemporary art and living bodies as vehicles for reviving the memory and significance of our collective past.

For his *Vintage Portrait* series, Thiam revives the interior "studio" of his forerunners by setting up a simple booth with a black background in the midst of urban chaos. The deceptively calm photos are composed by asking friends and passers-by to pilfer through his collection of archival photos, the "vintage portraits" that he has rescued from abandoned buildings and disinterested owners. He asks the sitter to position their chosen photograph over their own face, vivifying the ancestor at the expense of occluding themselves. Thiam views this as a corrective practice wherein he simultaneously educates Senegalese youth about the world of their great-grandparents and gives a new platform to the vintage photograph—both in the moment of creating his photograph and in its eventual dissemination through publication and exhibition. In this image (p. 70), a photograph by Mama Casset from 1960 features a woman adorned in a three-piece dress and head wrap and bedecked with gold ornaments around her hairline and wrists. Though the subject is unknown, the viewer is given enough clues about her sense of self—by her elegant costume, striking pose, and assured gaze—to emphasize her personhood and individuality. And even though the face of the young woman holding the photo is obscured, we still see a cohesive identity projected by her self-presentation: hair extensions formed into blue braids, a hoop earring, and a bevy of bracelets that feature the nation's colors of red, yellow, and green. Ironically, her screen-print shirt is adorned with a black-and-white photograph of a woman surrounded by an ornate vintage frame. Thiam's fear of Africans overlooking their own artistic heritage seems to manifest in this young woman's choice to sport a commercially-printed and distributed European portrait.

Where Viktor and Thiam's processes begin with the archives of European or African photographers, Amber N. Ford has built a practice based on hyperlocality, brandishing her camera in the service of documenting Black communities in Cleveland, Ohio. Beyond the themes in her work, Ford also pushes the boundaries of what constitutes photography, from the light-based development of cyanotypes to autonomous techniques (like scanning) to create digital images. This is a third method of photo-based artistry: synthesizing traditional camera-based techniques with other reproductive technologies and an expanded sense of portraiture.

For *TEXTURES*, Ford offers two oversized images printed on silk. *Pronto* (p. 160), referring to the "Pronto Quickweave" technique, is organized in horizontal registers, recalling a cutaway view of geological layers. Upon excavation, it becomes clear that the artist has fashioned multiple hairpieces into a stacked composition. In fact, these synthetic hair tracks are artifacts—extensions that once thickened and lengthened the artist's own hair. Transformed by this integration into Ford's personhood and self-presentation, the once-sterile hairpieces feel biologically activated, or at least implicated. Specks of dandruff, coils of stray hair, and uneven bits of glue along the seams betray the intimate nature of so-called "fake hair." For millions of women around the globe, the natural and synthetic hair industry is an integral component of self-fashioning. With competition between African-American, Korean, and Chinese distributors, this multibillion dollar industry is driven by more than mere accessories.[5] Ford highlights the deeply personal nature of hair—whether it sprouts from your own head or gets integrated later. *Pronto*, therefore, can be read as a kind of self-portrait, a portrait in which the body is absent. Like Althea Murphy-Price's fanciful prints of barrettes (p. 88, 89), Ford employs a synecdoche, isolating the hairpieces to encourage us to look more closely and recognize the biological, haptic qualities of (synthetic) hair.

There is no pressure to confine Black hair to a particular experience, or even to a uniform standard of presentation within a photograph (i.e. on the head, integrated with a corporeal subject). In creating this image by arranging her removed extensions on the scanner bed, Ford further undermines the traditions of image-making by removing the artist's hand. Where the artist creates distance between her body and this innovative photographic process, she minimizes the gap between her hair and the foreign extensions. Ultimately, the works in this series are printed on silk and installed in the gallery so as to be responsive to external stimuli. Ford manipulates the thingness of the hair tracks, digitizing the objects only to return them to three dimensions on silk. The new materiality of this expanded photography becomes further layered as we recall the various relationships between Black hair and silk (hair ties, durags, pillows, etc.).

As creative individuals who work with photography, in a traditional or expanded sense of the medium, these artists exemplify the diversity of responses to problematic representation of Black bodies and Black hair. While their artworks cannot erase the prevalent images that exoticize, primitivize, or pity Black peoples, they can call attention to such biases and undermine them, valorize the historic and contemporary authorship of Black visions and voices, and innovate vocabularies for delineating personal and communal experiences of Blackness.

DR. JOSEPH L. UNDERWOOD is an art historian and curator whose research focuses on artists from the African continent and the Diaspora. Rooted in the modern and contemporary periods, his projects focus on 1950-contemporary and encompass themes like (trans)nationalism, globalization, and biennialism. His research is especially focused on artists from Senegal and charting how their exhibitions have created transnational networks of influence.

1 Olu Oguibe, "Photography and the Substance of the Image," *In/Sight: African Photographers, 1940 to the Present* (New York: Guggenheim Museum, 1996), 232.
2 Emilye Crosby, *A Little Taste of Freedom: The Black Freedom Struggle in Claiborne County, Mississippi* (Chapel Hill: University of North Carolina Press, 2005).
3 *Lina Iris Viktor: A Haven. A Hell. A Dream Deferred*, ed. Allison K. Young (Milan and New Orleans: Skira Editore and New Orleans Museum of Art, 2019), 72.
4 See the exhibition *Africa Explores* (1991), curated by Susan Vogel for the Museum for African Art and the New Museum.
5 Emma Sapong, "Roots of Tension: Race, Hair, Competition and Black Beauty Stores," Minnesota Public Radio, April 25, 2017. <https://www.mprnews.org/story/2017/04/25/black-beauty-shops-korean-suppliers-roots-of-tension-mn>

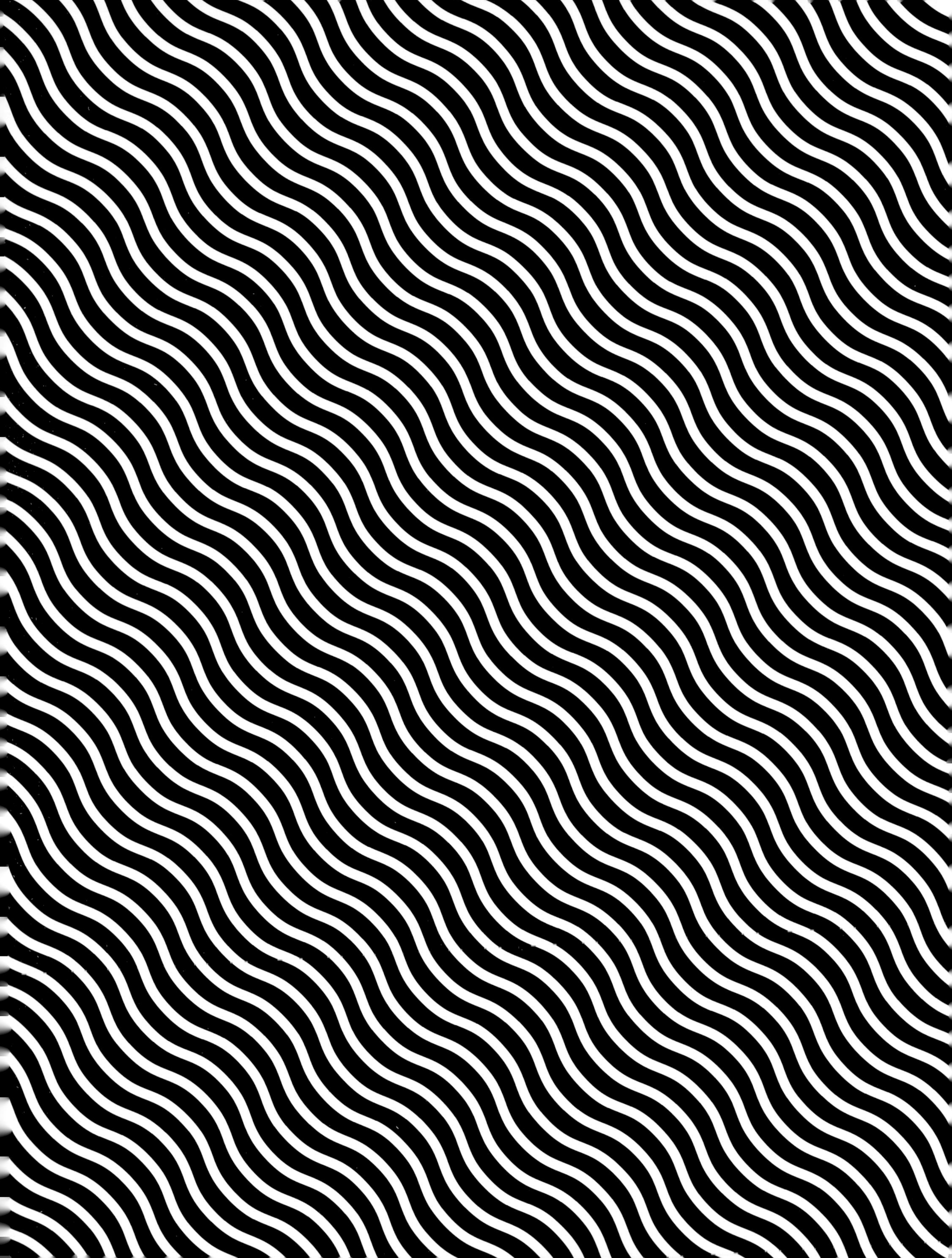

COMMUNITY & MEMORY

Memories have a strange way of combining the past and the present, like when a certain smell or sensation merges some slumbering thought with the current reality. Memories stem from everyday routines and exceptional life events—both integral to building our sense of self. Particular people and lived-in spaces tint our memories with nostalgia, changing the actual events and creating new memories that deviate from reality. For many Black people, their hair is woven into memories of mundane cleaning and care, highlights of self-discovery, and a sense of belonging within—or of alienation from—their social circles. How can something as commonplace as hair be so significant in rooting Black populations within spaces, communities, and families?

While the care, manipulation, and styling of Black hair has evolved throughout history, there are communal strands that carry through a variety of experiences. Because of the collaborative, multi-hand nature of styling—from braids to plaits to weaves—the memories around it are inherently personal and collective. In many African societies, hairstyles served as symbols to convey identities like ethnic group, marital status, or religious affiliation. For Black populations displaced by the transatlantic slave trade, these communal traditions were violently disrupted. The conditions of slavery demanded labor every day of the week, leaving no opportunity for individual or communal self-care routines. For example, in the context of U.S. history, slaves were given Sundays to tend to the needs of their family and faith, following the end of the legal slave trade in 1808. Only then were the communal traditions of hair care revived.

By the late nineteenth century, Black barbers transitioned from not only cutting the hair of White clientele to also serving Black patrons and establishing the barbershops and salons as gathering places in their neighborhoods. Black hair care gave rise to the first African-American millionaires, like Madam C. J. Walker (Sarah Breedlove), institutions of learning, like Annie Malone's Poro College for beauticians, and new inventions and formulae, like Willie Morrow's Afro-pick and California Curl products. The importance of salons and barbershops for Black communities around the globe is the cornerstone for artwork in this section—from Derrick Adams' *There is More Than One Beauty School*, to Nontsikelelo Mututi's *African Hair Braiding Salon Reader*. Other objects, like Annie Lee's *All that Glitters*, come from visual culture—a ubiquitous poster found in almost every beauty salon. The essence of Community & Memory is further echoed in *The Negro Motorist Green Book* series (and *TEXTURES*' related project that maps the oral histories of Black barbers and salon artists in our Northeast Ohio region, see p. 100) which helped African-Americans evade racial discrimination during the Jim Crow era by identifying safe businesses, ranging from hotels and restaurants, to barbershops and beauty parlors.

The artists in this section also complicate the relationships between communities and memories. Ibrahima Thiam disrupts the notion of continuity by superimposing vintage photographs over the faces of his community, questioning how we overlook links between the past and the present. Similarly, Devan Shimoyama undermines the nostalgia of barbershops as communal spaces by casting them as hypermasculine spaces where machismo presses against queer voices, creating a tense dynamic. With an emphasis on individual voices within communal experiences, this section of the exhibition demonstrates how, for thousands of years, Black hair has always been shaped by larger social contexts. From Egyptian court life, to antebellum slave plantations, to the rise of Black enterprises and the hair care industry, a sense of togetherness infuses the history of Black hair.

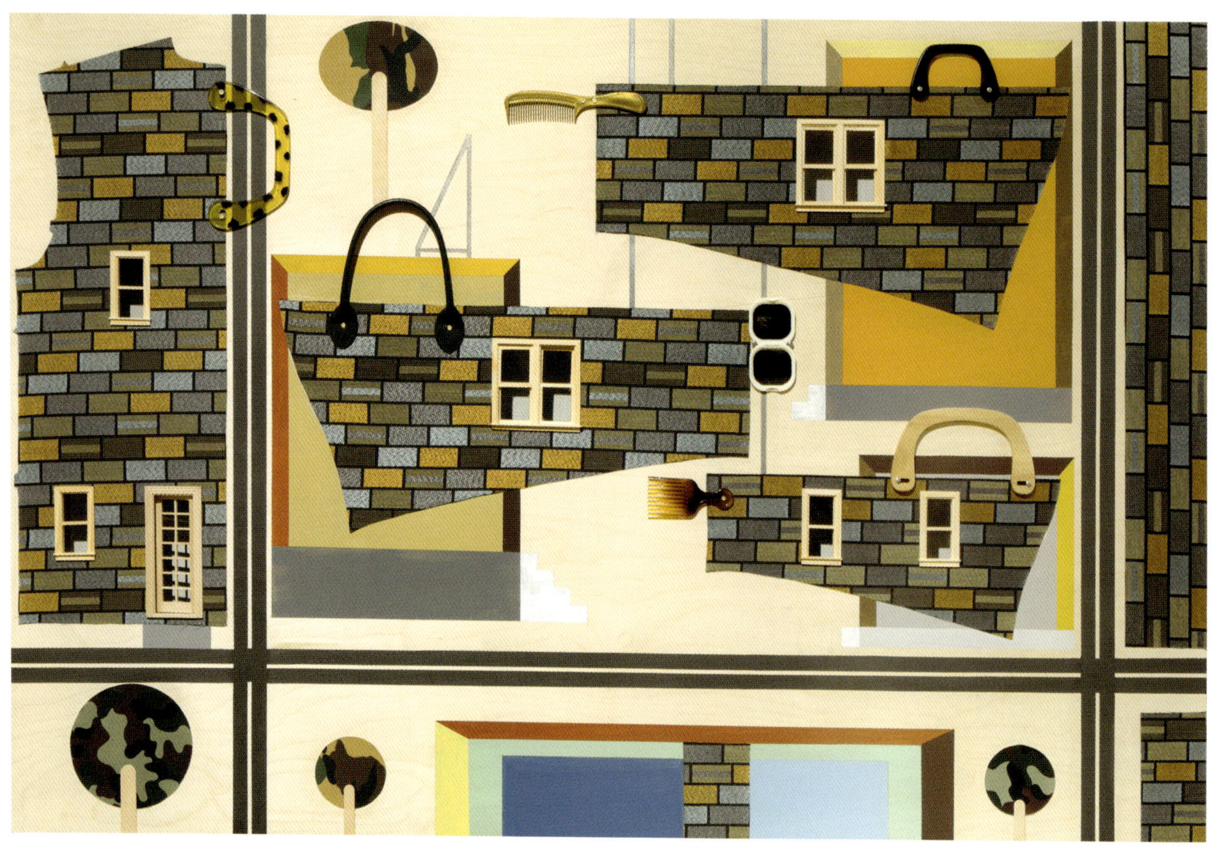

DERRICK ADAMS

There's More Than One Beauty School, 2018

Adams' 2018 exhibition, *Sanctuary*, drew inspiration from *The Negro Motorist Green Book*, a resource published between 1936 and 1966 that helped Black Americans navigate the United States safely. The *Green Book* listed hotels, restaurants, gas stations, and barbershops where Black clientele were welcome. Inspired by the historical context and the mid-century modern aesthetic, Adams created a series of shallow sculptural collages that addressed different industries from the American landscape.

There's More Than One Beauty School is a mixed-media assemblage of combs, picks, and mirrors, inviting us to reflect on the unrecognized labor of working-class Black Americans—before, during, and after the Civil War. The title also alludes to America's problematic history in promoting a singular definition of (female) beauty, a standard that consistently excludes people of certain races, skin color, or hair texture.

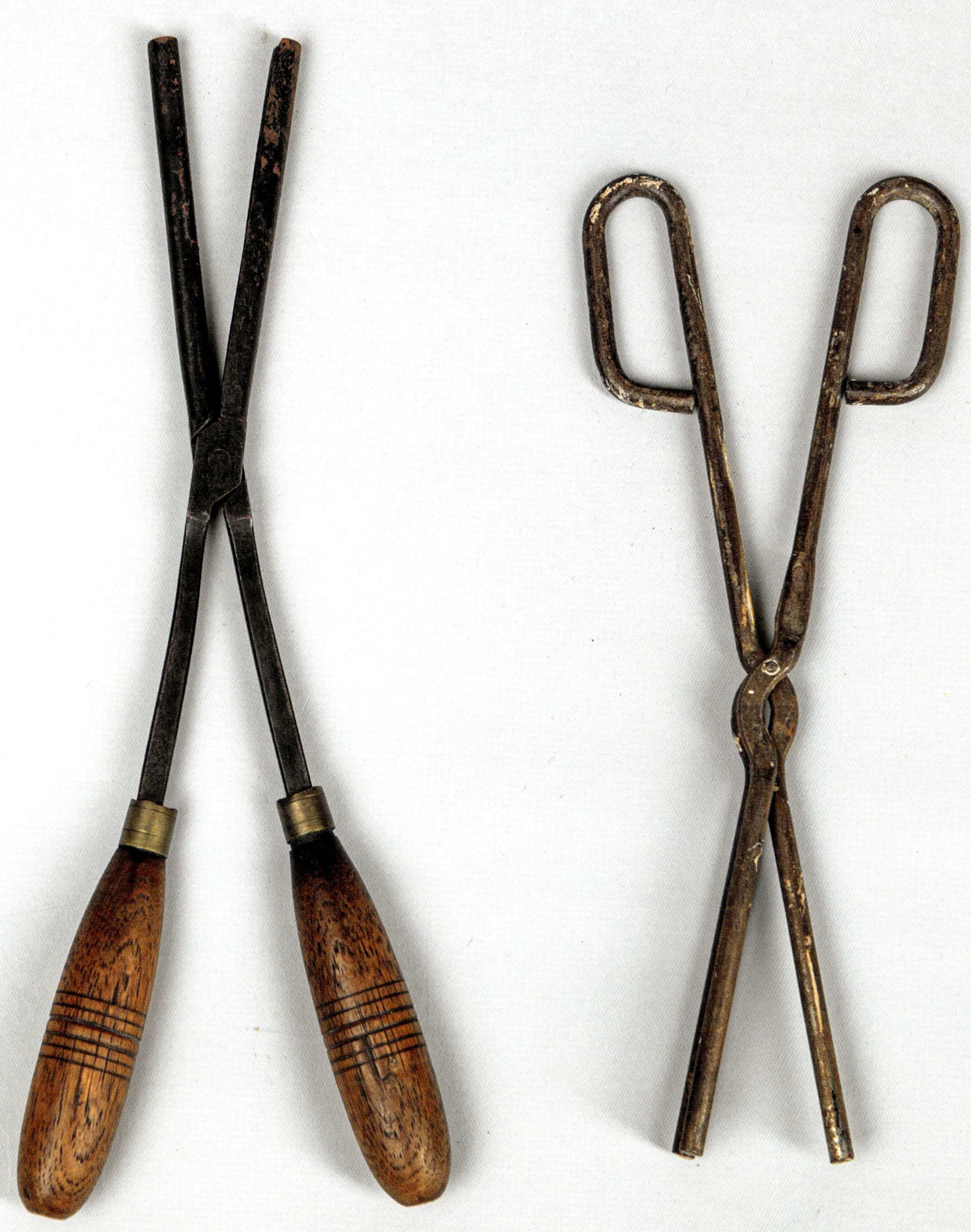

Marcel curlers, *ca.* 1890
Marcel curlers, *ca.* 1890

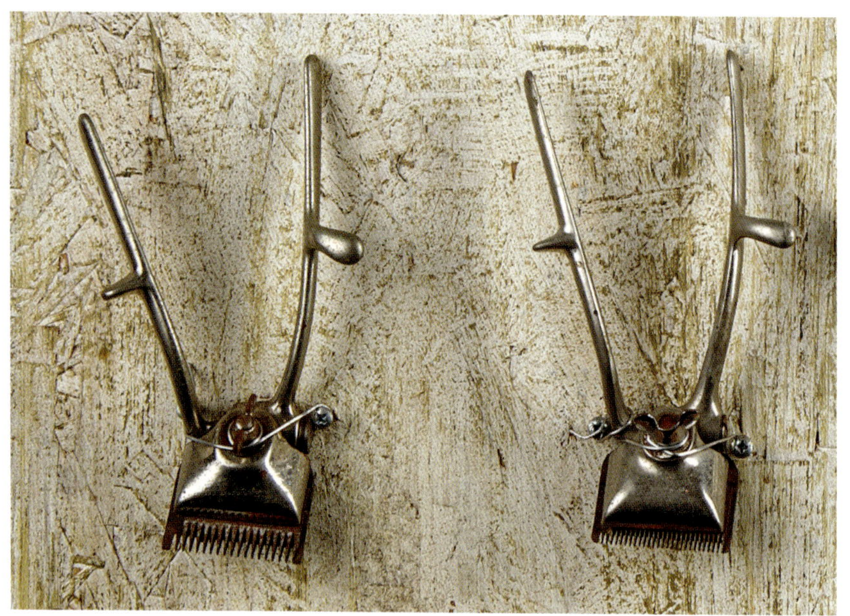

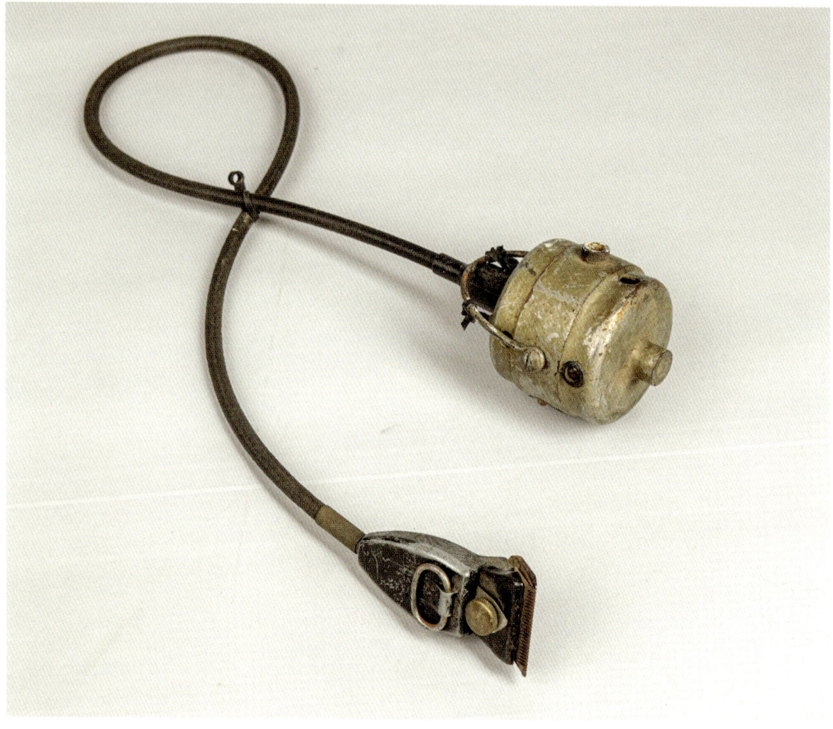

Second generation hand clippers, *ca.* 1900
Moore Electric Hair Cutter, *ca.* 1920

DEVAN SHIMOYAMA

Elijah, 2020

Known for his *Cry Baby* project, Shimoyama is a mixed media painter who frequently critiques the underlying prejudices of traditional Black masculinity, especially as it is perpetuated against queer bodies in barbershops. In working along these lines, the artist challenges the common perception that these are spaces of solidarity, free expression, and security. Beyond his cathartic images of tearful men getting a haircut, the artist explores themes of Black queerness, male vulnerability, and the tension between these worlds. Through a laborious process of layering—from paint to rhinestone to feather—Shimoyama crafts extravagant, seductive figures that are simultaneously personal and allegorical.

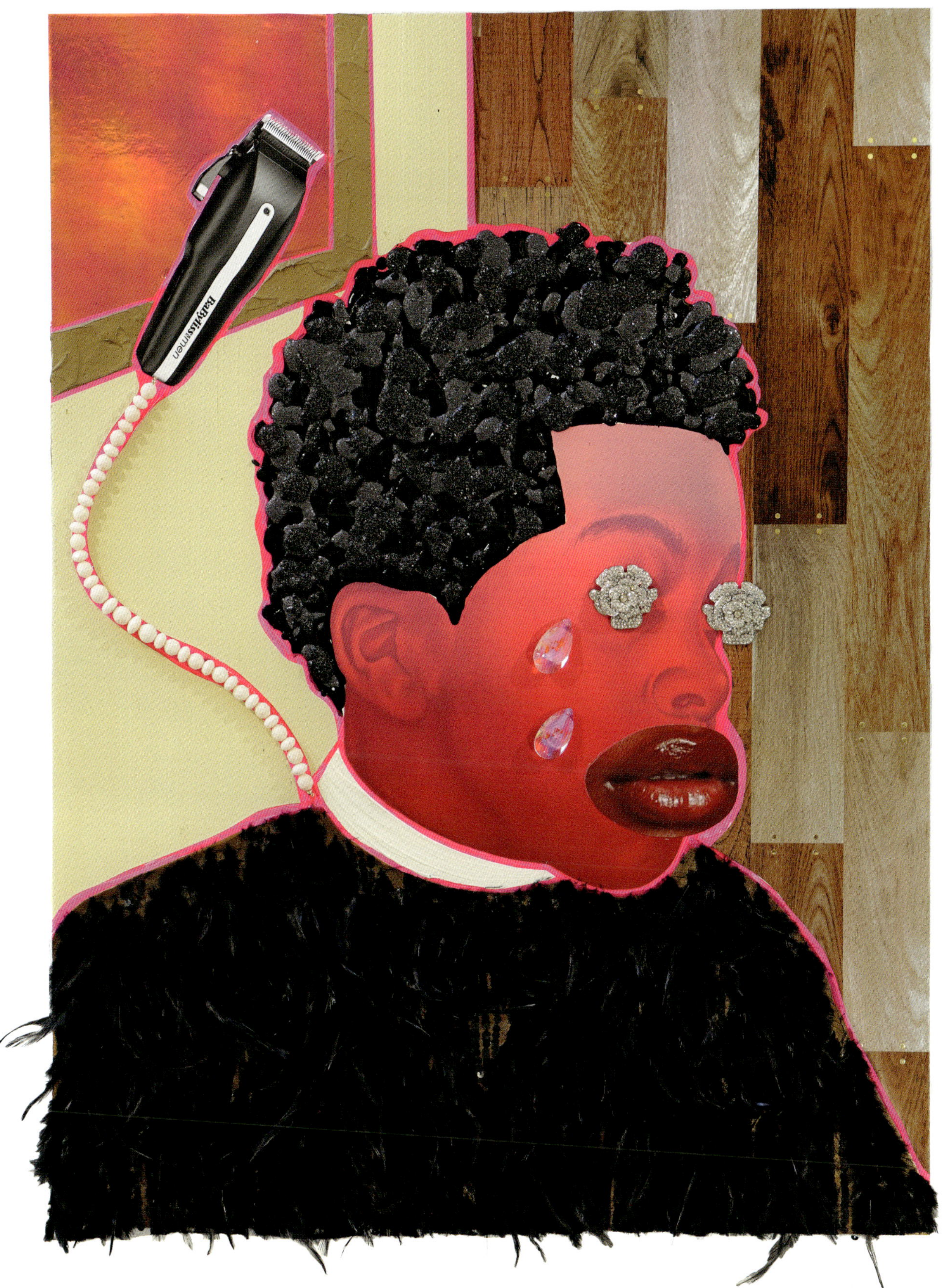
BaBylissmen

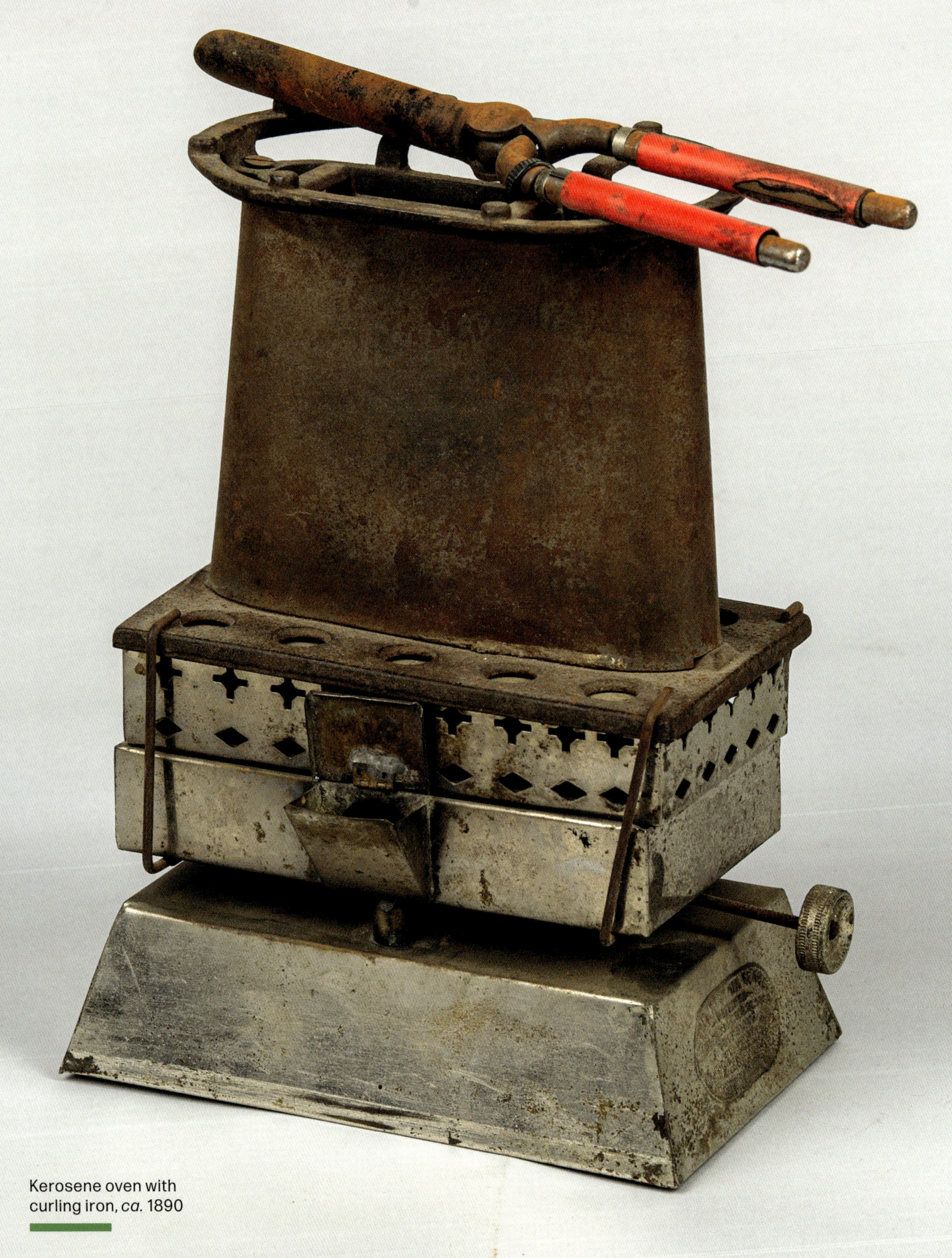

Kerosene oven with curling iron, *ca.* 1890

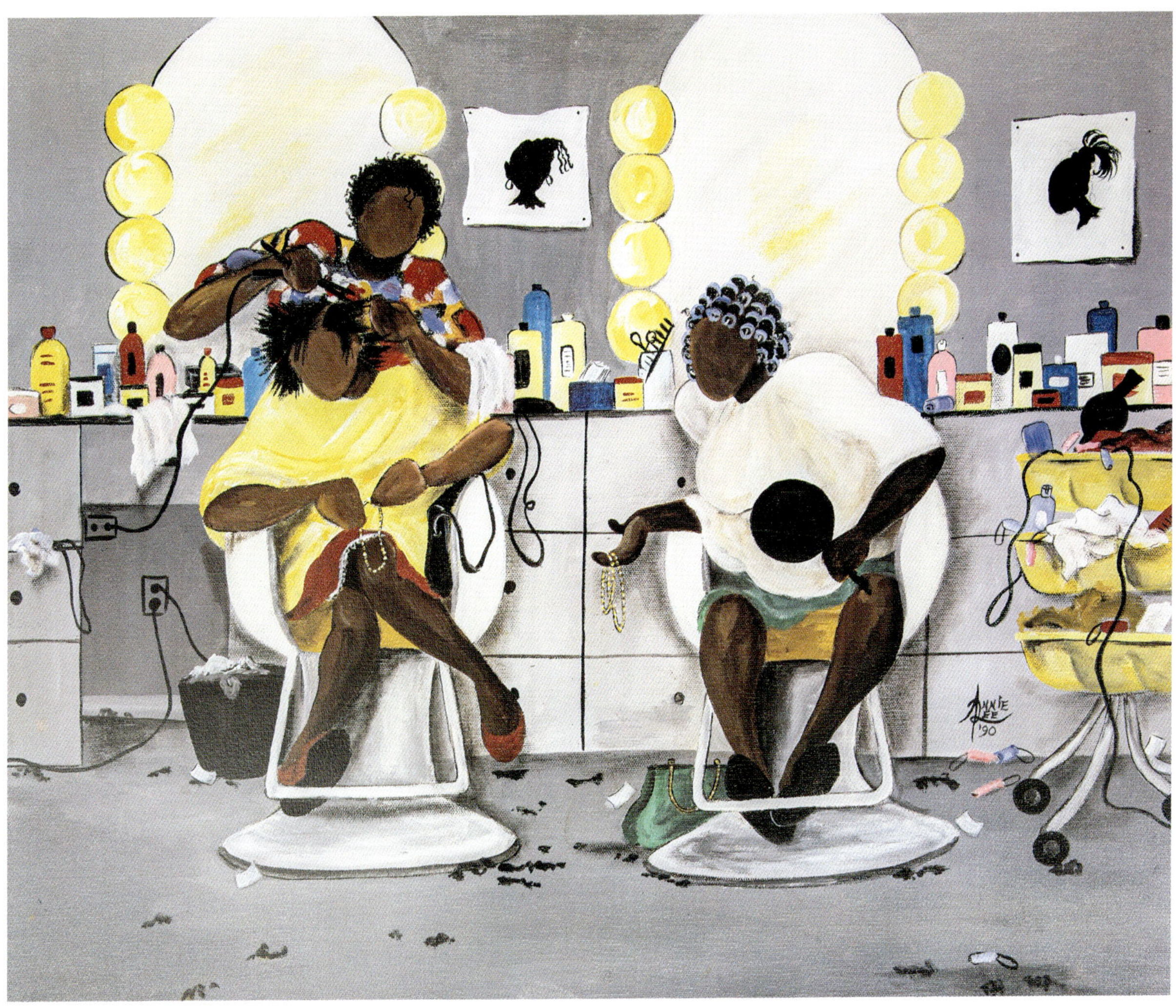

ANNIE LEE
All That Glitters

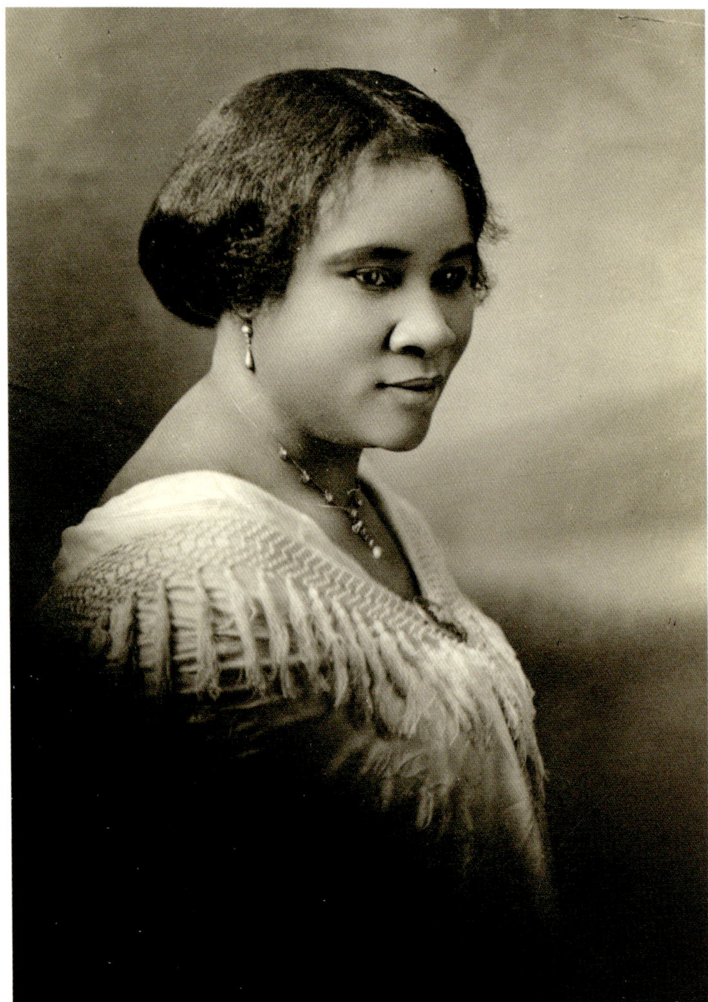

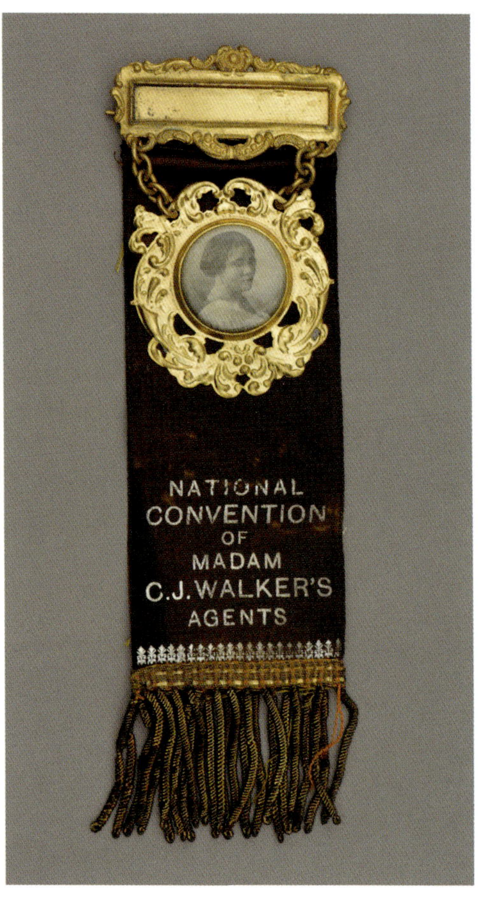

Walker Convention Badge, *ca.* 1930

Photograph of Madam C. J. Walker, 1914–1915

Madam C. J. Walker (Sarah Breedlove) was an entrepreneur and philanthropist, born near Delta, Louisiana to enslaved parents, Owen and Minerva Breedlove. As one of six children, she was the first born into freedom after the Emancipation Proclamation was signed. In St. Louis, Missouri, Madam C. J. Walker worked as a sales representative for Annie Turnbo Malone, one of the first African American millionaire hair care entrepreneurs. Miss Malone was also owner of the Poro Company and Poro College, a beauty school for "Race Women" (African American students) who would cater to Black clientele. Soon after resigning from Miss Malone's company, Madam C. J. Walker began developing her Wonderful Hair Grower products.

After several years of traveling around the United States selling and promoting her products, Madam C. J. Walker settled in Indianapolis, Indiana where she built a manufacturing plant for her products. In her company's complex she also built a salon and beauty school where she provided grooming services and educated up-and-coming sales agents. As a result of her strong work ethic and savvy business skills, she reached millionaire status. She became a vital component to the African American community by employing thousands of individuals who would not have been able to earn a living wage sharecropping former slave owners' fields. Madam C. J. Walker was and continues to be an unwavering representation of Black success and a shining example of how strong women can defy societal barriers. After her death in 1919, her brand and products reached new audiences in Cuba, Jamaica, Haiti, Panama, and Costa Rica.

The Indiana Historical Society holds the largest collection of Madam C. J. Walker artifacts. Their collection includes legal documents, hair products, advertisements, instructional books, and even brooches worn by former sales agents—a selection of which were chosen for *TEXTURES*.

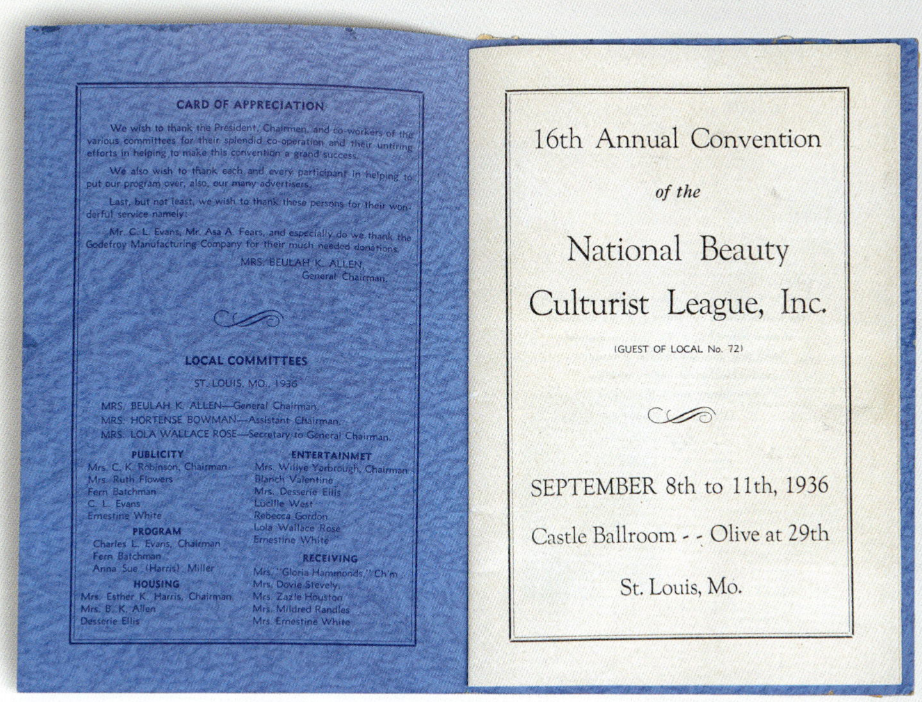

CARD OF APPRECIATION

We wish to thank the President, Chairmen, and co-workers of the various committees for their splendid co-operation and their untiring efforts in helping to make this convention a grand success.

We also wish to thank each and every participant in helping to put our program over, also, our many advertisers.

Last, but not least, we wish to thank these persons for their wonderful service namely:

Mr. C. L. Evans, Mr. Asa A. Fears, and especially do we thank the Godefroy Manufacturing Company for their much needed donations.

MRS. BEULAH K. ALLEN,
General Chairman.

LOCAL COMMITTEES

ST. LOUIS, MO., 1936

MRS. BEULAH K. ALLEN—General Chairman.
MRS. HORTENSE BOWMAN—Assistant Chairman.
MRS. LOLA WALLACE ROSE—Secretary to General Chairman.

PUBLICITY
Mrs. C. K. Robinson, Chairman
Mrs. Ruth Flowers
Fern Batchman
C. L. Evans
Ernestine White

PROGRAM
Charles L. Evans, Chairman
Fern Batchman
Anna Sue (Harris) Miller

HOUSING
Mrs. Esther K. Harris, Chairman
Mrs. B. K. Allen
Desserie Ellis

ENTERTAINMET
Mrs. Willye Yarbrough, Chairman
Blanch Valentine
Mrs. Desserie Ellis
Lucille West
Rebecca Gordon
Lola Wallace Rose
Ernestine White

RECEIVING
Mrs. "Gloria Hammonds," Ch'm.
Mrs. Dovie Stevely.
Mrs. Zazle Houston
Mrs. Mildred Randles
Mrs. Ernestine White

16th Annual Convention

of the

National Beauty Culturist League, Inc.

(GUEST OF LOCAL No. 72)

SEPTEMBER 8th to 11th, 1936

Castle Ballroom - - Olive at 29th

St. Louis, Mo.

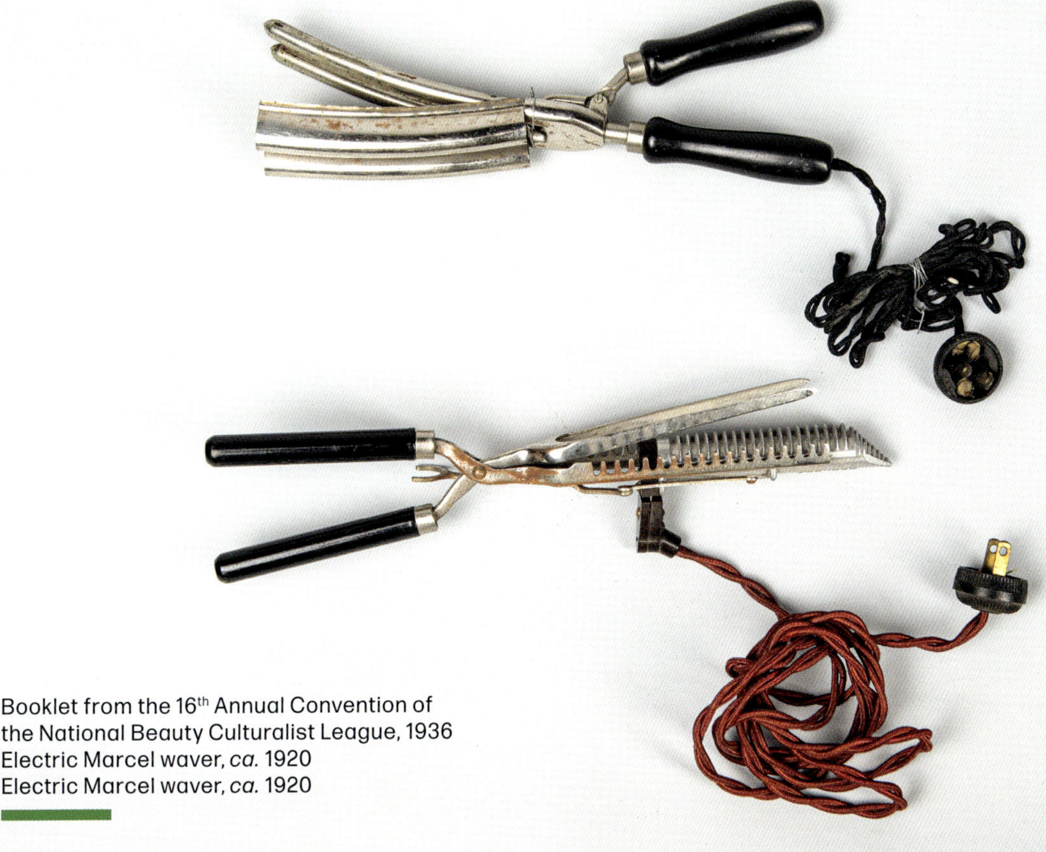

Booklet from the 16th Annual Convention of the National Beauty Culturalist League, 1936
Electric Marcel waver, *ca.* 1920
Electric Marcel waver, *ca.* 1920

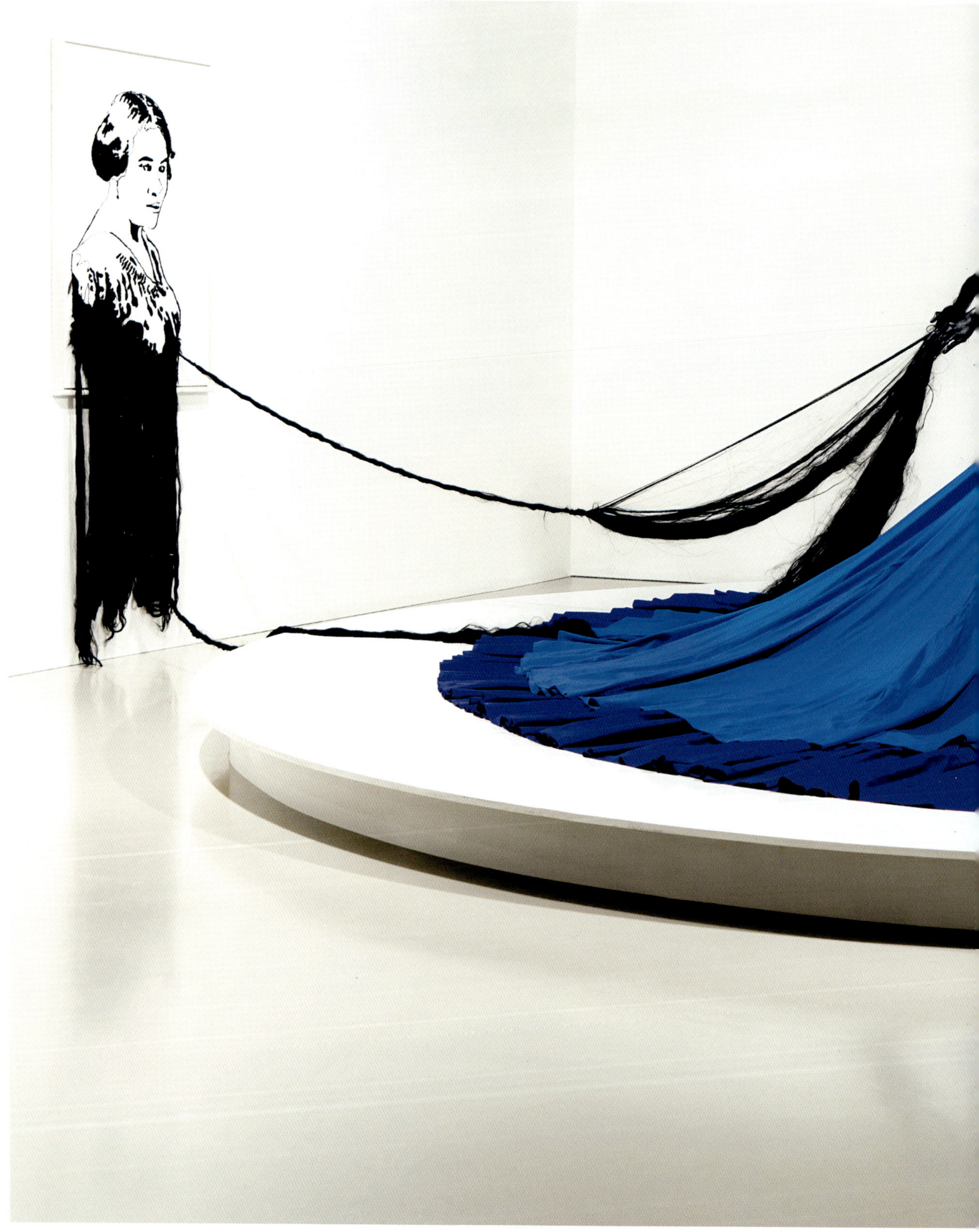

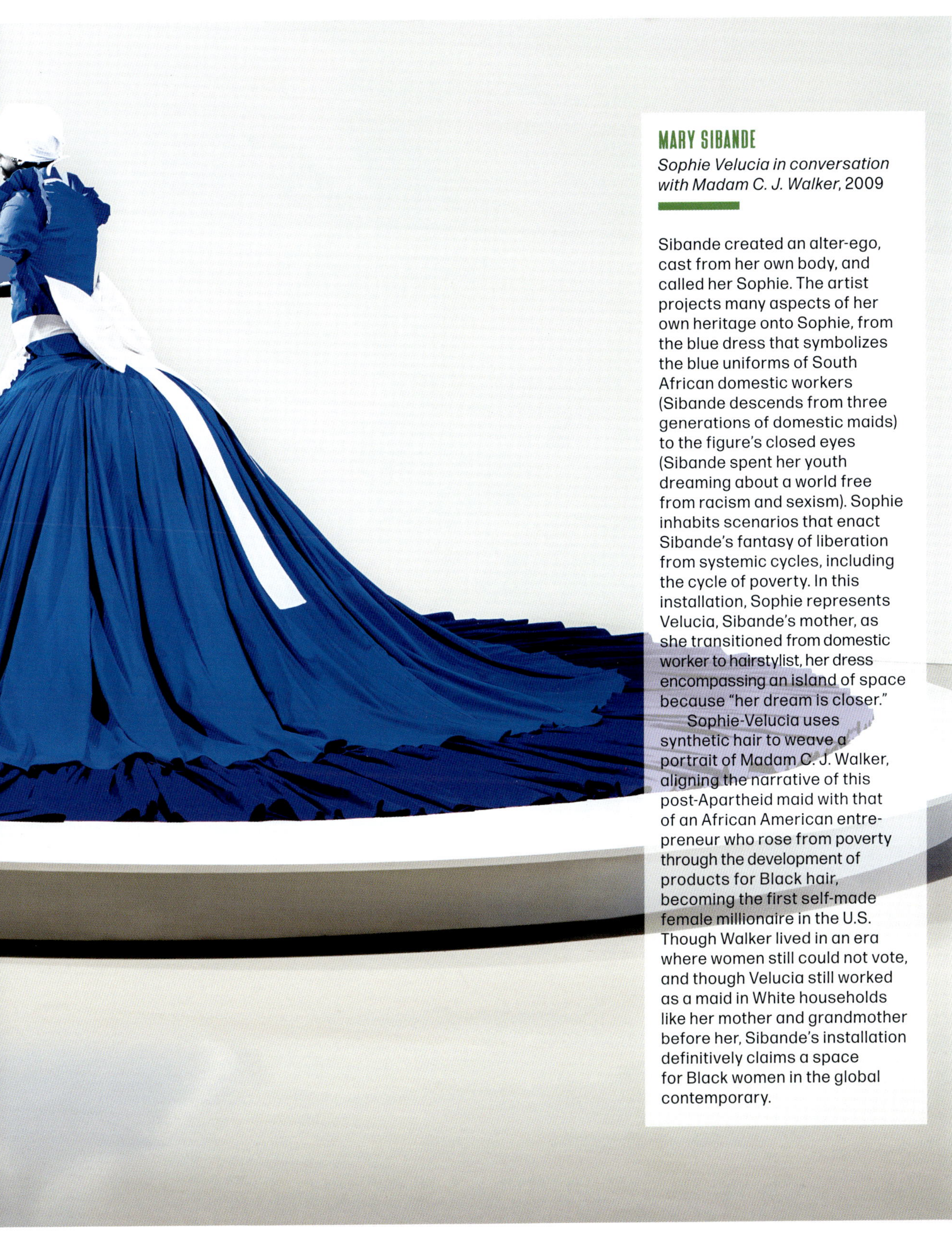

MARY SIBANDE

Sophie Velucia in conversation with Madam C. J. Walker, 2009

Sibande created an alter-ego, cast from her own body, and called her Sophie. The artist projects many aspects of her own heritage onto Sophie, from the blue dress that symbolizes the blue uniforms of South African domestic workers (Sibande descends from three generations of domestic maids) to the figure's closed eyes (Sibande spent her youth dreaming about a world free from racism and sexism). Sophie inhabits scenarios that enact Sibande's fantasy of liberation from systemic cycles, including the cycle of poverty. In this installation, Sophie represents Velucia, Sibande's mother, as she transitioned from domestic worker to hairstylist, her dress encompassing an island of space because "her dream is closer."

Sophie-Velucia uses synthetic hair to weave a portrait of Madam C. J. Walker, aligning the narrative of this post-Apartheid maid with that of an African American entrepreneur who rose from poverty through the development of products for Black hair, becoming the first self-made female millionaire in the U.S. Though Walker lived in an era where women still could not vote, and though Velucia still worked as a maid in White households like her mother and grandmother before her, Sibande's installation definitively claims a space for Black women in the global contemporary.

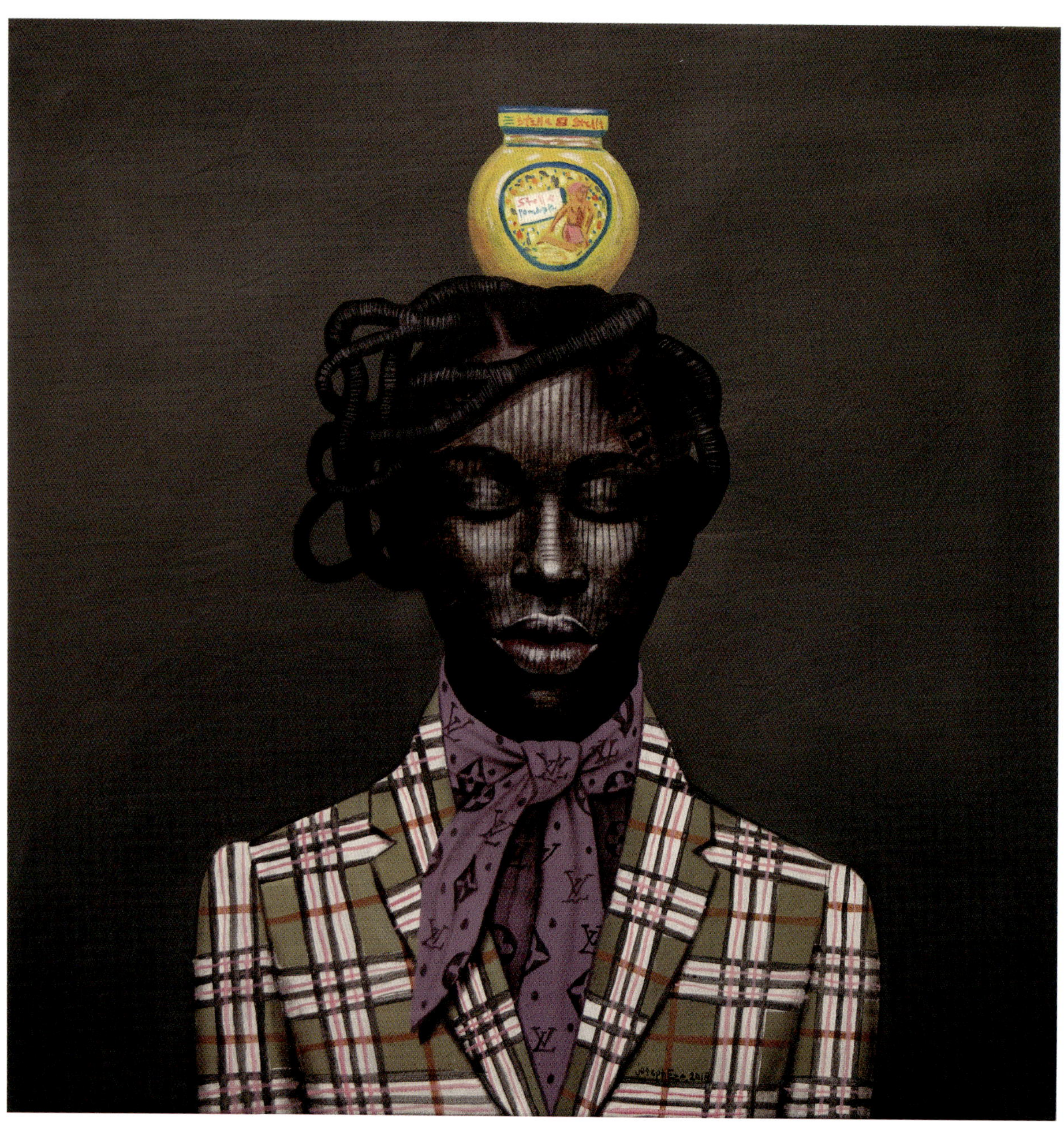

JOSEPH EZE

Stella Pomade #3, 2018

As a skincare product developed by PZ Cussons Nigeria, Stella Pomade used to be in every household. Though it has largely been replaced by imported foreign products, the iconic canister and its range of scents remain nostalgic for a generation of Nigerians. In this collage, Eze evokes the spirit of his mother by layering newspaper and acrylic paint to create a stunning model. Along with the luminous skin from the pomade, Eze recalls his mother by threading the model's hair—a style she frequently wore. Threading is a protective hairstyle that allows hair to grow and stretch naturally, even though thread is wrapped around small sections of hair from root to end. Balancing the worlds of fashion, advertisement, and fine art, Eze's practice always delivers a compelling, culturally-nuanced image.

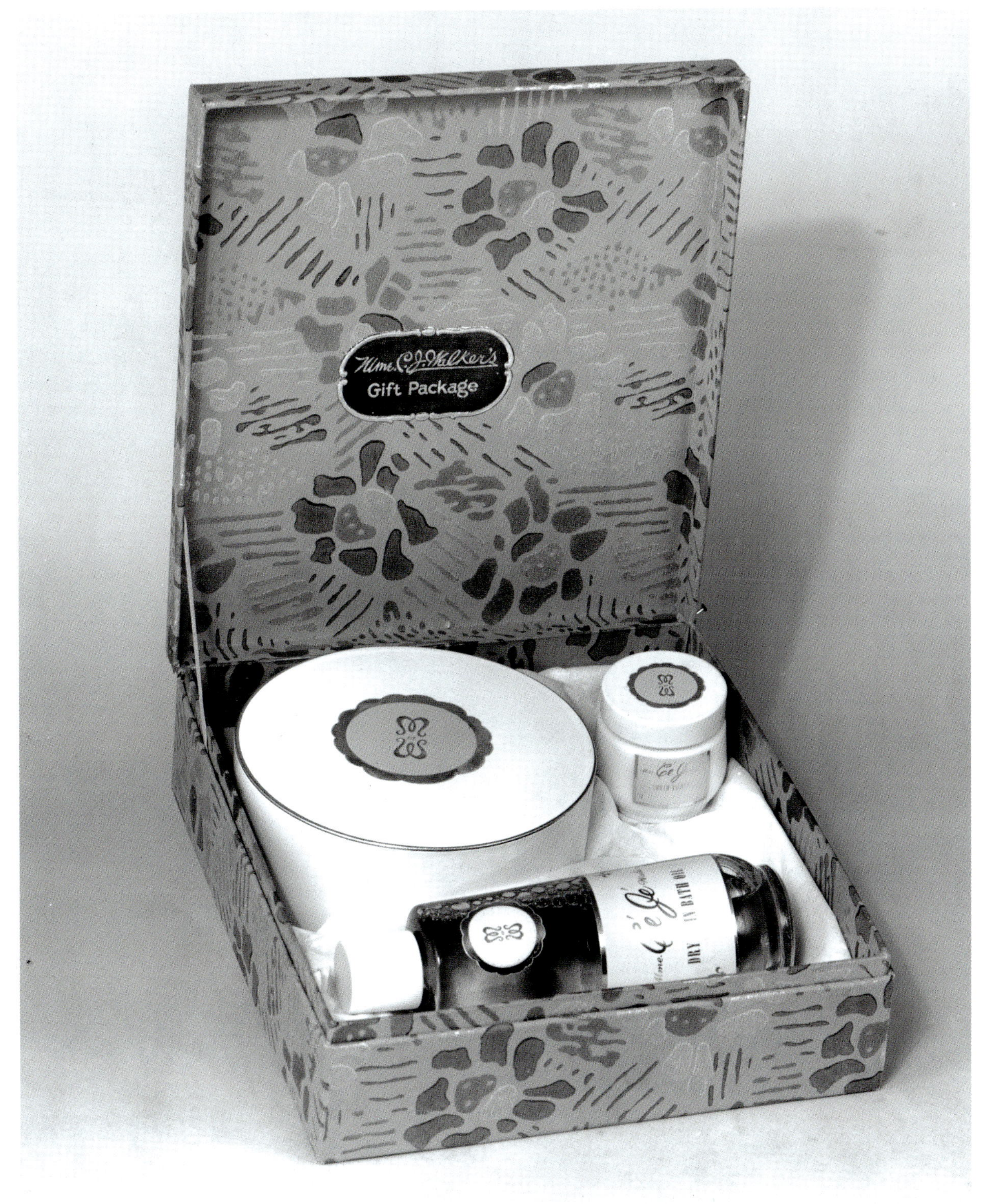

Madam C. J. Walker's Gift Package, *ca.* 1925

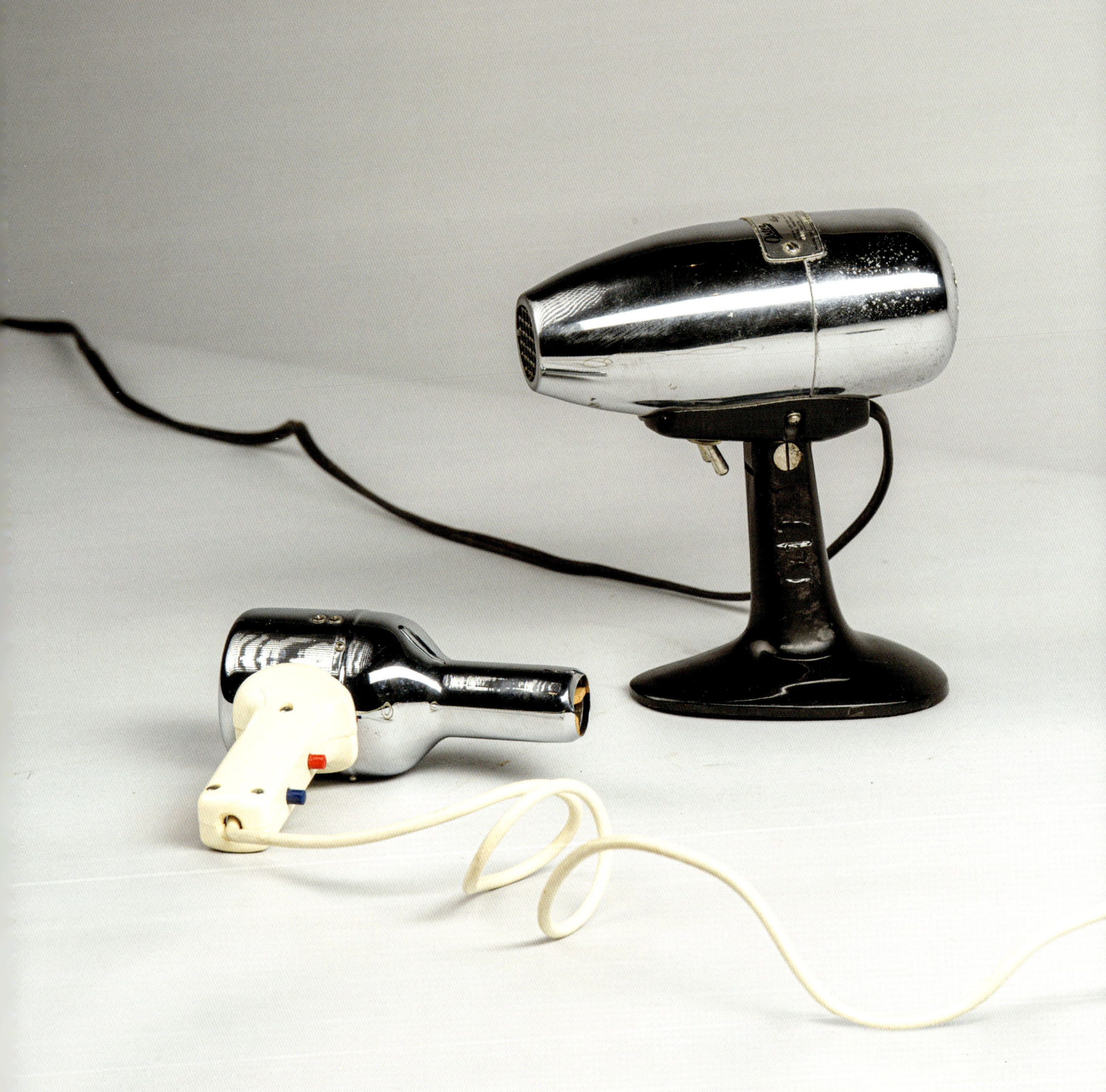

Hand hairdryer, *ca.* 1920–1930
Hand hairdryer, *ca.* 1920–1930

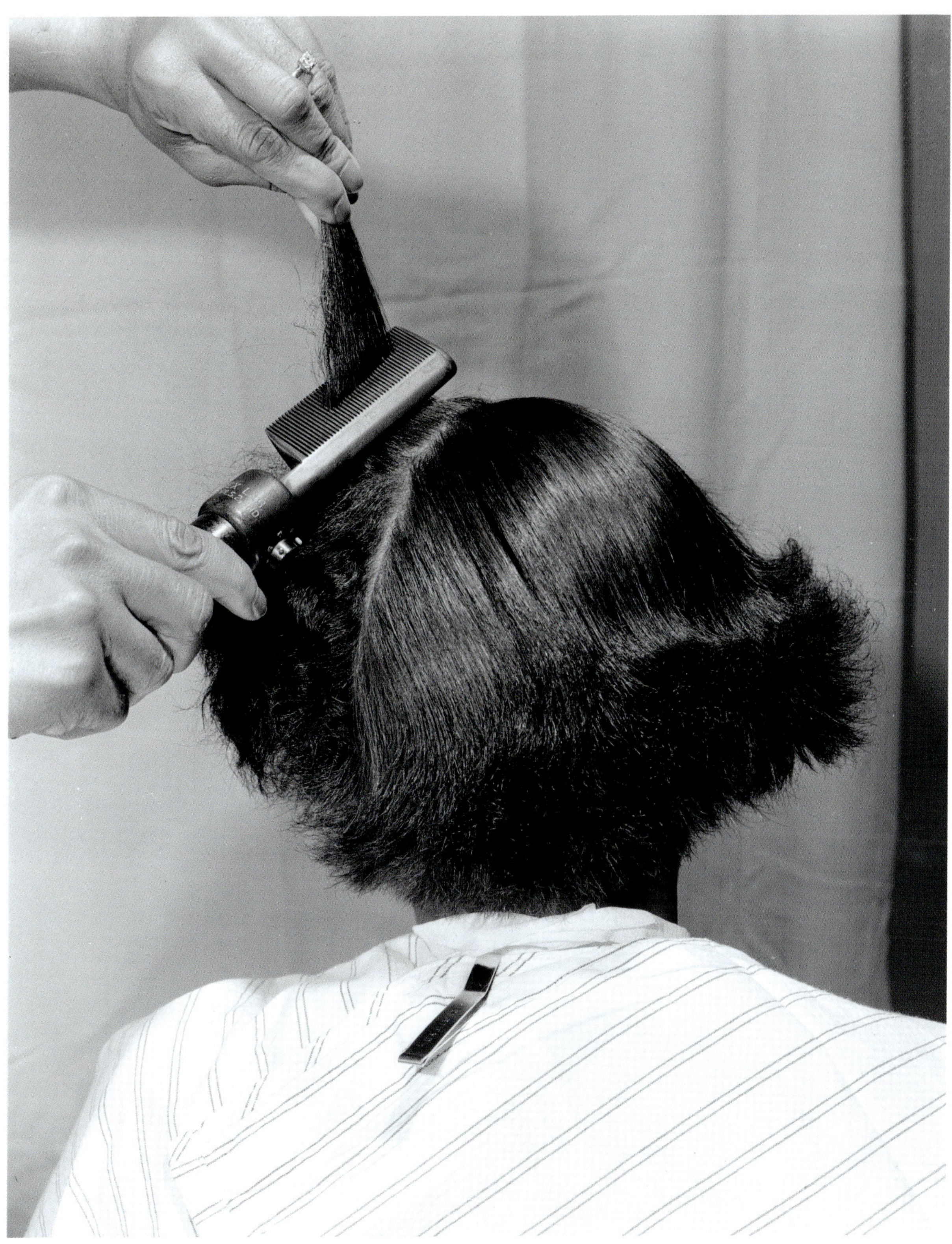

Hot Comb Demonstration, 1915

ASSORTMENT OF COMBS

(top) Yaka, Yaka, Akan, Asante, Ivorian, Baule, Congolese, Congolese, Congolese (bottom) Nande, Luba, Mangbetu, Surinamese, Saramaka, Ndyuka, Ndyuka, Chokwe, Congolese

Combs are one of the earliest tools for grooming and self-care. Ranging in size, the comb could serve as a prestige object, depending on the quality of the carving, the rarity of the wood, or the ornateness of its design. Whether in Africa or the Diaspora beyond, the comb has been an absolute necessity. From a tool used for everyday management to a symbol of Black pride and solidarity, hair combs and picks are ubiquitous among Black populations. Some highlights include:

Duafe, Akan, Ghana (Wood)

These combs were traditionally gifted during special occasions, like births, weddings, or coming of age ceremonies. Typically, the more elaborate belonged to women and were decorated with references to proverbs.

Baule, Ivory Coast (Wood)

One of the largest ethnic groups in the Ivory Coast, the Baule people, believe their finely sculpted objects can foster spiritual connections. The *Mblo* masks have influenced many of their decorated objects, including this wooden comb. These combs represented an elevated social status and were used for both styling the hair and decorating it.

Ndyuka, Suriname (Wood)

The combs carved by Ndyuka and Maroon artists feature intricate knot patterns. Typically carved by men as a gift to their partners, the combs were mostly regarded as prestige objects. Though they were rarely used, a finely carved or oversized comb conveyed the status of a woman and her lover.

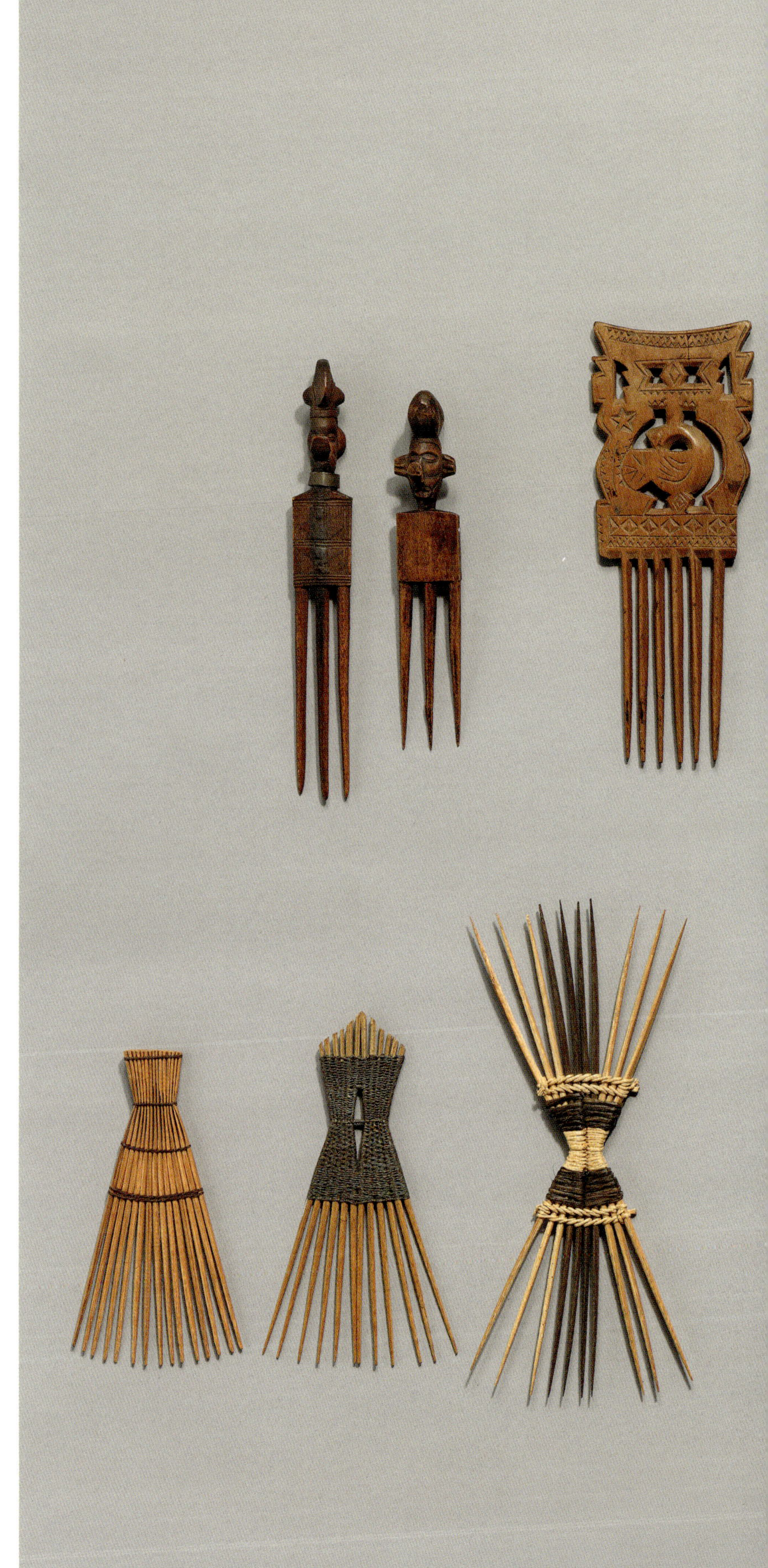

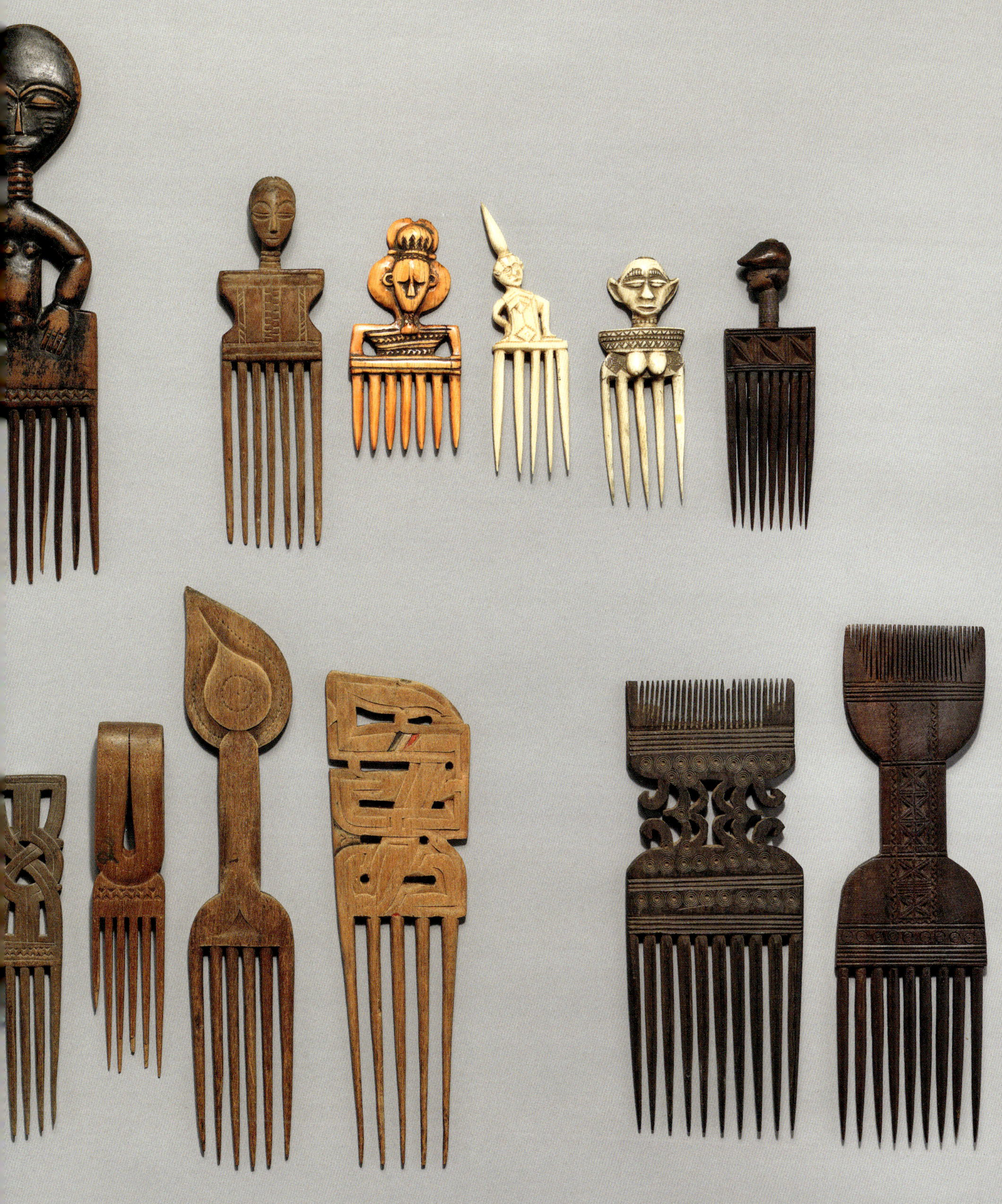

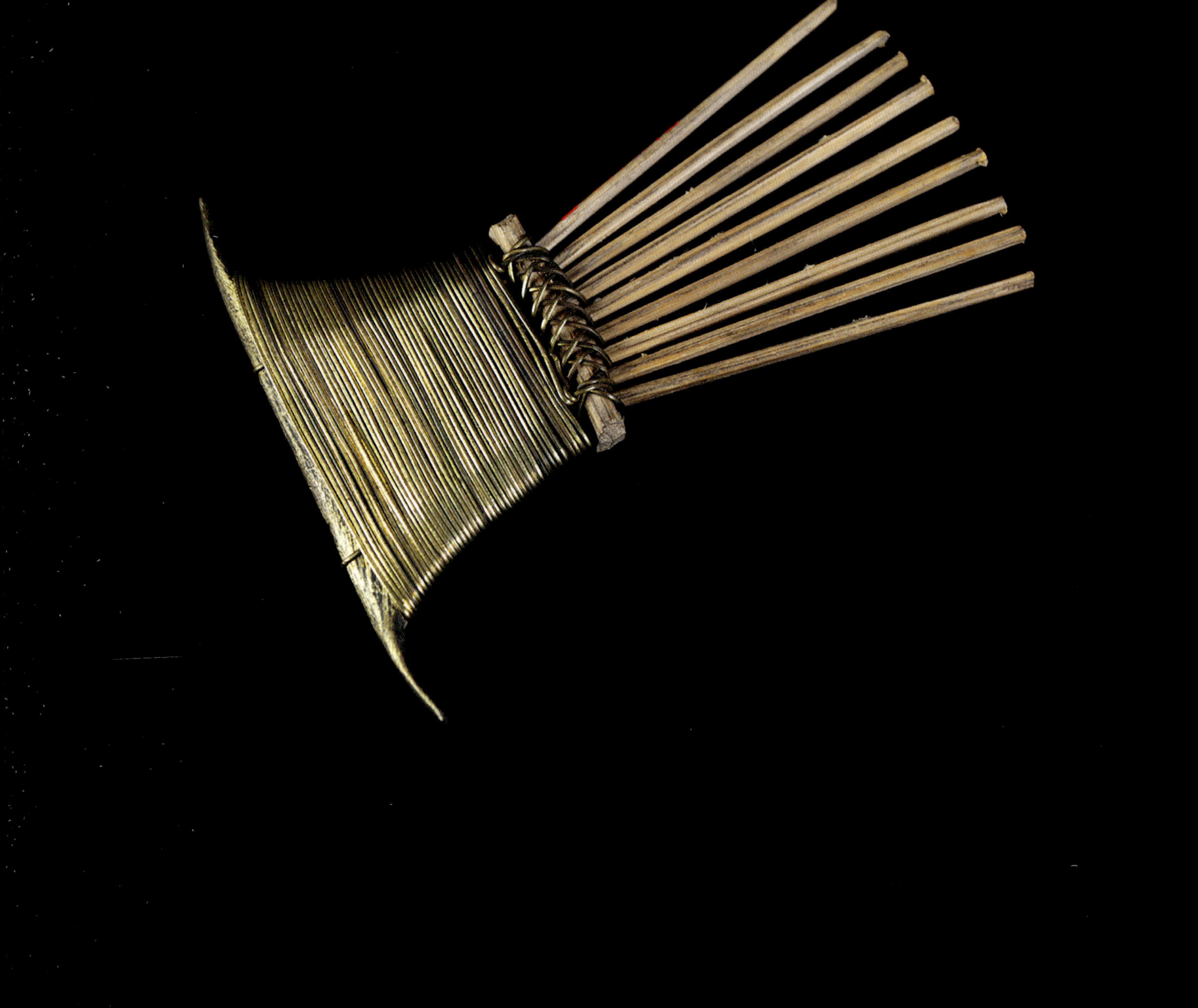

UNIDENTIFIED AFRICAN ARTIST
Combs

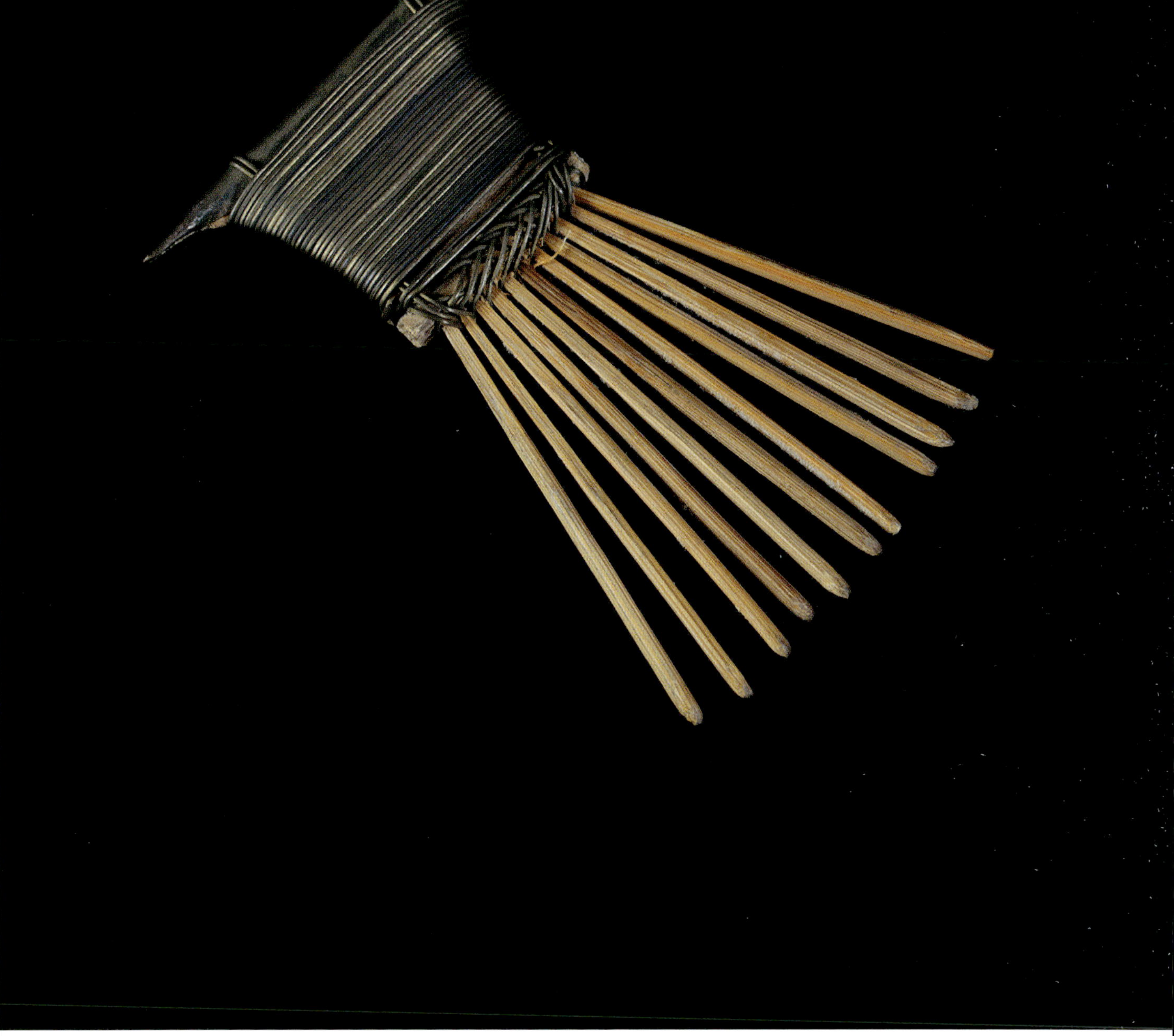

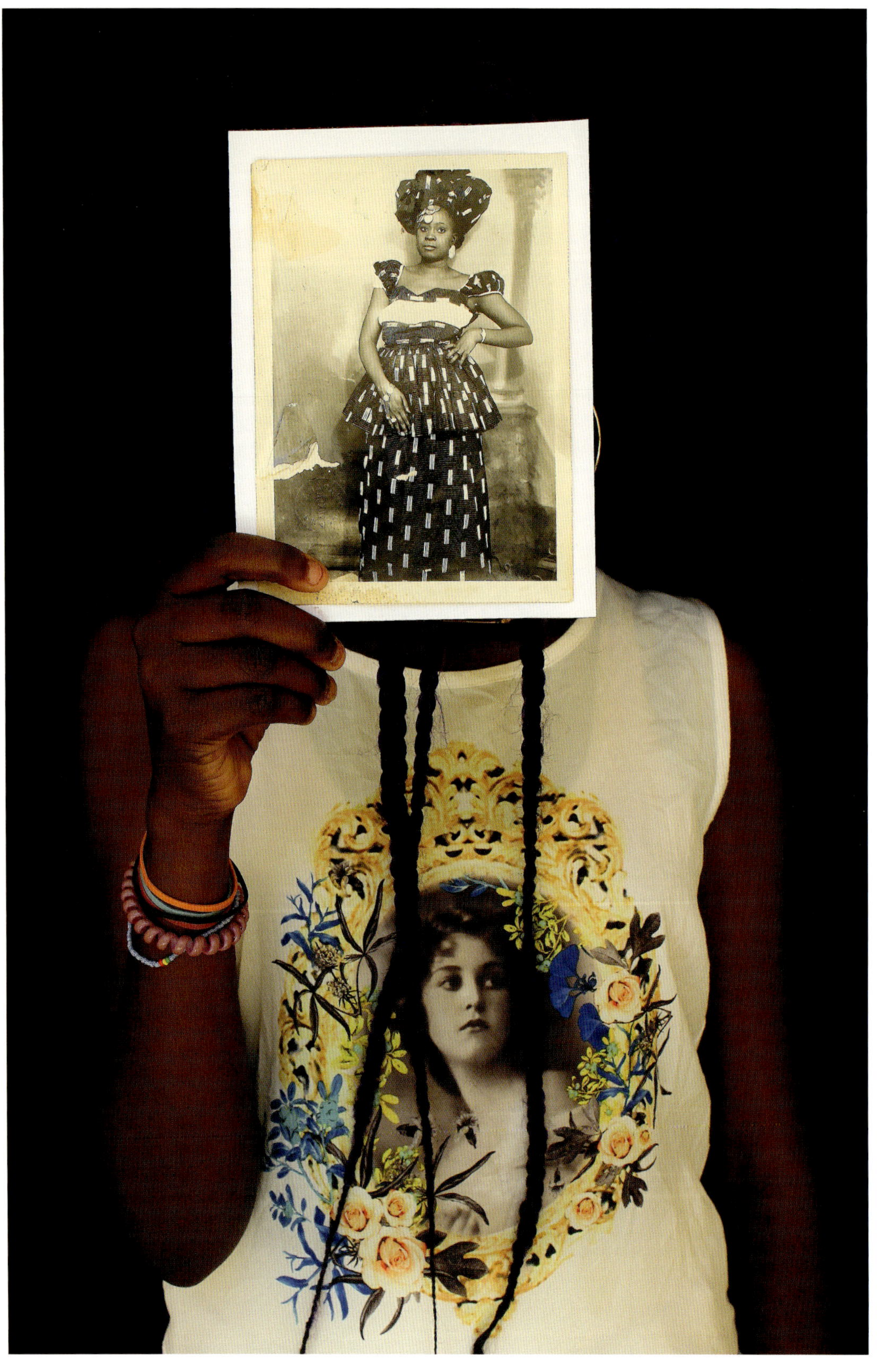

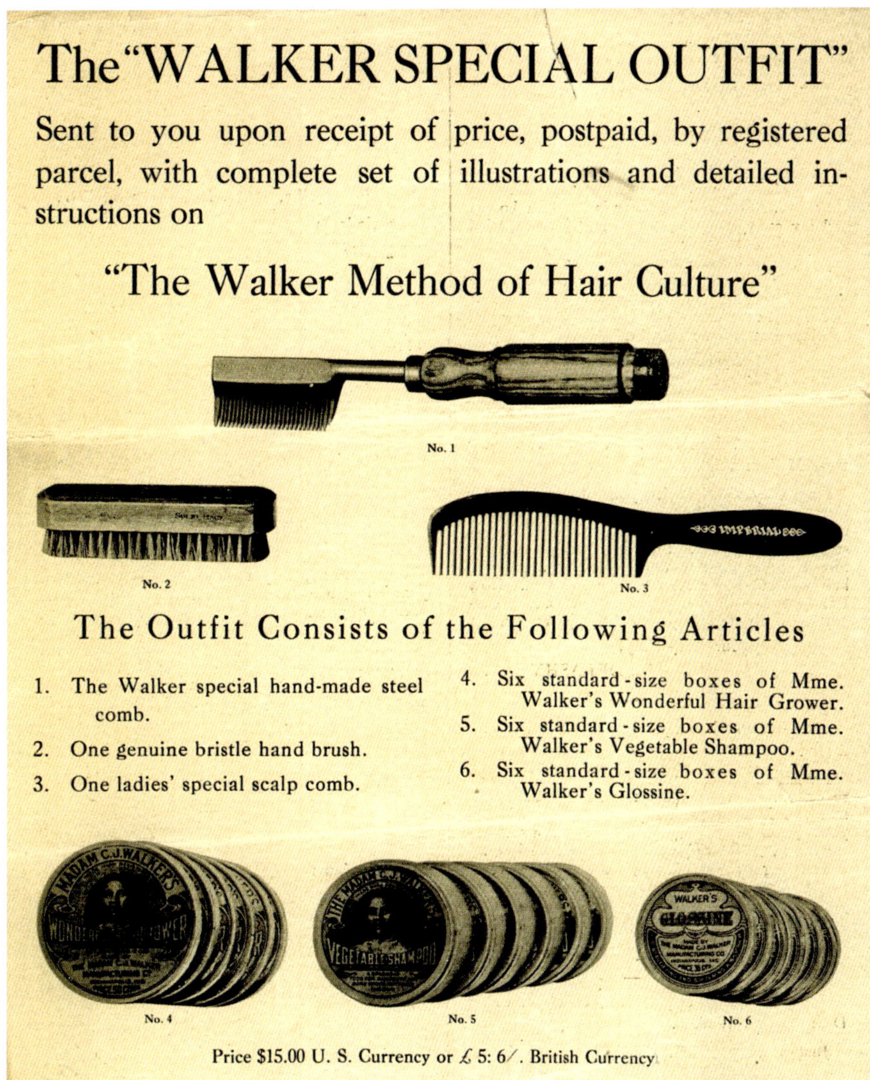

Walker Special Outfit, 1930s

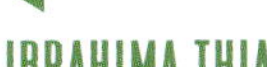

IBRAHIMA THIAM

Selection from *Vintage Portrait* series, 2017

Our natural instinct when seeing a piece of art is to find the subject's face and look into their eyes. However, this impulse is thwarted in Thiam's *Vintage Portrait* series. The artist gives new life to historic photos from 1900 to 1980s Senegal by having family, friends, and passers-by pose with their face hidden by an archival photo. Dedicated to archiving the rich tradition of photography in Senegal and to finding novel ways to encourage Africans to safeguard their history and heritage, Thiam deftly balances the past in the present.

In this image, the young woman has chosen to feature a 1960s studio portrait. However, even with her face hidden, Thiam's camera captures some of the same biographic details about her that the studio photographer documented for his sitter: the manner of dress, an assortment of accessories, and the styling of the hair. Each woman's hair adornment—from elaborate wrap to purple-dyed extensions—reflects their particular historical moments and social context.

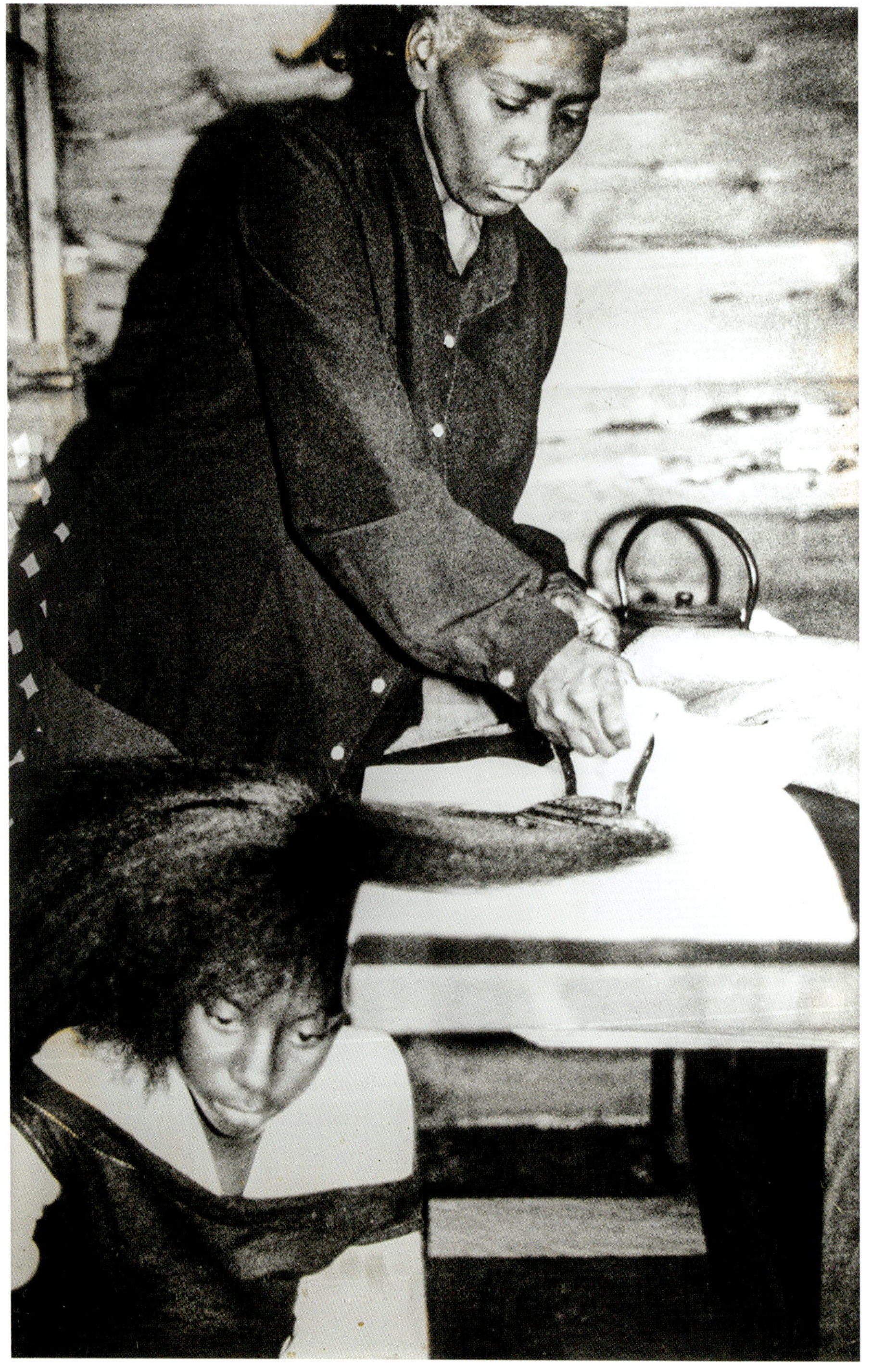

Unknown photographer, *Hair being straightened with an iron*

After the abolition of slavery in 1865, Black people were free but continued to face enormous hardships as they transitioned into the United States economy. Assimilation and acculturation became necessary evils for survival. Ideologies around colorism (preferential treatment of those with lighter skin over those with darker skin) started during the slave era and were major hurdles for many. Bleaching creams became a household item for many Black families. Paired with colorism was the preference of straighter hair (what Dr. Ellington coined as texturism), thus Black people went to extreme measures to rid their hair of its natural kinky texture. They used household clothing irons, hot towels, hot knives, spoons, or forks as tools to transform their hair into a more "acceptable" style. In 1872, the hot comb was invented by Frenchman François Marcel Grateau. By 1906, entrepreneur Madam C. J. Walker helped to popularize the hot comb in the United States which she sold as a package with her hair serums.

CHARLES BOHANNAH
Seated Woman, *ca.* 1940

Born in Brooklyn in 1910, Bohannah put his artistic career on hold to join the war effort, employing photography to show the realities of combat. After World War II, he resumed painting, using oils to create expressive landscapes, figurative portraits, and still lifes. *Seated Woman* follows a pattern seen in many of his portraits by depicting women with natural hair and a commanding presence at rest in a nondescript setting. The light source shines down from the left, highlighting the sitter's face as her shoulders open toward the light. With expressive brushstrokes, Bohannah conveys the texture of her hair, the softness of her skin, and the energetic twist of her torso. Despite the anonymity of the subject, the self-assured woman casts a resolute gaze at the viewer.

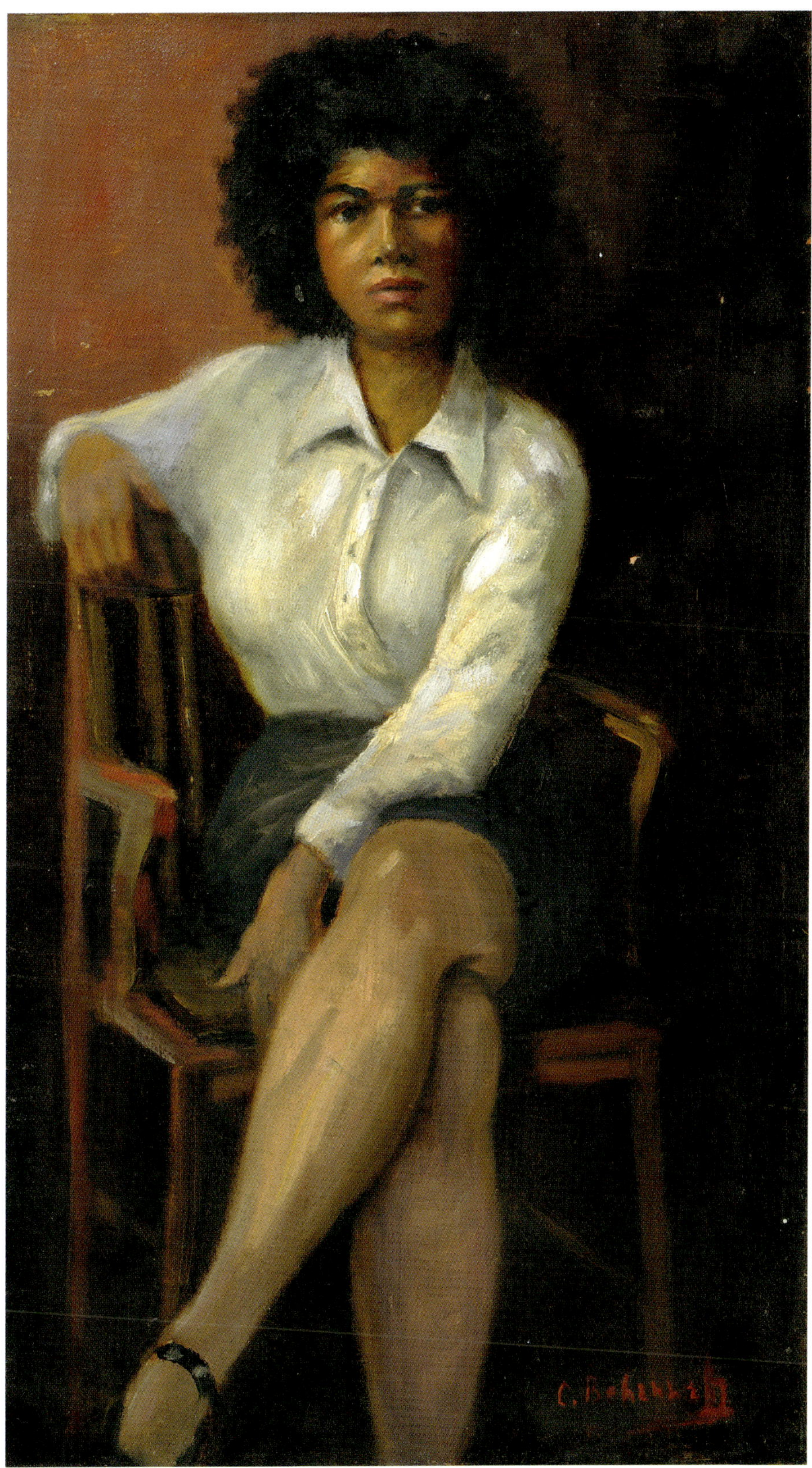

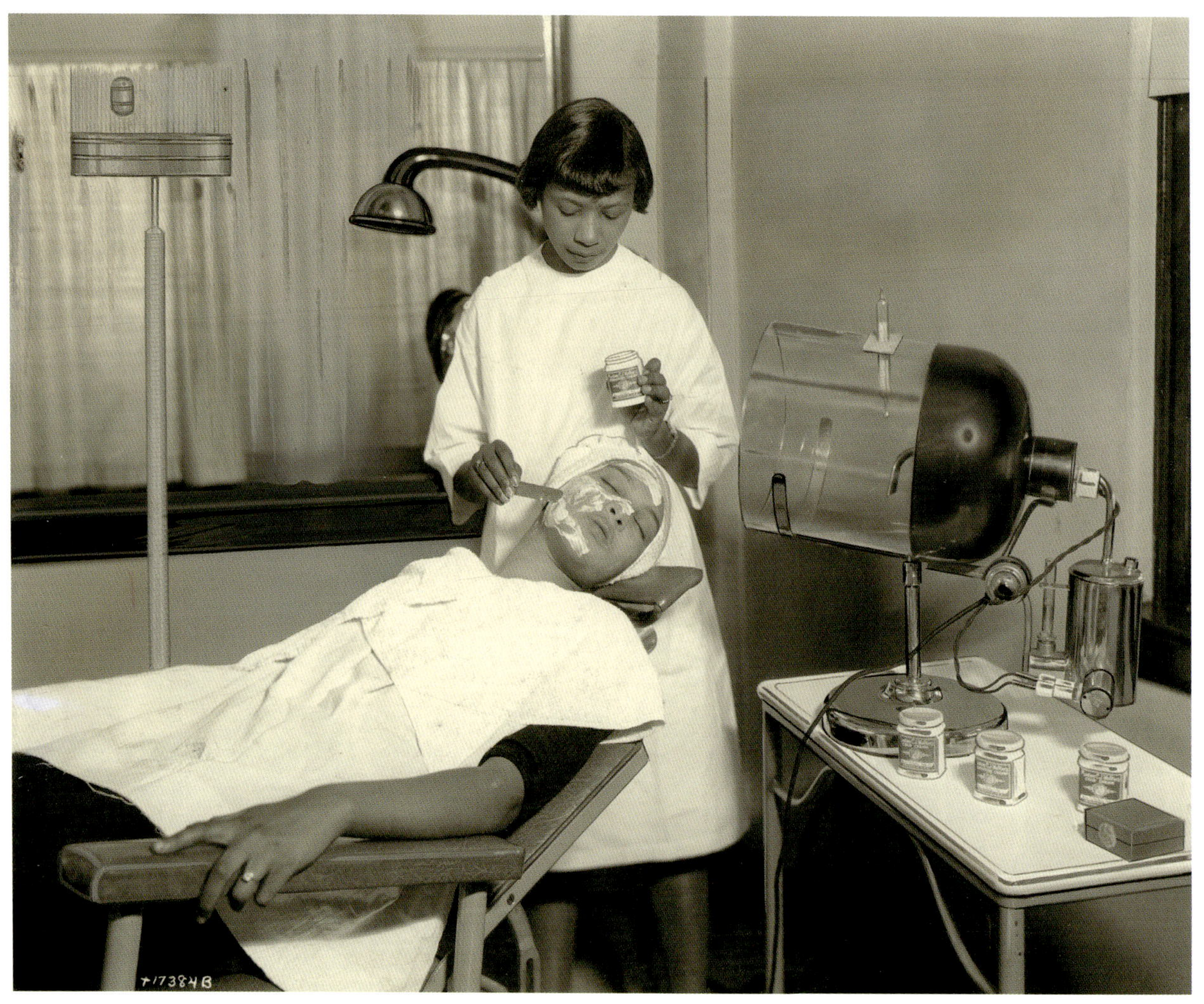

Vanishing Cream Facial, *ca.* 1920

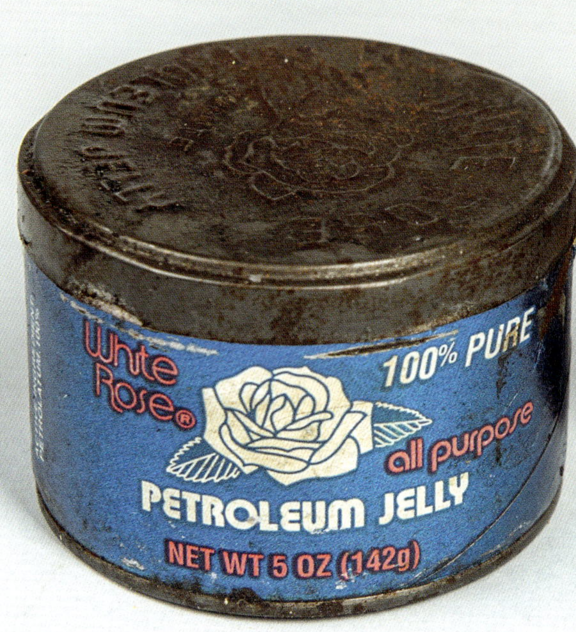

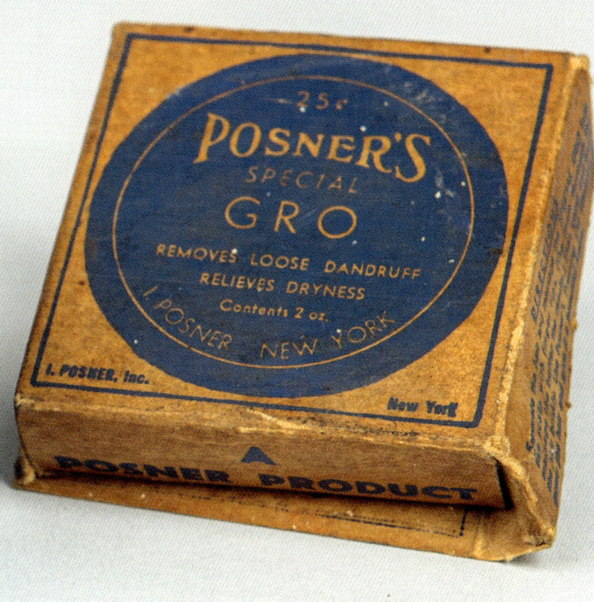

White Rose Petroleum Jelly, *ca.* 1980
Posner's Special Gro hair conditioner, *ca.* 1960

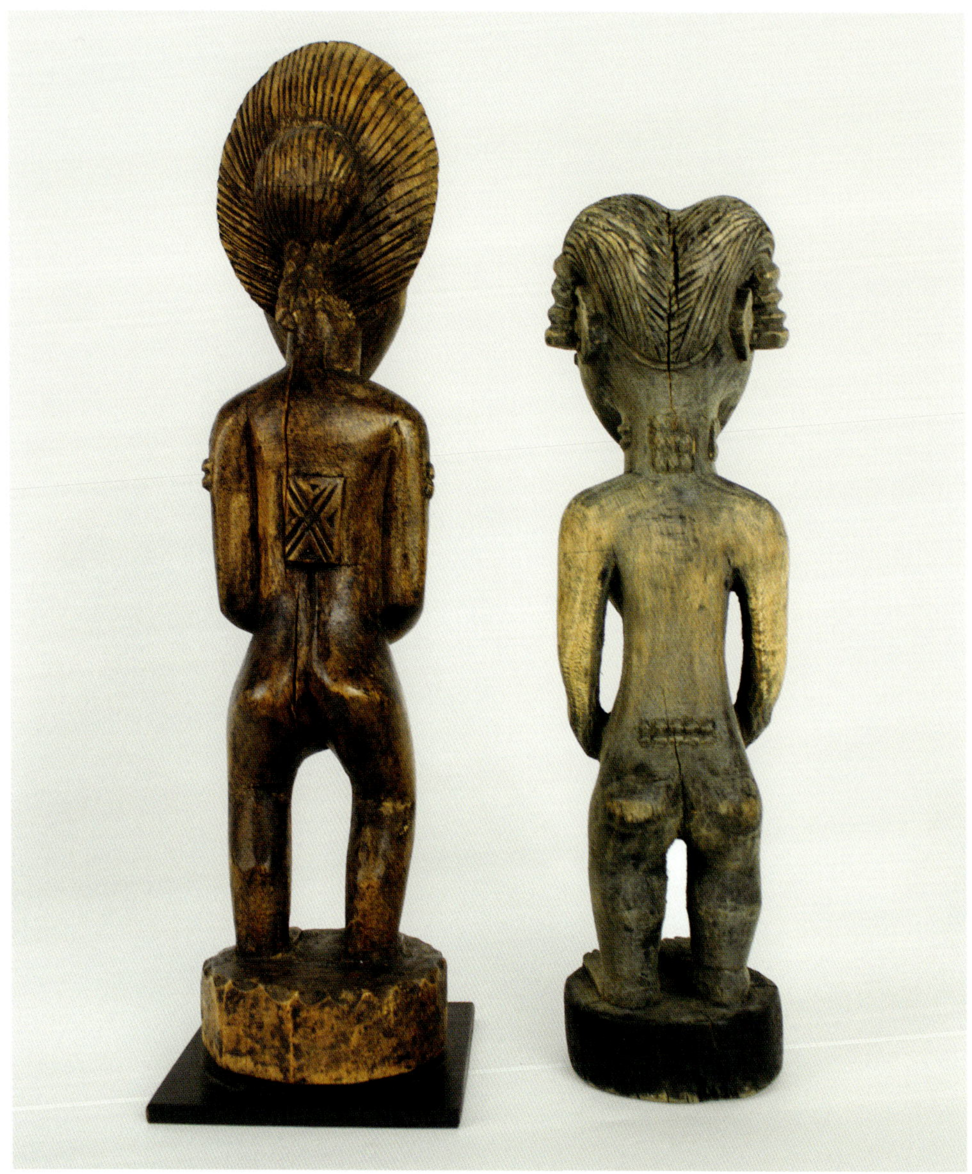

(L) UNIDENTIFIED BAULE ARTIST
Male Figure, 20th century

(R) UNIDENTIFIED AKAN ARTIST
Female Figure, 20th century

Hair has been valued in most African societies for its aesthetic qualities and its ability to communicate social hierarchies and communal identities. Particular hairstyles are like signs and signals, conveying the wearer's ethnic or familial identity, social status, religious affiliation, or stage of life. Translating these styles onto figural sculptures—sometimes the most finely carved aspect of the whole statue—demonstrates the value of hair as a physical feature and the necessity of the social codes woven into it.

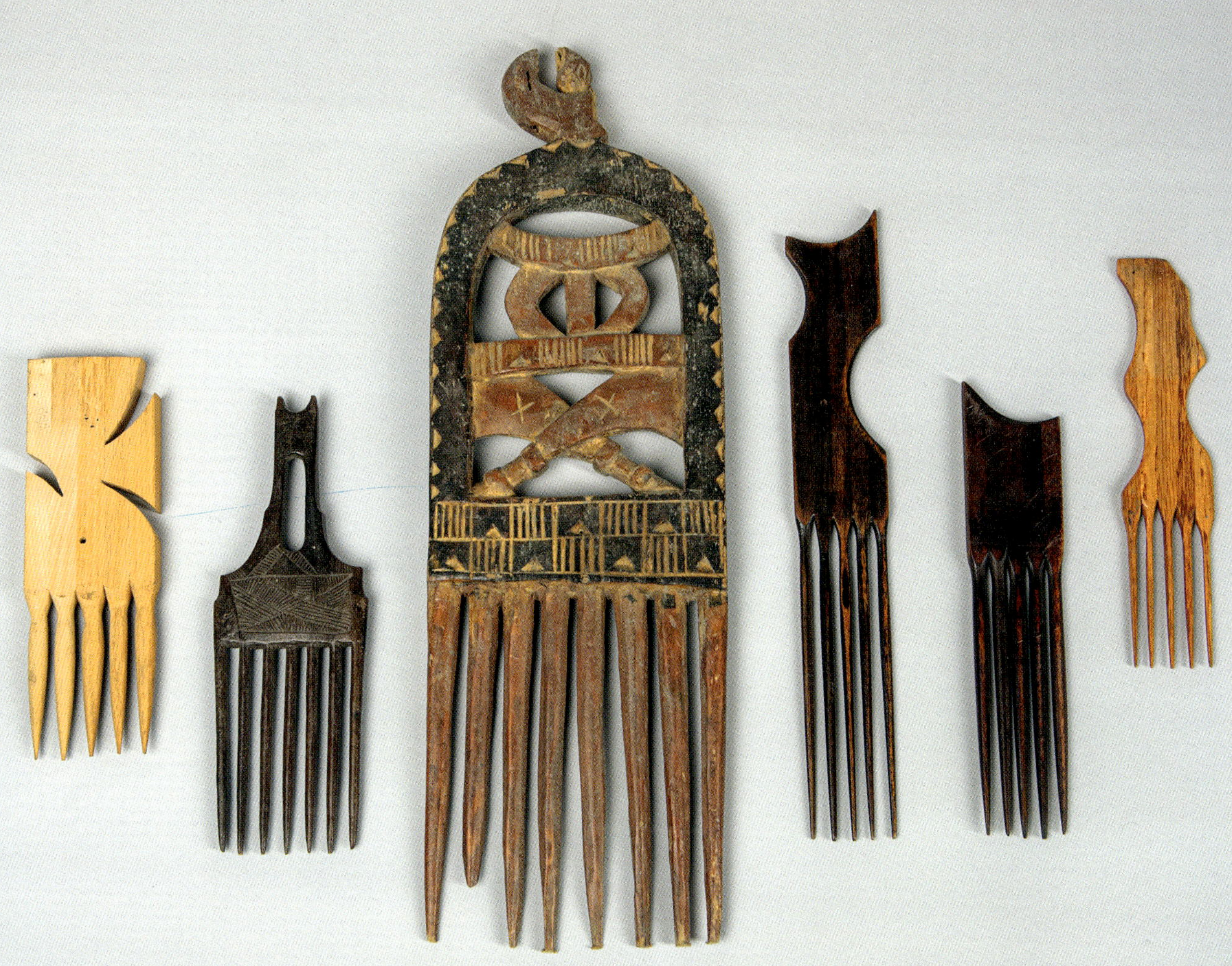

Selection of African combs from the collection of Dr. Willie Morrow

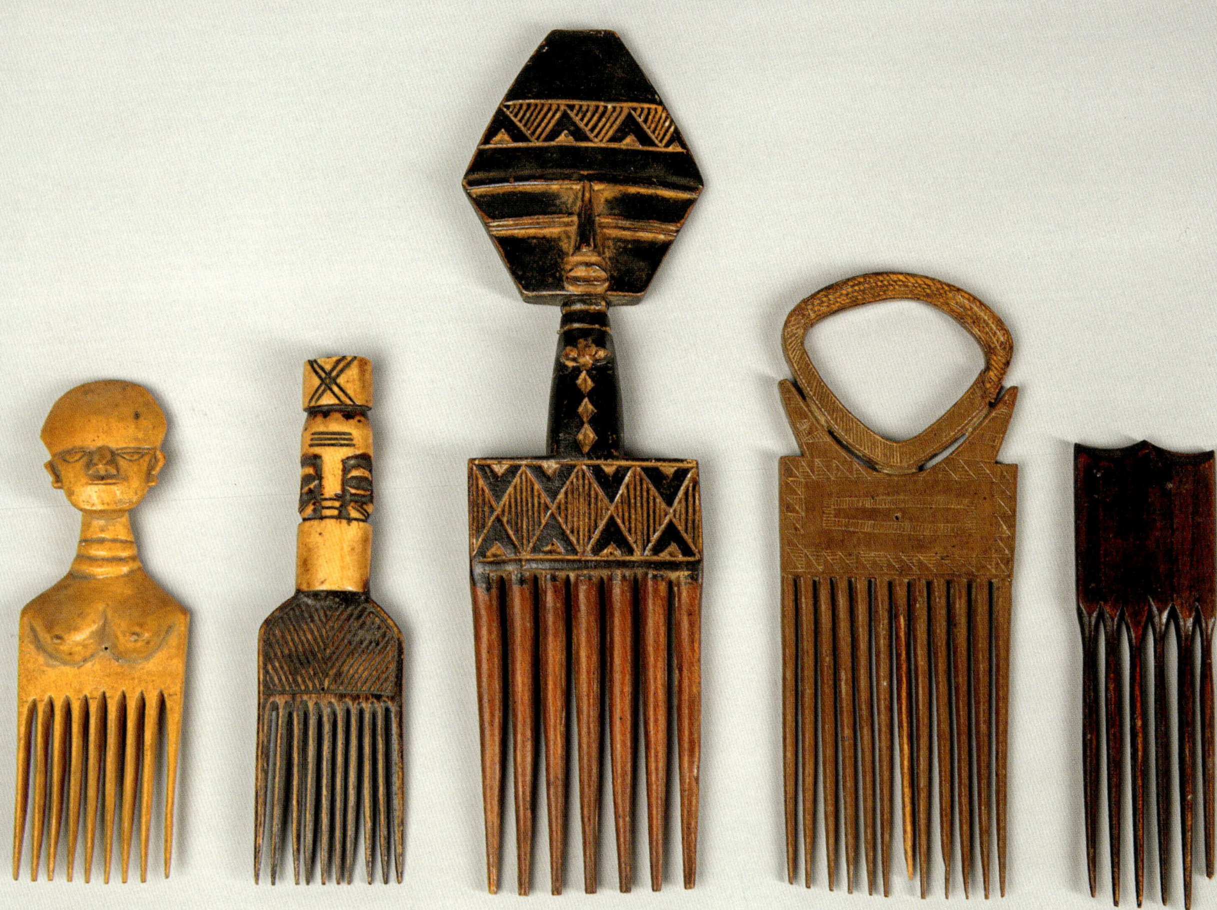

Selection of African combs from the collection of Dr. Willie Morrow

ANDREW ESIEBO

Nuance Abidjan from the *Pride* series, 2012
Nuance Mali from the *Pride* series, 2012

Representing barbershops across West Africa, Esiebo's *Pride* series examines these intimate spaces as multi-layered expressions of urban aesthetics. Found on every other street corner in major cities, the small tin barbershop can accommodate only one or two patrons at a time. While most of *Pride* documents the people and locations associated with this profession, *Nuance Mali* and *Nuance Abidjan* differ in their almost clinical examination of the tools gathered for the cutting and styling of hair. The innovation of the barbers is signaled by their breadth of styling devices—some traditional, some unexpected. The sporadic arrangement of the picks, razors, combs, and clippers suggests their frequent use even as Esiebo's camera fixes them in space like a seventeenth-century still life. Though Esiebo is known for his photographs on male queerness in Africa, the *Pride* series is based on the barbers' immense pride for their craft, citing their career as the key to their financial independence and their shop as the hub for their local communities.

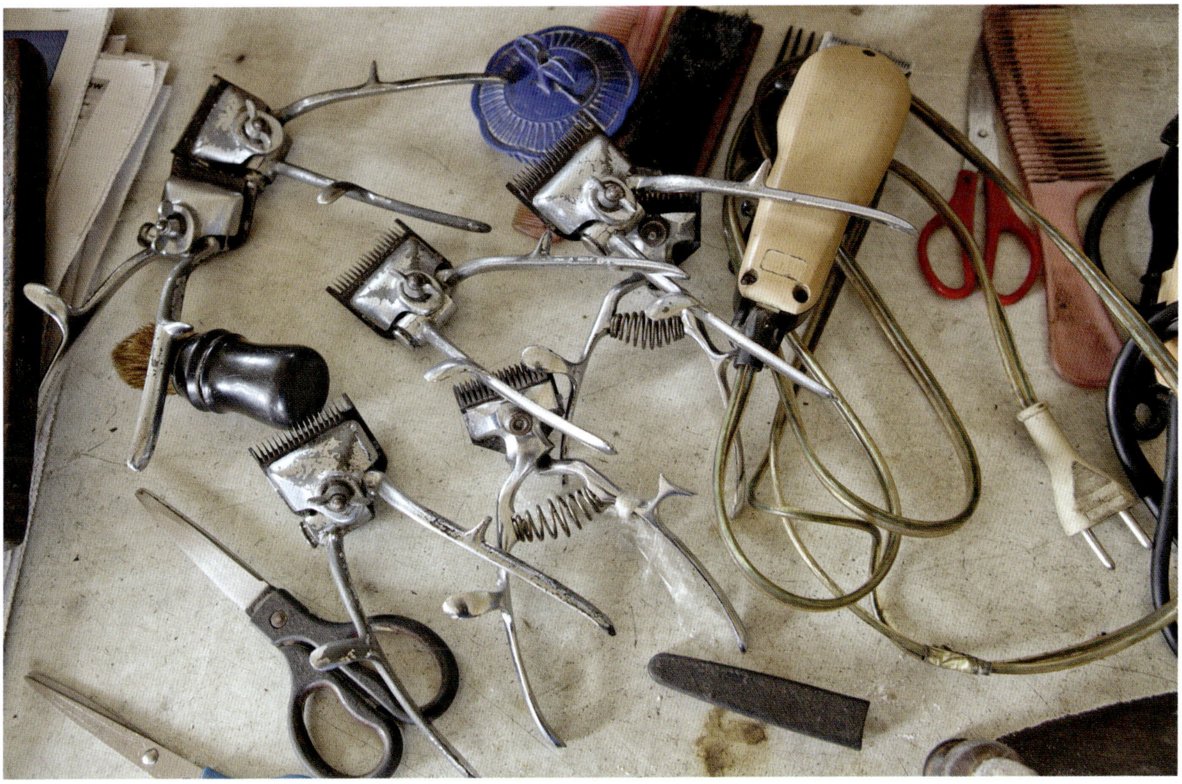

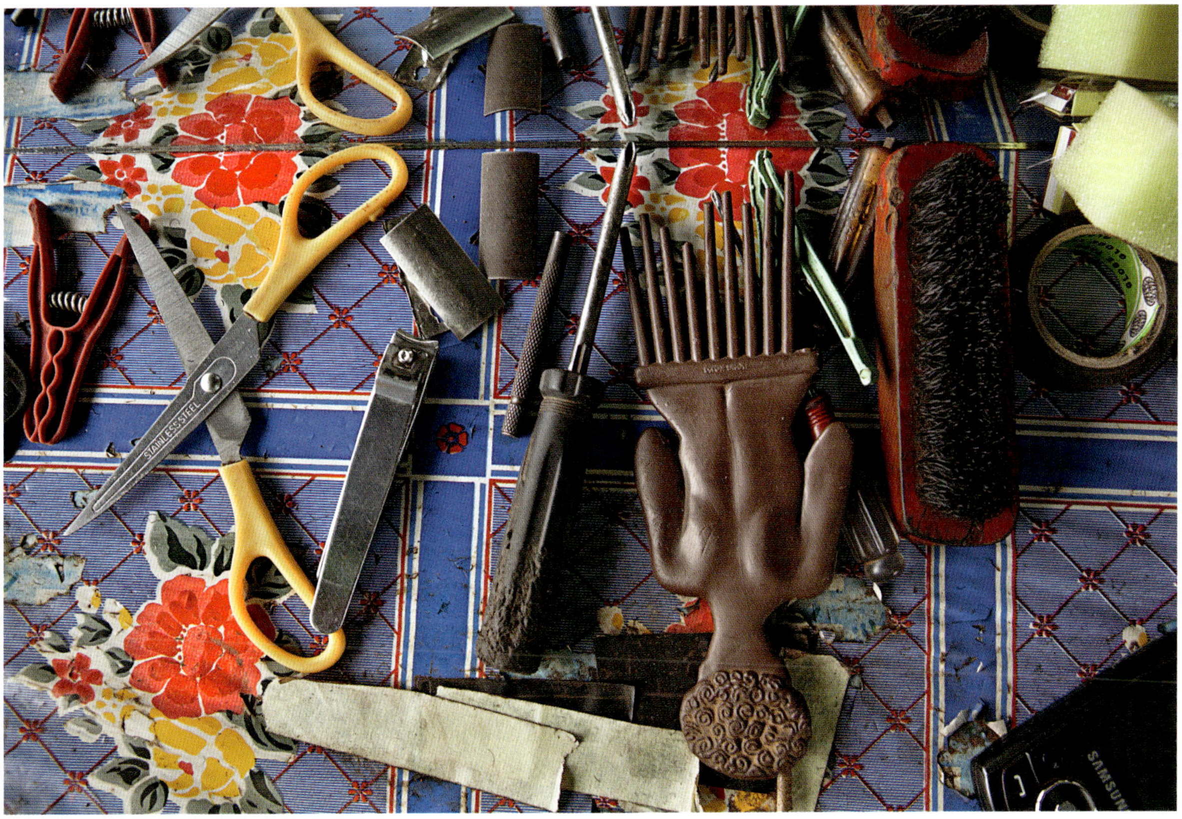

Due to challenges arising from the COVID-19 pandemic of 2020, the planned loans of Egyptian artifacts from the Metropolitan Museum of Art and the Brooklyn Museum were cancelled. To honor their role in this exhibition, and to maintain the integrity of the curatorial vision of demonstrating the long history of hair on the African continent and in its Diaspora, the editors have decided to include two of the nine examples that should have been in the physical installation. Though the exhibition visitors may not be able to see these particular ancient objects alongside the contemporary artworks, we hope that situating them together visually in this catalogue is fruitful for the reader.

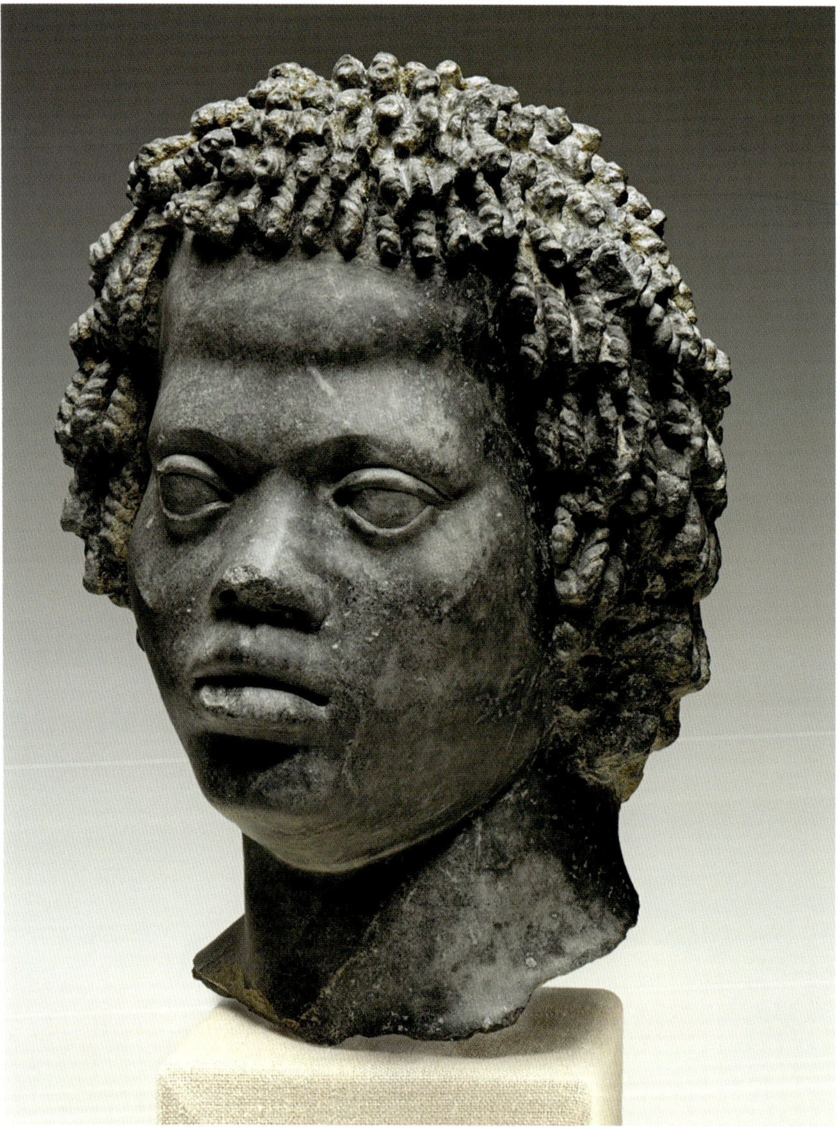

UNIDENTIFIED EGYPTIAN ARTIST
Head of a Man with Tight, Curly Hair, late 2nd century BCE
Marble, "Bigio Morata"
11 × 7.7 × 7.5 in. (27.9 × 19.6 × 19.1 cm)
Collection of The Brooklyn Museum, Charles Edwin Wilbour Fund

Though the origin of this head is disputed, probably coming from Greece or Asia Minor rather than Egypt, the sculptor's intention to recreate the texture of tightly coiled Black hair is unmistakable. With hyperrealistic detail, the features of this man are very different from the proportions and conventions of canonical Egyptian art. Likely based on the Nubian population of Sub-Saharan Africa, this remnant would have belonged to a full figure.

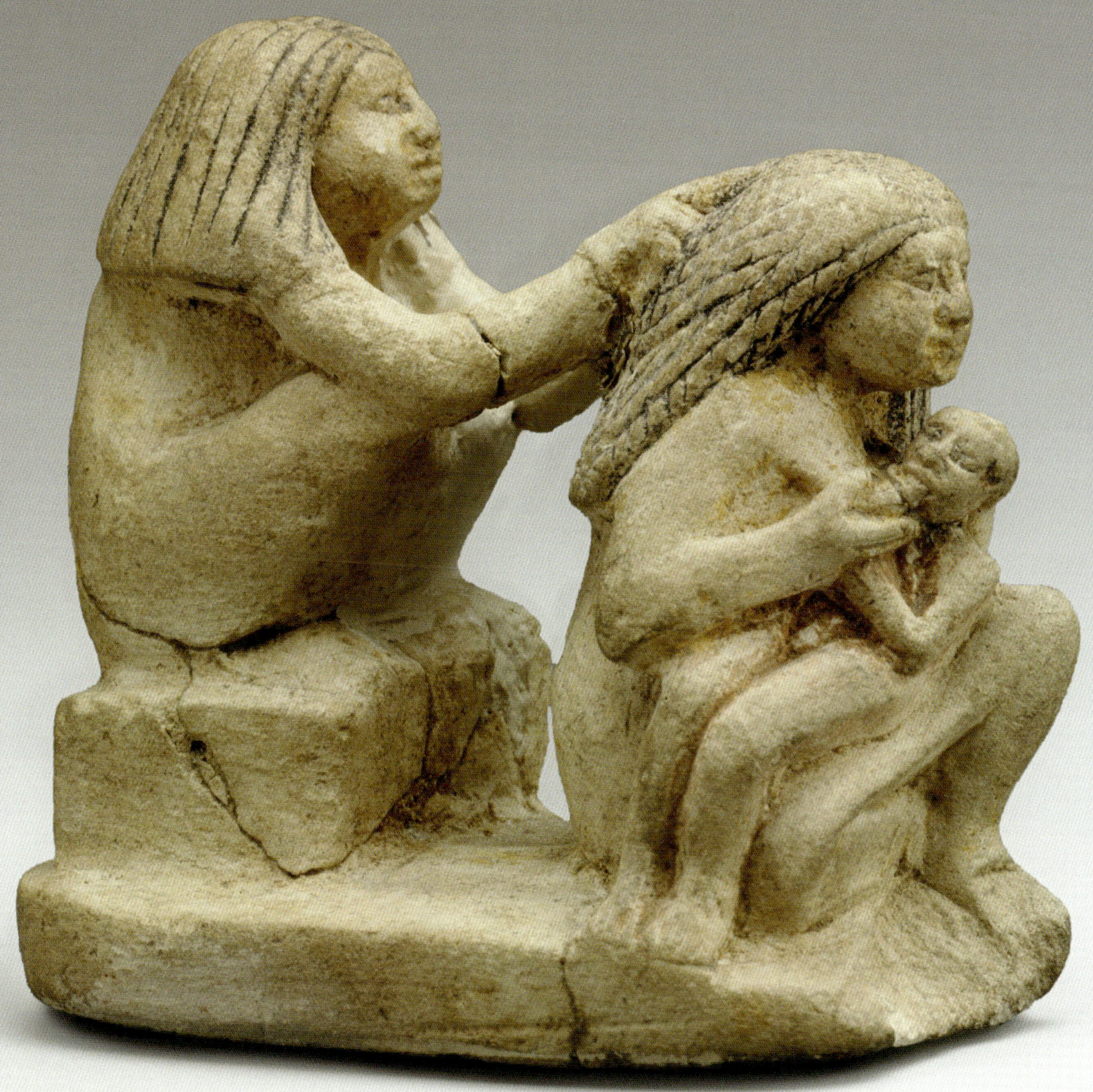

UNIDENTIFIED EGYPTIAN ARTIST
Group of Two Women and a Child,
ca. 1981–1500 BCE
Limestone, paint
2.8 × 1.7 × 3.25 in. (7.1 × 4.3 × 8.2 cm)
Collection of The Metropolitan Museum of Art,
Rogers Fund, 1922

This artifact depicts a scene from life in an Egyptian harem: two women, one of whom is breastfeeding her child while the other braids her hair. This statuette shows not only the proliferation of the culture surrounding Black hair and the art of braiding, but also the gendered nature of hair care and styling throughout history. These small artifacts are common in funerary offerings and many show diverse styles of hair, some even with holes drilled into the crown of the head so that actual locks of hair could be inserted. The time and care dedicated to sculpting figures and the detailed appearance of their braids demonstrates the importance of this practice in ancient Egyptian culture—almost four thousand years ago.

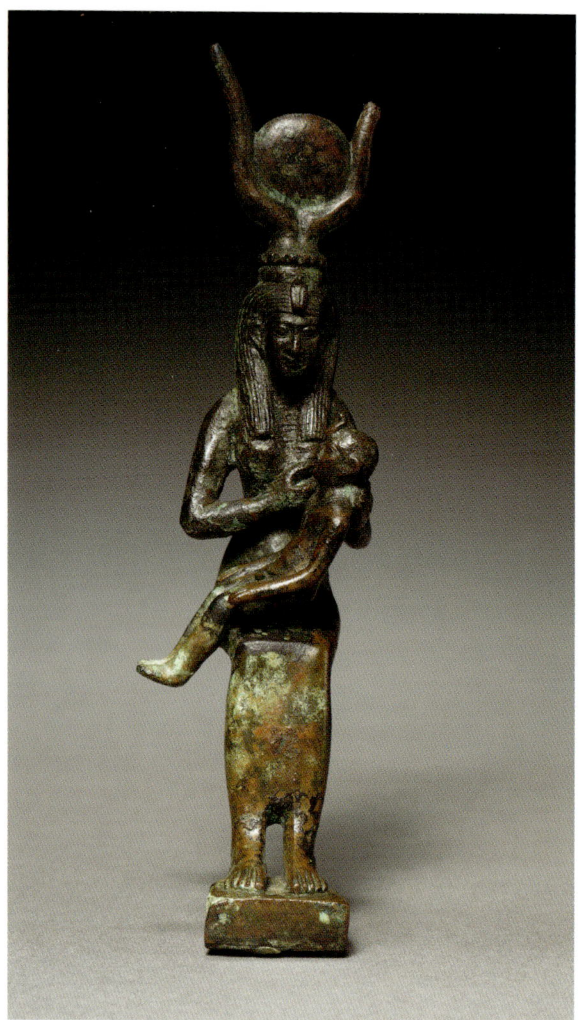

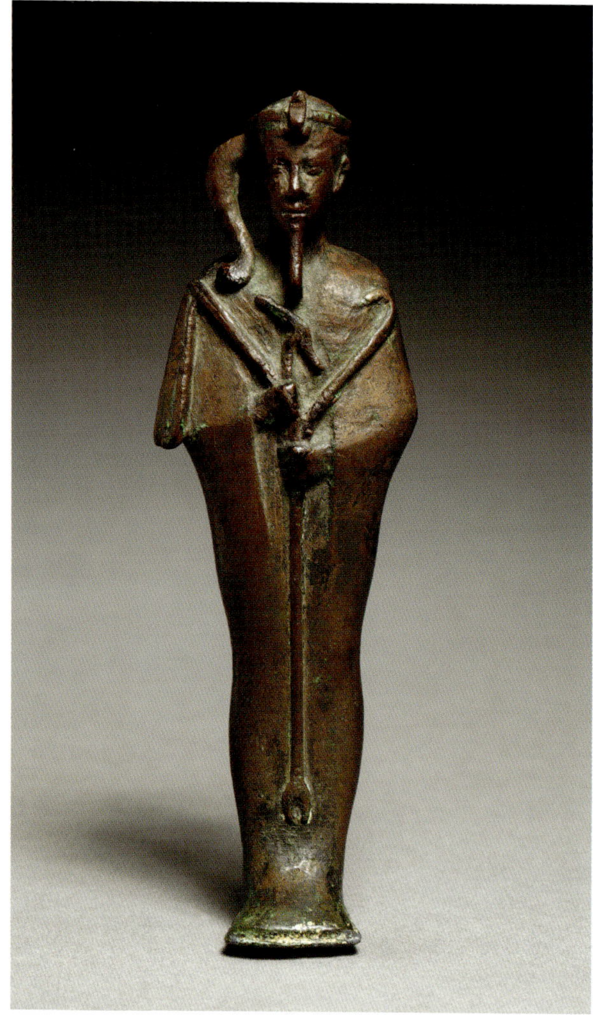

UNIDENTIFIED EGYPTIAN ARTIST

Statuette of Isis and Horus, 305-30 BCE
Egypt, Greco-Roman Period, probably Ptolemaic Dynasty
Bronze, solid cast
6.8 × 1.8 × 2.6 in. (17.3 × 4.6 × 6.5 cm)
Collection of the Cleveland Museum of Art, Bequest of John L. Severance, 1942.774

UNIDENTIFIED EGYPTIAN ARTIST

Statuette of Khonsu, 664-525 BCE
Egypt, Late Period, Dynasty 26 or later
Bronze, solid cast
2.1 × 1.4 × 6.9 in., with tang (5.4 × 3.7 × 17.4 cm, with tang)
Collection of the Cleveland Museum of Art, Gift of the John Huntington Art and Polytechnic Trust, 1914.572

According to mythology, Isis left Egypt to search for her missing husband, only to lose hope at the shore of a river. Amidst her grief and mourning, some maidens approached Isis to comfort her and, as these women bonded, Isis began to care for their hair and teach them how to plait it. As one of the most prominent maternal figures in Egyptian mythology, Isis' story is significant for how it addresses common haircare practices as a foundational social dynamic. Her fellow deity, Khonsu, is famous for his distinctive hairstyle—a single lock of hair on the right side of his head. This style was associated with youthfulness, as it was popularly worn by children. As the Egyptian deity of the moon, Khonsu is connected to women's fertility—a further association with children that might explain his 'sidelock of youth' hairstyle.

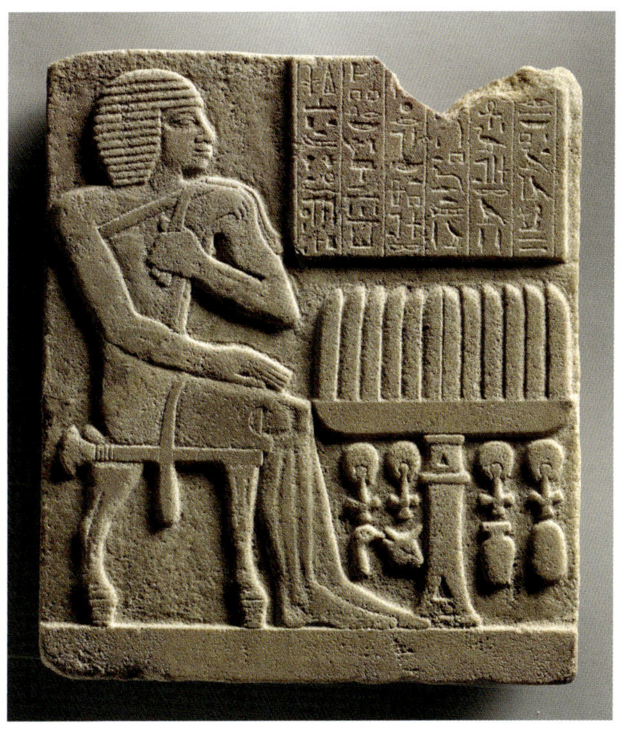

UNIDENTIFIED EGYPTIAN ARTIST
Stele of Djedatumiufankh, 664-525 BCE
Egypt, Late Period, Dynasty 26
Brown quartzite
10.8 × 9.8 in. (27.5 × 25 cm)
Collection of the Cleveland Museum of Art, Gift of the John Huntington Art and Polytechnic Trust, 1920.1977

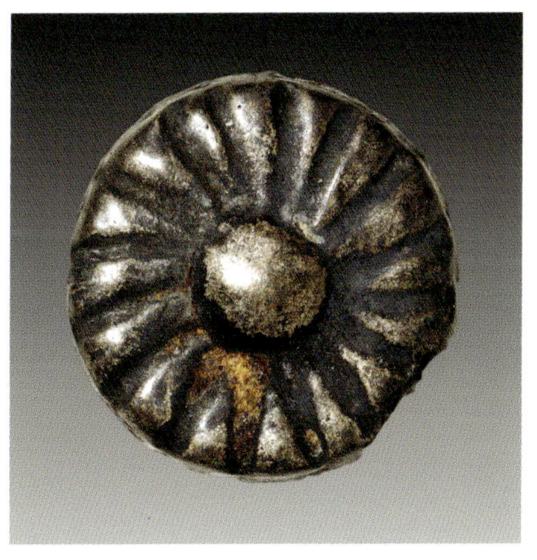

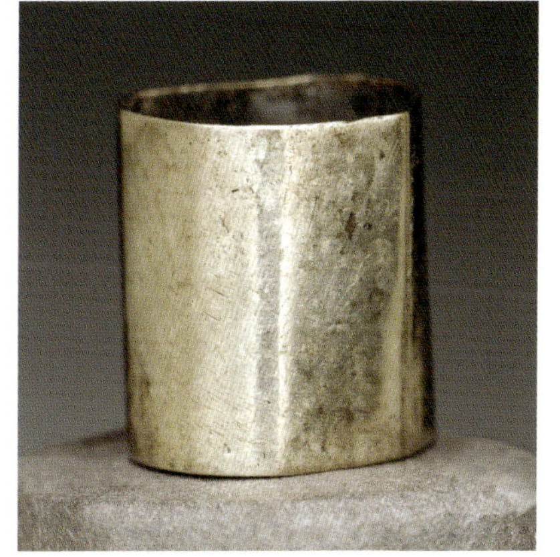

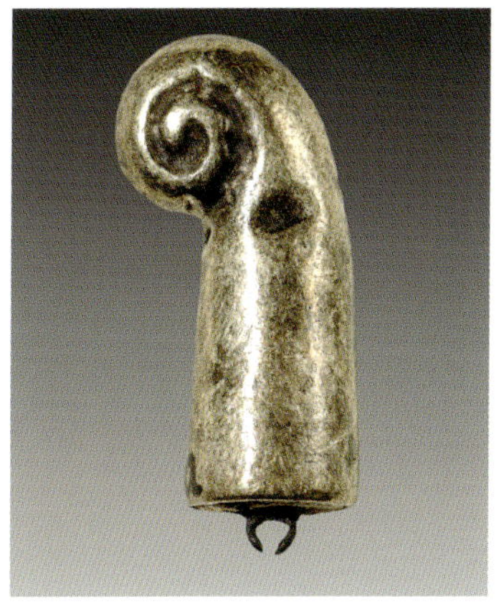

UNIDENTIFIED EGYPTIAN ARTIST
Wig ornamentation elements (rosette, cylinder, sidelock), 1980-1801 BCE
Egypt, Middle Kingdom, Dynasty 12
Silver
Between 0.5-1.0 in. (1.2-2.5 cm)
Collection of the Cleveland Museum of Art, Gift of the John Huntington Art and Polytechnic Trust, 1914.795

Though the first hair extensions in Egypt date back to c. 3400 BCE and were primarily woven into women's hair, the appearance of wigs—which were much more difficult to construct and, therefore, more elite—coincided with the rise of a stratified hierarchy for men in the Egyptian court. Given the sparse details in many carvings, like the *Stele of Djedatumiufankh*, the hairstyle stands out for receiving so much attention from the sculptor. A man's hair (from the styling technique to the overall presentation) projected his social status and his ritual purity. Wigs were frequently adorned with ivory pins, gold amulets, and ornaments fashioned from precious metals—like these silver sidelocks, rosettes, and cylinders which were woven into the hair or integrated onto textile panels that laid over the hair.

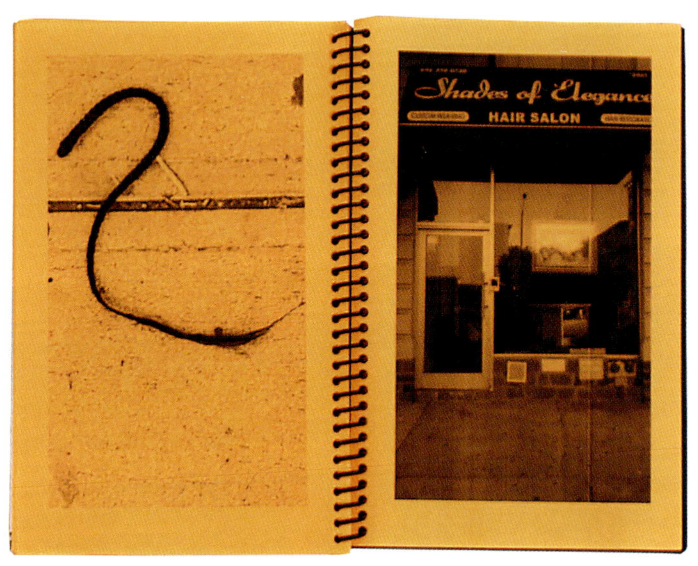

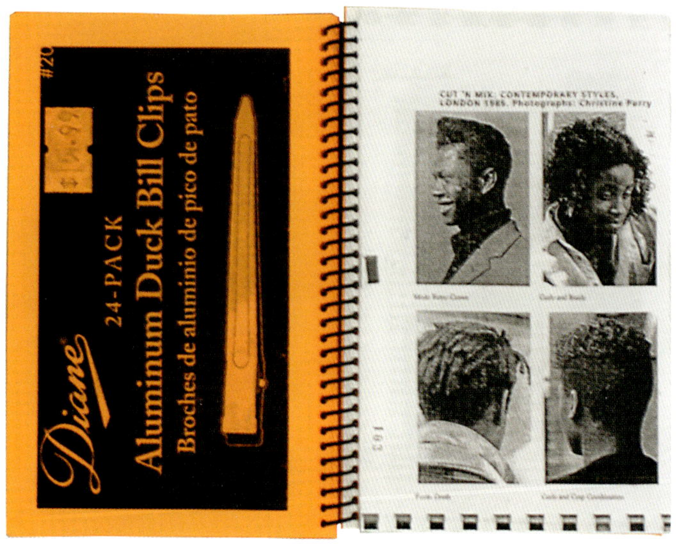

NONTSIKELELO MUTITI

African Hair Braiding Salon Reader, 2014

As an agent of change, Zimbabwean-born interdisciplinary artist Nontsikelelo Mutiti has crafted a body of work that is rarely limited by gallery walls. From interventions in museums, to vinyl installations in unexpected places, Mutiti's practice is design-based and socially engaged. For these reasons, Mutiti is also completing a new commission for *TEXTURES*, a limited edition takeaway print that was created in collaboration with Ohio community partners for distribution during the exhibition's programming.

For the gallery space, Mutiti is restaging parts of the *African Hair Braiding Salon Reader*, a booklet featuring collages, drawings, writing, and photography- all laser printed on spiral bound, electric orange paper. Based on conversations and the visual culture of salons in Zimbabwe, this booklet is usually displayed in a deconstructed format alongside physical objects from the salon's environs. Since the artist's work usually exists in multiples, the stories and ideas contained therein are democratized and, thus, easily distributed. With an eye toward engagement from the public, Mutiti is committed to fostering exchange.

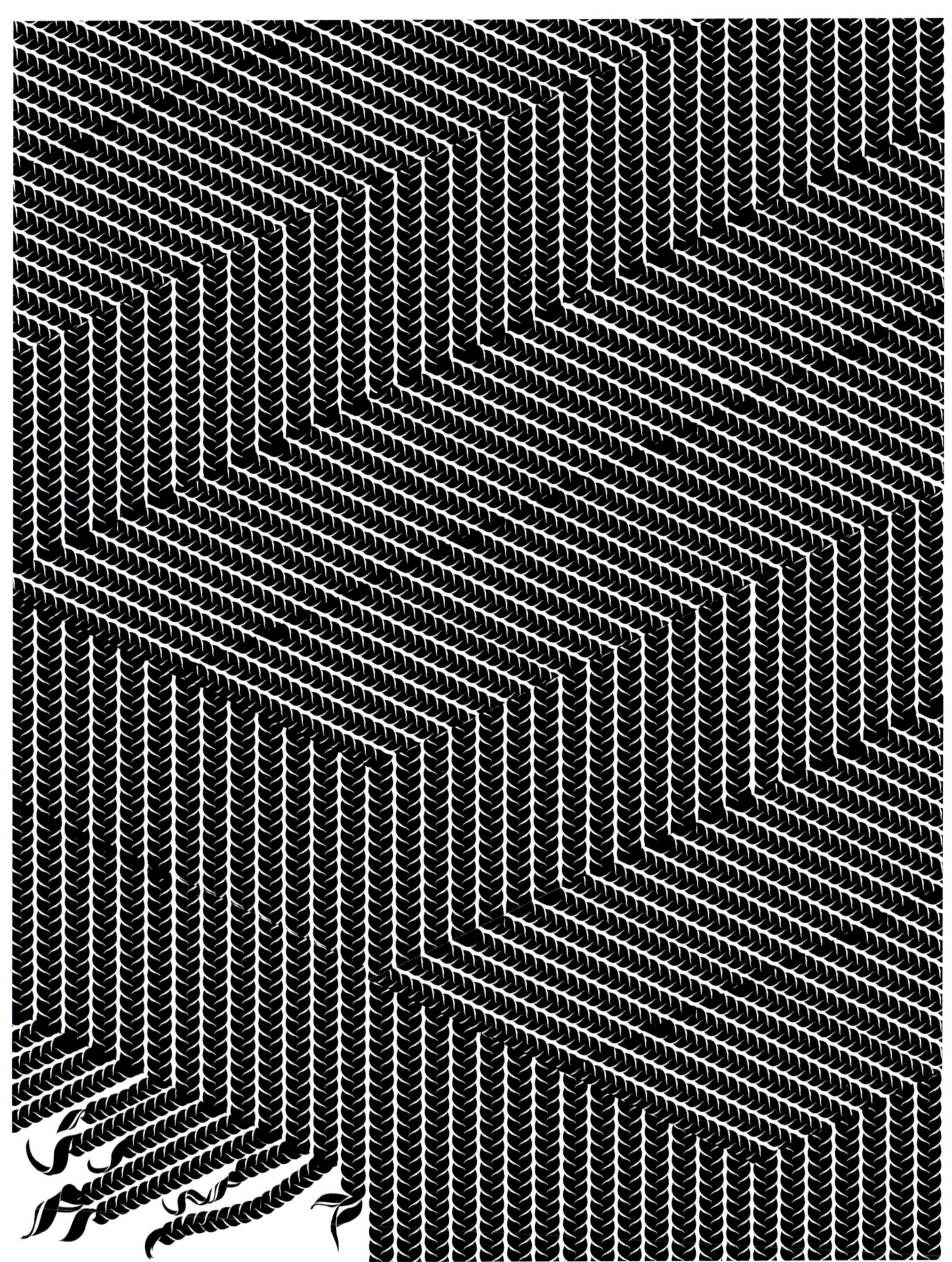

NONTSIKELELO MUTITI
Cassamance #2, 2020

Beauty and Success!

Both May be Yours ~ So Easily
There's No Excuse for Not Having Them

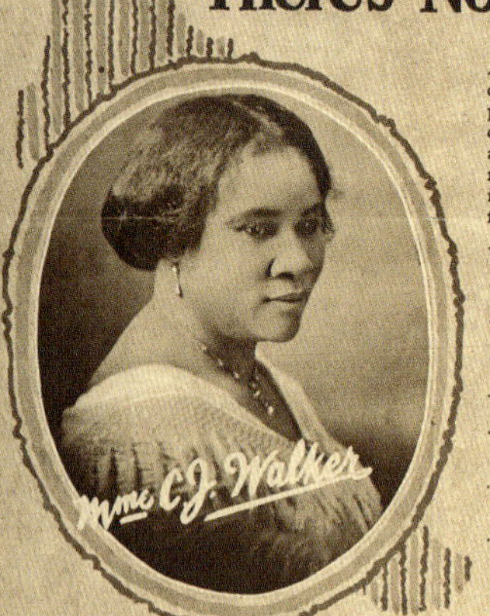

America should be proud of the achievements of her colored citizens. In the short span of sixty years we have accomplished more than any race beginning with similar handicaps. "Freed" in 1866, we were still enslaved by poverty and illiteracy. Now, everywhere are to be seen negro businesses, skilled negro workmen, professional men and women in ever-growing numbers. During the past sixty years the following stupendous changes have taken place:

...from only a few negroes who could read and write, the thirst for education now enables nine-tenths of us to do so.

...from 700 backwoods huts 47,000 churches have arisen, valued at ninety-eight million dollars;

...600 colored teachers have increased to 48,000 in five hundred colleges, normal and public schools;

...12,000 negroes who owned their own homes have increased to 700,000;

...the gross wealth of negroes has increased from twenty million dollars to two billion dollars;

...from menial labor we have evolved into the arts, sciences, literature, education, and other phases of American civilization in no small way;

...70,000 of us conduct our own business, while many other thousands are working into the weave and web of American commerce.

...we have our Tanner, Dunbar, Roland Hayes, Ernest Just, Booker Washington, and many others.

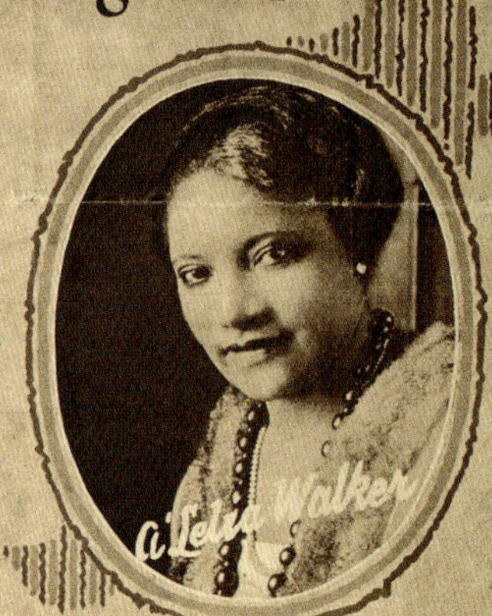

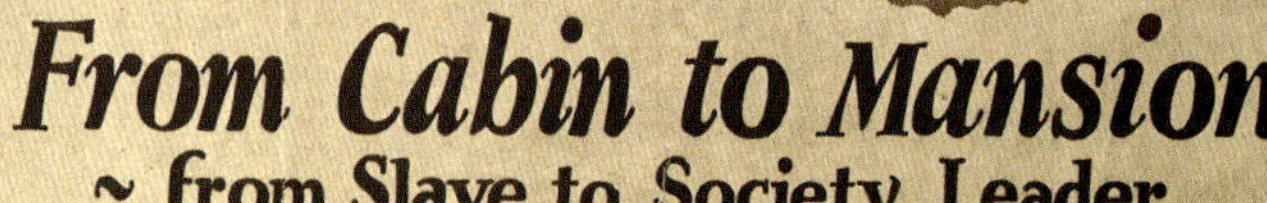

~ from Slave to Society Leader
~ from Poverty to "The Greatest Benefactress of Her Race"

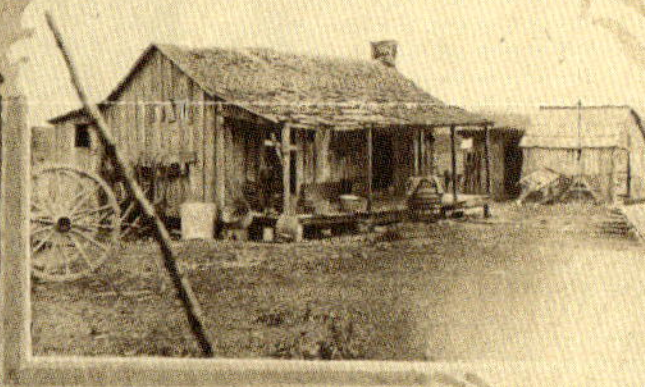

Cabin Where Madam Walker Was Born

Born of slave parents in the little cabin shown at left (Delta, Louisiana), Madam C. J. Walker forged ahead to success and influence.

At the age of seven years she was left an orphan by the death of her parents; at fourteen, alone and hopeless, she married in order that she might have a home.

When she was twenty years of age and had one child, a little girl, her husband died and left her on her own resources. She reared and educated her daughter and developed the line of Walker Hair and Toilet Preparations now so famous all over the world.

Improve Your Position!

Consider this woman who started with absolutely nothing and left a great factory and thriving business in all parts of the world, a beautiful home in Indianapolis, a mansion on 136th Street in New York City and a residence fit for a king at Irvington-on-the-Hudson.

Surely this is a fine example of the latent ability to be found in the colored race. Madam Walker applied herself to the tasks in hand, persevered in the face of obstacles and reached enviable achievements.

Let her life be an inspiring lesson, a beacon light to point the way to bigger and better things *for you*. For that, after all, was Madam Walker's main desire—to see her own race prosper and succeed as never before.

Make More Money!

Having for her motto, "The Improvement of the Outward Appearance of Her Race," Madam Walker proved herself its greatest benefactress by developing eighteen preparations that have helped in the remarkable progress of negroes everywhere.

Furthermore, she arranged her estate so that it would be wisely administered, and two-thirds of the profits should always go towards helping colored education, religion and charity.

You Too Can Enjoy a Lovely Complection

Mme. C. J. Walker's
None genuine
Mme C. J. Walker
without this signature
Hair Preparations

Such charms as a clear, lovely complexion and a velvety skin are now within the reach of every one. All women crave beauty as the flowers seek the sunlight. There is no need for ugly, pimply skins or short harsh hair when Madam Walker's preparations are so easy to use and so reasonable in price.

It is often said that "a woman's appearance is an index to her character." Don't let it be said of *you* that your appearance indicates carelessness, uncleanliness, or ignorance.

Beautiful Hair ~ a Woman's Crowning Glory

Money could not buy the luxurious heads of hair possessed by most women who stand out as leaders in their respective communities, or who wield the most influence, get the best positions, travel widely, etc.

These women properly value and appreciate the tremendous advantage given to any member of the colored race by a beautiful crown of hair. If you have this advantage naturally, then by all means cultivate and keep it.

If your hair is not naturally pleasing, then profit by Madam C. J. Walker's assistance and let her world-renowned hair preparations do for you what they have done for thousands of others.

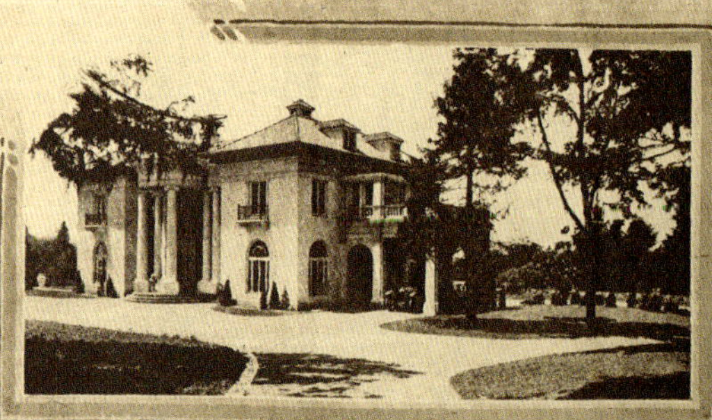

Villa Le Waro, Irvington-on-the-Hudson
The half-million dollar palatial residence of America's foremost colored woman

Beauty and Success! Madam C. J. Walker advertisement, 1920s

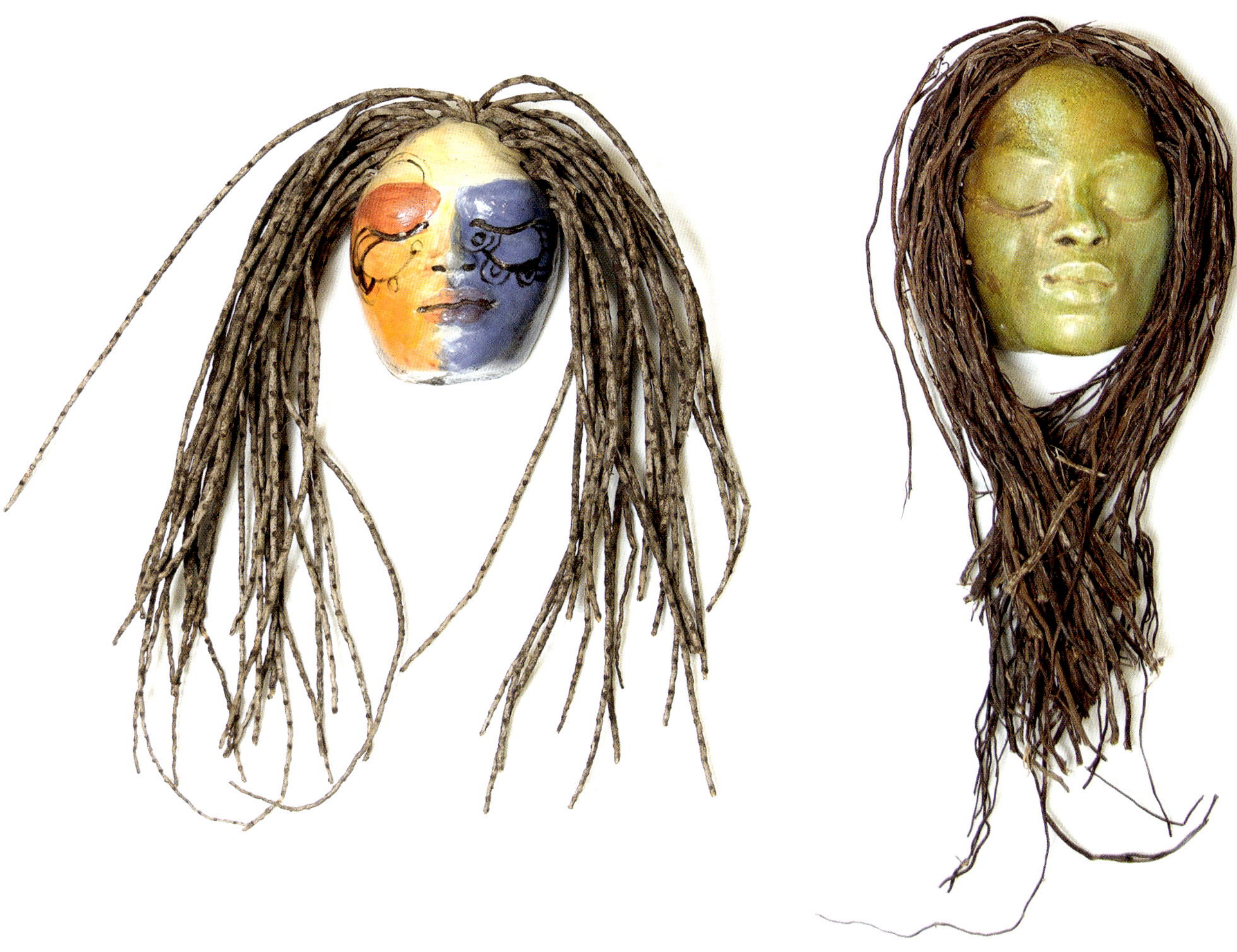

NAKAZZI HUTCHINSON

Untitled, 2018
Humble Youth (Yute) from the *Roots Mask* series, 2017

As part of the *Root Mask* series, these works were created from clay sourced in Westmoreland, Jamaica and organic materials that evoke popular hairstyles of Jamaican people. The serene faces contrast with the vegetal elements that envelop the form. In crafting from natural resources, Hutchinson foregrounds an Afro-centric identity while safeguarding the multiracial and multiethnic environments within Caribbean cultures. As the artist often phrases it: "Out of many, one People." Through the creation of this series, she made the very thing she wanted to see—art that reflected her own people and their complex cultural identities. Playing on the term "root," Hutchinson references both our natural resources and the diasporic conditions of the Black Atlantic whose "roots" lie in Africa.

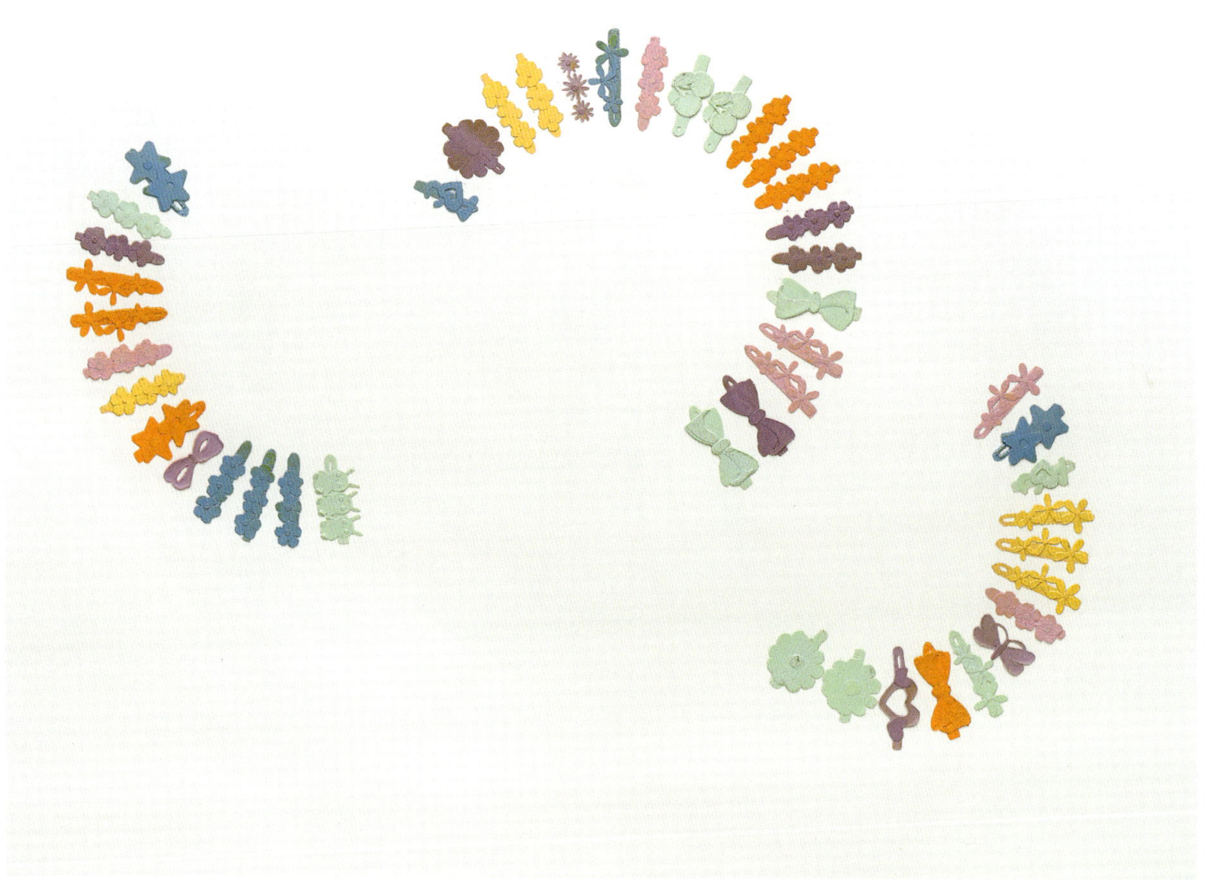

ALTHEA MURPHY-PRICE

Barrettes no. 1, 2017
Barrettes no. 2, 2017

Light and airy, the compositions of these screen prints are whimsical, but succinct. The barrettes in Murphy-Price's prints come from the world of young Black girls. Even though the artist avoided depicting any human subjects or hair, these images evoke a visceral reaction in many viewers. A great unifier between generations, hair care is a dedicated time to connect physically and emotionally between family members. Whether it is nostalgia for maternal figures who spent hours caring for their hair, or a recollection of a particular barrette as a childhood momento, the plastic clips have an uncanny ability to provoke memories.

With her geometric, ordered patterns, the artist's barrettes are similar to microbiological forms—like the configuration of DNA or protozoa under a magnifying lens. The *Barrettes* series imaginatively captures the world through a child's eyes and points us toward the microbial qualities of hair. However disparate these readings may seem, they both speak to life, and generations of exchange, at their core.

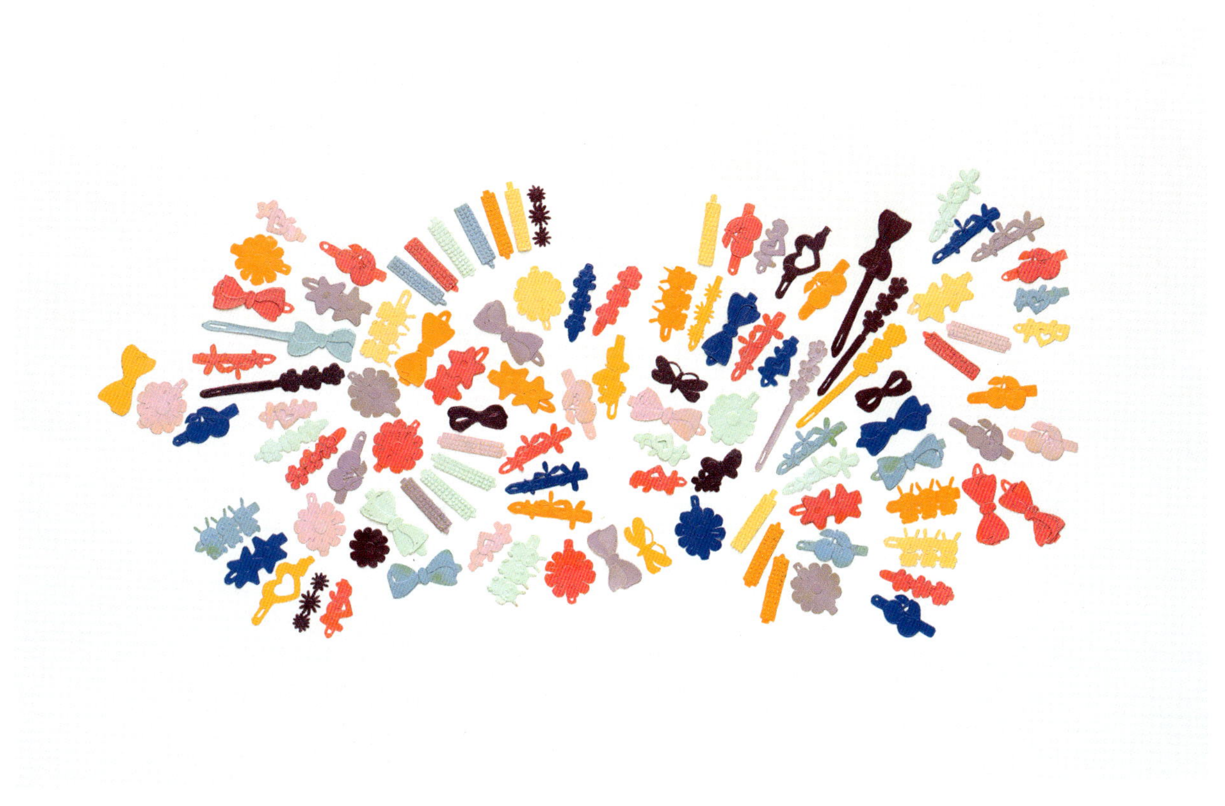

WALKER NEWSLETTER

VOL. V Indianapolis, Ind., October 1953 NO.VII

NEW PRODUCTS!!!

YES SOMETHING NEW HAS BEEN ADDED!!!

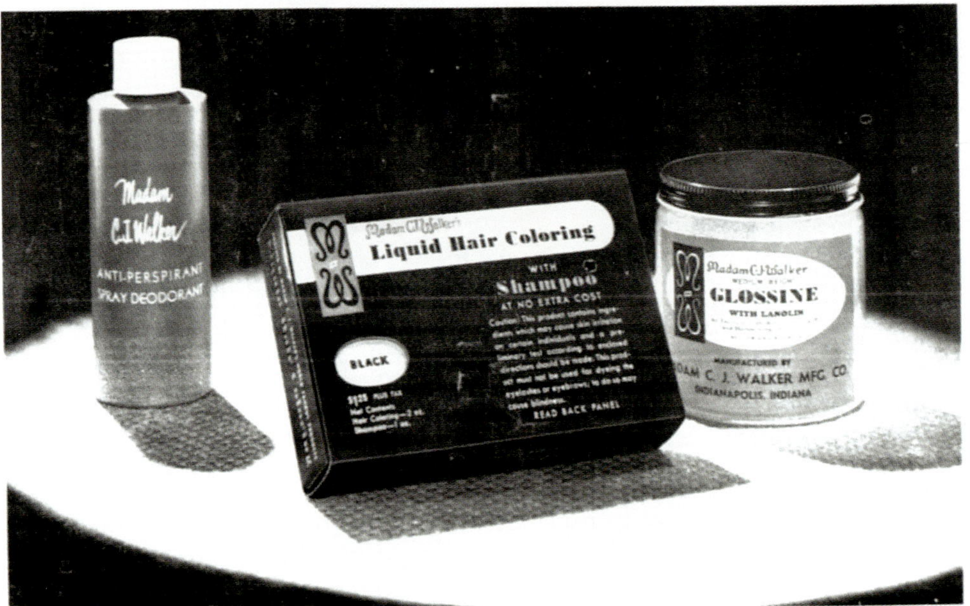

New Spray Deodorant and Anti-Perspirant, New Hair Coloring (with Shampoo at no extra cost) New Family Size Medium Glossine (with Lanolin) placed on market by Walker Company!

Here they are! Three of Mme. Walker's newest and finest products!

(1) Family-Size Medium Glossine - premier light-bodied pressing oil and hair dressing, containing Lanolin - at 75¢ plus tax.

(2) New Hair Coloring in (Black, Off-Black, Brown, Warm Brown, Auburn, Ginger, Coppertone) with Shampoo at no extra cost - only $1.25 plus ta

(3) New Anti-Perspirant and Spray Deodorant-checks perspiration, saves fabrics, eliminates odor (just spray on!) only $1.25 plus tax.

And here are your prices:

Retail (each)	Prices to Agents and Beauticians (Wholesale) Quarter Dozen	Half Dozen	Dozen
Family Size Glossine 75¢ plus tax	$2.00	$3.50	$6.00
Anti-Perspirant $1.25 plus tax	$3.00	$5.50	$10.00
Hair Coloring (Name shade desired) $1.25 plus tax	(Not sold in quarter Doz. lots)	$6.00	$10.00

ORDER TODAY! ORDER TODAY! ORDER TODAY!

Walker Newsletter, vol. V, no. VII, October 1953

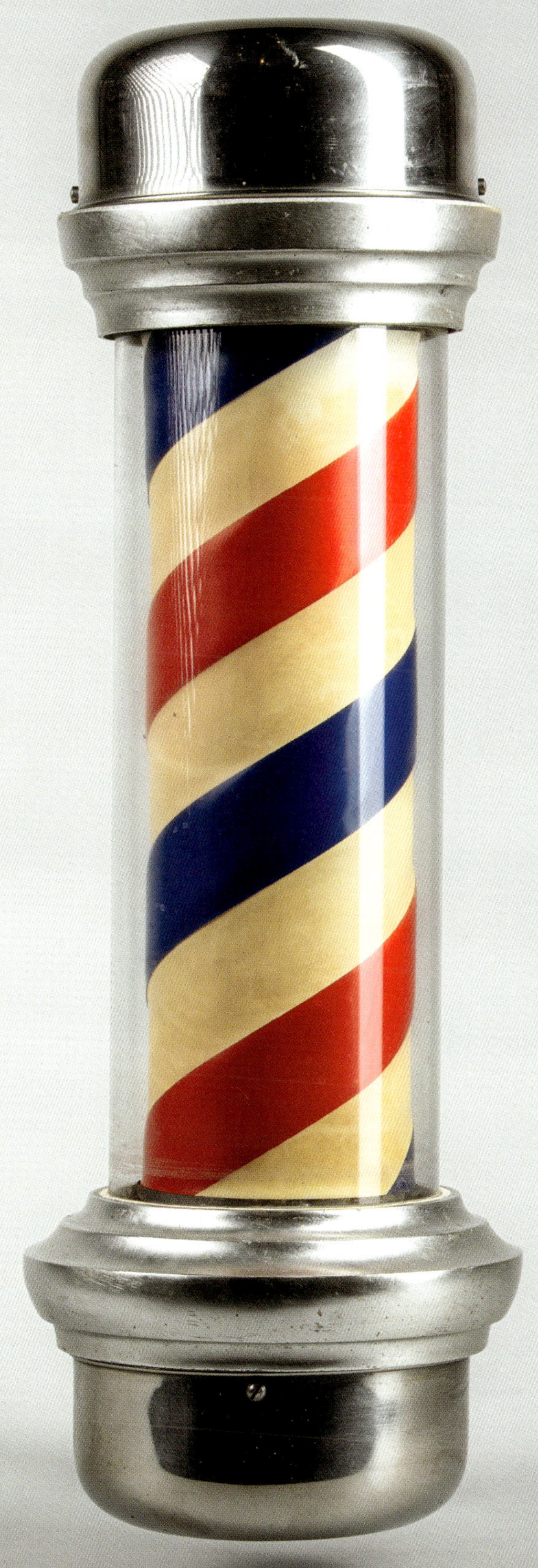

Barber pole from Dr. Willie Morrow's first barbershop, *ca.* 1950

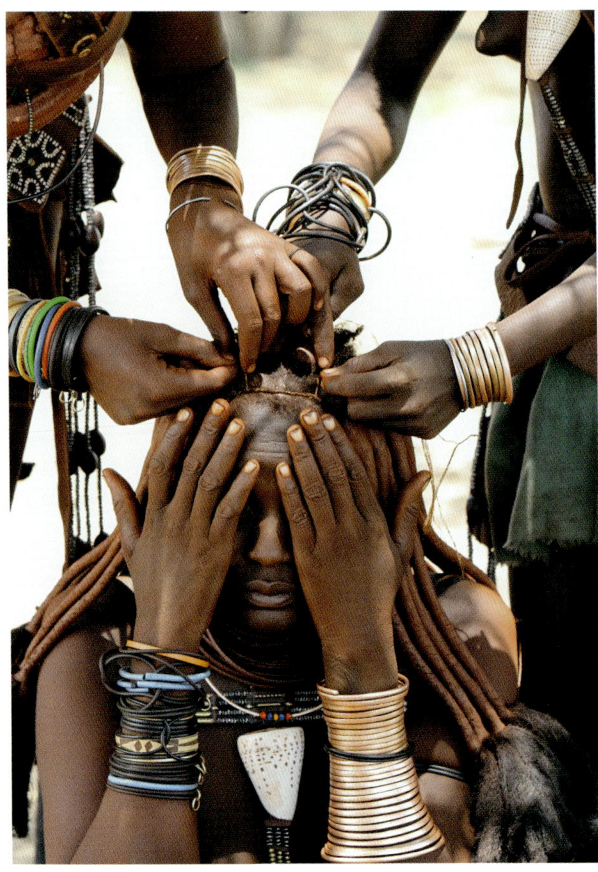

WOODROW NASH

Untitled, *ca.* 2010

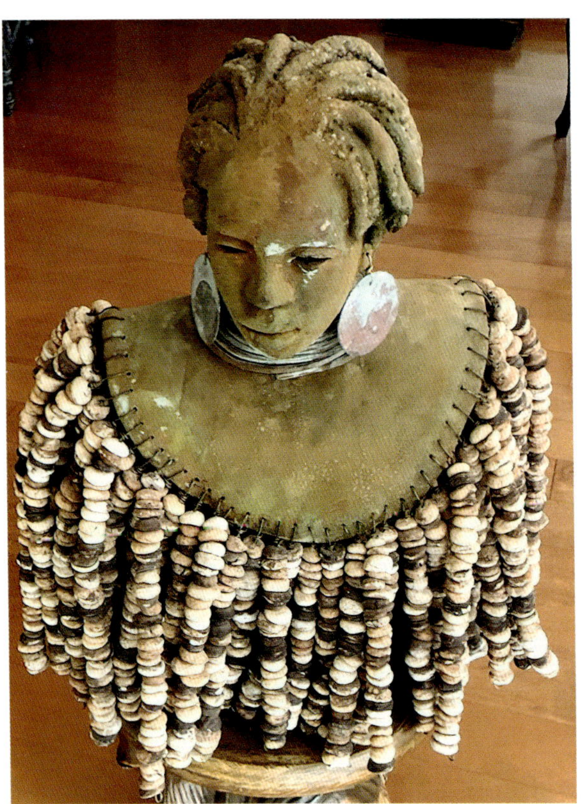

SHARA K. JOHNSON

Himba Hands, 2016
Otjize, 2016

These photographs by travel blogger and photographer Shara K. Johnson are from her trip to Namibia, where she met some Himba women. *Otjize*, the title of one of her photos, is the paste made from butterfat and red ochre that Himba women apply to their hair and skin to give themselves an iconic red hue. This paste is applied mostly for aesthetic purposes, but the hairstyles themselves are an important aspect of social development for Himba women. Hairstyles are crafted by close relatives, as seen in *Himba Hands*, and typically incorporate woven hay, goat hair, and other hair extensions to add length to their styles. Capturing these images as a White American woman, Johnson's case poses the question of how to approach artwork created by outsiders who photograph indigenous cultures. Since the invention of the camera, photographers have gone into many African spaces to capture scenes like the Himba's cosmetic traditions. With images destined for consumption by Western audiences, one must consider the balance between appreciation and patronization—even if the images are strikingly beautiful and created with complimentary intentions.

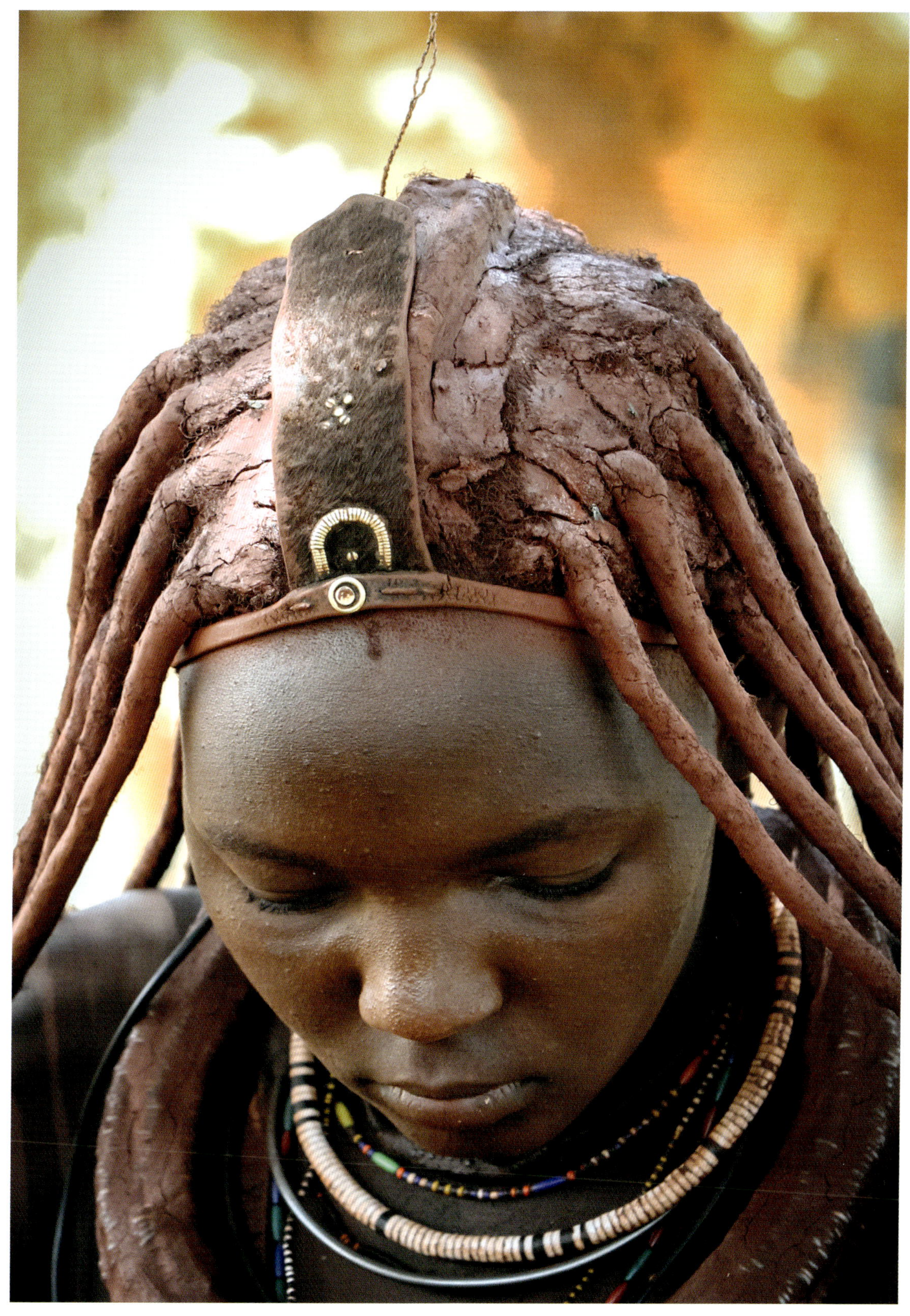

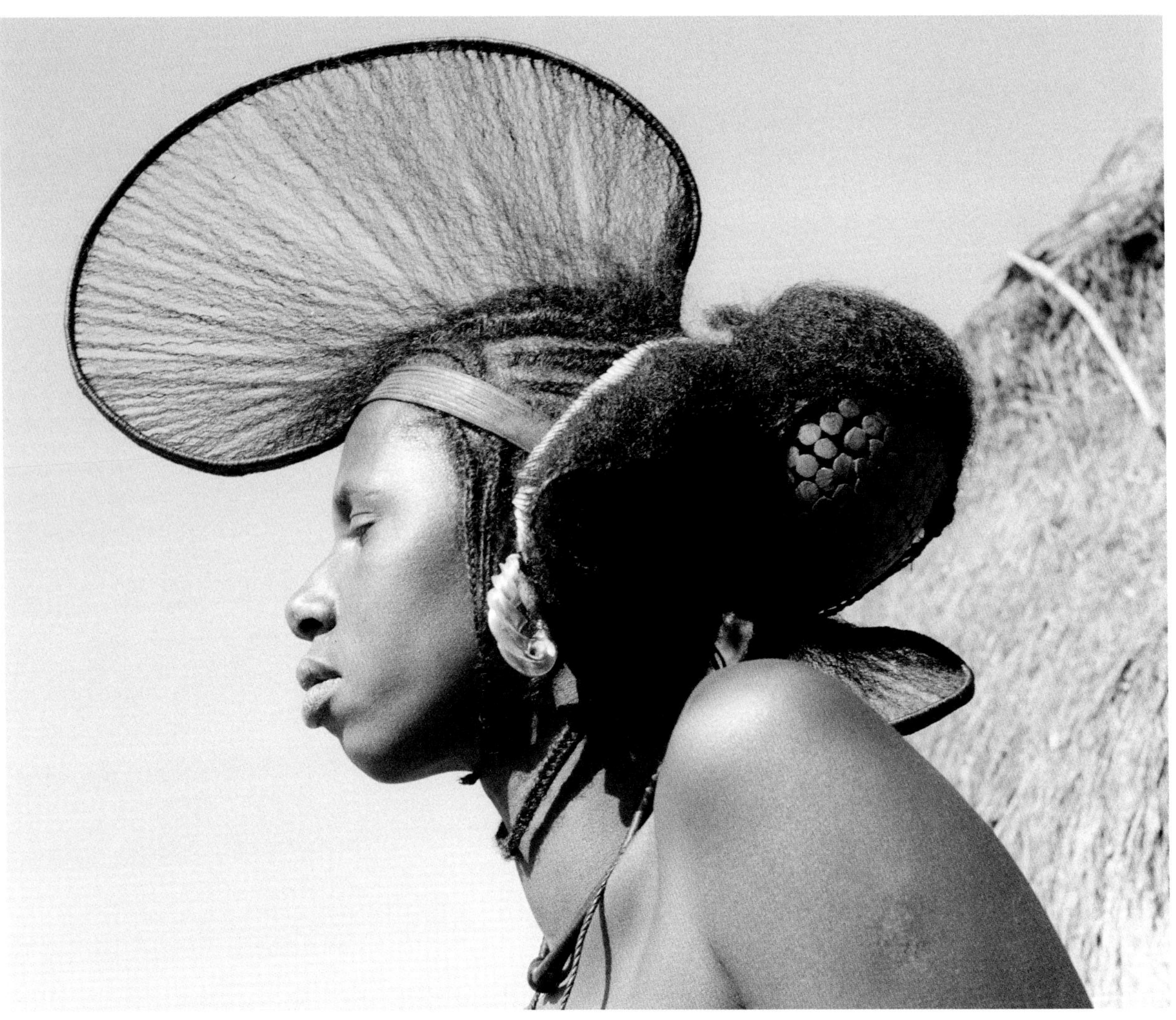

HECTOR ACEBES

Fulani (Foula) Woman, Guinea, 1953 (printed 2003)
Maasai Man, Tanzania, 1953 (printed 2003)

In the Maasai culture, male warriors are the only ones allowed to grow out their hair. The photograph *Maasai Man, Tanzania* emphasizes his braids to signify his status. The Fulani woman's hairstyle is known as a *jubaade* (or *dyubade*) in which the hair is stretched across a strip of bamboo to form a crest, which can be enlarged by weaving in the hair of ancestors as extensions. Coiffures like these play an integral role in the lives of the Fulani people and highlight the continued presence of ancestors among the living. These two photographs, taken by Colombia native Hector Acebes in 1953, place the subjects above the viewer, conveying prestige and respect, even as their individual identities are obscured by the ethnographic focus on their hair and jewelry. The angle at which Acebes took the photos reveals his desire to maintain eye contact with his subjects and establish a connection. His collection of images, although somewhat controversial for their colonial gaze, is notable for how it utilized compositional strategies to give his subjects some agency.

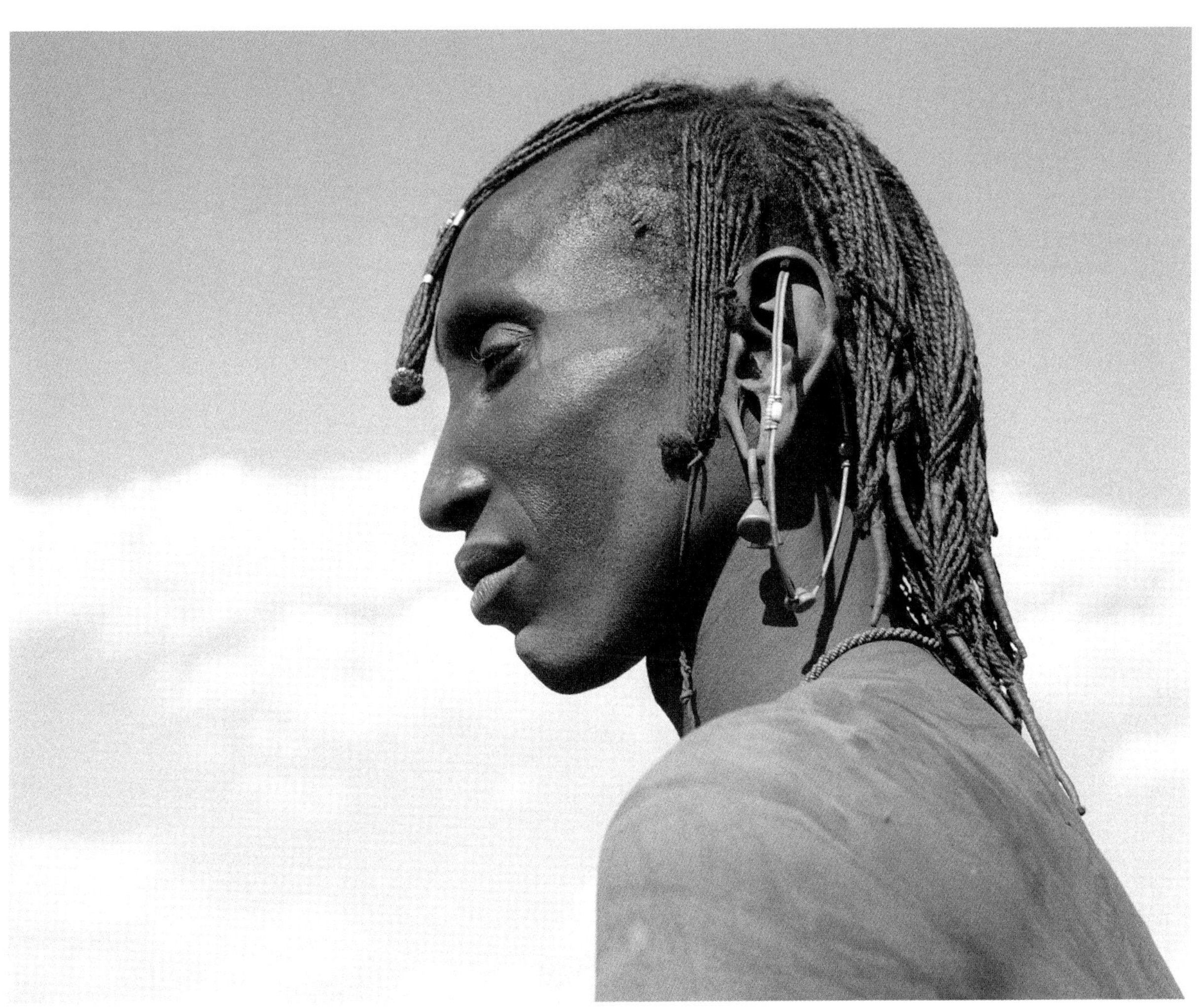

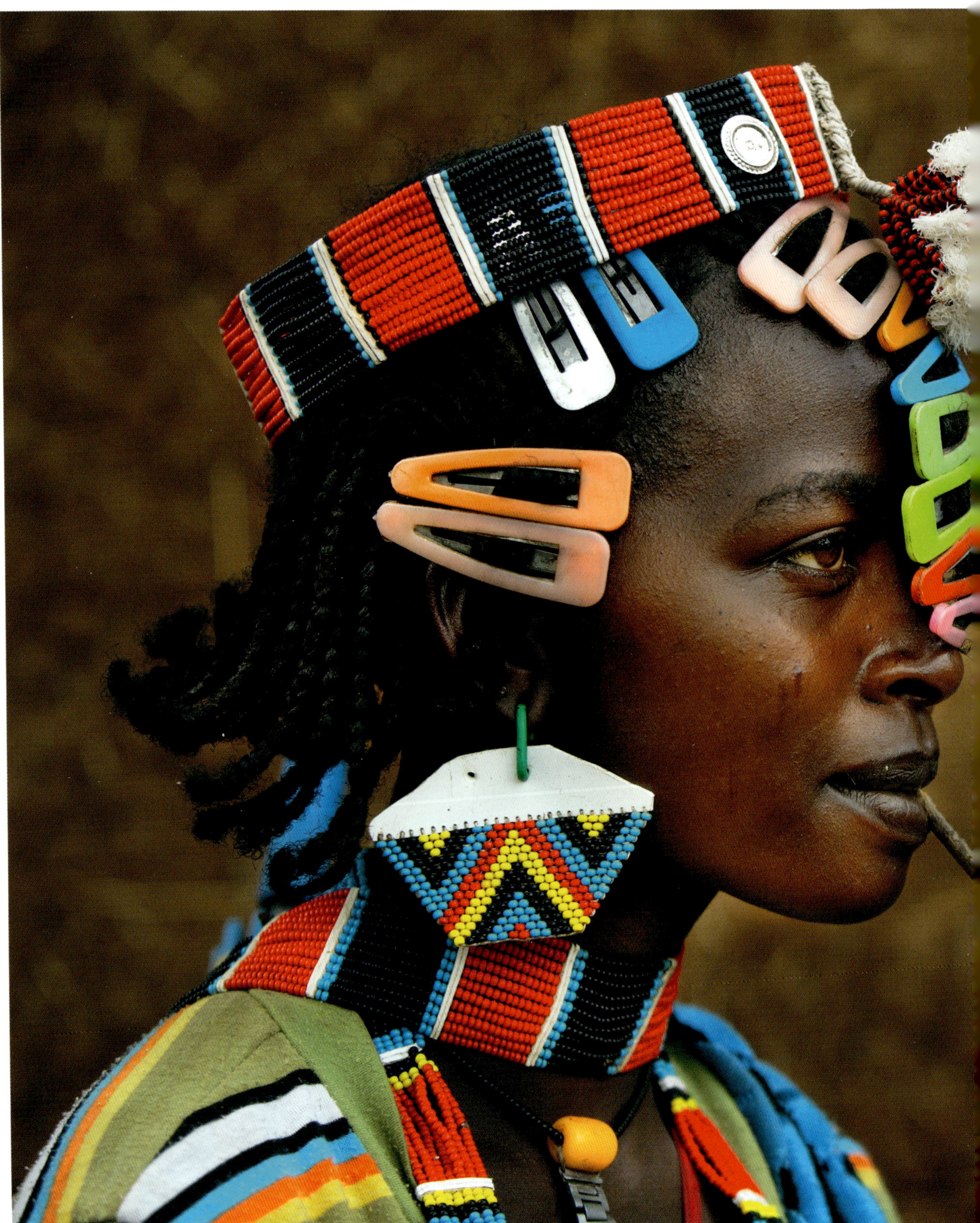

ERIC LAFFORGUE

Miss Biremuda, Bana Tribe Girl, Key Afer, Ethiopia, 2012

Taken from Lafforgue's larger series on Ethiopia, these subjects represent the Afar and Bana peoples—both known for unique hair care and hairstyling traditions. Mr. Awol Mohammed (next page) sports the *asdago* style (similar to the Afro) and the color and sheen of his hair can be attributed to ghee (clarified butter). For the Afar peoples, ghee protects hair from the intense heat of the sun and keeps it moisturized. Bana women, like Miss Biremuda, also use ghee in their hair, typically applying it as an adhesive for the decorative beads and other vibrant accessories.

As a French photographer, Lafforgue's documentary photographs blend portraiture with ethnography as he highlights the individual sitter, but also foregrounds the unique cultural aspects that are sure to spark curiosity among non-indigenous audiences. From their dress to their hair and their body modifications, the subjects in Lafforgue's images are simultaneously gorgeous individuals and ethnic or cultural types.

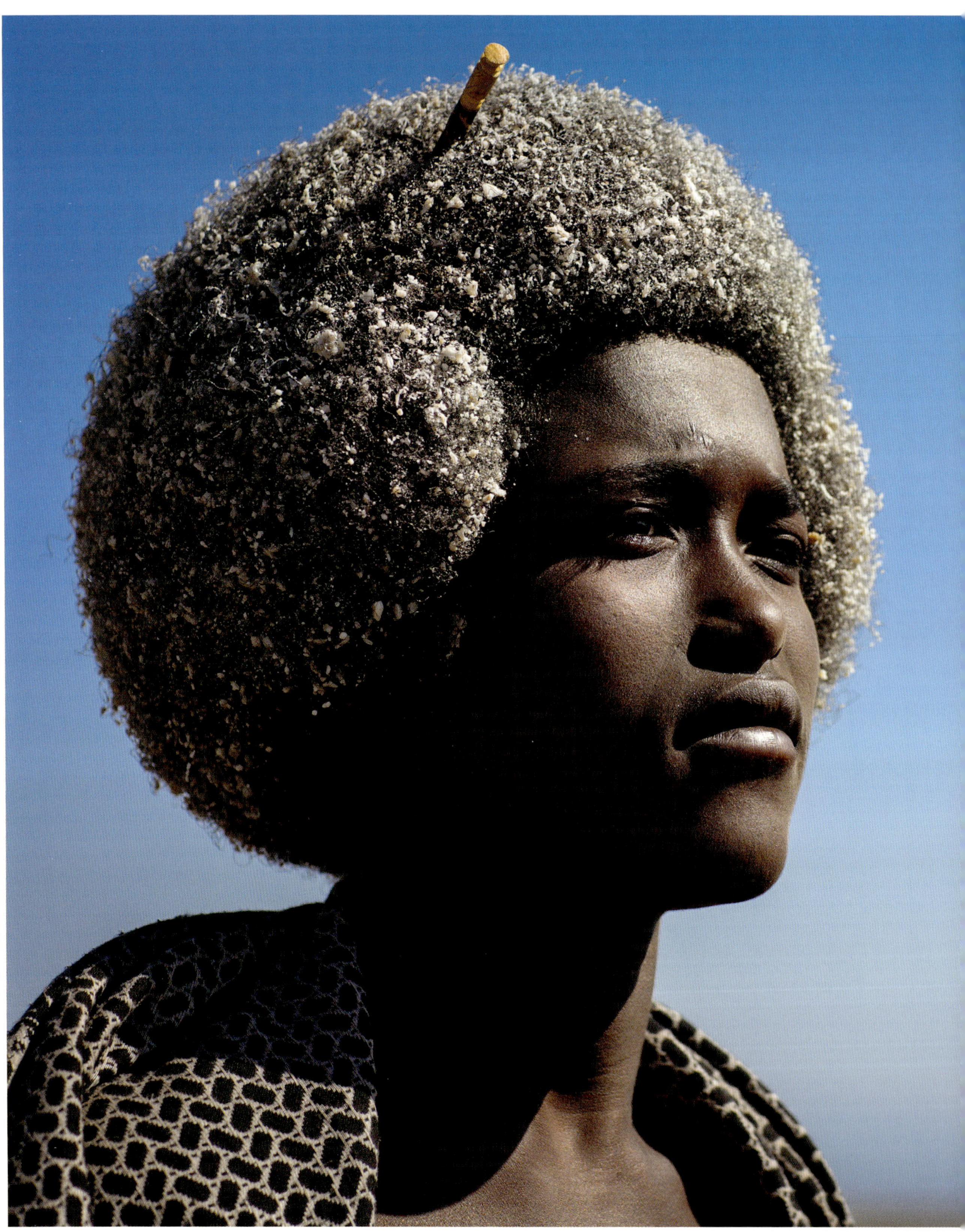

ERIC LAFFORGUE
Mr. Awol Mohammed, Afar Tribe Man with ghee on his hair, Mille, Ethiopia, 2014

THE DIGITAL GREEN BOOK PROJECT

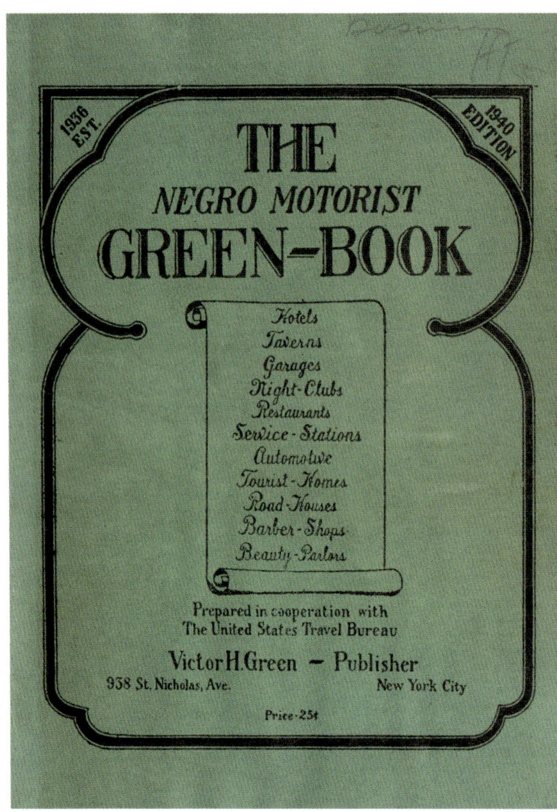

The Negro Motorist Green Book, 1940
Victor H. Green & Co.
4.9 × 6.7 in. (12.5 × 17 cm)
Schomburg Center for Research
in Black Culture

THE DIGITAL GREEN BOOK PROJECT

In tandem with the development of the *TEXTURES* exhibition, the curators conceived of a project that would document the modern-day landscape of Black hair care. Inspired by Victor Green's *Green Book*, published between 1936 and 1966, the curatorial team made a regional map and identified the Black-owned barbershops and beauty parlors. The original *Green Book* was organized by state, city, and service so that African-American travelers could easily identify welcoming businesses despite the prevalence of Jim Crow laws. In addition to hotels, restaurants, and auto repairs shops, Green knew an essential service that his readers would need was specialized care for Black hair.

Therefore, our digital version focuses on the people and places that constitute today's network of communities, businesses, and philosophies. From certified cosmetologists to multi-generational businesses, *The Digital Green Book Project* reflects the long heritage of Black hair care business and archives it for future audiences. The video interviews will be available in the exhibition, allowing barbers and salon artists to recount their own journeys into the hair care community and to offer their reflections on select artworks. Developed in collaboration with the Wick Poetry Center and the Each + Every design team, these videos will be accompanied by important hair-related texts with which visitors can interact. Longer edits of the interviews will also be made available online, in an archived compilation for public reference. For more information, visit www.kent.edu/museum.

"If this guide has proved useful to you on your trips, let us know. There will be a day sometime in the near future when this guide will not have to be published. That is when we as a race will have equal opportunities and privileges in the United States. It will be a great day for us to suspend this publication for then we can go wherever we please, and without embarrassment. But until that time comes we shall continue to publish this information for your convenience each year."
The Negro Motorist Green Book (1949)

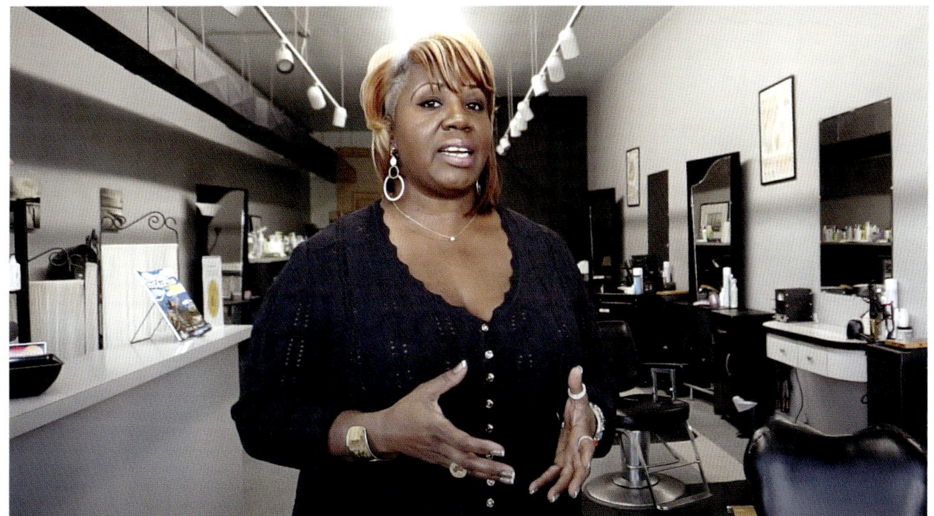

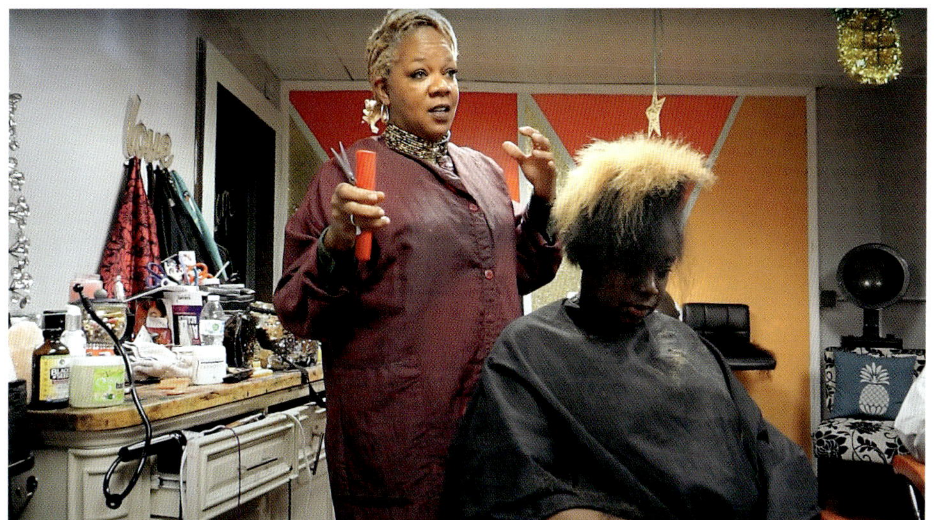

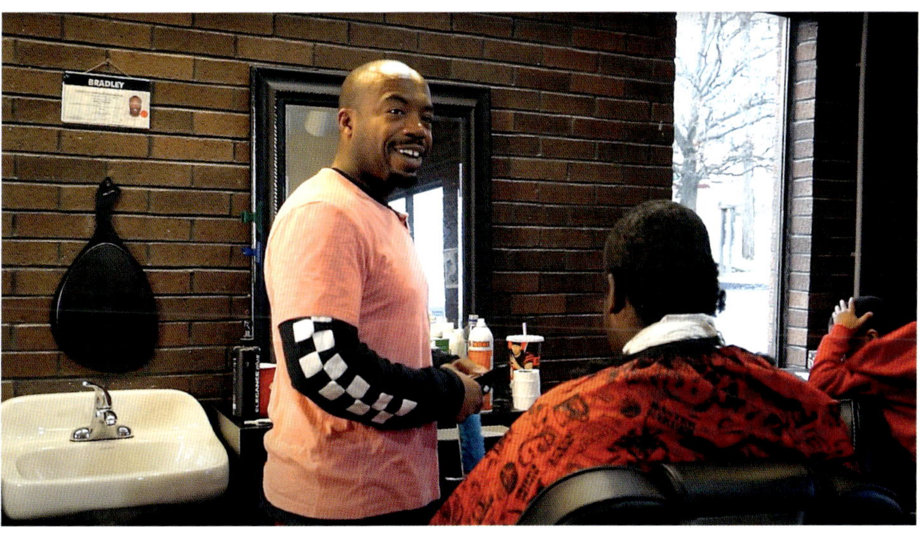

Stills from interviews with Ladosha Wright (Reverence Design Team, Cleveland Heights, Ohio), Maria-Lynn Ogletree (Natural Roots Styling Studio, Cleveland, Ohio), and Bradley Robinson (Headmasters, Kent, Ohio) as part of *The Digital Green Book* project, 2018–2020

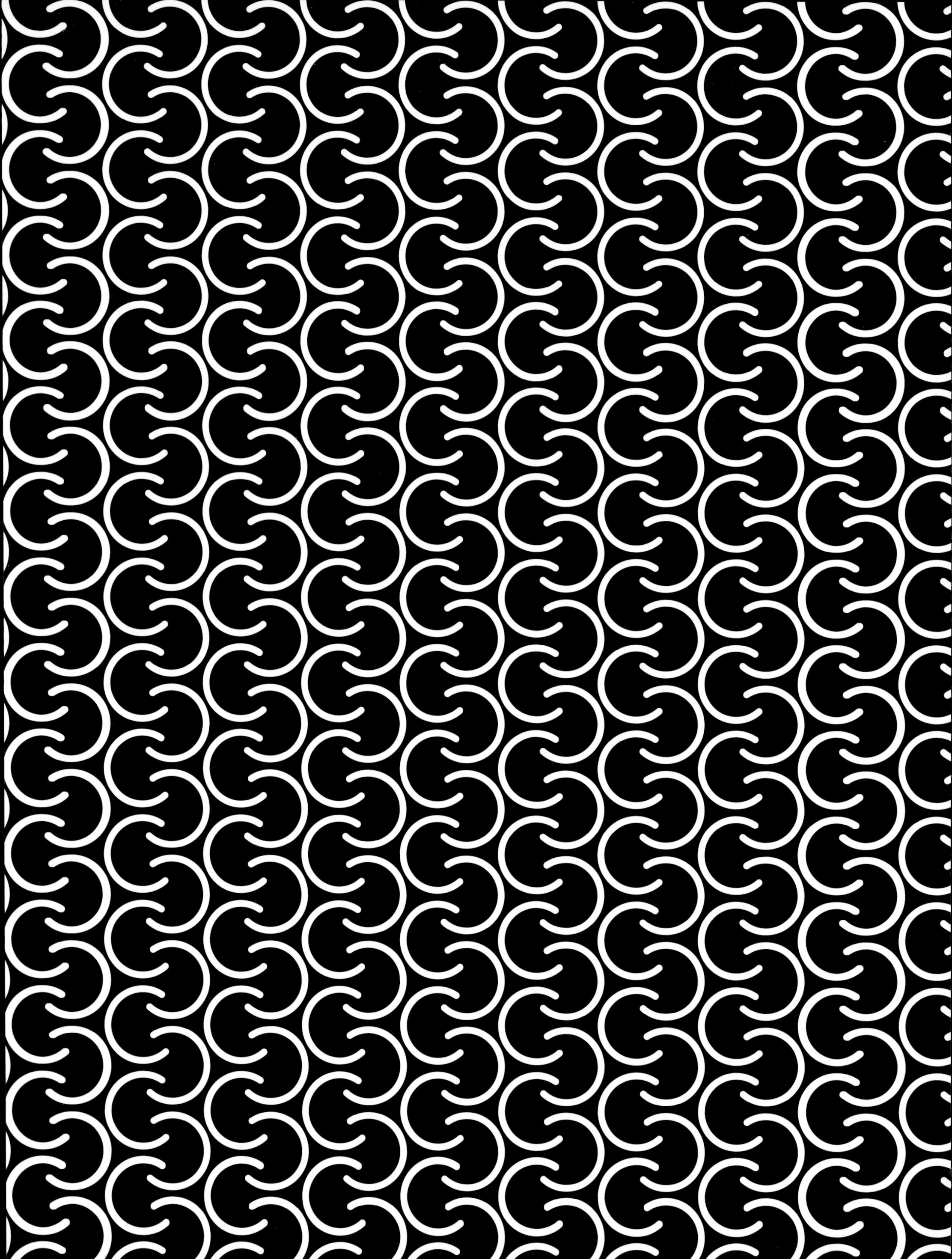

HAIR POLITICS

In our current climate of news cycles, it seems that everything is political or politicized. But even throughout history, Black hair has frequently been the subject of political debate, whether or not it was meant to be—on topics ranging from Afros and raised fists, to girls in braids sent home from school or employees being fired for having "unprofessional" hair. Recent news headlines are only the latest manifestations of the politics surrounding Black bodies and how they express themselves. Within this thematic section of *TEXTURES*, there is an element of politics woven into every work of art and functional object on display. Black people have been pushed to justify themselves as citizens, as leaders, as artists, and even as humans. From struggles aimed at changing legislation to the racial politics of carving a space for self-expression, Black hair is an unavoidable visual signifier that has been leveraged, disdained, celebrated, and scrutinized for centuries.

Many Black individuals have experienced the oppressive realities that politics assign to their hair. Faced with mainstream society's perception of "dirty" dreadlocks or "unkempt" Afros, one wonders if Black hair (or Black bodies) could ever be politically neutral. In the last twenty years the United States has evolved its understanding, thanks to the Natural Hair Movement (a community of Black women celebrating, educating, and supporting each other's choice to wear their natural hair texture) and, more recently, to a recognition of the "Black Joy" concept. However, one cannot deny the persistent prejudices—both within and outside Black communities—against hair textures and styles considered to be too closely related to Africa and antebellum stigmas.

Coiffing, cutting, and curling Black hair has been a political issue on the African continent (where a hairstyle might signal political rank, or a religious affiliation), in the Caribbean (where free women in the eighteenth century wore elaborate madras cloth headwraps because hats were forbidden for non-whites), and in North America (where Afros and braids signified self-love and resistance to the status quo in the 1960s). Even within Black communities, the ideologies surrounding hair are contentious, with debates and stigmatization surrounding "good" and "bad" hair. Hair has been used as a vehicle to discuss a variety of other geo-political issues.

For example, note how Deborah Anzinger uses hair as a metaphor for ecological impacts and asks where governments around the globe are implicated by pursuing economic growth at any cost, or how Sonya Clark's act of dismantling and reconstructing flags powerfully symbolizes the eradication of Black narratives from United States history and political groups. Although the politics of hair textures and how we style them are complicated, it remains a personal way to engage with communal, national, and political positions. Whether it is boldly proclaimed by embracing kinks and curls, or subtly stated by purchasing hair products from a particular manufacturer; whether you were actively protesting discriminatory policies, or you just went to school and found yourself the poster child of a national debate, Black hair is a nexus around which national policies and international economies turn.

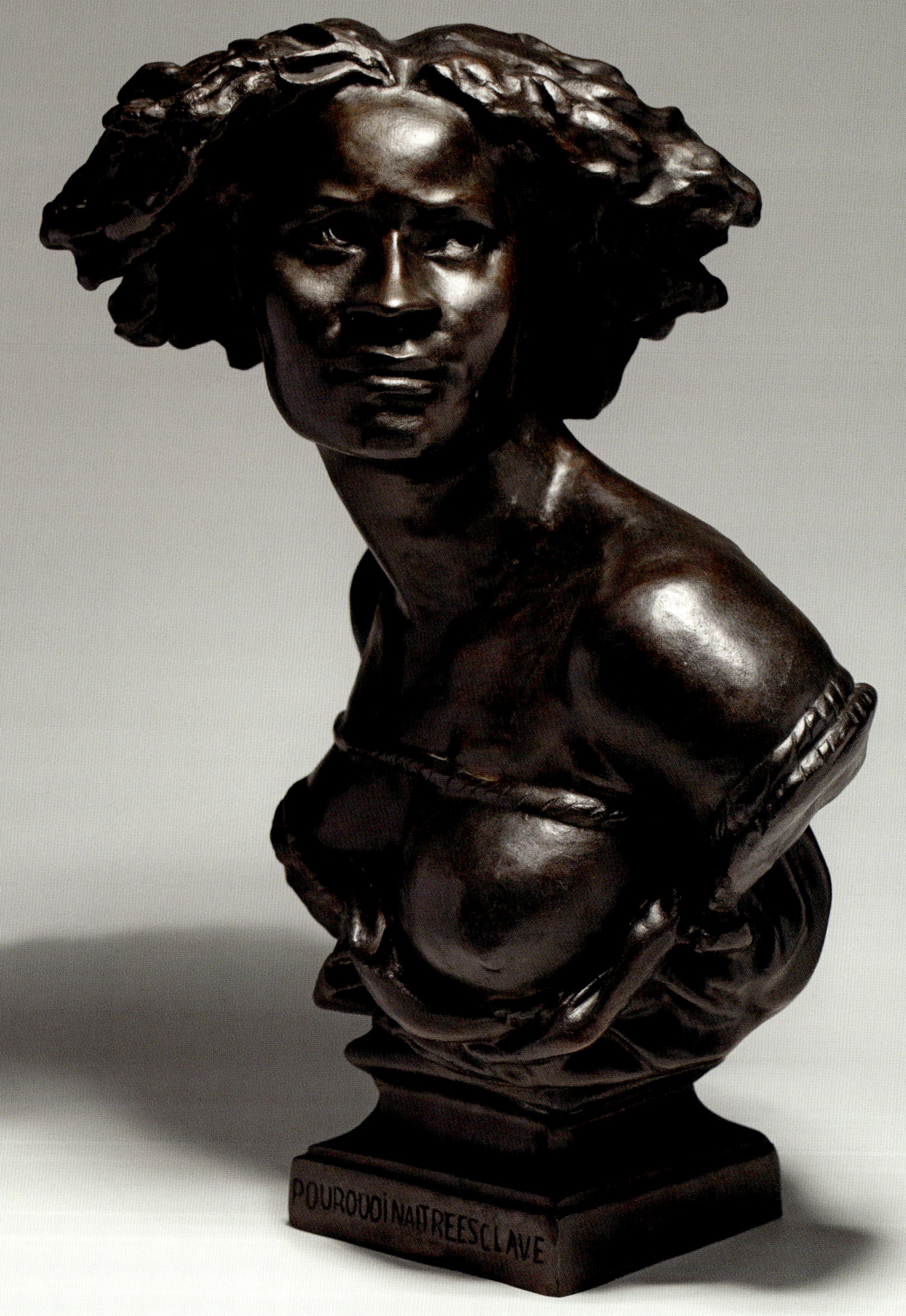

JEAN-BAPTISTE CARPEAUX
Woman of African Descent (or *La Négresse*), 1868 (recast 1979)

With shoulders, arms, and breasts bound by ropes and a slightly contorted frame, the bronze bust *Woman of African Descent* (or, historically, *La Négresse*) was a preparatory piece for naturalist sculptor Jean-Baptiste Carpeaux's final project *Fontaine de l'Observatoire* (Paris). The fountain presents four women holding up a globe, signifying the four races as allegories for the four continents of the world, with *La Négresse* representing Africa. Though she is restrained by the rope and her status as an enslaved woman, her hair flows freely—a stark contrast to the hairstyles of the other women in the fountain. Because of the textured hair and the tilt of the woman's head, a rich array of blacks and browns are revealed by the light that dances on the bronze surface.

Sculpted only twenty years after France banned slavery, this bust was inscribed with the phrase "Pourquoi Naître Esclave" ("Why Be Born a Slave"), signaling the artist's horror at the institution of slavery and its regrettable effect on the African continent.

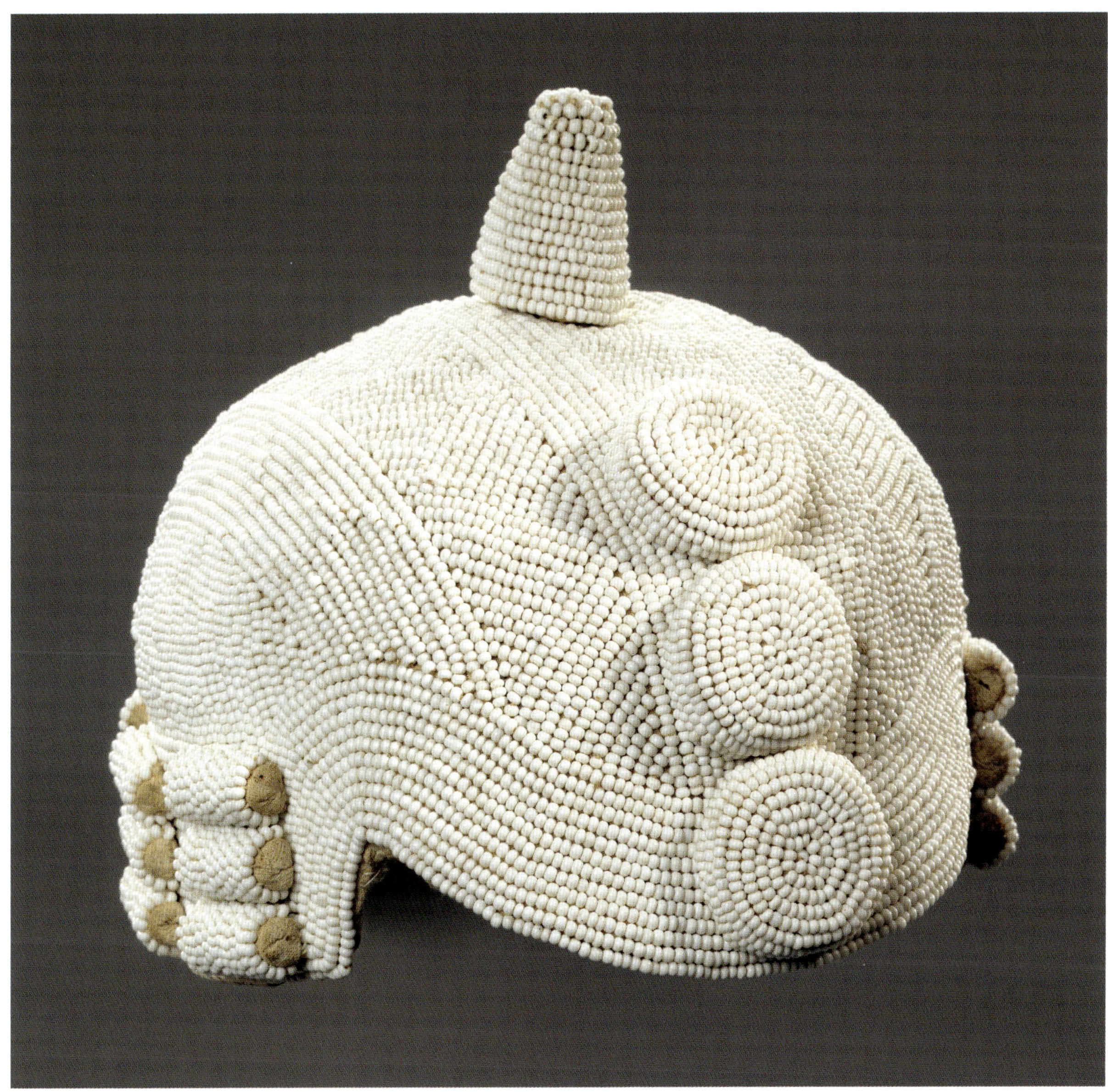

UNIDENTIFIED YORUBA ARTIST

White Beaded Cap (*orikogbofo*), 1988

In Yoruba society, finely beaded crowns are worn by an *oba*, or king, to demonstrate his authority within the community and his elevated spirituality. Compared with the traditional vertical *Ade* crown, this particular *orikogbofo* headdress reflects the influence of British culture as a result of Britain's colonial rule over Nigeria. Though it was modeled after the cap and curl style of a barrister's wig, it also resonates with symbolism from Yoruba culture. A person with *ewu* (white hair) should be esteemed for reaching the pinnacle of wisdom, and the disks on the forehead recall several ancient African societies as well as the circular faces on *Ade* crowns.

While several pieces in this exhibition reflect on foreigners' regard for Black hair as they traveled in Africa, this beaded cap shows an inversed relationship: what did Black artists in Africa think about the hair textures and styles they encountered from European cultures?

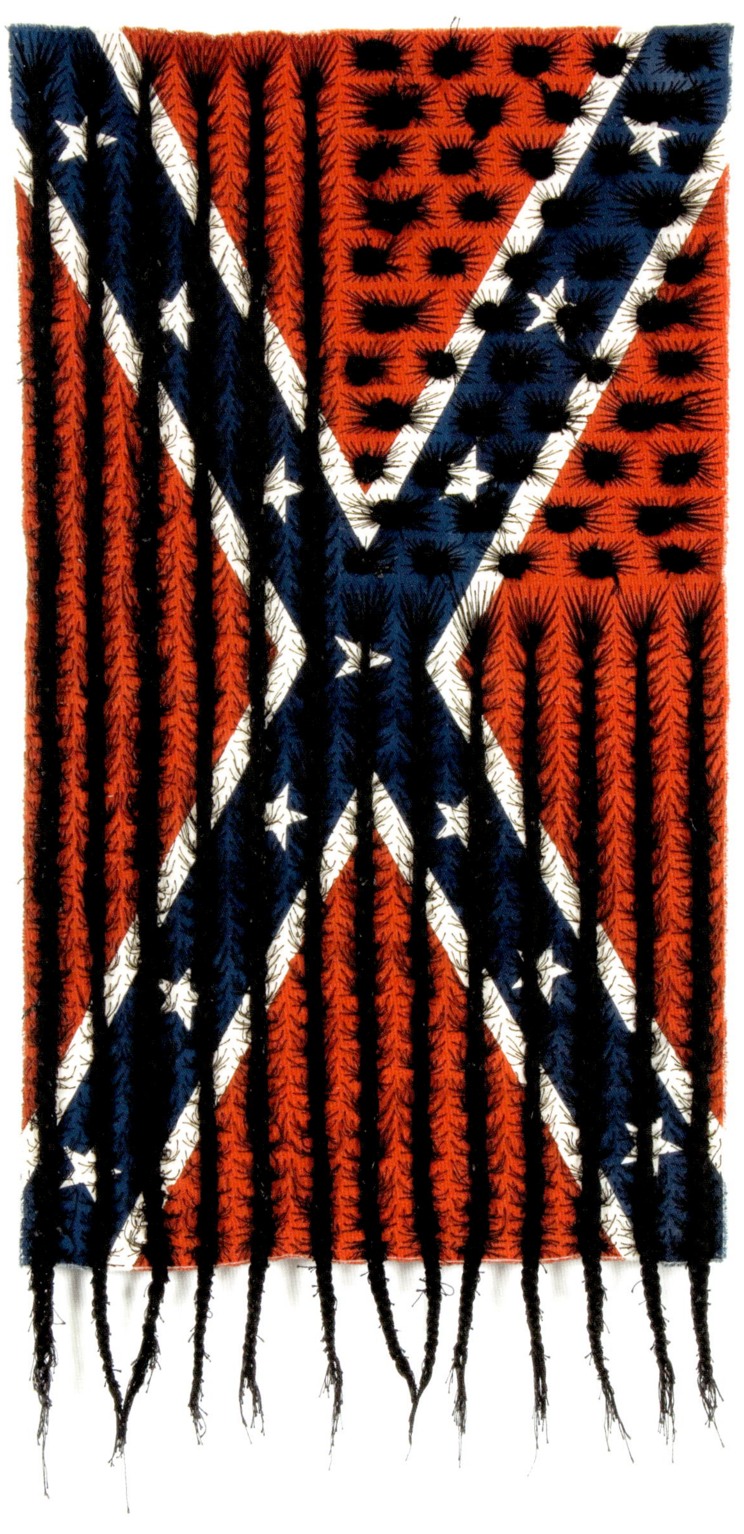

SONYA CLARK

Black Hair Flag, 2010

"Hair was the first fiber that people manipulated for aesthetic and functional reasons," Clark notes. Her practice has become synonymous with a mixing of Black hair with textile arts. *Black Hair Flag* is a combination of cloth, paint, and thread wherein Clark reimagines the Confederate flag, a symbol that remains popular in parts of the United States. After painting an image of the flag, she wove black thread into cornrows and constructed Bantu knots (knots of twisted hair) to recall the stars and stripes of the American flag. Under the Confederacy, there were strict rules regarding how Black people could wear their hair and that legacy endures even today in certain spaces. Not only does the braiding over the flag physically reclaim it, but it also explores the idea of symbols within the United States. The thread evoking Black hair binds together these two visions of America—hair acts like the thru-line of American chronology, reminding us that some of today's discrimination has roots in the dehumanization that occurred throughout the nation's past.

Corn shuck/grinder, *ca.* 1850

Enslaved Africans were not given the consideration of taking care of their bodily hygiene, including hair care. Often their hair would become extremely matted which resulted in scalp disease. Ringworms and pus from the disease would cake in their hair, leaving the hair even more unmanageable. Thus, shaved heads became popular among men and women. In 1808, the slave trade was outlawed, and traders were no longer allowed to take Africans from their homelands. Eventually, slave owners saw personal hygiene as an important factor in increasing the lifespan of previously purchased slaves. Sunday was given as a day for rest, religion, and personal hygiene. Enslaved Africans used whatever tools they had available such as carding combs and ground cornmeal, which was used to rid the hair of dirt and oils by combing the husks through the hair.

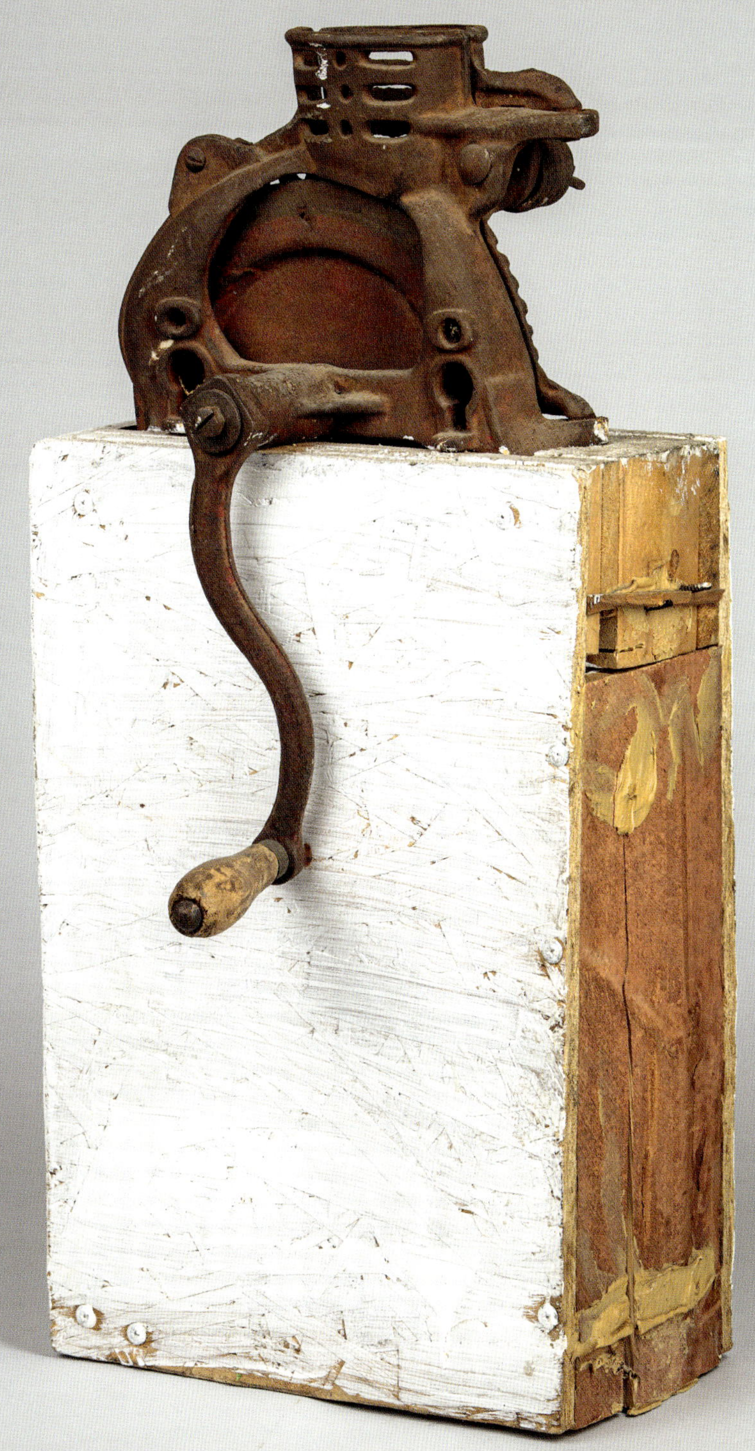

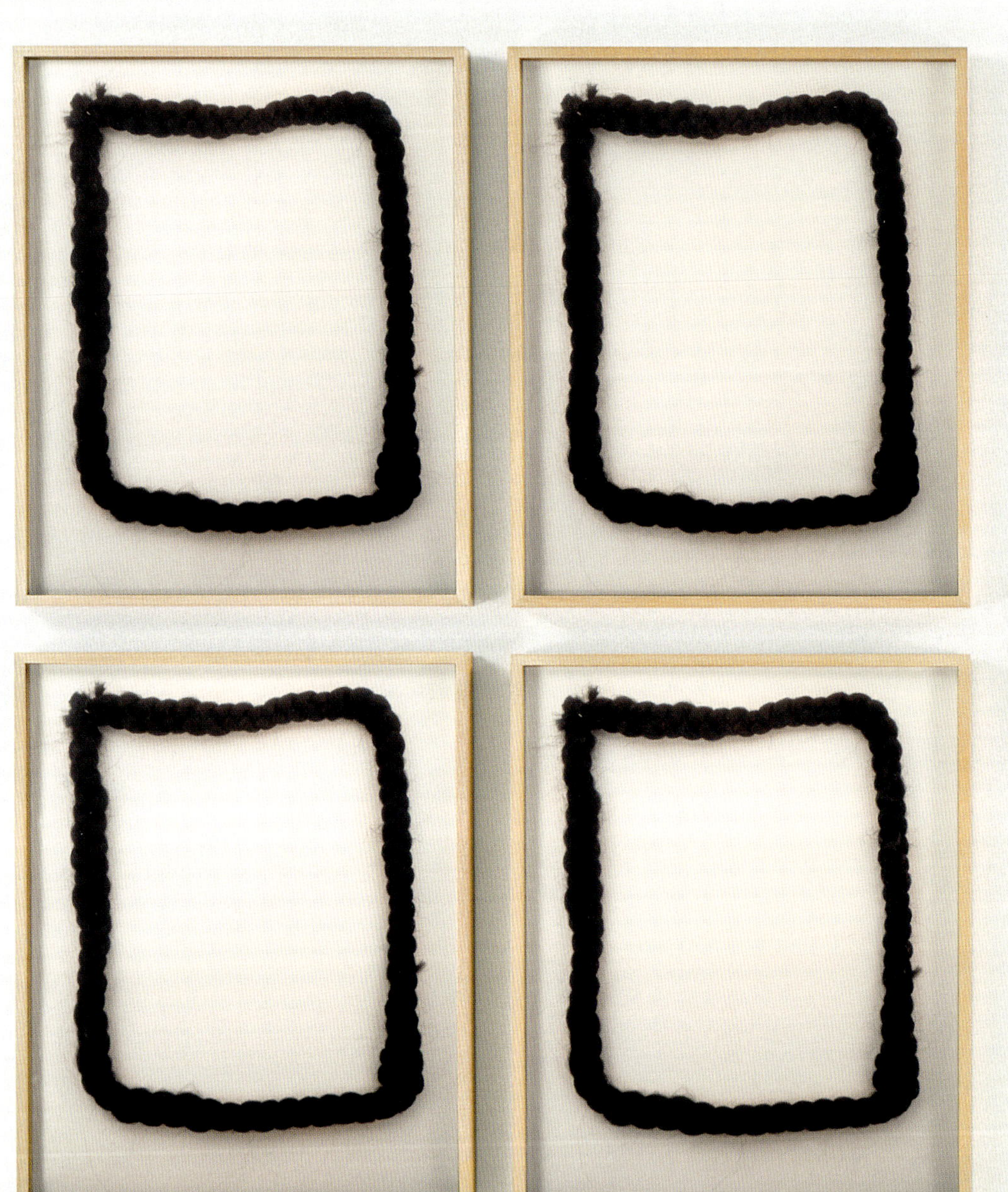
Their story doesn't
square with yours;
try and
square the two.

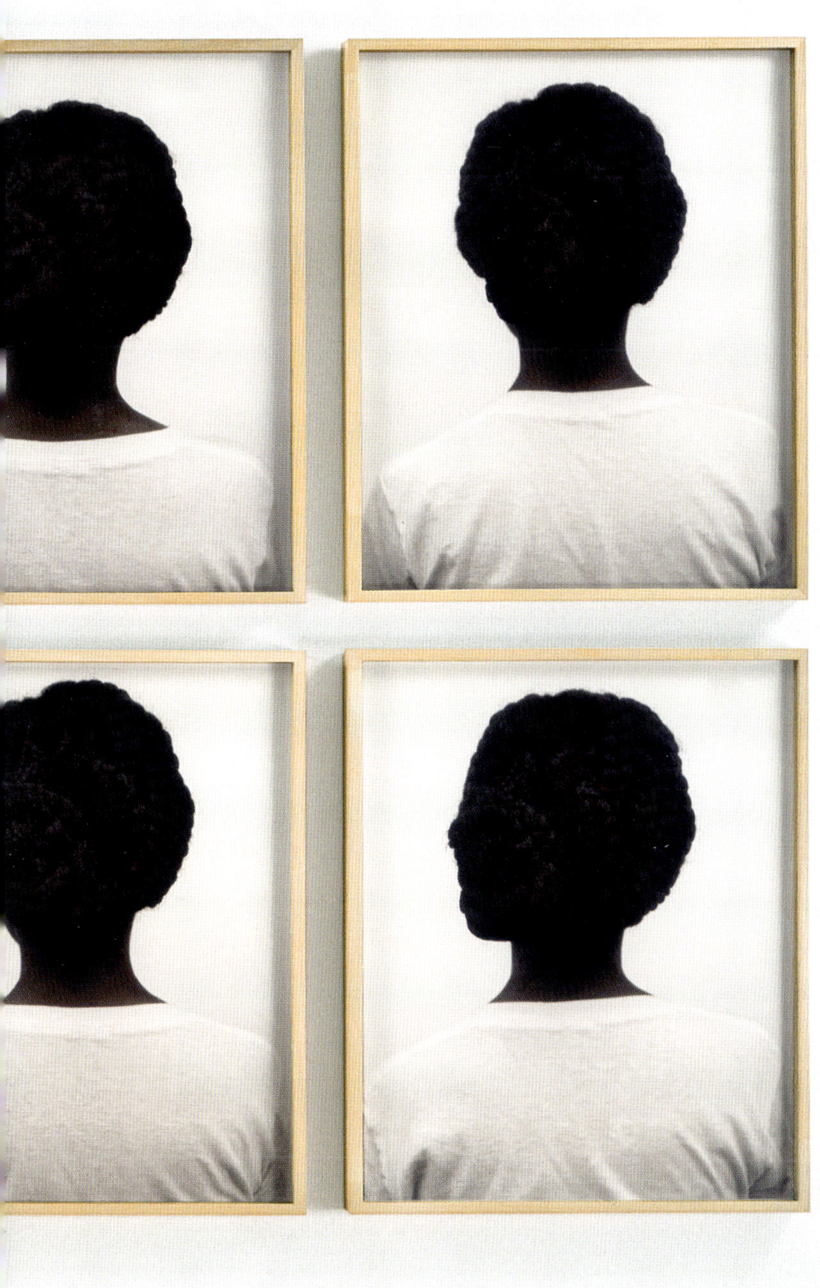

LORNA SIMPSON

Square Deal, 1990

The expression 'square deal' refers to an honest, fair transaction. Simpson's *Square Deal* features eight Polaroid prints, four of which show the dorsal silhouette of an anonymous woman, while the other four show singular braids laid out in a square. Between the two groups, an engraved plaque reads "Their story doesn't square with yours try and square the two"—implying misunderstanding at best, and deception at worst. The artist suggested the work addresses the murky nature of origin stories: "Family stories are often told in code and in such a roundabout way, and as the stories are passed down they take on heroic and mythological proportions."

Given her prominence as one of the first Black conceptual photographers to emerge in the late 1980s, Simpson's hallmarks were a dauntless evocation of Black (women's) lives in the United States and the incorporation of text alongside or within photos. As with most of her works, the text in *Square Deal* does not lead the viewer to a clear interpretation. In trying to determine whose story doesn't square with whose, we might see the hair braids as nooses for the four heads, recalling several historic lynchings that resulted from a dispute in accounts. Between each element of this work—anonymous women, hair braids, and ambiguous text—tensions arise from the open-endedness of the connotations.

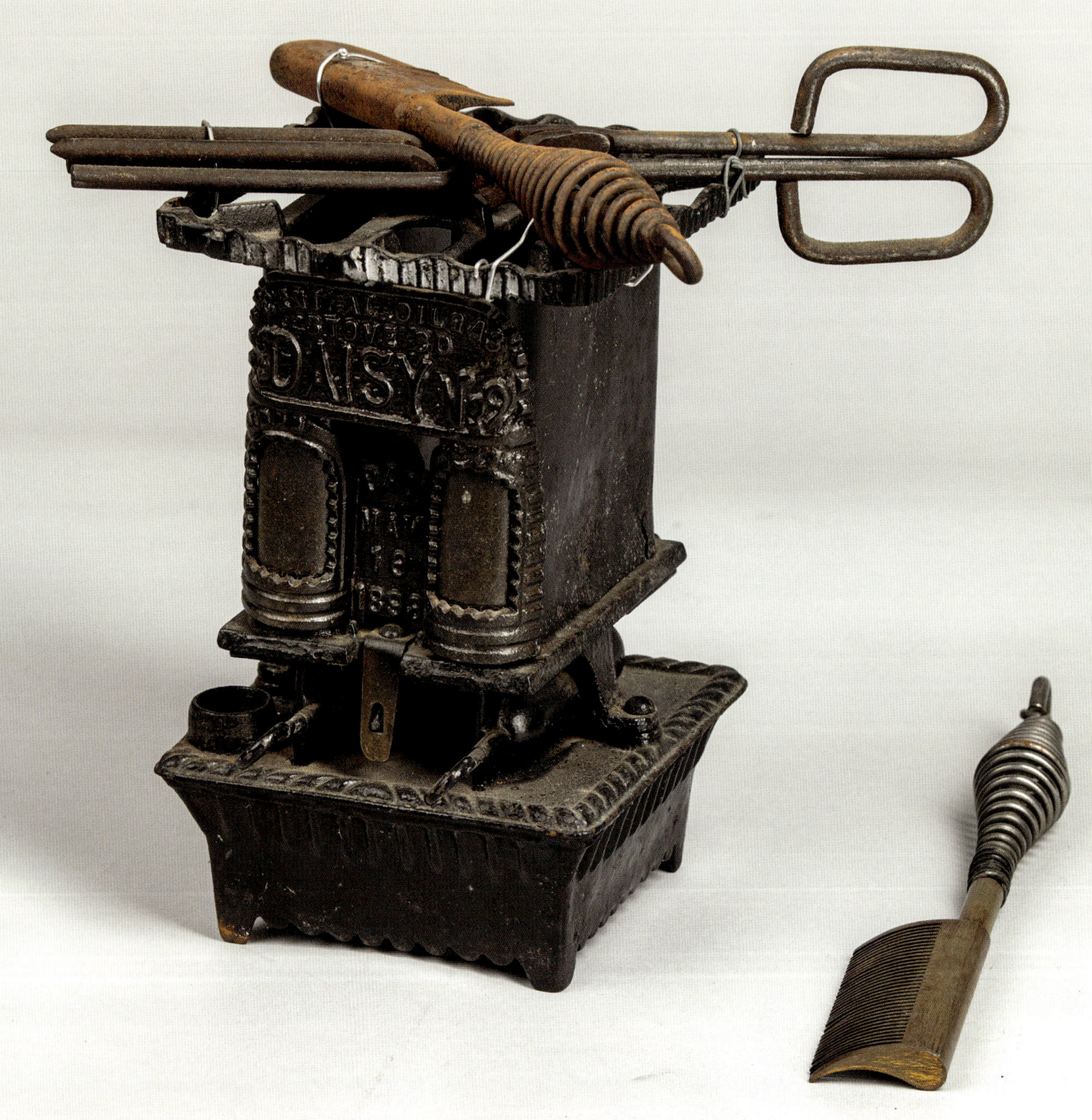

Stove with hot comb and three-barrel Marcel curler, *ca.* 1920

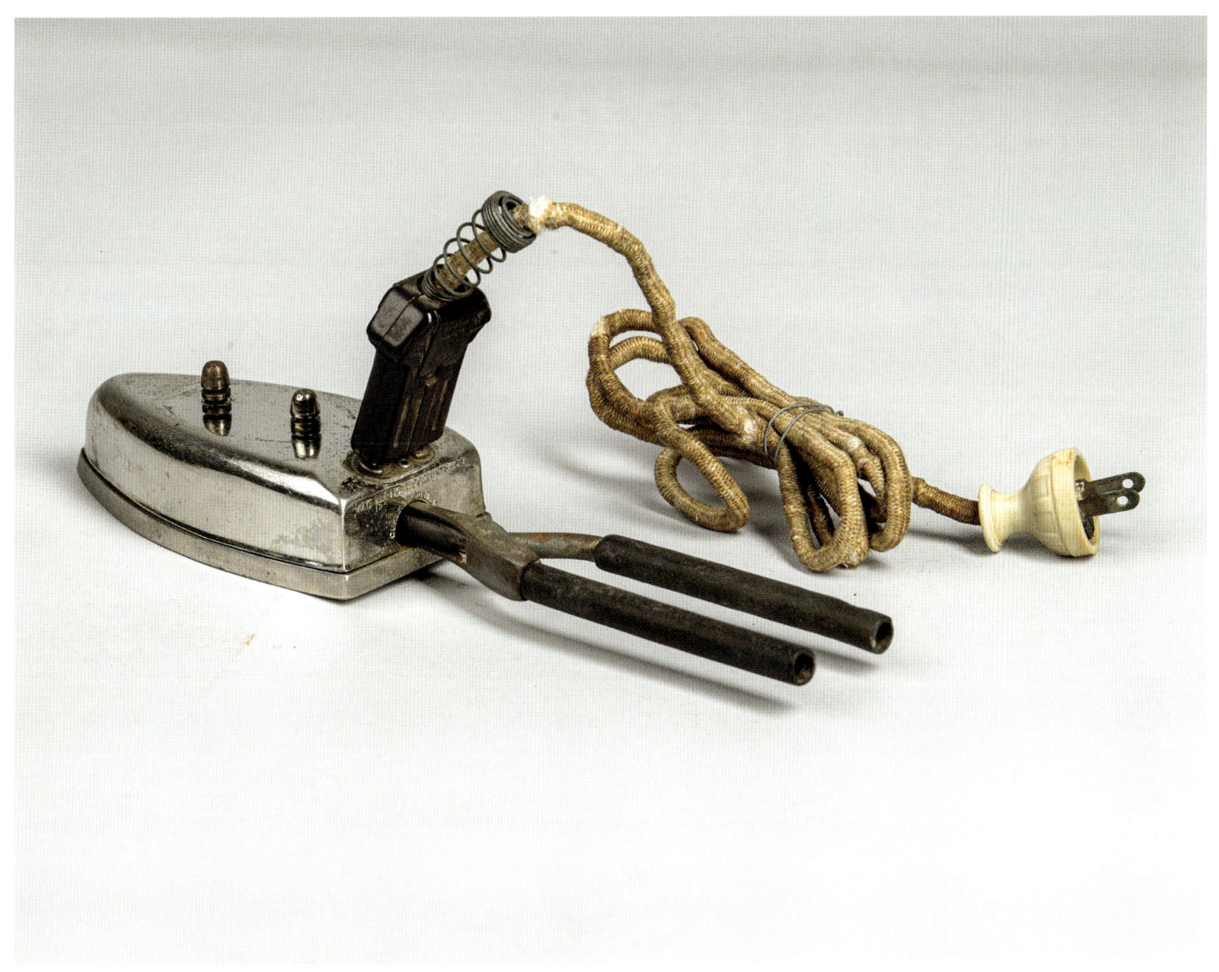

Electric pressing iron with curling implements, 1920s

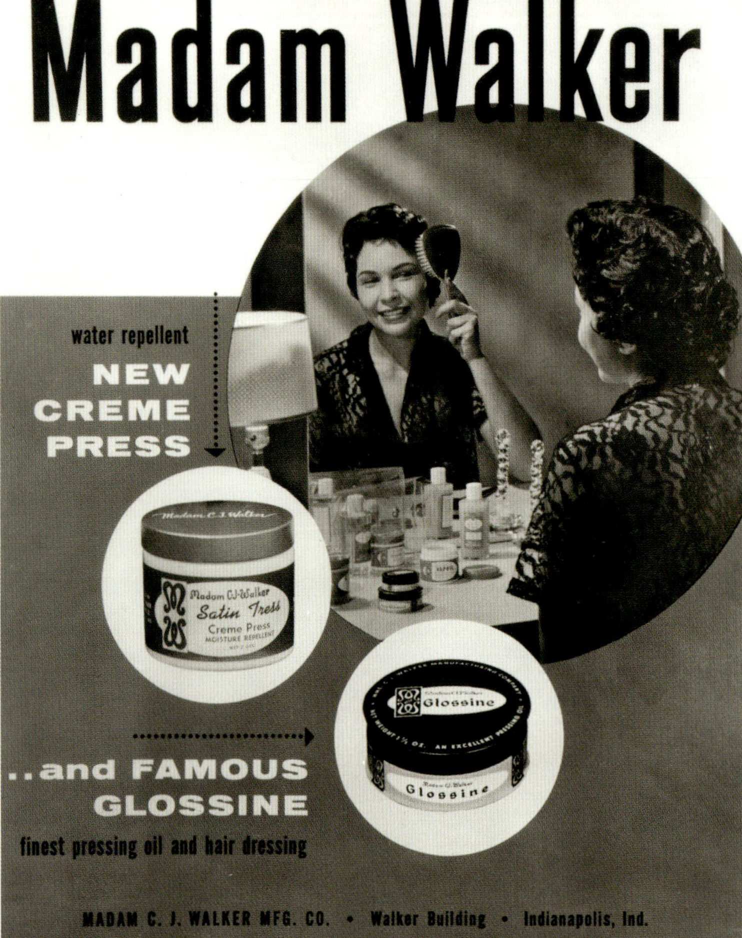

Madam C. J. Walker's
Advertisement *ca.* 1907

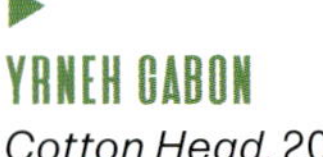

YRNEH GABON

Cotton Head, 2016

An interdisciplinary artist, Gabon makes art about historical contexts, socio-political ideas, and environmental issues. Across his performances and artworks, the Jamaican-born artist has decried systems that perpetuate climate change and biases that foster violence against Black albinos in Africa.

Cotton Head is a clay sculpture wherein actual stalks of cotton serve as the figure's hair. The connotations of cotton are manifold, from the failed experiments to cultivate the crop in the Caribbean, to the back-breaking labor of enslaved African Americans across the South. Despite some similarities in the texture of Black hair and cotton bundles, the substitution of the crop of "King Cotton" for this Black man's "crown" (a term sometimes used to describe one's hair) is off-putting and uncanny. Indeed, even these terms belie the question of authority—who has the power to subjugate another person in the name of morality, tradition, or profit?

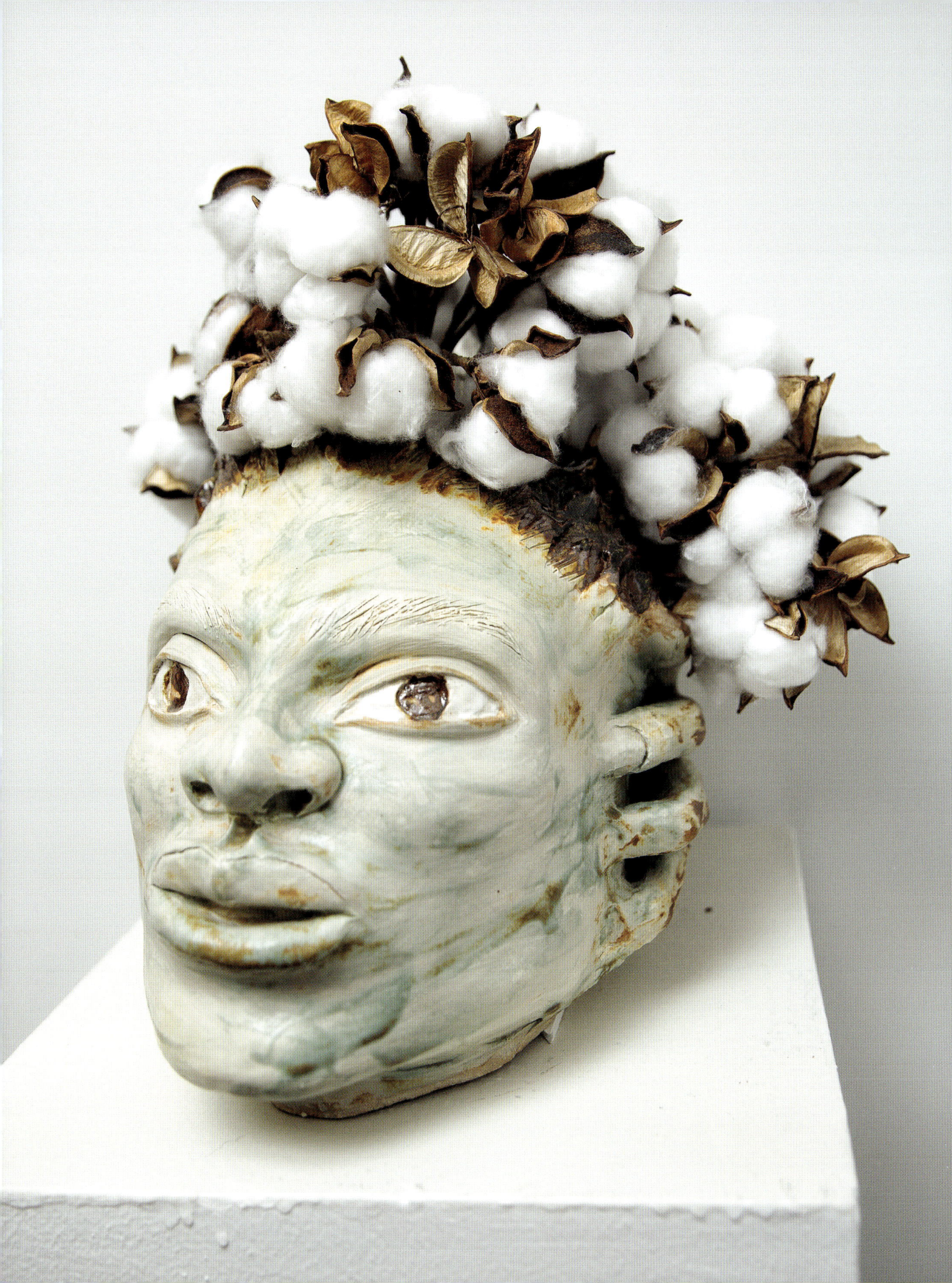

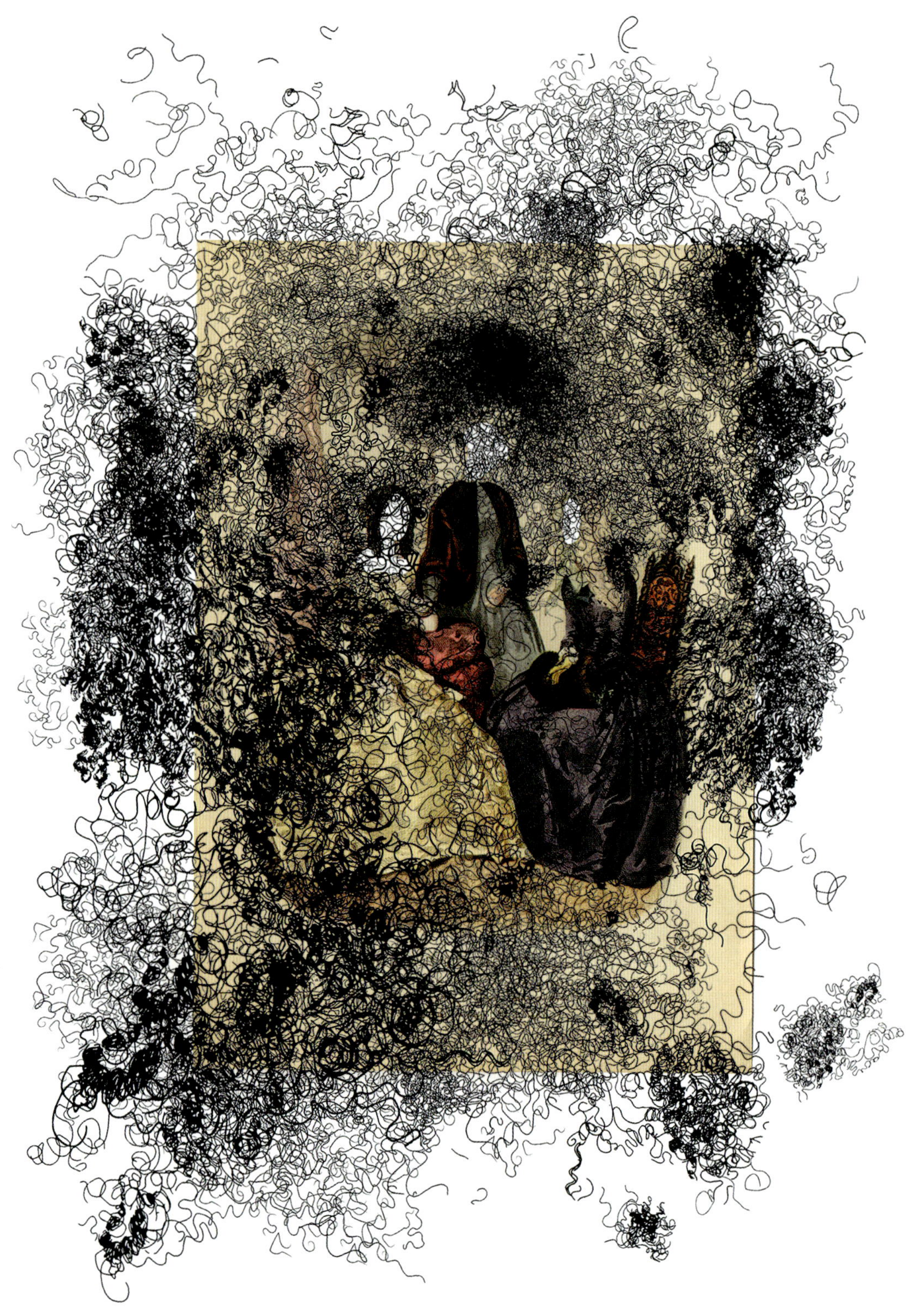

SHARON NORWOOD
The Root of the Matter XII, 2017

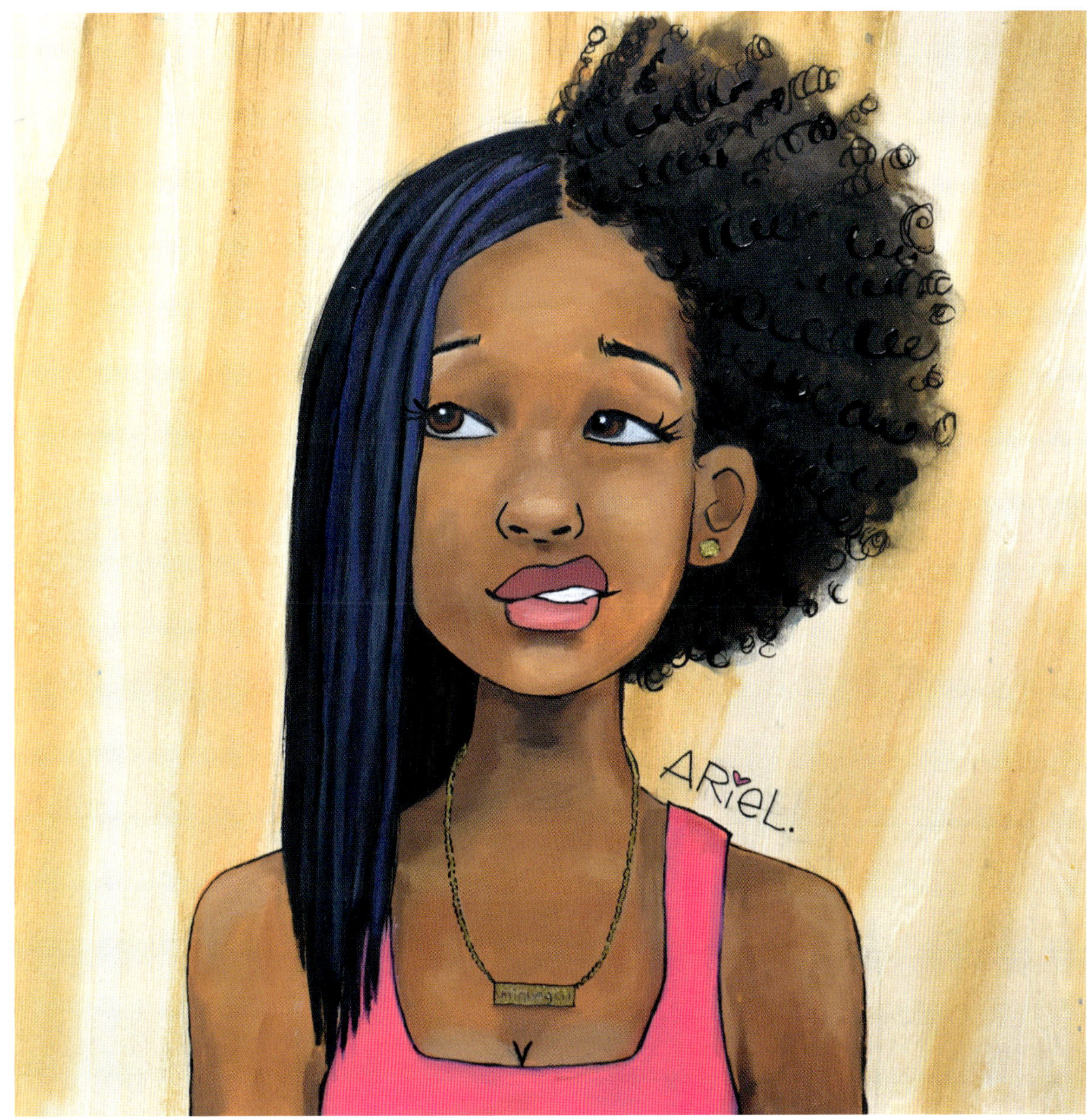

KETURAH ARIEL

Internal Battle, 2013

The decision: natural hair or straightened? Negotiating the practical, social, and financial aspects of this decision is complicated, a reality which many women can attest remains hidden. Ariel's work, *Internal Battle,* brings this dilemma into the open, depicting a young woman agonizing over the decision. As an artist, designer, and entrepreneur, Ariel's work can be found in illustrations for children's books and popular magazines. However, in her paintings the artist is committed to depicting circumstances that often go unseen, giving visual space to the common, day-to-day experiences that remain invisible to a majority of the population. She creates paintings in which some viewers find a comfortable familiarity and realize they are not alone. After listening to a friend's confession of her struggles to grow out her natural hair, Ariel was inspired to create *Internal Battle* as a vehicle for solidarity among women who seem to face criticism for whatever choice they make in the styling and presentation of their hair.

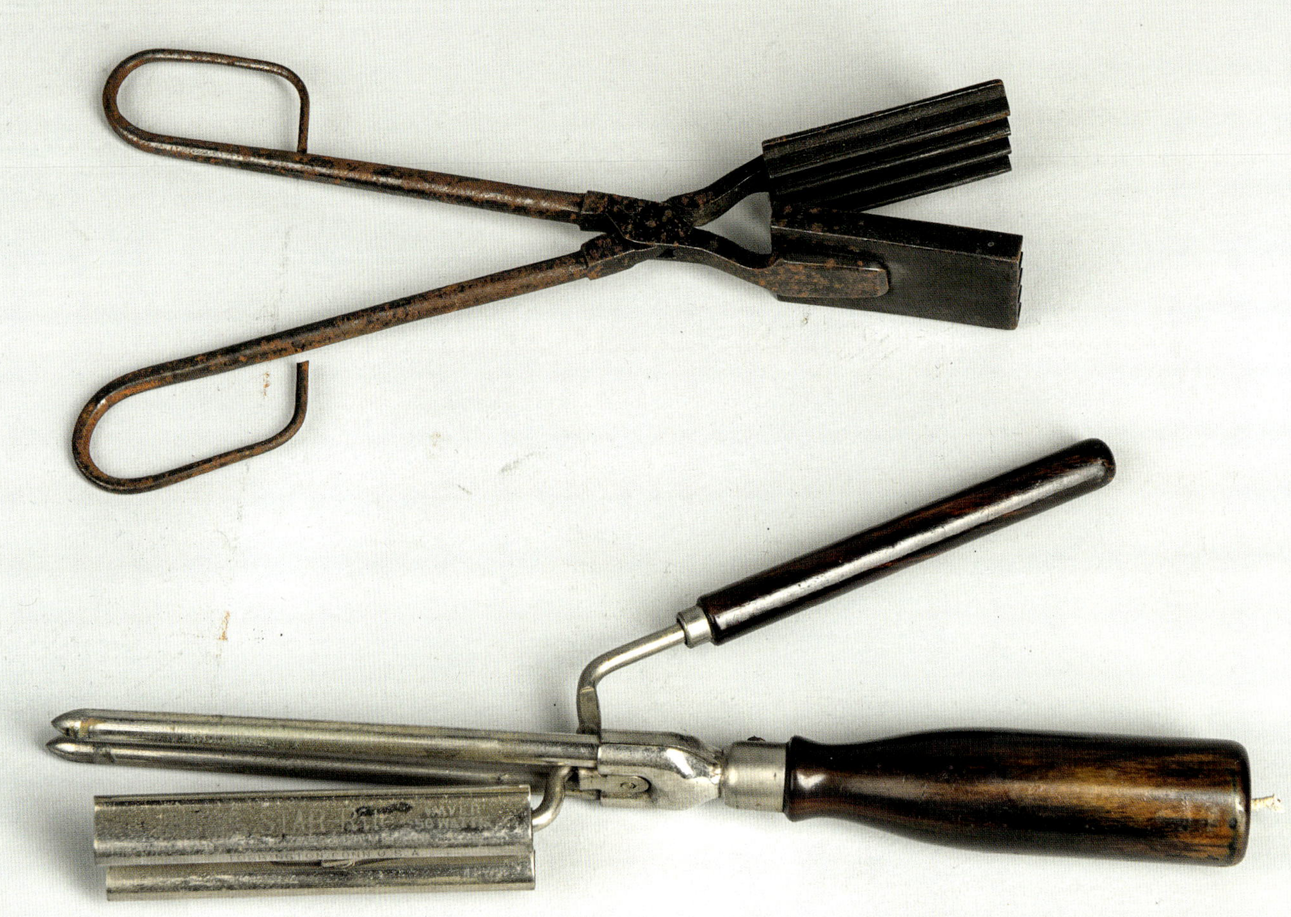

Crimpers from the stove set, *ca.* 1920

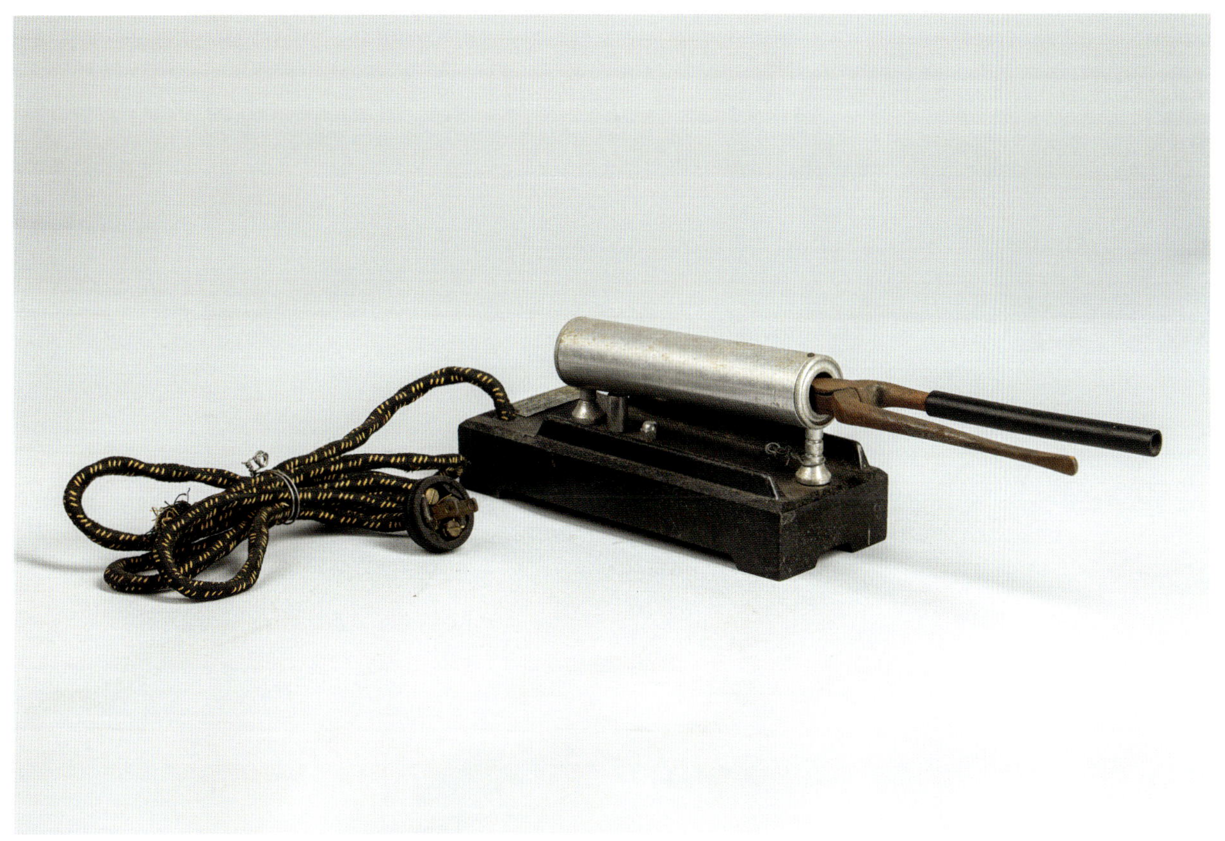

Electric stove with removable Marcel curler, *ca.* 1920

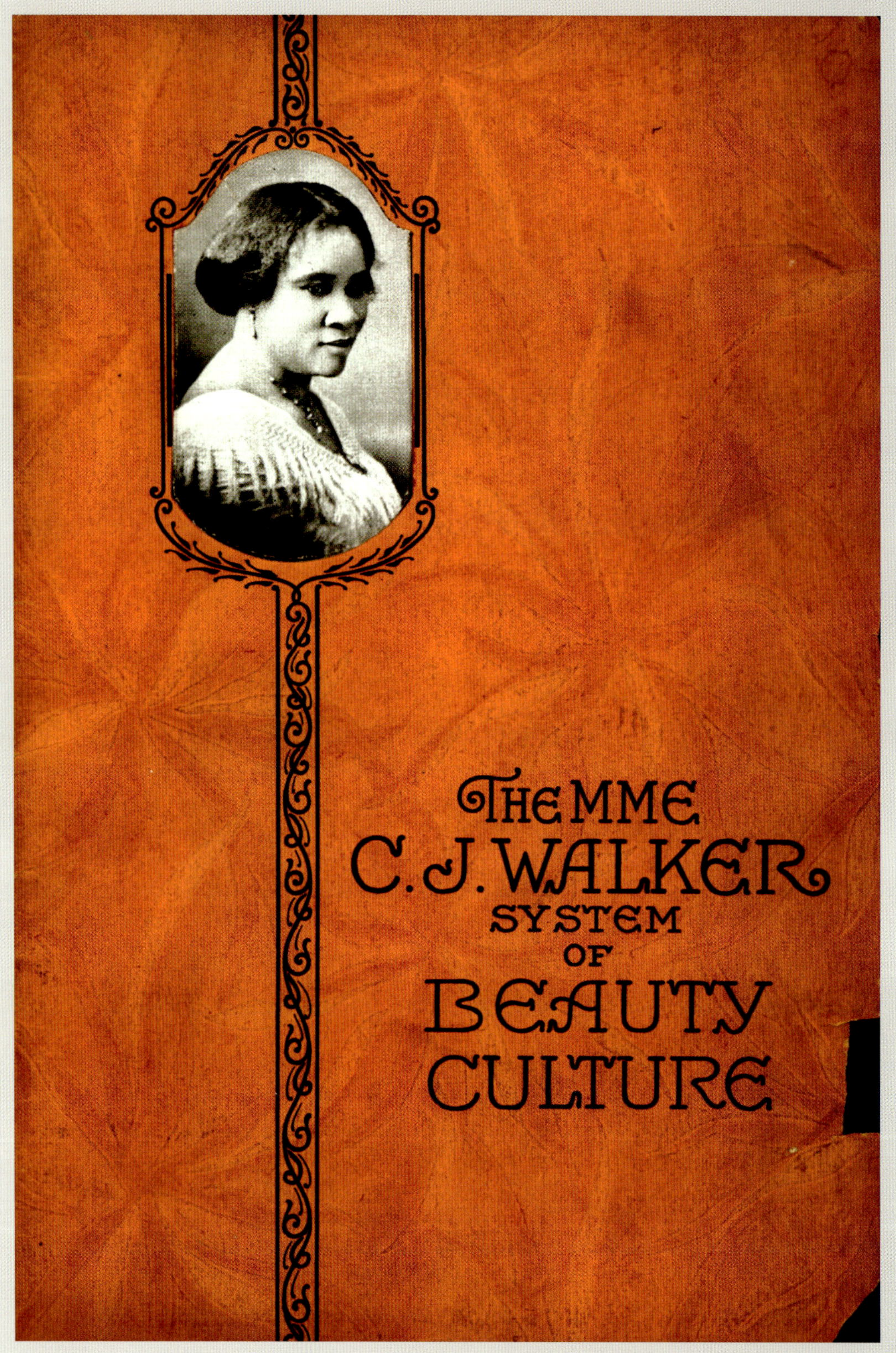

The Madam C. J. Walker System of Beauty Culture, 1928

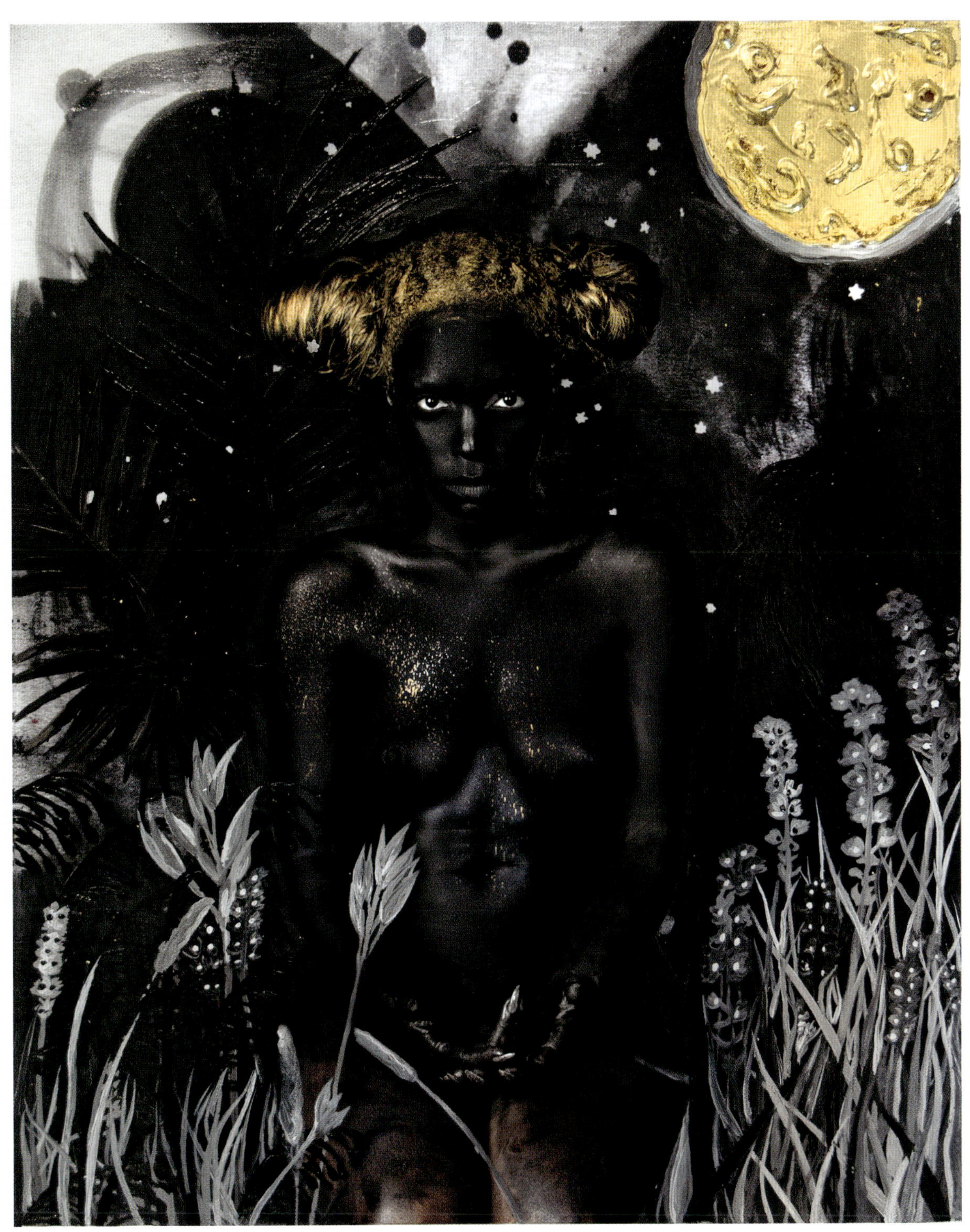

LINA IRIS VIKTOR
The Massacre of the Innocents… No. XXIV
(from the *Dark Continent* series), 2017

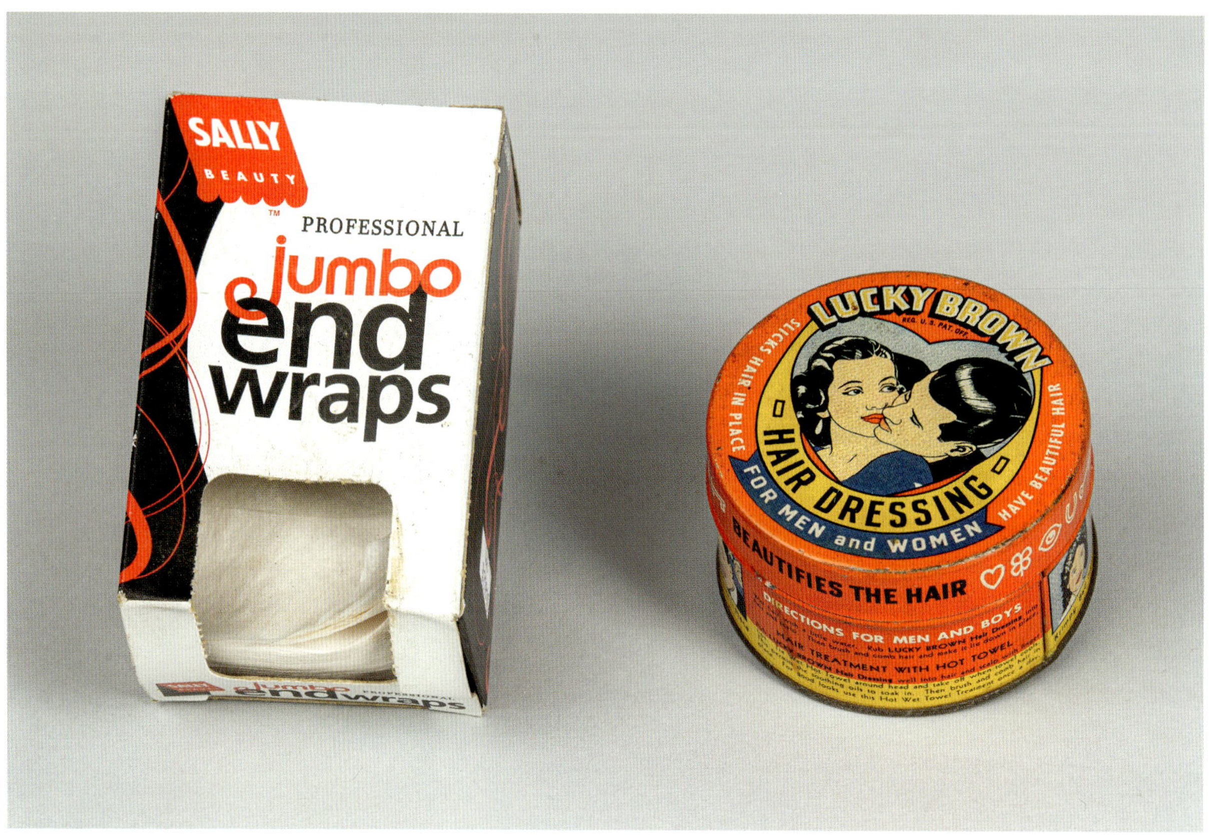

Sally Beauty professional jumbo end wraps, *ca.* 1990
Lucky Brown Hair Dressing, 1937

▶
Wanted by the FBI: Angela Davis, 1970

Angela Davis is one of the most famous figures to come out of the Civil Rights Movement and, arguably, her hairstyle is just as recognizable. As a passionate activist and member of the Communist Party, Davis was wanted by the FBI for kidnapping and murder, charges for which she was later acquitted. These iconic images were plastered across the country, leading the Afro hairstyle to become associated with militant and disruptive behavior. This resulted in the further oppression of Black women who sported their natural hair during this time period—a reality that has lingered into society today. With nostalgic trends harkening back to the styles of the 1970s, the Afro has re-entered mainstream culture, though largely devoid of its political roots. The experience of Davis is an example of cultural politicization. Though she did not wear the Afro as a political statement, the circumstances she faced and the way her image was spread made it political.

WANTED BY THE FBI

INTERSTATE FLIGHT - MURDER, KIDNAPING

ANGELA YVONNE DAVIS

FBI No. 867,615 G

Photograph taken 1969

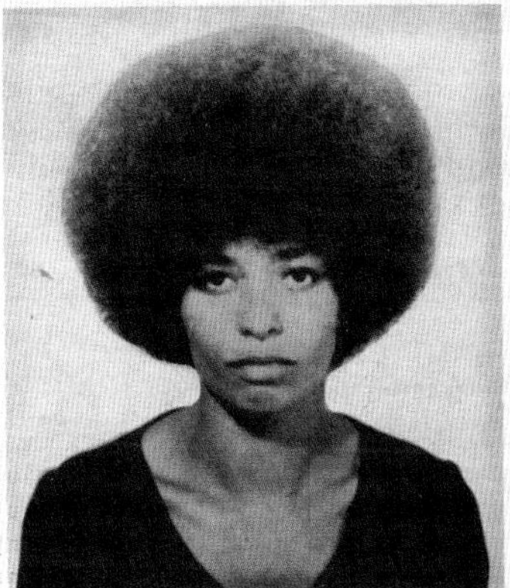

Photograph taken 1970

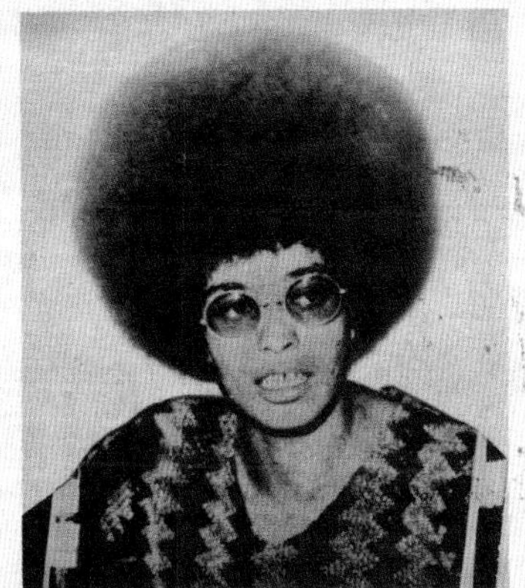

Alias: "Tamu"

DESCRIPTION

Age:	26, born January 26, 1944, Birmingham, Alabama	**Eyes:**	Brown
Height:	5'8"	**Complexion:**	Light brown
Weight:	145 pounds	**Race:**	Negro
Build:	Slender	**Nationality:**	American
Hair:	Black		
Occupation:	Teacher		
Scars and Marks:	Small scars on both knees		

Fingerprint Classification: $\frac{4\ M\quad 5\ Ua\ 6}{I\ 17\ U}$

CAUTION

ANGELA DAVIS IS WANTED ON KIDNAPING AND MURDER CHARGES GROWING OUT OF AN ABDUCTION AND SHOOTING IN MARIN COUNTY, CALIFORNIA, ON AUGUST 7, 1970. SHE ALLEGEDLY HAS PURCHASED SEVERAL GUNS IN THE PAST. CONSIDER POSSIBLY ARMED AND DANGEROUS.

A Federal warrant was issued on August 15, 1970, at San Francisco, California, charging Davis with unlawful interstate flight to avoid prosecution for murder and kidnaping (Title 18, U. S. Code, Section 1073).

IF YOU HAVE ANY INFORMATION CONCERNING THIS PERSON, PLEASE NOTIFY ME OR CONTACT YOUR LOCAL FBI OFFICE. TELEPHONE NUMBERS AND ADDRESSES OF ALL FBI OFFICES LISTED ON BACK.

J. Edgar Hoover

DIRECTOR
FEDERAL BUREAU OF INVESTIGATION
UNITED STATES DEPARTMENT OF JUSTICE
WASHINGTON, D. C. 20535
TELEPHONE, NATIONAL 8-7117

Entered NCIC
Wanted Flyer 457
August 18, 1970

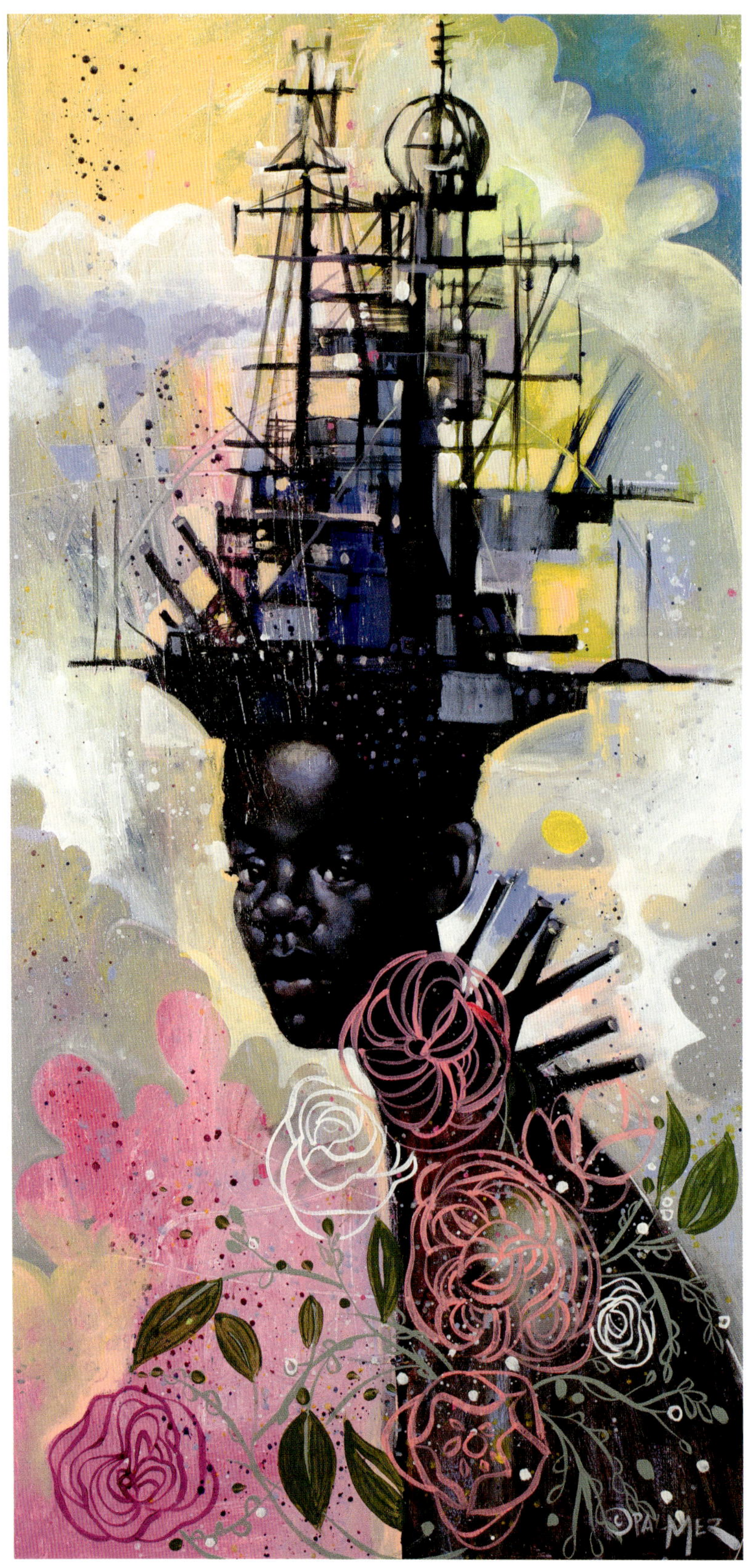

CHARLY PALMER

Battleship 3, 2016

Charly Palmer does not shy away from political commentary—in fact most of his art discusses what it means to be Black in America. By titling his series with loaded terms like *Protest* and *Silenced*, he constructs visual narratives inspired by communal history and personal life experience. His figurative art depicts Black bodies merging with a range of motifs, from flowers to the American flag, teasing out the interplay of beauty and conflict. His *Battleship* series exemplifies this commitment to exploring opposing dynamics, bringing in soft colors alongside floral patterns, but juxtaposing them with a warship balanced on each figure's head. Some individuals stand resolutely while others sink into the water below. *Battleship 3* is the most striking of the series, as the subject is weighed down by the battleship that replaces her hair—a metaphor for the politicization of Black hair. This can come, of course, from outside Black communities, but it also happens whenever Black individuals weaponize their hair to put down others' preferences of natural or synthetic styles or textures.

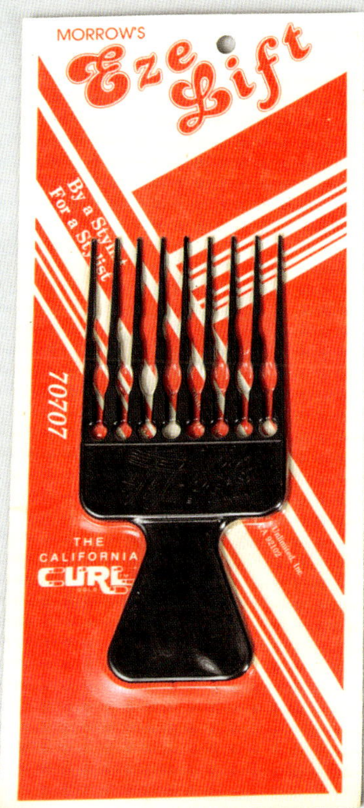

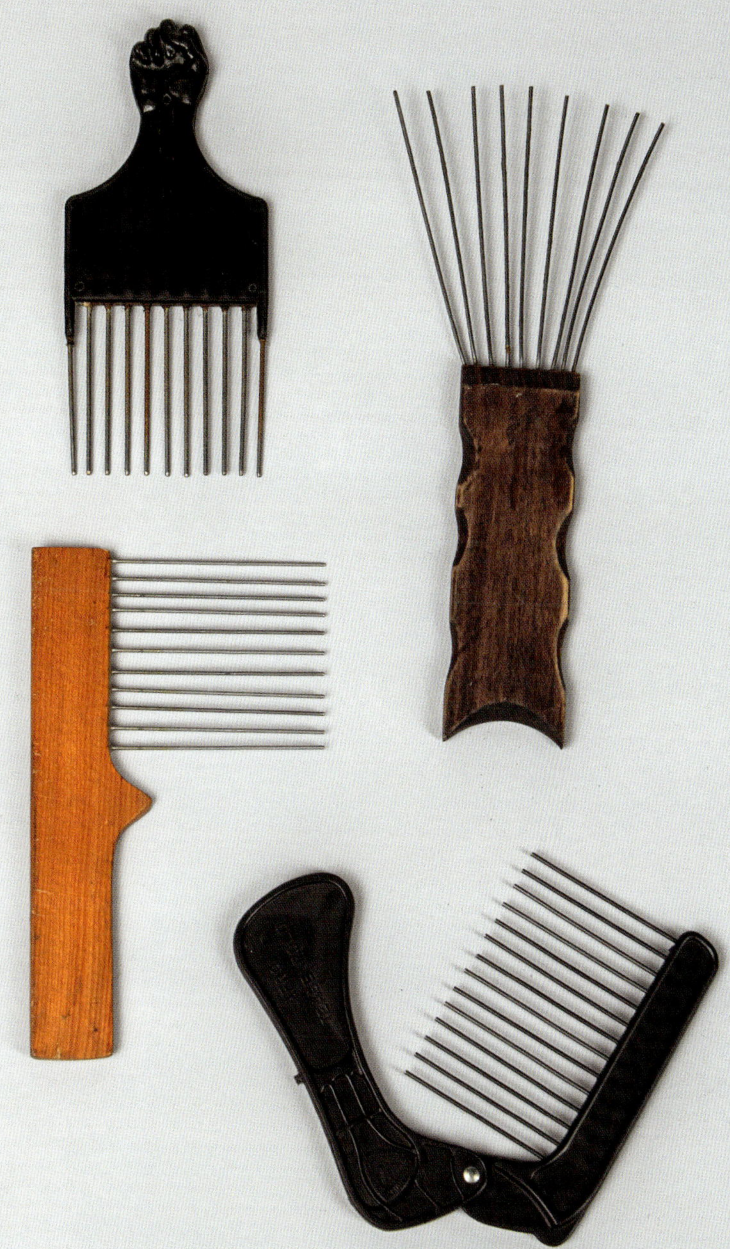

Selection of Picks from the collection of Dr. Willie Morrow, 1962–1974

The Afro pick is a symbol of revolution, similar to the connotations of the hairstyle for which it was created. In the 1960s, pulling inspiration from centuries-old wooden African combs, Dr. Willie Morrow carved the first Afro picks and distributed them commercially in the United States. He proudly told the curators that a portion of the sales from these picks went to help fund Civil Rights demonstrations and protests. The popular Afro pick with a raised fist as the handle was patented in 1969 by two African Americans, Samuel H. Bundles Jr. and Henry M. Childrey (Tulloch). These inventors, just like Dr. Morrow, were responding to the Black consciousness movement, where people sought various means to signify their Black pride. In 1977, Dr. Morrow patented the plastic Afro Comb, a modern rendition of his earlier models.

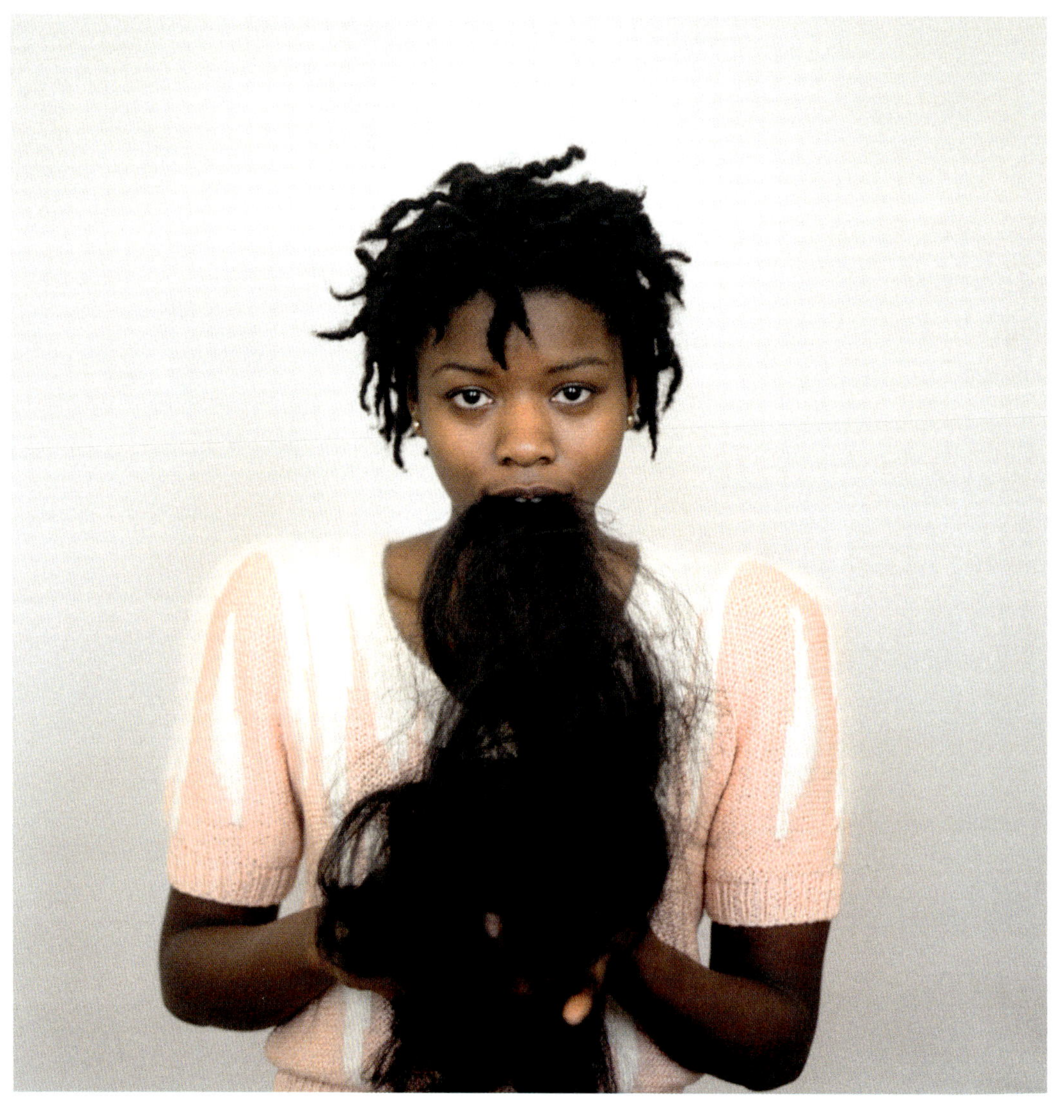

NAKEYA BROWN
Hair Portrait #3 from the *Refutation of "Good" Hair* series, 2012

Brown uses her platform to emphasize the importance of social politics, hair rituals, and Black cultures through photography. In her critically acclaimed work, the artist communicates across the barriers that divide cultures and dismiss Black hair and beauty. Instead of depicting these unsavory tensions, Brown cleverly highlights the universal themes that the barriers threaten to hide. With clean pastel colors, a simple composition, and an outward-facing subject, her images present the viewer with a sense of nostalgia and relatability.

In this photograph, Brown opposes the "Black hair is bad hair" stereotype that pervades many mindsets, even within Black communities. The contrast between the hair on the woman's head and the hairpiece she is beginning to ingest conveys the discomfort of being forced to pursue a certain vision of "good" hair—a synthetic hairpiece, straightened, devoid of kinks or curls. Her naturally textured hair might recall the misconceptions that have circulated for centuries; it is "coarse," "unmanageable," and "undesirable." The woman confronts the viewer with her gaze as she imminently begins to choke on a standard being forced down her throat. With this series, Brown unabashedly declares that Black hair is beautiful as it is.

APRIL BEY

Creamy Chris, 2013

A transplant from the Caribbean to the West Coast, Bey is a mixed media artist who offers insightful commentary on what it means to navigate the world as a Black woman. From portraits in wood to fabric collages, Bey's focus on certain materials conveys as much significance as the artwork's subject matter.

This print is inspired by the mixed response to comedian Chris Rock's 2009 documentary *Good Hair.* The film's title refers to an American social debate as to which textures of hair fall into the categories of "good" or "bad." In this film, Rock follows the journey of Black hair from the first straightening tools, to the sudden prevalence of hair extensions, to the destructive nature of relaxers. While *Good Hair* includes the perspectives of professional hair stylists, product creators, and celebrities, many believe that the perspectives of everyday women were ignored. In fact, given the rise of social platforms like YouTube, many women were already speaking to these issues, and later described how Rock's film co-opted their experiences and insights without appropriate credit. After an affluent Black man profited from stories of (mostly) Black women's haircare, the beauty community took their criticisms to the internet. With a more physical, artistic response, Bey took a promotional image for the film and covered it with hair relaxer to highlight its toxic connotations. Fashioning Rock as a clown and choosing a font with a circus-like flair, the artist emphasizes how the comedian's excessive jokes made a mockery of Black hair instead of sharing the platform like an advocate would.

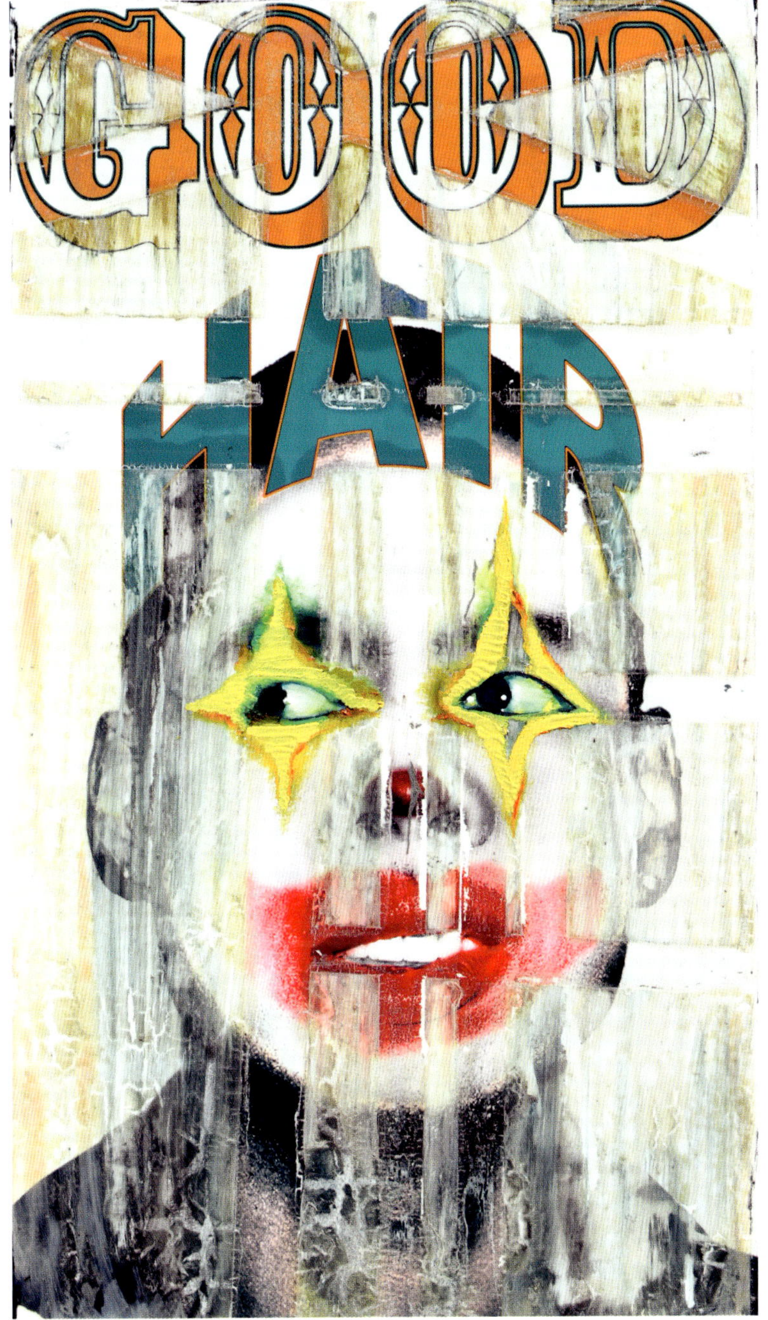

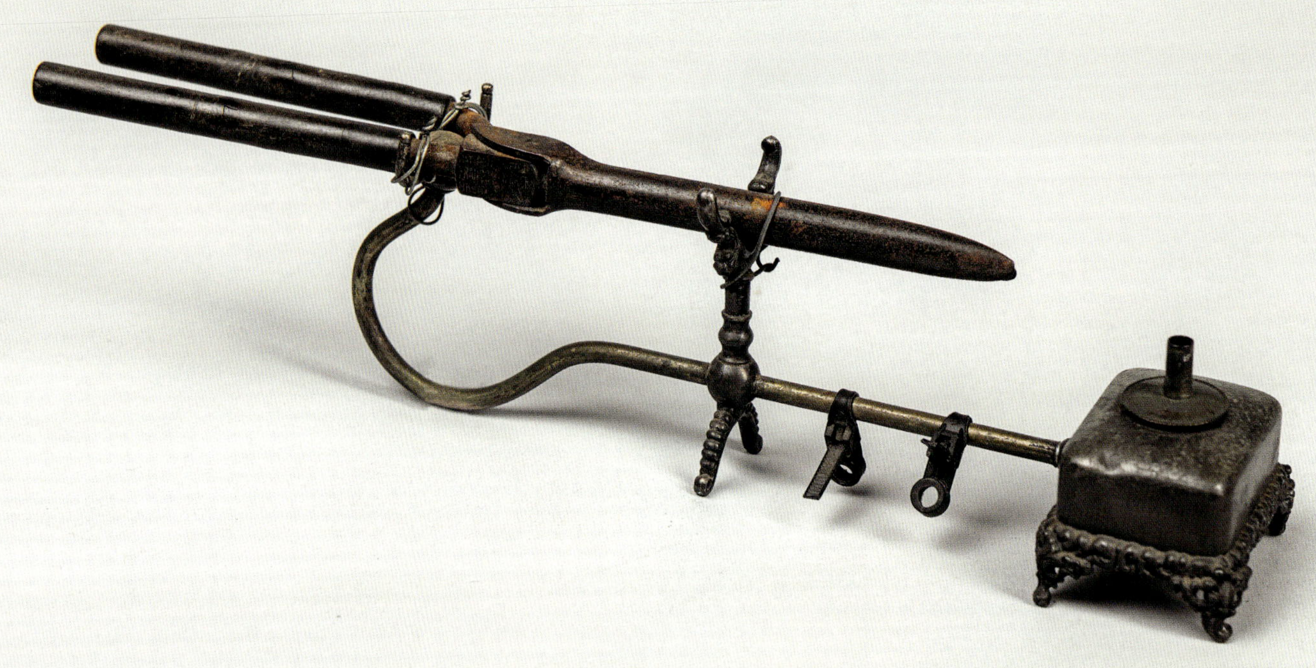

Steam curling iron, 1890

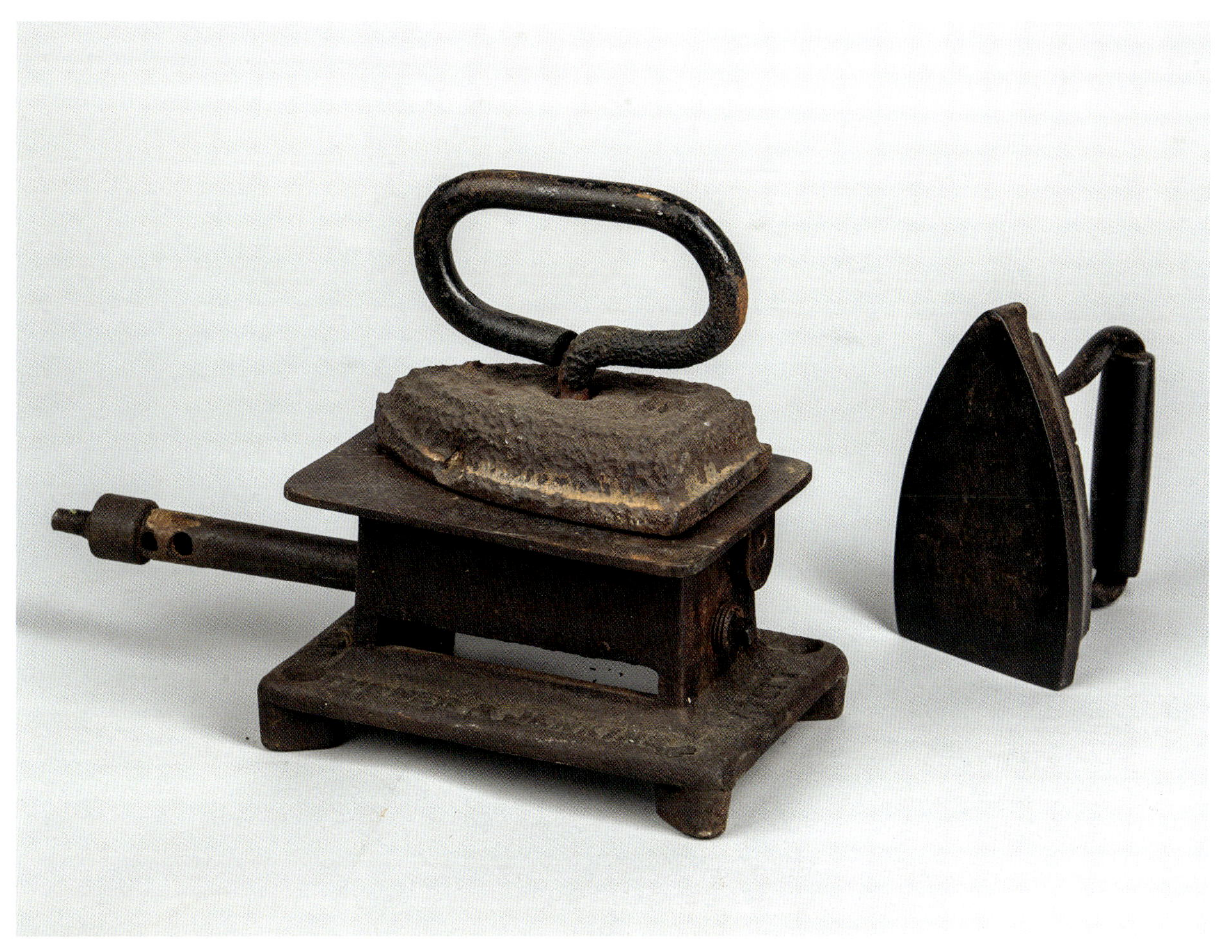

Electric pressing iron, *ca.* 1920

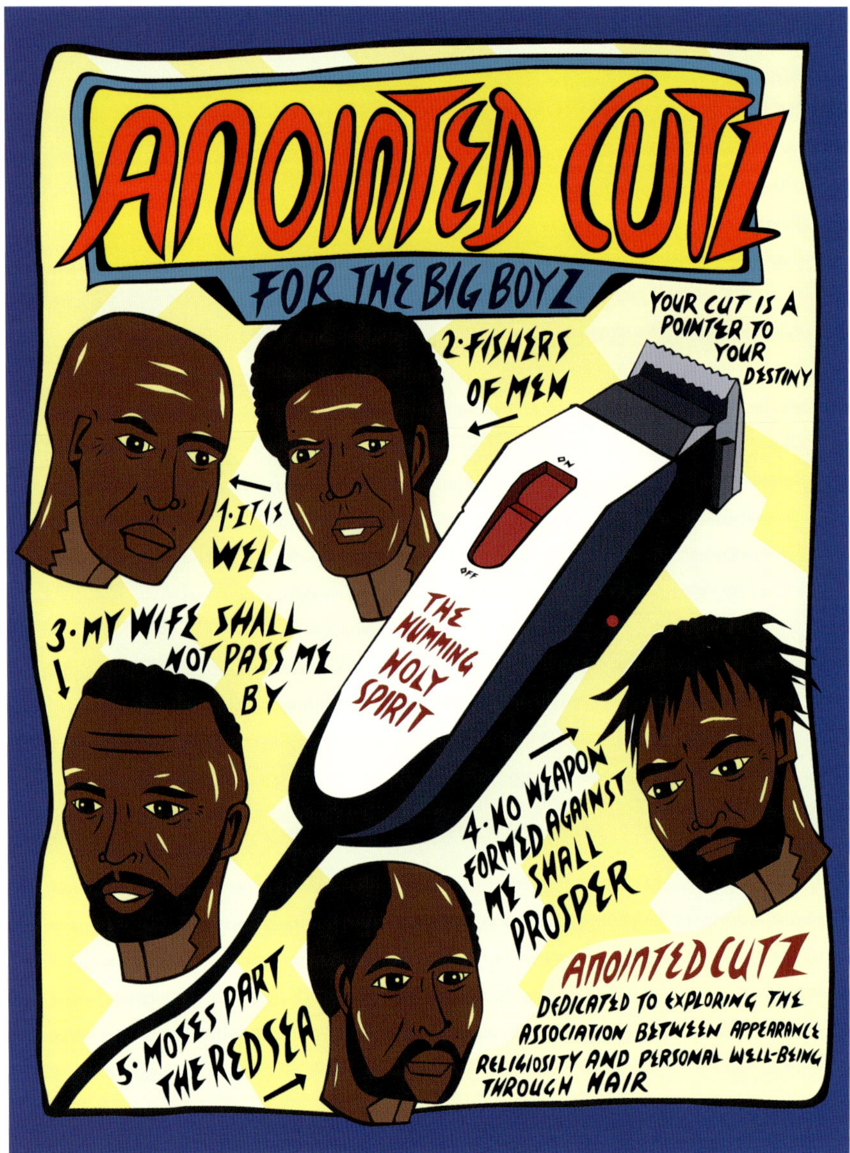

KARO AKPOKIERE

Annointed Cutz, 2013

A native of Lagos who now splits his time with Berlin, Akpokiere is an illustrator and graphic designer whose art takes its inspiration from everyday thoughts, sights, and objects. Rather than working within a defined set of themes, he allows his experiences and his love for design to generate images that range from political to humorous, and from societal to intimate. Though the aesthetic is rooted in comic strips, Akpokiere is one of several African artists who are co-opting this style to convey Black lives with an impactful visual language. *Anointed Cutz* shows Akpokiere's penchant for satire, as he notes "the association between appearance, religiosity, and personal well-being" through popular Nigerian hairstyles. Referencing biblical phrases that are popular among Christians, this image combines a common format of African barbershops (many have painted signs on the exterior that feature several heads with an array of possible hairstyles) with a social critique on Nigerian clergy and televangelists who have branded themselves so distinctly that they might as well ask their followers to adopt a specific hairstyle.

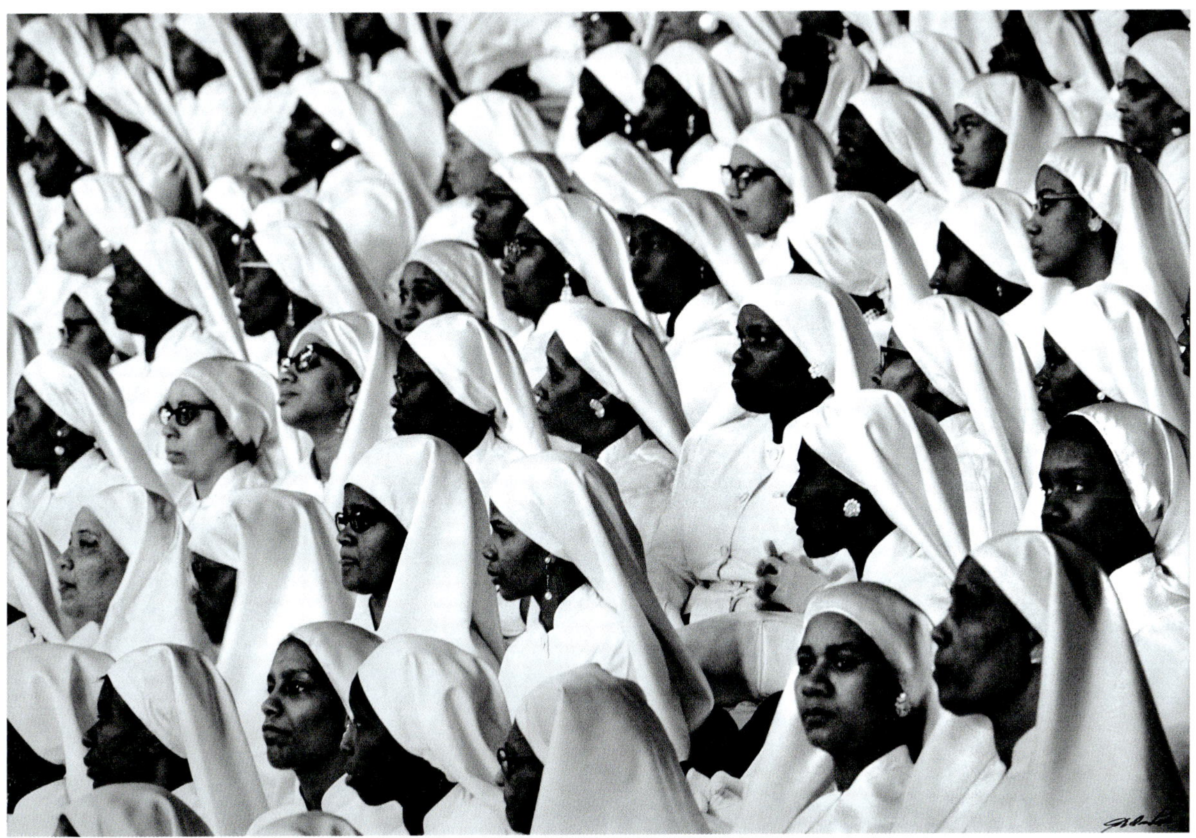

GORDON PARKS

Muslim Women in Chicago, 1970

A large group of Black Muslim women fill the frame of Gordon Parks' camera. Working for *Life* magazine, Parks is widely recognized for his pivotal role in documenting Black life in America, and was seen by his White counterparts as the only way to gain access to the growing community of Black Muslims in the United States. There is a dual political reality within this image as both Black hair and the women's hijabs were considered semi-taboo methods of dress and self-expression—or even as anti-establishment. With the hair of each woman covered, their faces become more prominent, representing both solidarity in faith and individuality as women. The unity created by the women's matching outfits and similar postures is undeniable, fostering a sense of strength and cohesion as a largely disenfranchised group.

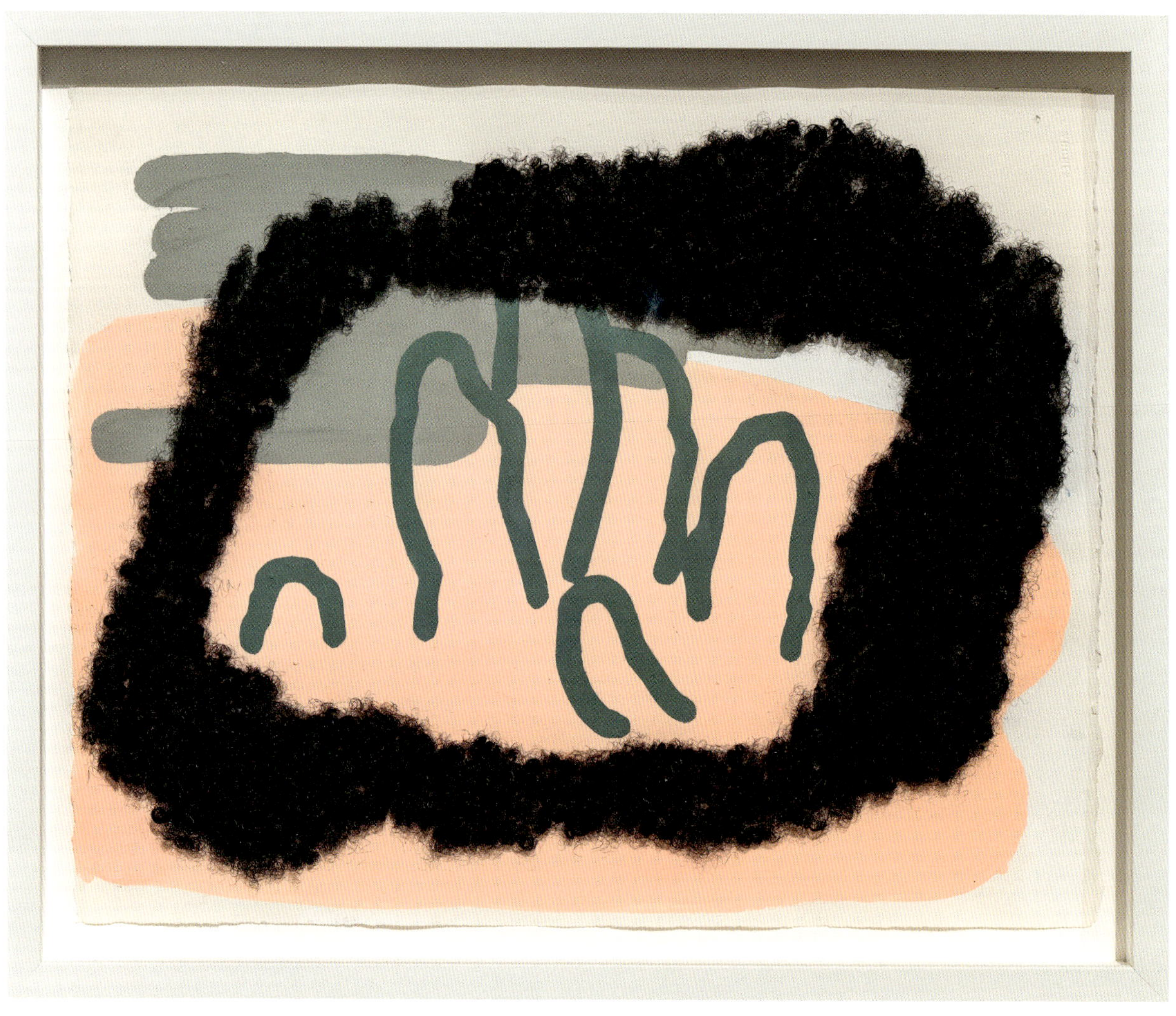

DEBORAH ANZINGER

Growth Index #3, 2019

Anzinger is a student of contrast. Exploring the relationship between humans and their environments from her vantage point in the Caribbean, she uses natural ecological resources with contrasting associations to reshape how audiences think about the historic and current sociological structures: "The ecological paradigms and aesthetic syntax of these inherited understandings is what I attempt to erode and reshape through my current work."

With her *Growth Index* series, the artist subverts our understanding of the mechanics of everyday life, from environmental factors, to social hierarchies, to economic inequalities. Her abstract forms recall protozoan organisms, underwater seascapes, and topographical maps as she renders each scene in saturated colors that loosely reflect the flora and ocean of Jamaica. While the title refers to the universal implications of capitalism and its growth markets, the physical incorporation of "Afro kinky hair" draws attention to the unseen impact of unbridled growth, most directly affecting the habitats and livelihoods of communities of color. With this context, Anzinger's collages point toward an overheated ecosystem, rising sea levels in the Caribbean, and an uncertain "growth" trajectory.

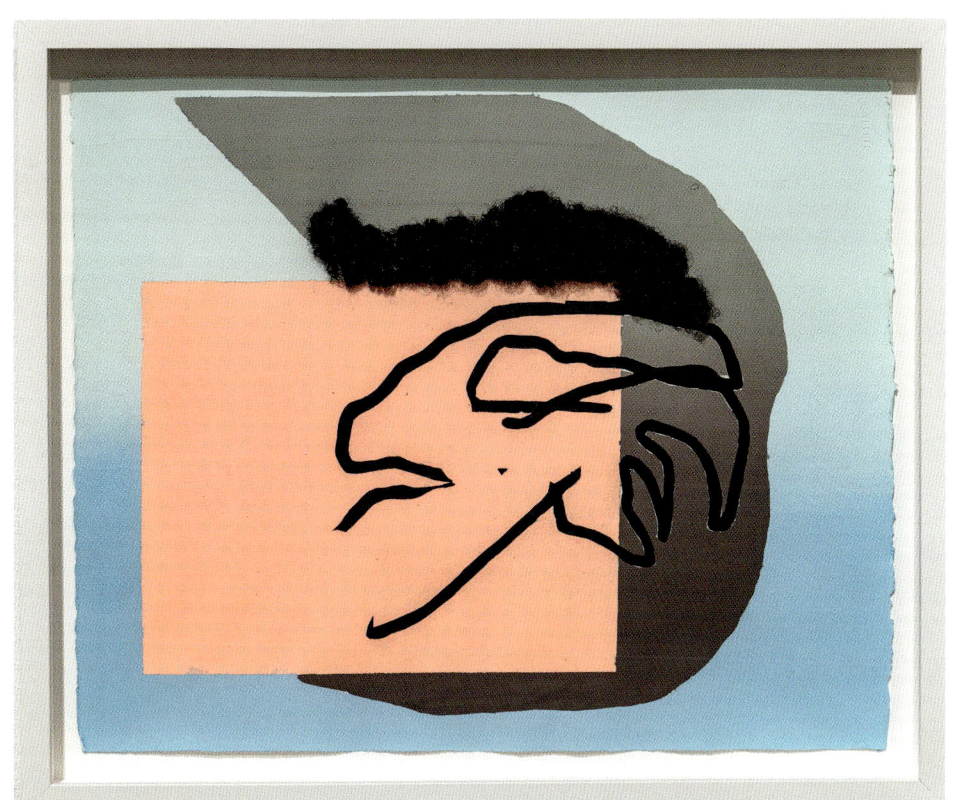

DEBORAH ANZINGER
Growth Index #4, 2019

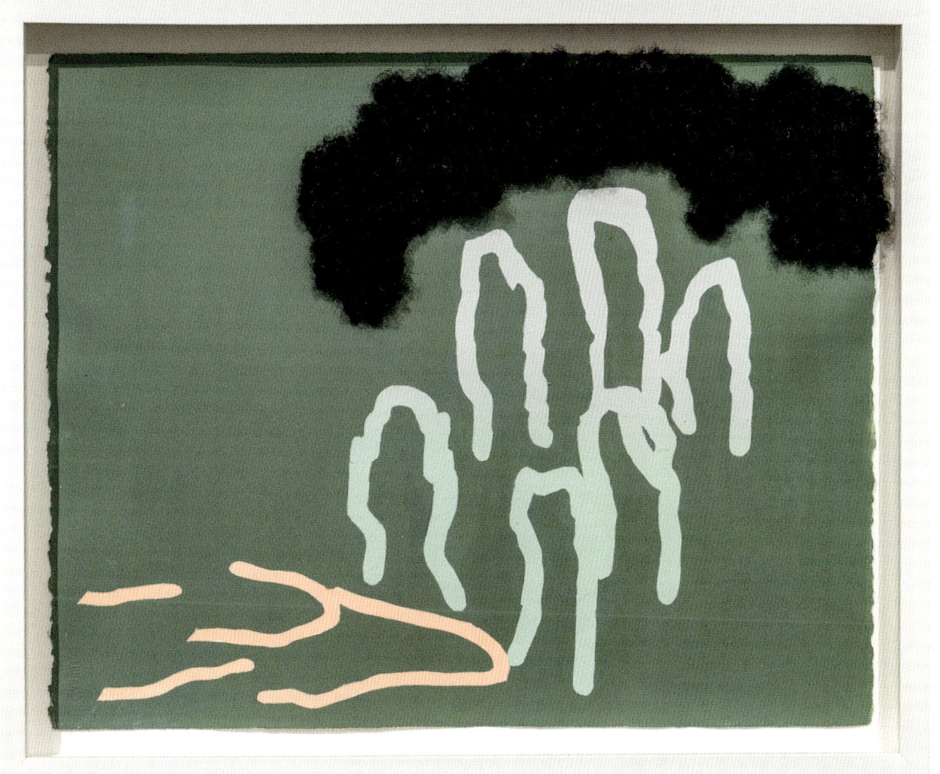

DEBORAH ANZINGER
Growth Index #5, 2019

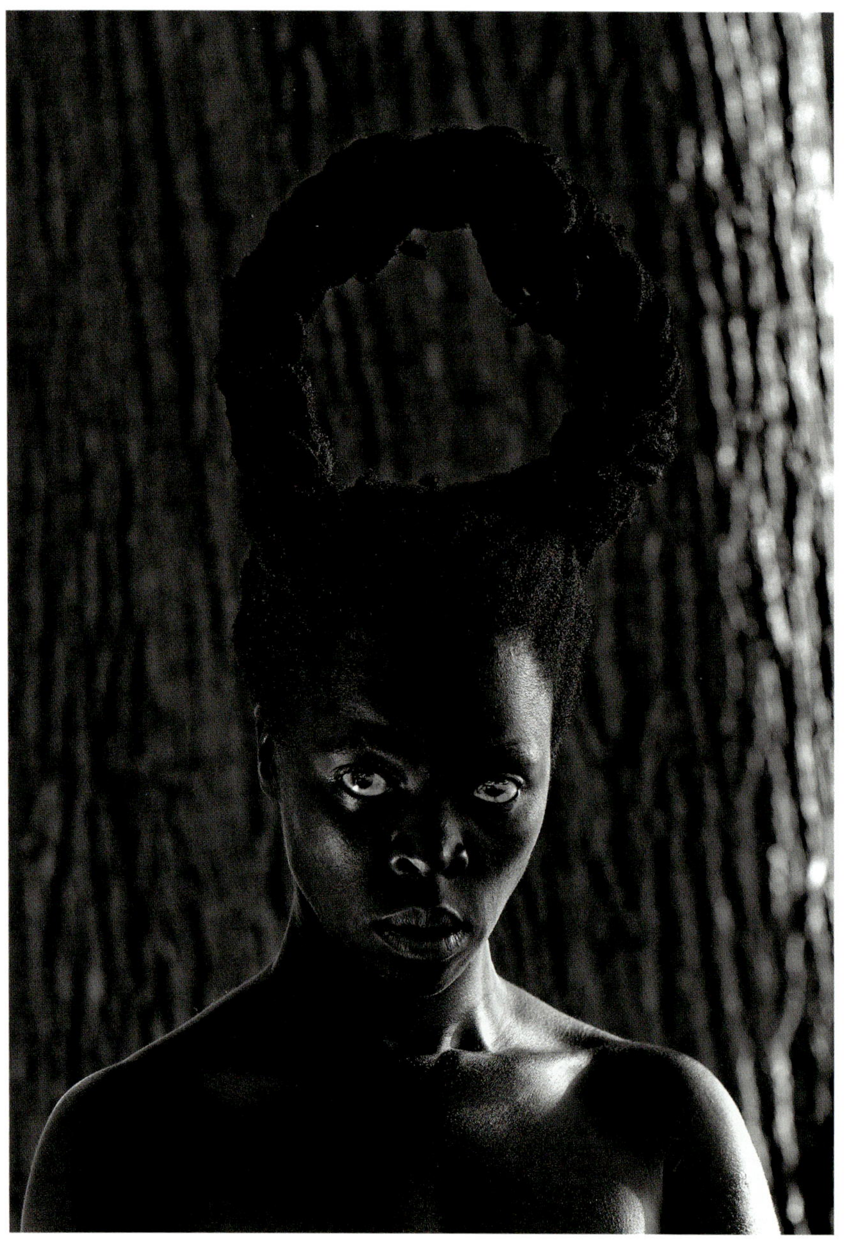

ZANELE MUHOLI

Zibuyile I, Syracuse, 2015
Zinathi I, Johannesburg, 2015

Muholi tends to categorize their work as visual activism more than as art. Their first major project, *Faces and Phases*, portrayed lesbian and transgender individuals from South Africa in order to humanize these communities in the face of extreme violence and discrimination. Muholi's newest series, *Somnyama Ngonyama* (or, *Hail the Dark Lioness*), speaks with a global audience in mind. In a collection of 365 self-portraits that respond to problematic archives of images from *National Geographic* and colonial photography, Muholi uses deeply-pigmented tones to proclaim the beauty of Black skin. Now the subject of their own work, Muholi rectifies an absence of Black faces in art and condemns the biases against Black skin and hair, especially as faced by LGBTQ+ people. In these two photographs, Muholi exaggerates the darkness of their skin tone and uses their hair, adorned with found objects and accessories, to comment on people, events, and moments related to the city where the photo was taken. For example, *Zibuyile* is an isiZulu expression that means "the dowry cows have come back" or "they are back," likely referring to the practice of *Lobola* tradition wherein a husband is responsible for paying the bride's family.

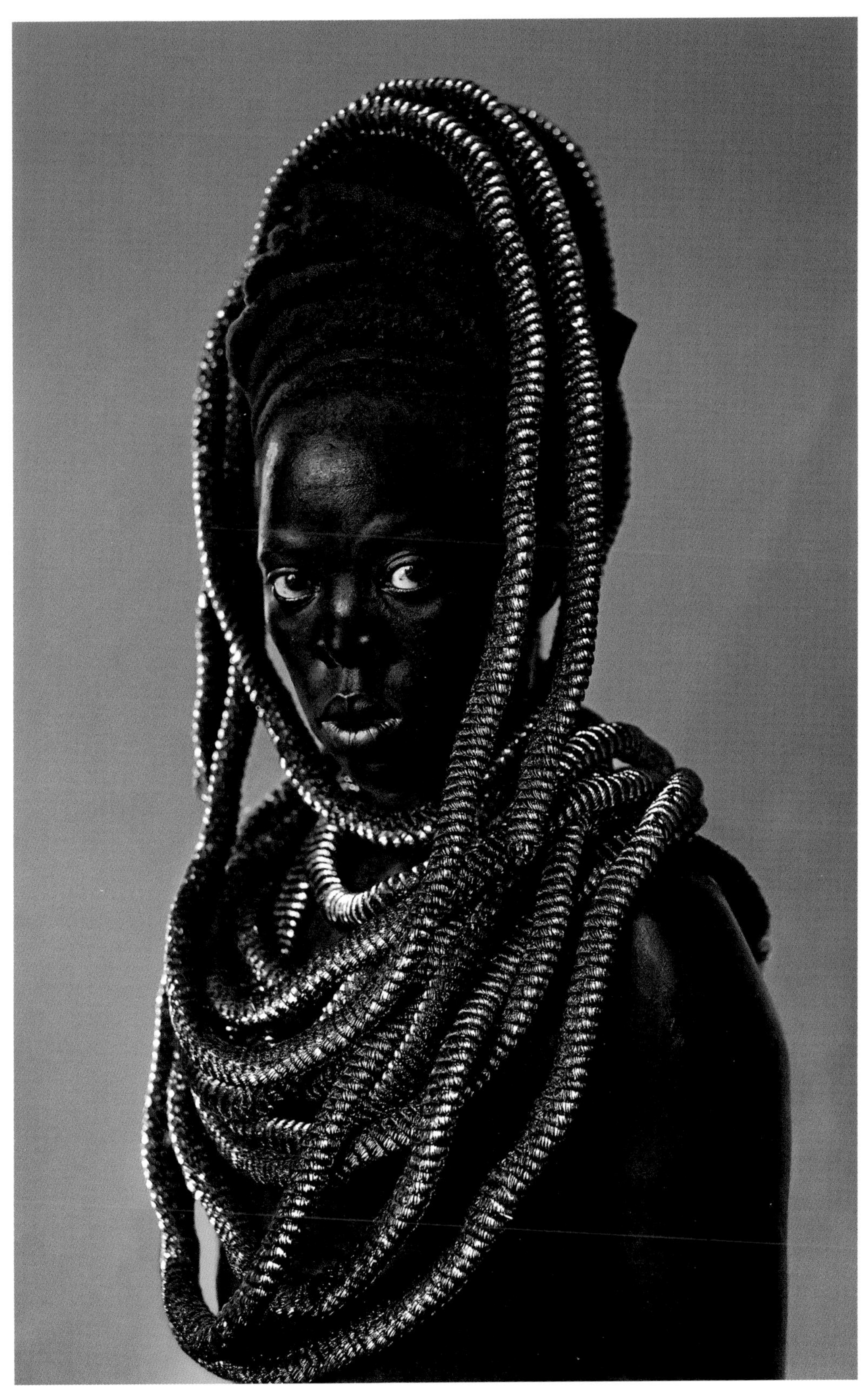

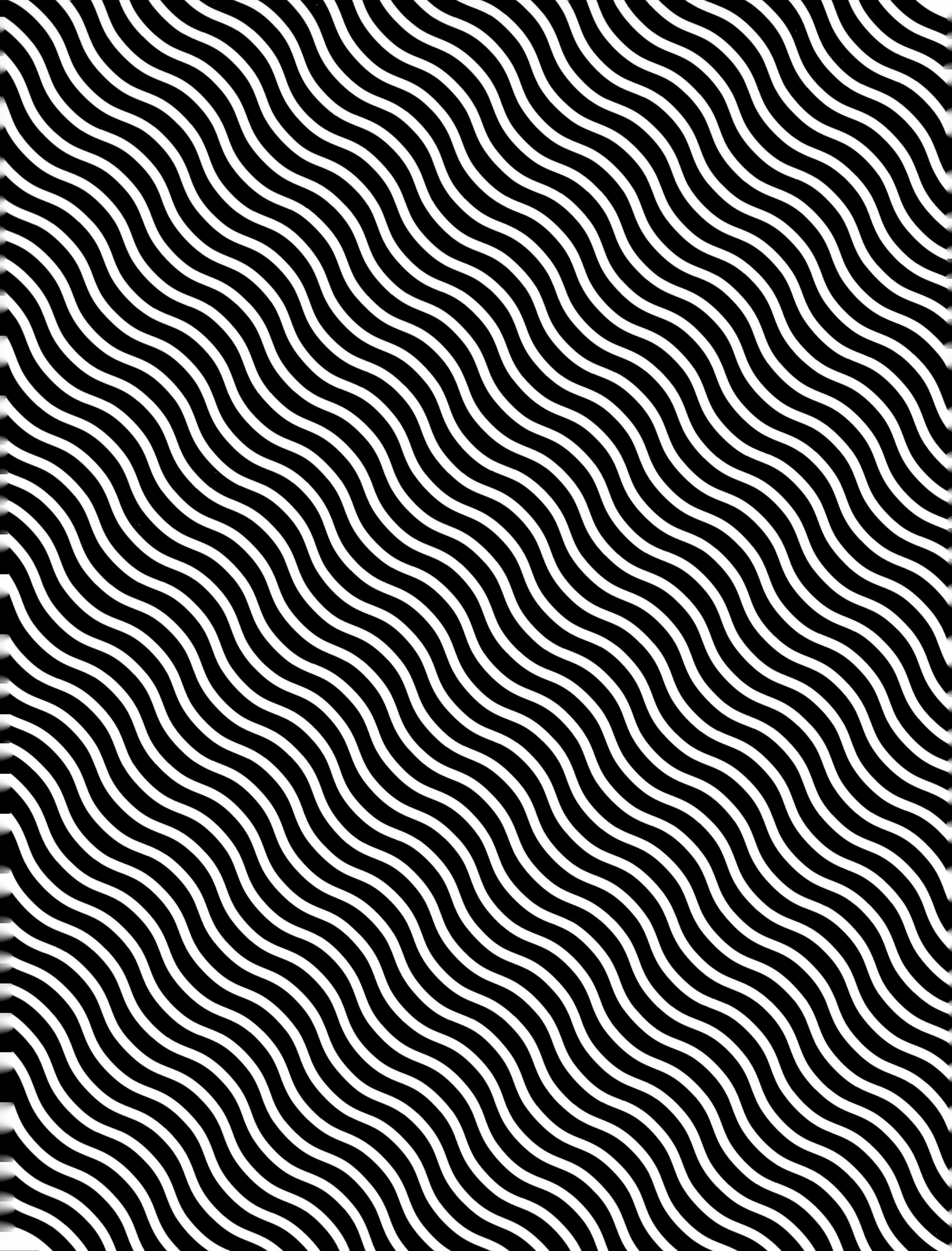

BLACK JOY

Black Joy is a celebratory representation of self-love and cultural pride. Related to the concept of Black Excellence, Black Joy foregrounds aspirational imagery that expresses the magic, wonder, and spirit of thriving while being unapologetically Black. It is an outright refusal to endure societal discrimination and a colonized state of mind. Black Joy is grabbing onto a piece of freedom. It connects folks to one another, it gives back to its community, and it says "yes" when the world has said "no" time and time again. Black Joy is rooted in earlier concepts, like the pride of Black Power and the "shine" of the AfriCOBRA (African Commune of Bad Relevant Artists) artist group. Adapting to cultural need, it has shapeshifted from the powerful fist on Afro picks in the 1960s to the two-strand twists and TWAs (teeny-weeny Afros) worn by Black women today. Having a cathartic effect, Black Joy offers healing and liberation when people celebrate the skin—and hair—they are in today.

The *Black Joy Project* is a social media movement founded by writer, poet, and organizer Kleaver Cruz. Beginning in 2015, the *Black Joy Project* became a way to combat the overwhelming negative depictions of Black people in the media. From starving orphans, to underserved communities, to crime stories, mass media around the world follow a long legacy of colonial biases against Black bodies. From pity and pandering to racism and contempt, these depictions are so culturally engrained that they have become heavy shadows, weighing down entire communities. Into this void, Kleaver launched his first post: a photo of his mother, a rebellious smile, and the #BlackJoy hashtag. Though Kleaver sought to dedicate one small corner of space to positive imagery from the lives of Black people, he ultimately ignited a celebration across the realms of social media.

Similar movements and hashtags from recent years include #BlackGirlMagic (an expression that celebrates the power, success, and resilience of Black women and girls), #MelaninPoppin (a movement that counters colorism in the Black community by honoring all skin tones, not just lighter ones), and #NoWeaveNecessary (a trending hashtag that celebrated Zozibini Tunzi's crowning as Miss Universe, even though she defied convention by rocking a beautiful, short, natural hairstyle!). Initiatives like these are reclamations of public (cyber) spaces where Black voices can resonate from the continent to the Diaspora. Juxtaposed against the traumatic cycle of news headlines and all the cases of discrimination spread on social media platforms, the *Black Joy Project* has been a digital breath of fresh air.

Whether the artists in this section are celebrating the radiance of melanin-saturated skin—as evidenced in the lustrous photos of Charlotte Mensah's *Afrofuture* collection—or the curly coil of textured hair—as highlighted in the sculptural installation by Lebohang Motaung—Black Joy is abundant! As we reflect on Egyptian artifacts (the earliest representations of self-care from the African continent), the Black Pride Movement of the 1960s, #BlackJoy and the other self-affirmation movements of today, this exhibition is a testament to the fact that giving voice and presence to the joy of Black folks will never go out of style.

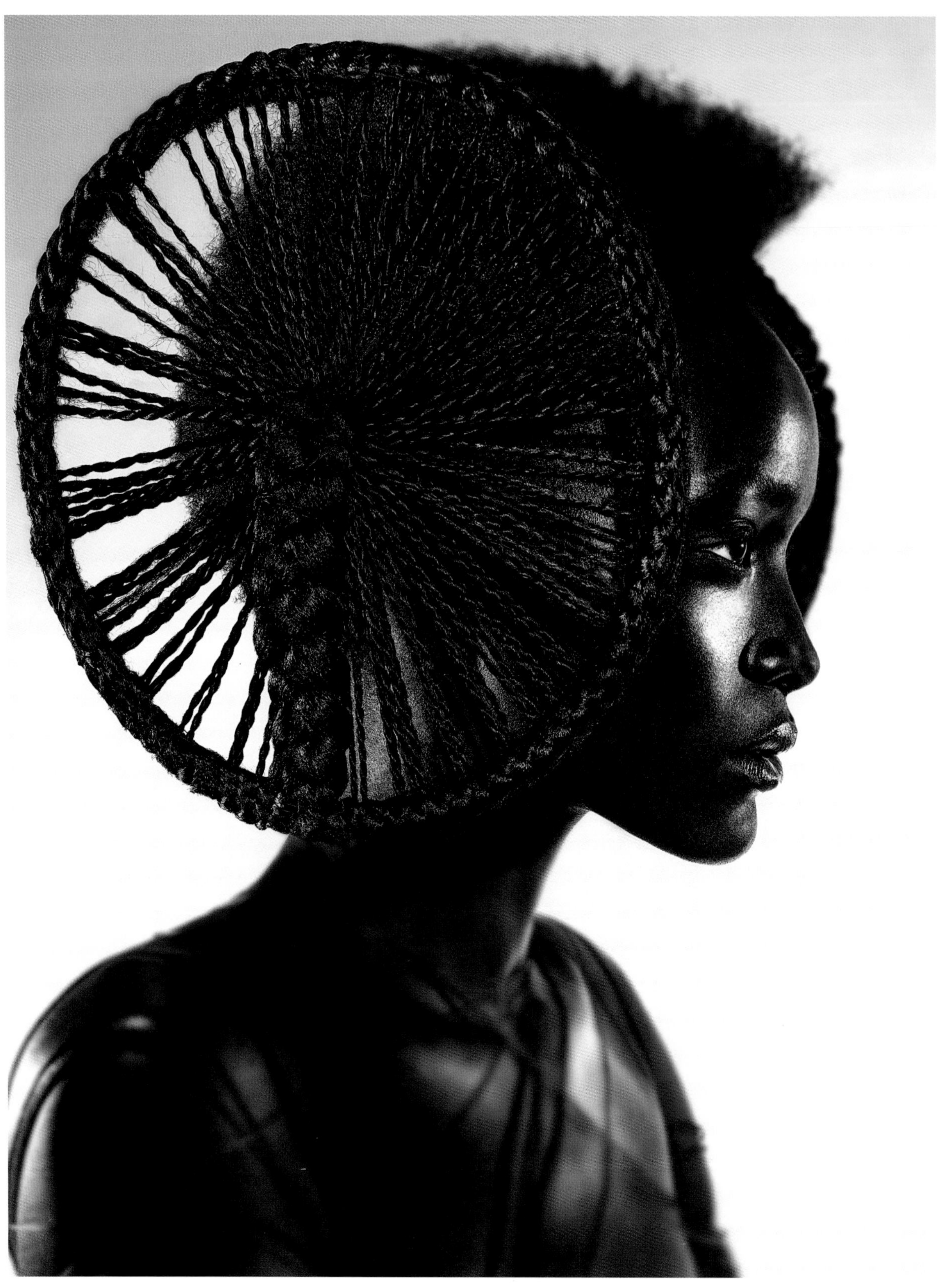

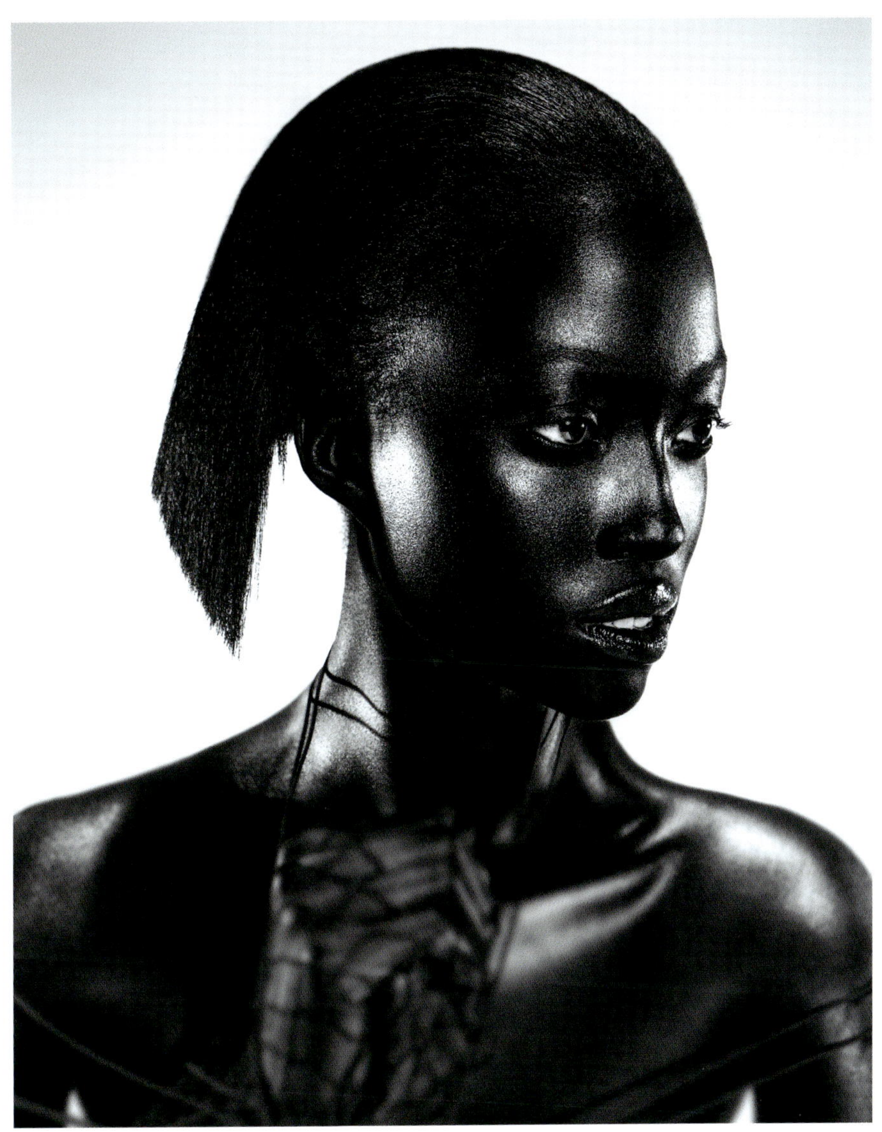

CHARLOTTE MENSAH

Hairstyles from the *Afrofuture* collection, 2017

In 2018, hair stylist Charlotte Mensah became the first Black female stylist to be inducted into the British Hairdressing Awards' Hall of Fame. While honored, she pointed to the irony of how long it took for a Black woman to be included, given the dynamism of Black women's hairstyling for centuries. The two photographs from the *Afrofuture* collection display Mensah's vision of versatility, an inherent quality of Black hair. Many of her styles are sculptural in nature, similar to those featured in the photographs of J. D. 'Okhai Ojeikere. As an advocate of natural hair, Mensah approaches all styling from a belief in the acceptance of self and others.

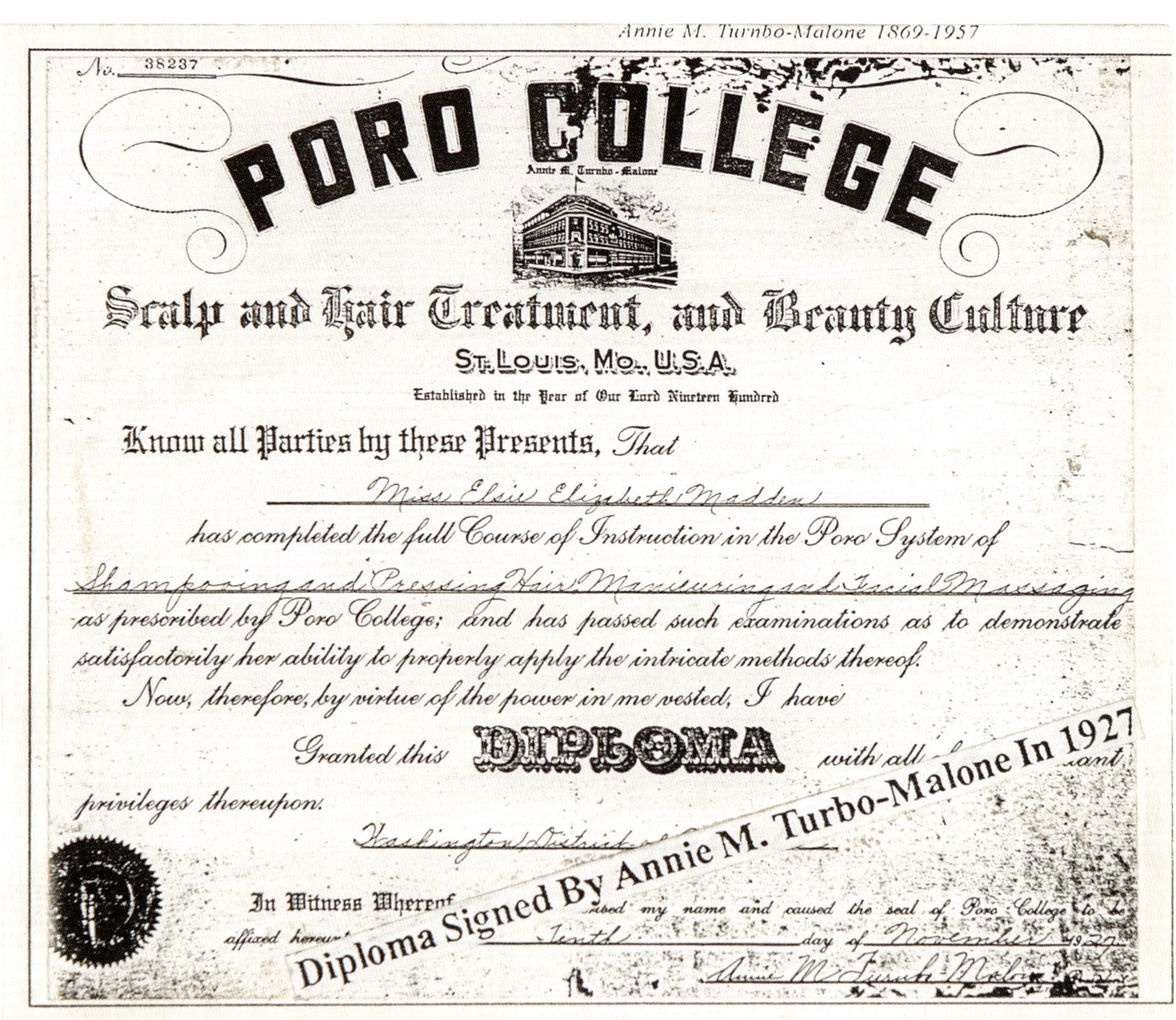

Annie M. Turnbo-Malone 1869-1957

No. 38237

PORO COLLEGE

Annie M. Turnbo-Malone

Scalp and Hair Treatment, and Beauty Culture

St. Louis, Mo., U.S.A.

Established in the Year of Our Lord Nineteen Hundred

Know all Parties by these Presents, That

Miss Elsie Elizabeth Madden

has completed the full Course of Instruction in the Poro System of

Shampooing and Pressing Hair, Manicuring and Facial Massaging

as prescribed by Poro College; and has passed such examinations as to demonstrate satisfactorily her ability to properly apply the intricate methods thereof.

Now, therefore, by virtue of the power in me vested, I have

Granted this DIPLOMA with all ... privileges thereupon.

Washington District ...

In Witness Whereof ... my name and caused the seal of Poro College to be affixed hereu... Tenth day of November 1927

Annie M. Turnbo Malone

Diploma Signed By Annie M. Turbo-Malone In 1927

Poro College Diploma signed by Annie M. Turnbo Malone, 1927

Annie Turnbo Malone was a chemist, entrepreneur, and philanthropist who created the first marketed "Wonderful Hair Grower" serum for Black women. She started her company at the turn of the twentieth century, and moved the business to St. Louis, Missouri in 1902. In 1918, Malone established Poro College, a cosmetology school and training center for Black women. By the mid-1950s, she had thirty-two branches of Poro College throughout the United States. This leading educational institution graduated more than 75,000 women and one famous man—Chuck Berry, graduate of the 1952 class.

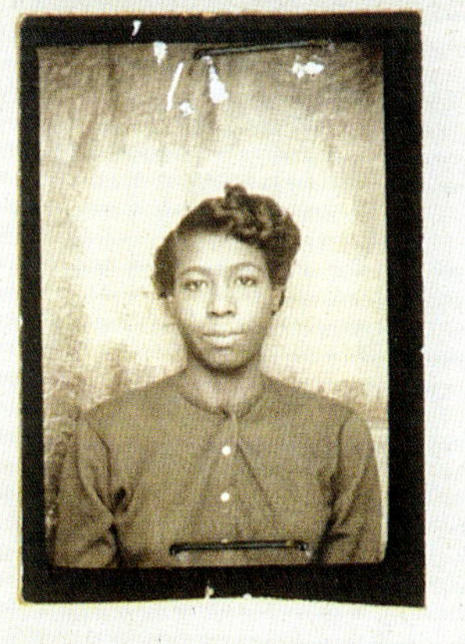

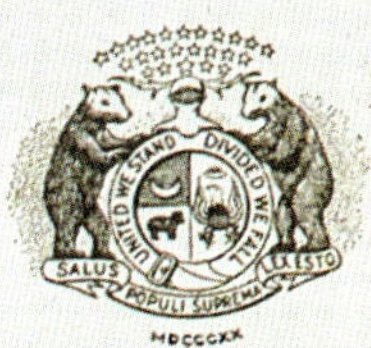

MISSOURI STATE BOARD of COSMETOLOGY
PERMANENT LICENSE

Registration No. EX-4358 License No. 20380

MRS. LARZENE LEIGH

Has complied with the requirements of law and is entitled to practice

COSMETOLOGY, HAIRDRESSING AND MANICURING

unless this license is revoked for a good and sufficient reason.
License is not valid unless Registration fee is paid annually.

PRESIDENT SECRETARY

I 8352 THE LAW REQUIRES THIS LICENSE TO BE CONSPICUOUSLY POSTED

Missouri State Board of Cosmetology Permanent License

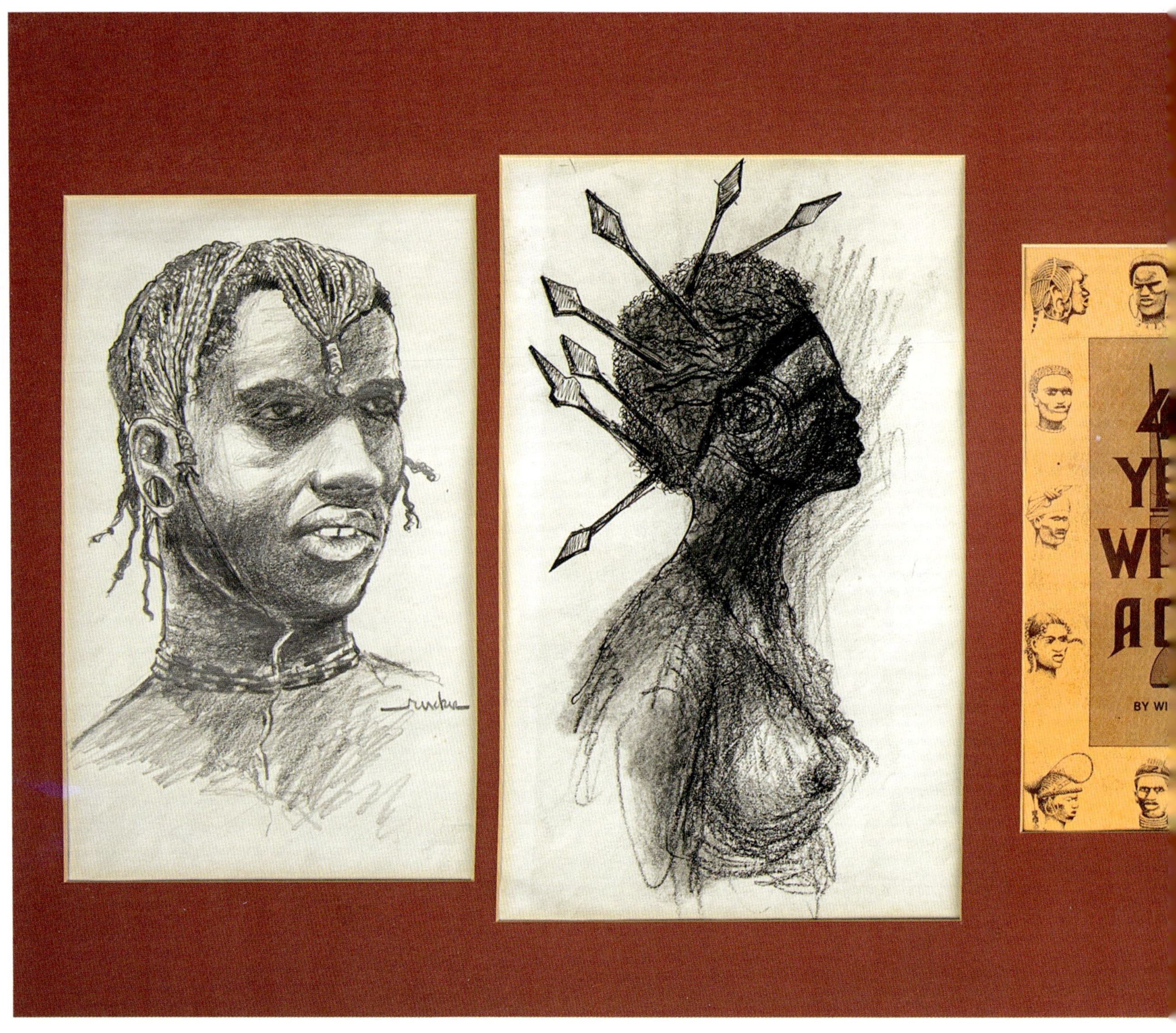

Sketches from *400 Years Without a Comb*, 1971–73

"The African's few personal possessions consisted of ornaments for the hair and the comb. The comb represented an expression of its creator and reflected tribal status, family traditions, or expressions of affection. When he was removed from his motherland to become a slave in faraway lands, his comb was left behind, not to be found for 400 years."

400 Years Without a Comb: The Untold Story was published in 1973 by Dr. Willie Morrow. This work is a compilation of historic photographs, illustrations, and texts detailing the journey of Black hair from the 1700s in Africa, through the slave era, and up into the early 1970s. With Dr. Morrow's desire to educate his community, he had the book produced into a documentary in the 1980s. Dr. Morrow's books have been translated into multiple languages, and he was hired by several national military groups as an expert consultant on Black hair care for their officers.

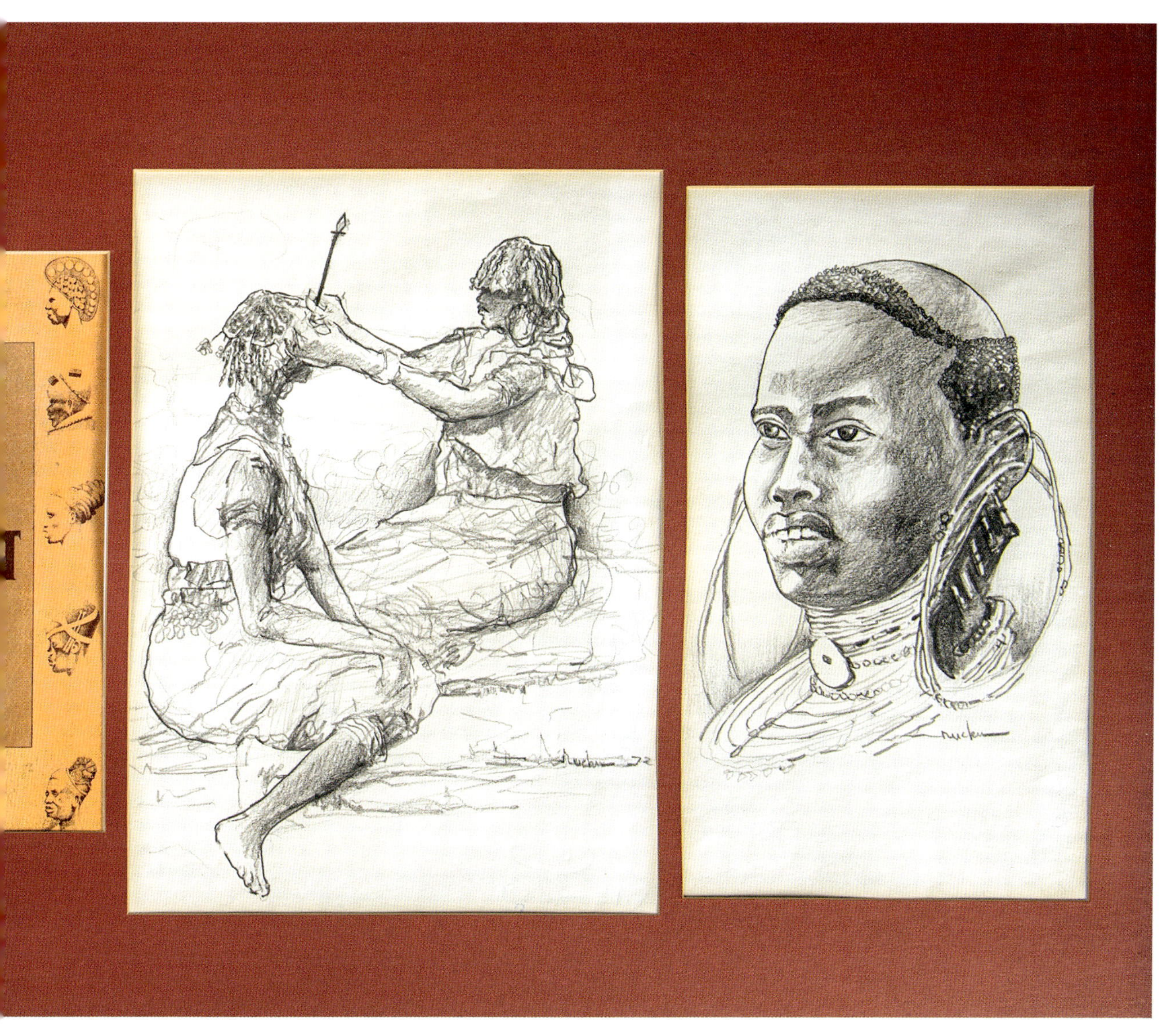

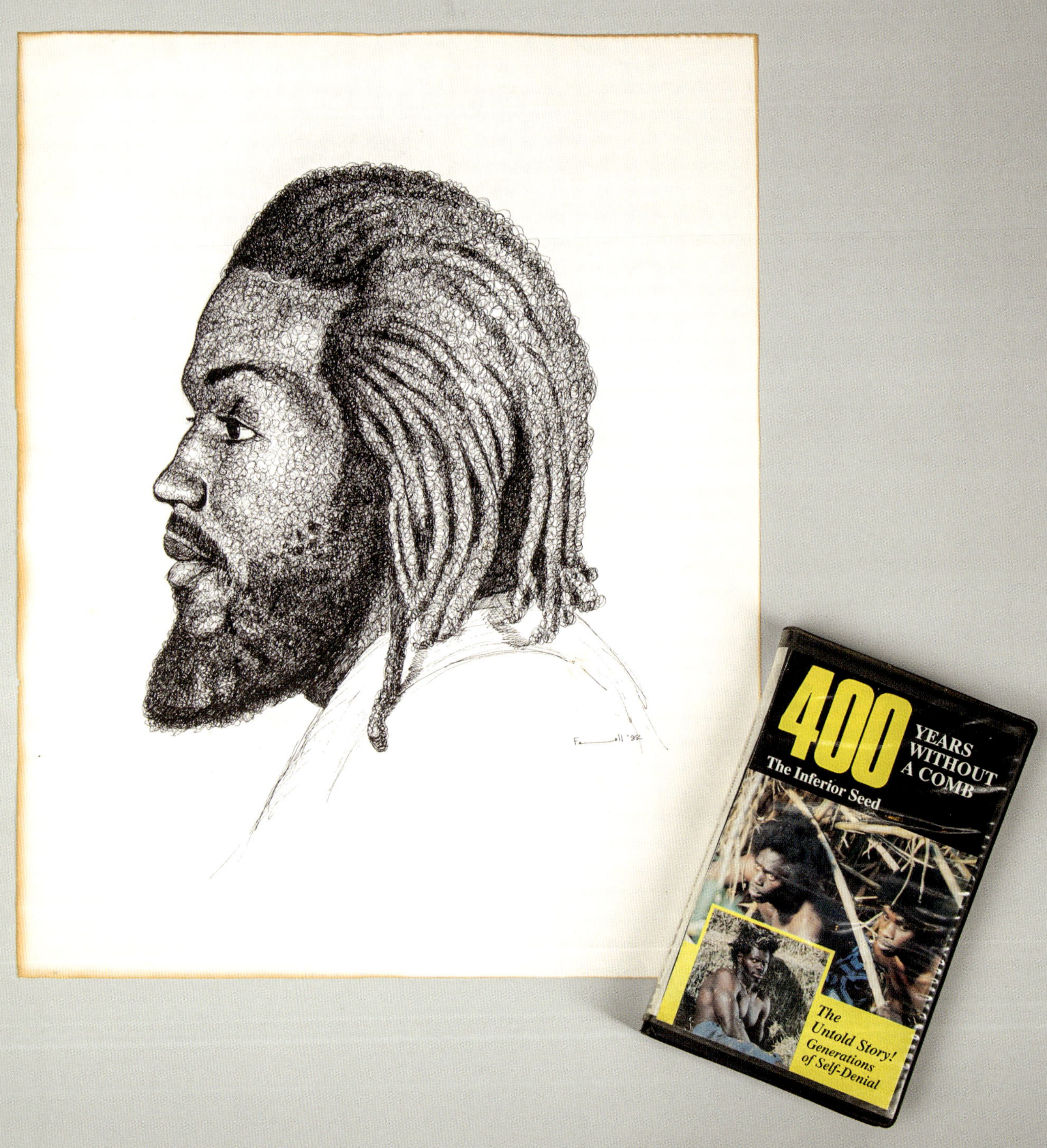

Drawing of Man with Dreadlocks, 1982
400 Years Without a Comb: The Inferior Seed, 1989

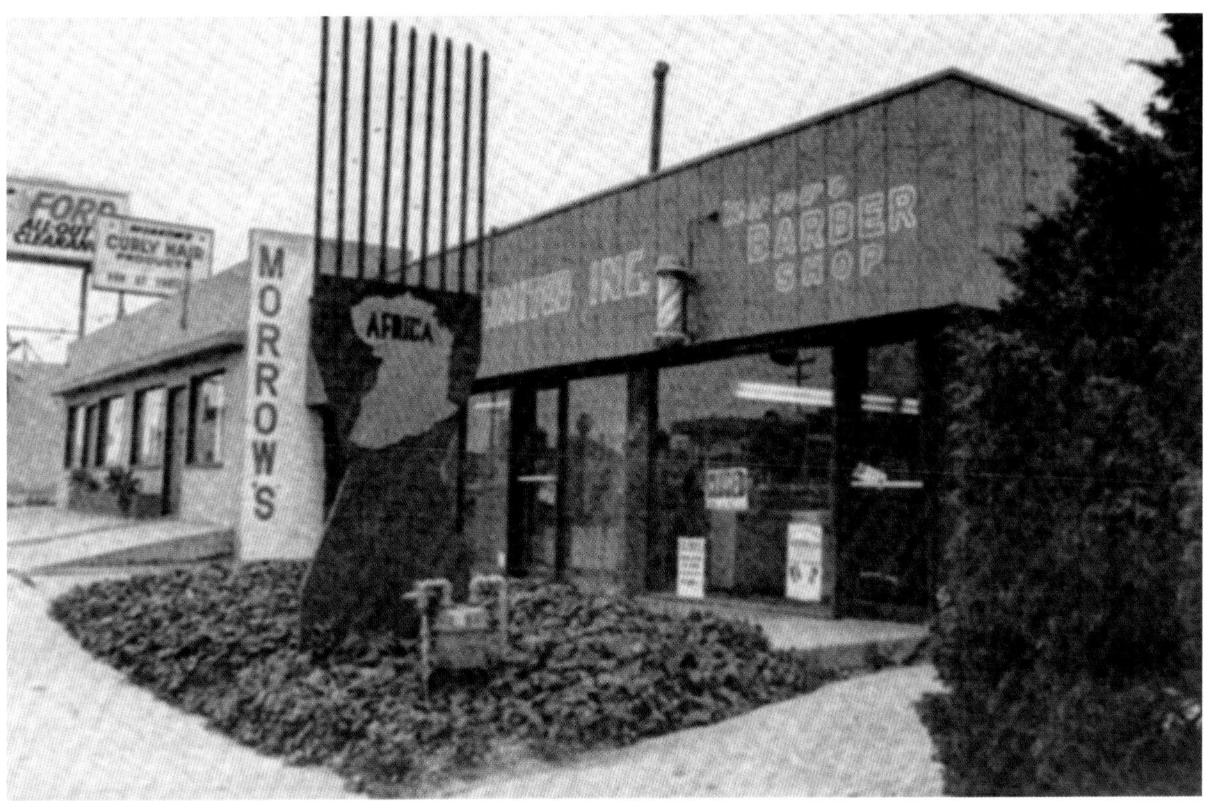

Photograph of Dr. Willie Morrow's
Barbershop in San Diego, 1960s

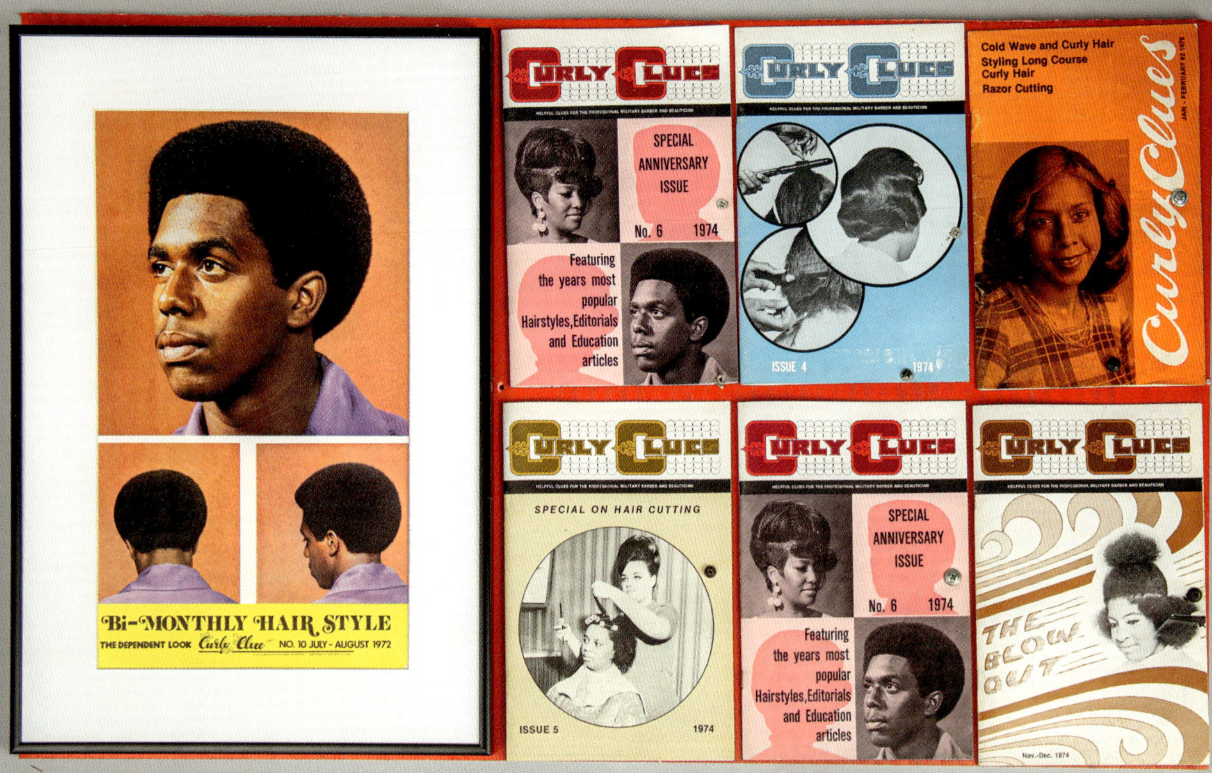

Curly Cues booklets, 1974

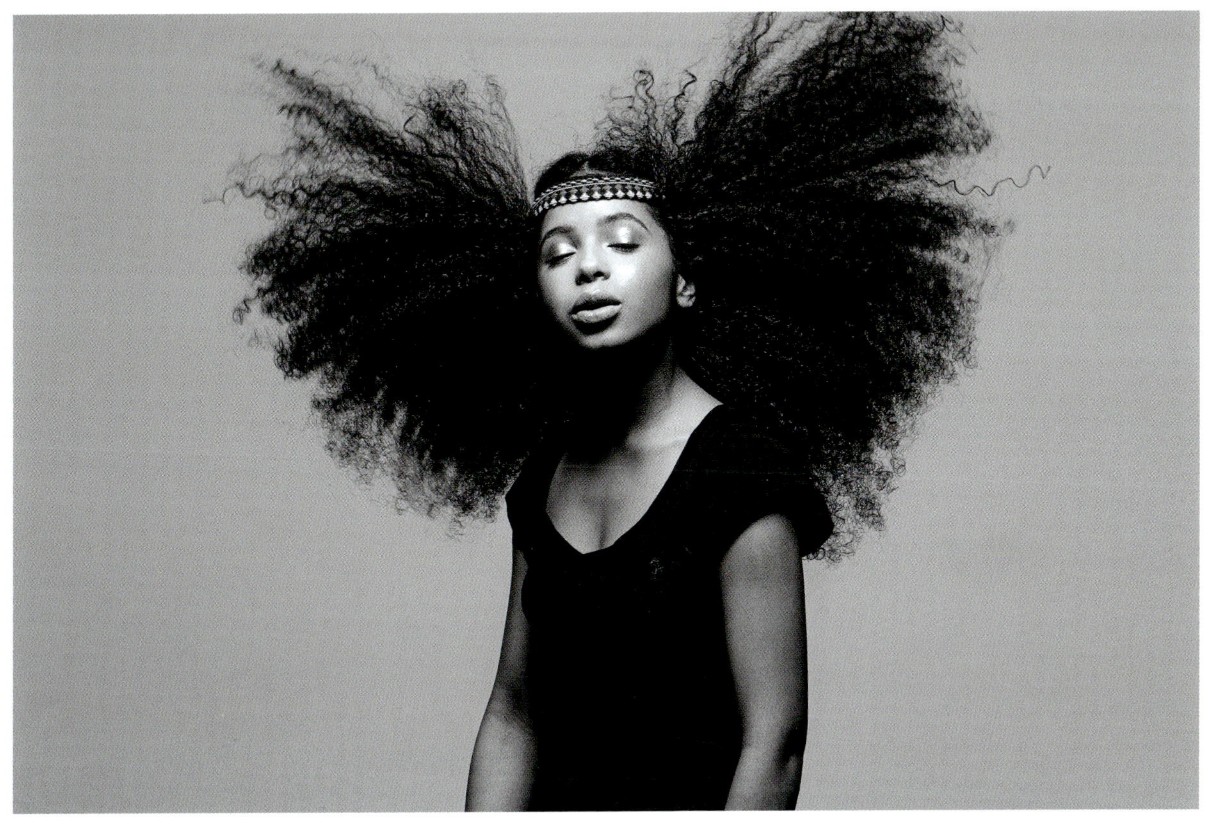

GLENFORD NUÑEZ

The Coiffure Project: A portrait of Zaruta, 2011

The photo stems from a book, *The Coiffure Project*, wherein Nuñez explores the means by which Black people express themselves with natural hair. Placing his subjects against a plain background, this particular composition allows the woman and her hair to be the sole focus of the viewer. High contrast between the model and the background gives prominence to the different textures within Zaruta's hair. Almost alive with movements, individual strands radiate from her head and rhythmic curls form waves of lush hair. As a photographer between the worlds of fashion and art, Nuñez captures the revival of the Natural Hair Movement and its diversity of styles.

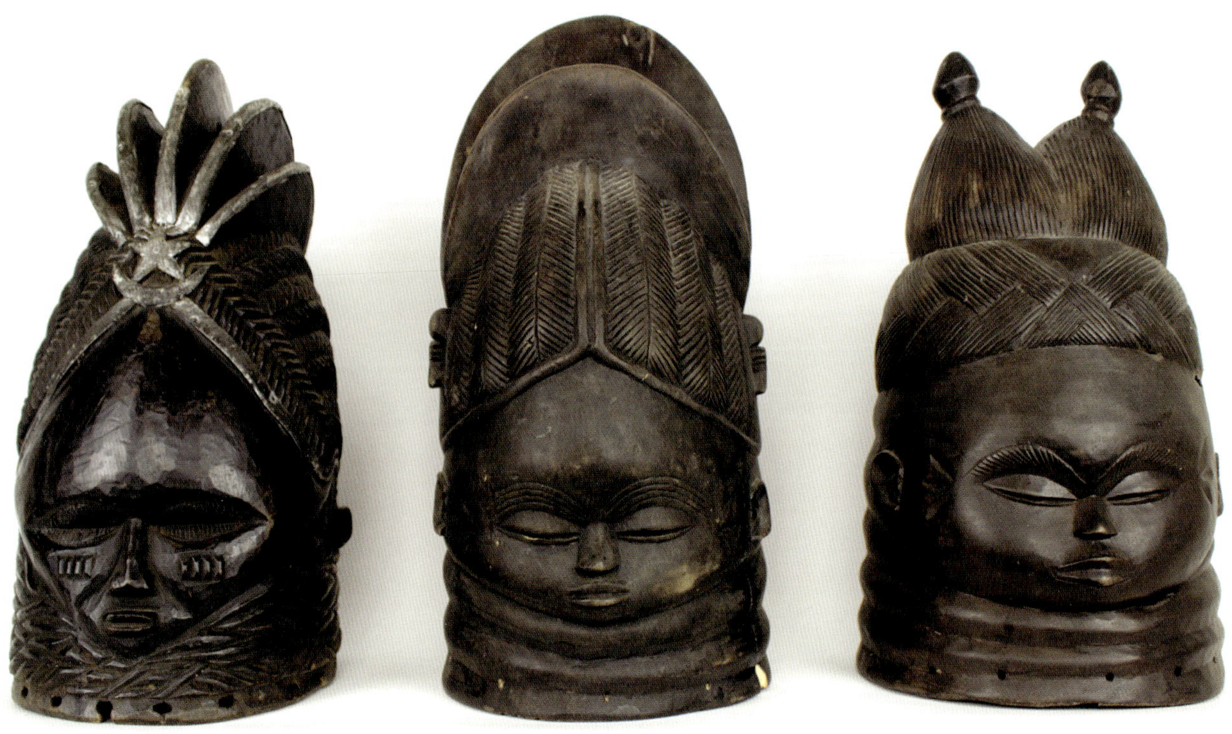

UNIDENTIFIED MENDE ARTISTS

Sowei (bundu) Helmet Masks, 20th century

Unique among all the masquerade traditions of West Africa, the secret Sande society is dedicated to, and danced by, women from the Mende people group. Though the wooden *bundu* masks were carved by men, they were animated by women in a coming-of-age ritual for adolescent girls. The form of the mask depicts the ideal physical and moral traits that the young initiates will strive for in adulthood: lustrous black skin and neck rolls to represent health, and miniaturized ears and mouth to reflect femininity—and to remind them to avoid gossip. The Sande masks are also popular for the diversity of hairstyles found across the hundreds of known examples. Crests, braids, and twists are formed into complex sculptural hairstyles, many of which are also adorned with ornaments. While most of the mask's physical attributes were fairly standardized across the Mende groups, the fantastical hairstyles remained the primary area where the carver enjoyed creative license.

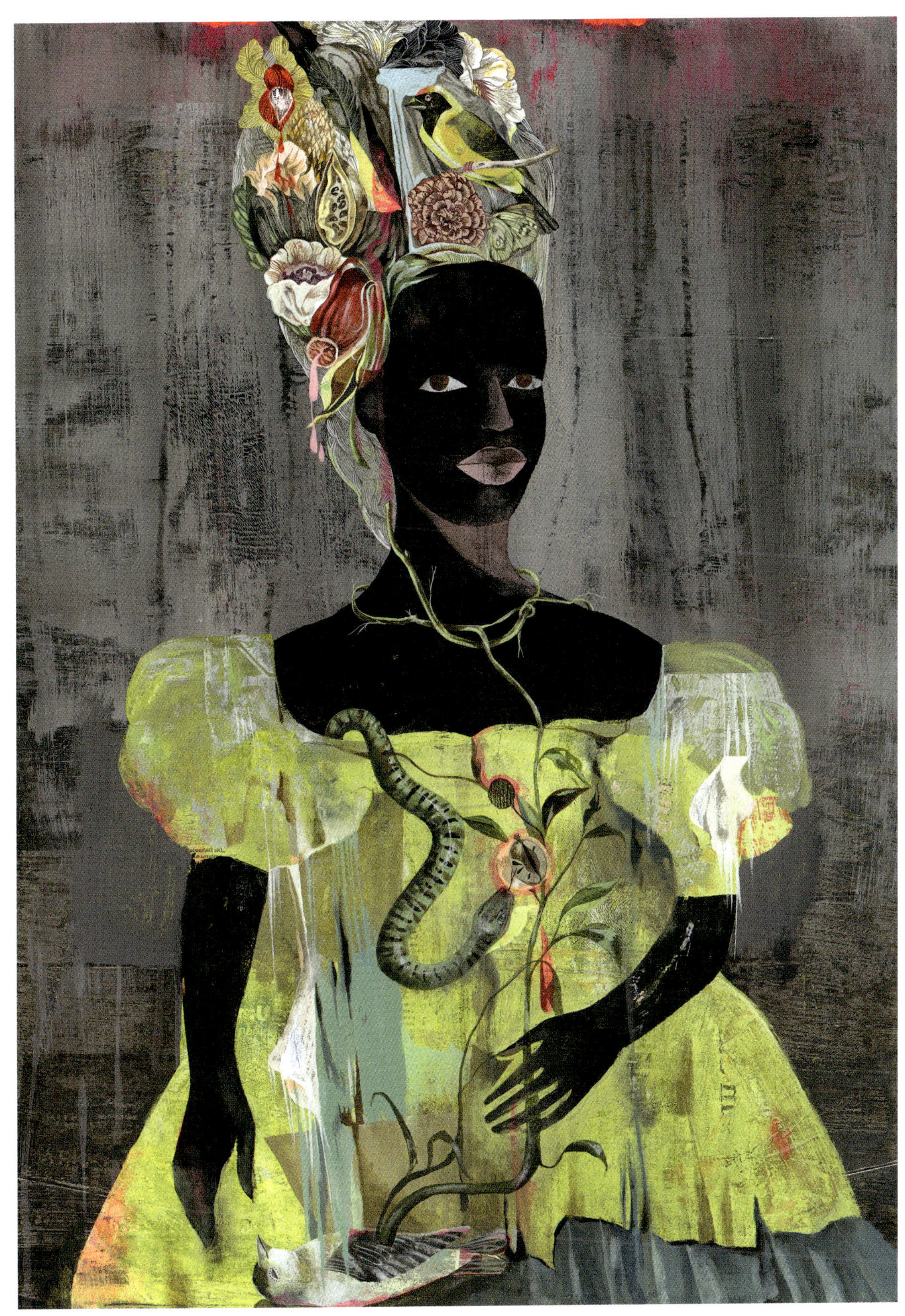

OLAF HAJEK
Black Antoinette #001, 2017

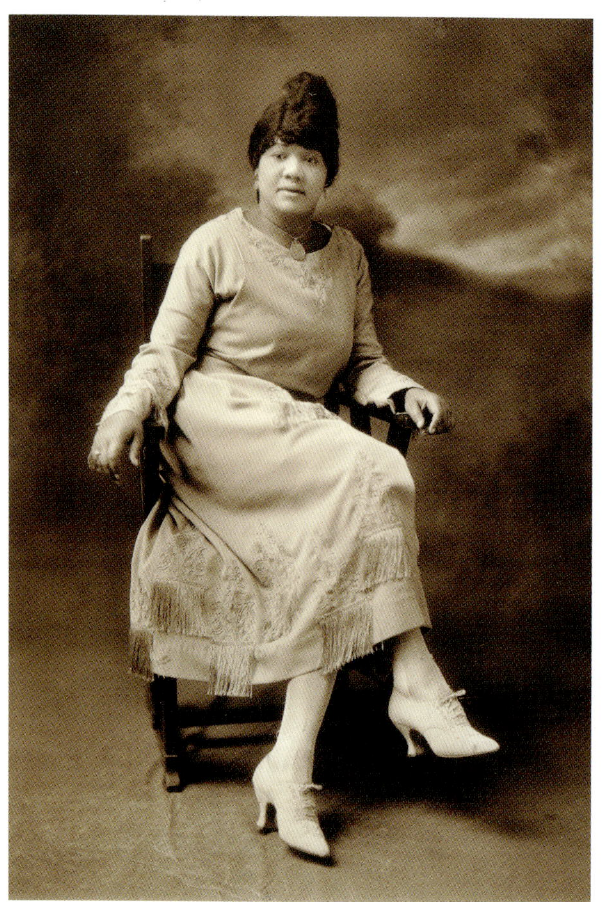

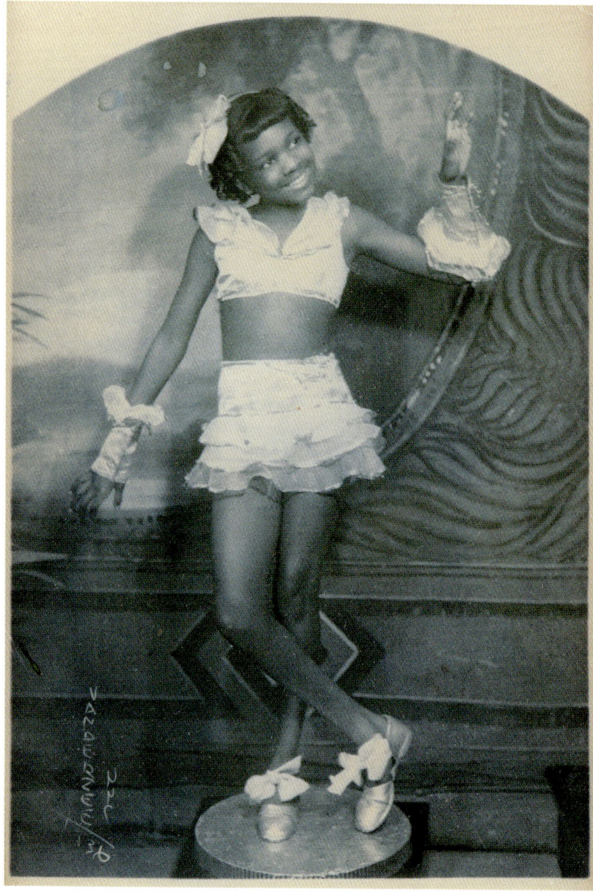

JAMES VAN DER ZEE

Harlem, ca. 1940
Portrait of a Black Girl in a Dance Outfit, 1936

Van Der Zee opened his first studio in the early 1900s, making him one of the first renowned African-American photographers in the United States. As key records of the Harlem Renaissance, Van Der Zee's photographs depict a vibrant and glamorous view of Harlem before World War II. He photographed notable figures traveling through Harlem, but also its residents, institutions, and the local community events. The artist is credited with documenting the rise of a new African American middle class. Van Der Zee used backdrops and props that aligned with the Edwardian and Art Deco styles in fashion at the time. He presented the subject in a state of joy, refinement, and success. The photographs in this exhibition exemplify this aspirational spirit and elevate the sitters to present as agents of their own livelihood. The young girl's warm expression animates *Portrait of a Black Girl in a Dance Outfit*, mirroring the fineness of her costume. In *Harlem,* the woman sits elegantly, presenting her stylish shoe to the viewer. The sophistication exhibited by the sitter, from her coiffure to the quality of her dress and accessories, is a prime example of how Van Der Zee documented Harlem's rich culture in the midst of countless caricatures of Black citizens.

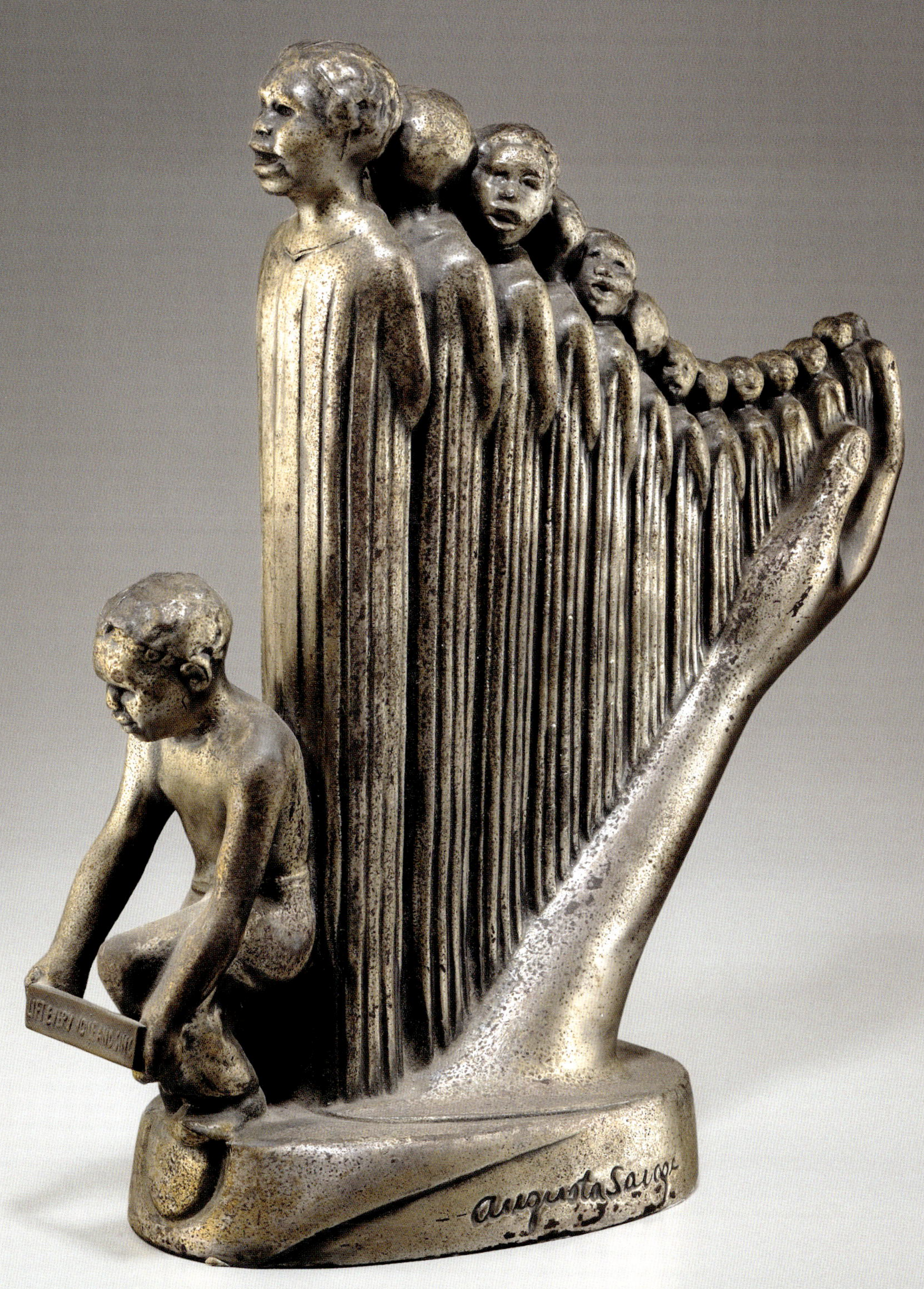

AUGUSTA SAVAGE
Lift Every Voice and Sing, 1939

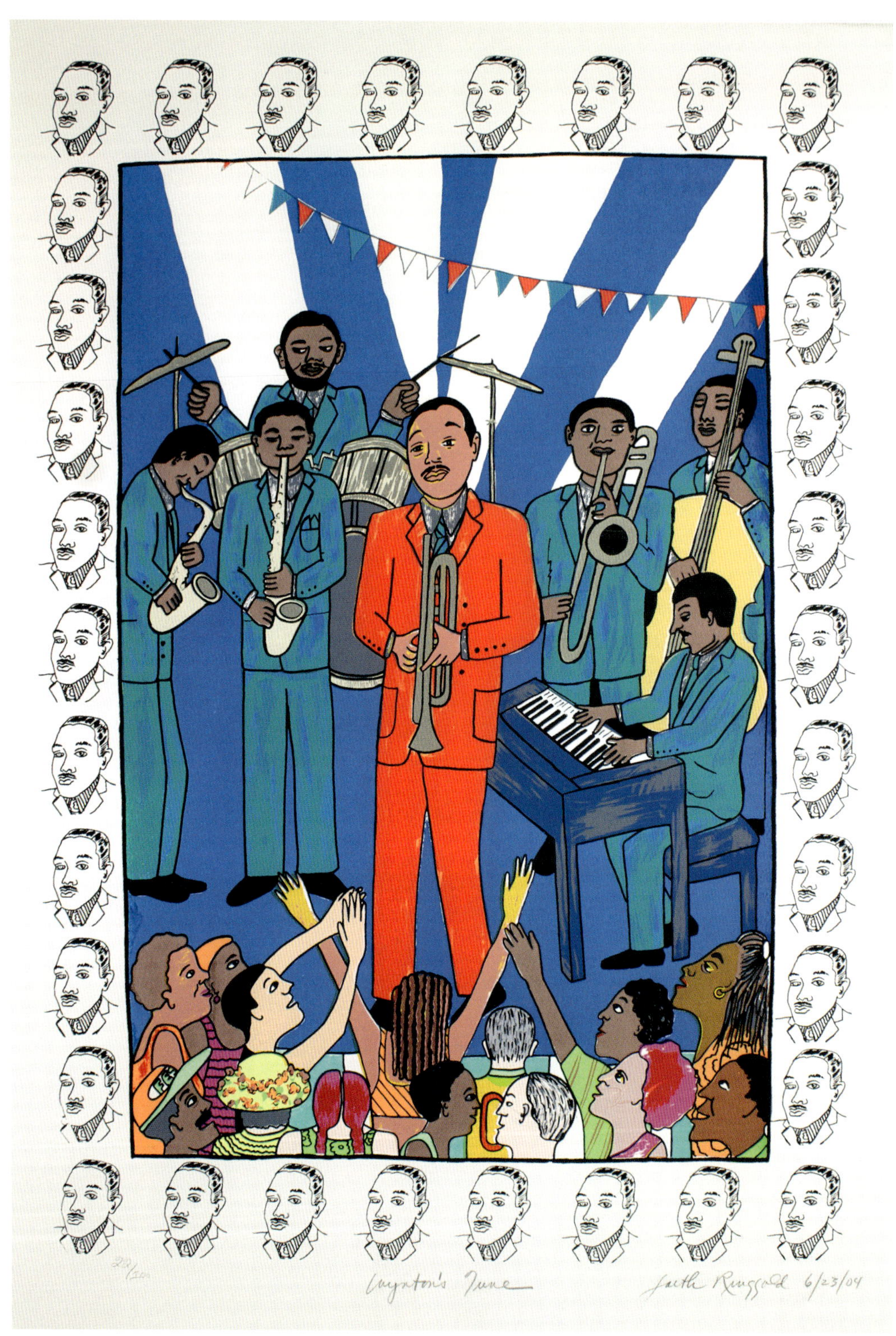

FAITH RINGGOLD
Wynton's Tune, 2014

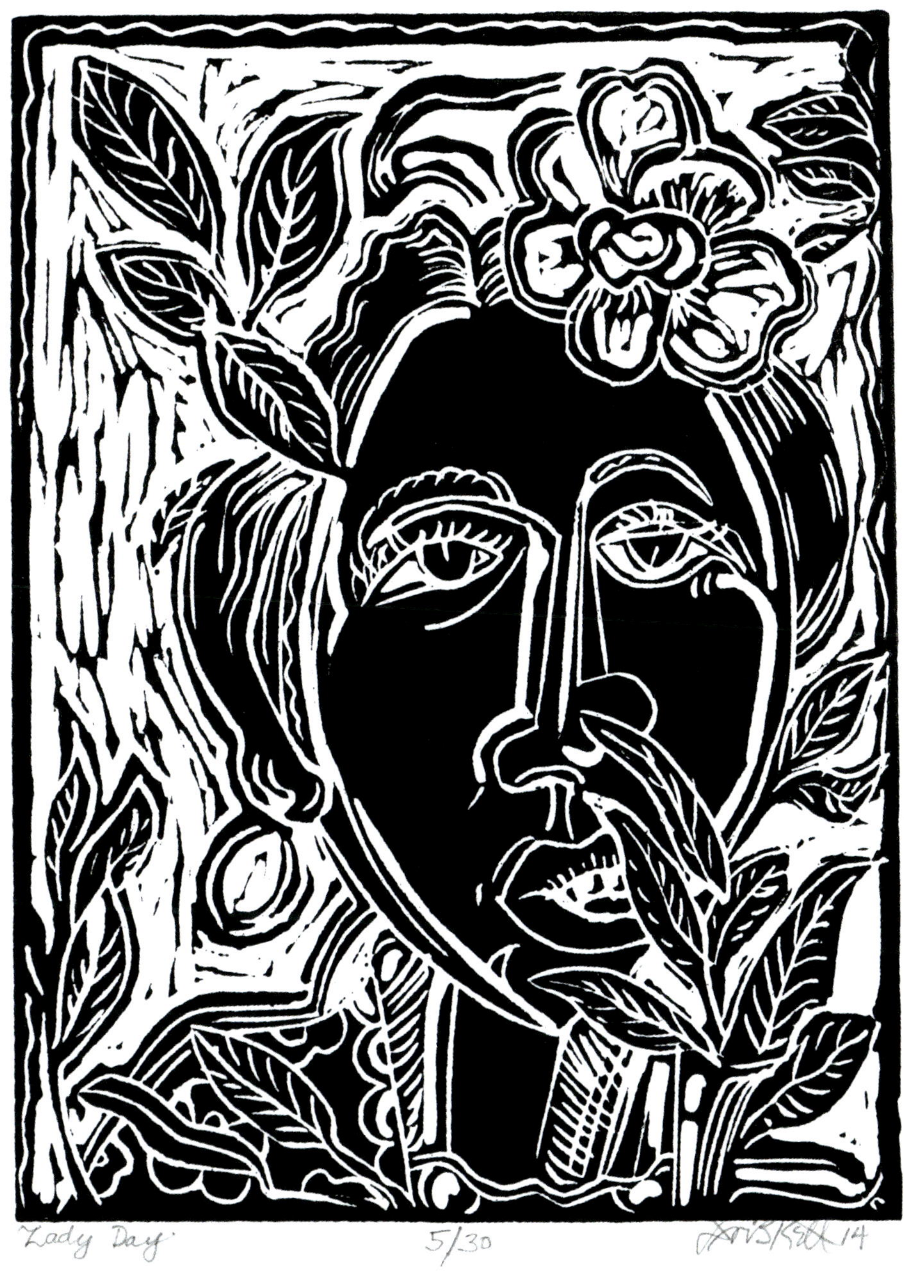

DAVID DRISKELL
Lady Day, 2014

Author, artist, art historian, and educator, David Driskell has illuminated the beauty and creativity of Black makers since the 1950s. Influenced by the work of African American artists like Jacob Lawrence and Romare Bearden, he combines facets of identity and specific cultural references to create works that inspire and uplift. In *Lady Day,* Driskell carves an expressive woodblock print portrait of jazz singer Billie Holiday within a frame of leaves. In memorializing Black lives through his artmaking and writing, he championed a vision that challenges the very idea of what constitutes American art: "I wanted to add to what was there so that nobody could say that you can define American art without including people of color, women, and other so-called minorities."

NELSON STEVENS

Spirit Sister, 2013

Famous for his involvement in the AfriCOBRA (African Commune of Bad Relevant Artists) artist group in the 1970s, Nelson Stevens is a revolutionary artist. Stevens would later work as a university professor after receiving his MFA from Kent State University and working with AfriCOBRA colleagues in Chicago. His paintings and prints espoused the values of the AfriCOBRA manifesto, namely the aesthetic principles of free symmetry, shine, and dynamic "cool-ade" color. His figures clamor with mouths agape, shouting, singing, or protesting for the right to just be. *Spirit Sister*, a portrait of one of his former students, conveys the frantic energy of both Stevens' style and the political turmoil that characterized that era of American history. Celebrating natural hair as a marker of Afro-identity, Stevens saw the artist's role as an instructor to the community. It was aspirational imagery that moved beyond commercial galleries and dusty museums, choosing to instead vivify Black minds that were seeking psychological emancipation as much as their civil rights.

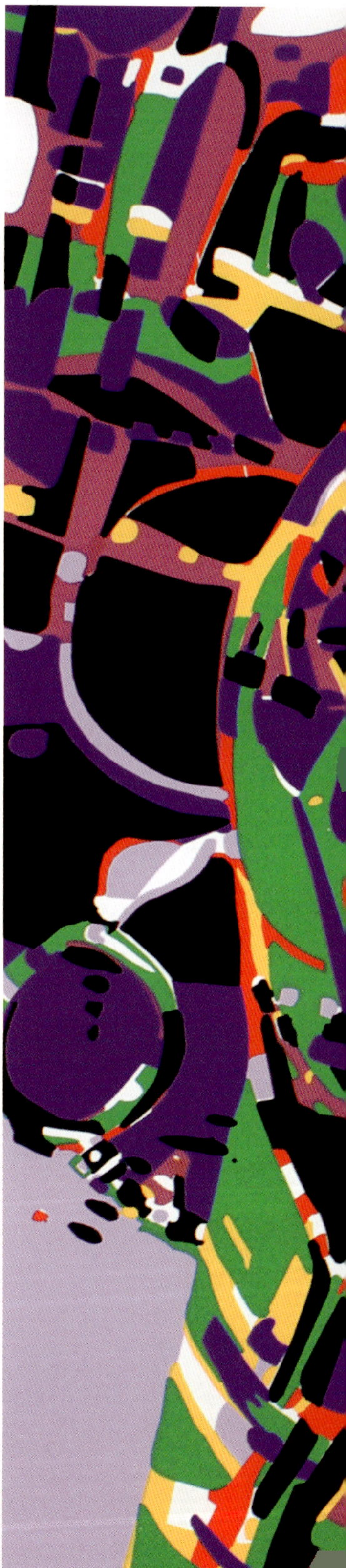

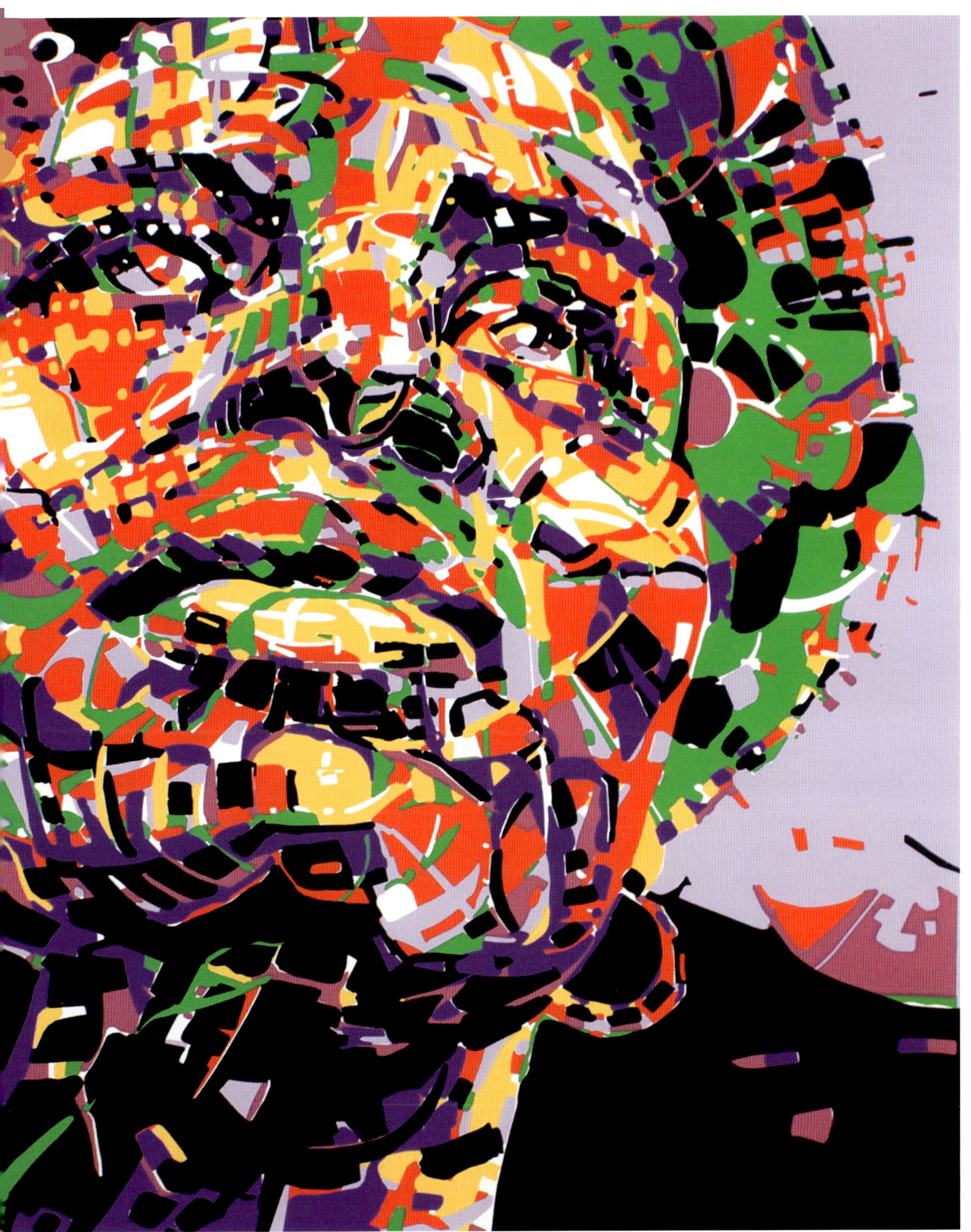

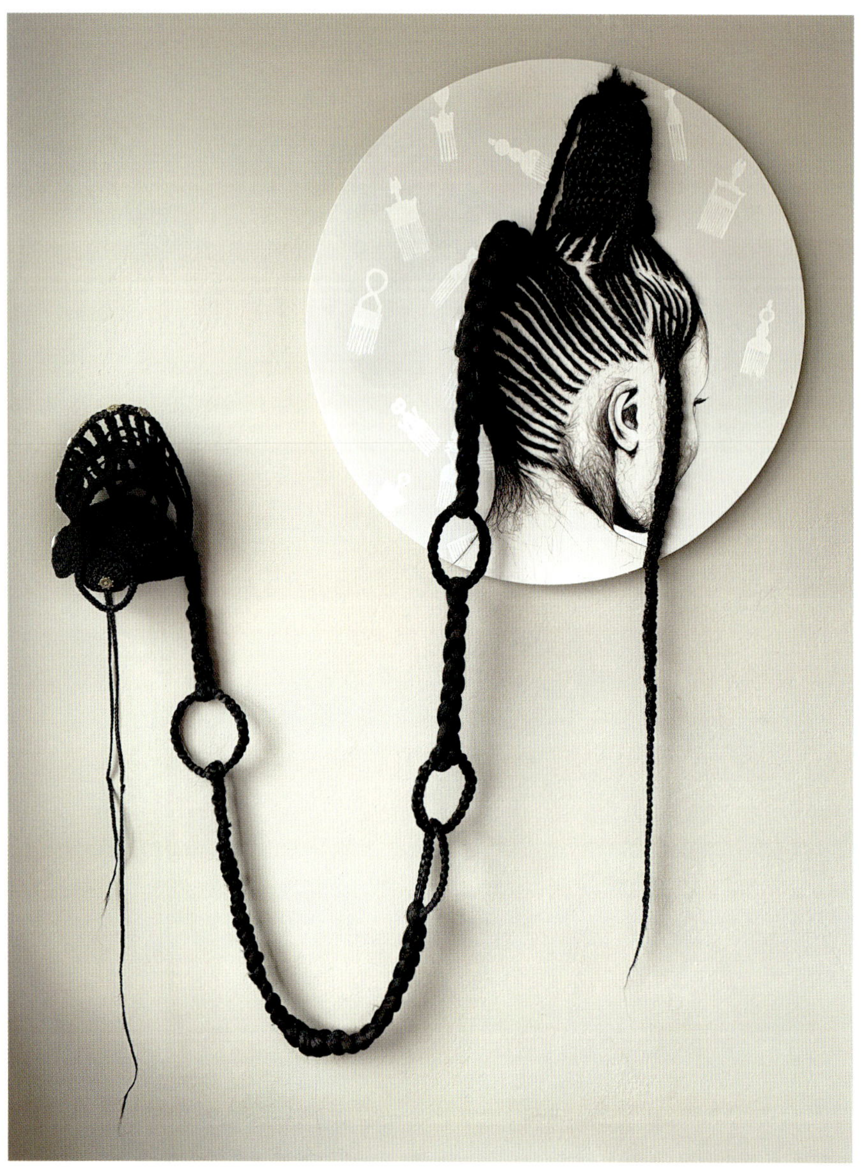

LEBOHANG MOTAUNG

Braided from the Roots, 2020

As both a hairstylist and an artist, Lebohang Motaung is an innovator when it comes to hair. She not only sees personal hairstyling as a form of art, but also shapes her art practice to imitate the skills of a hairstylist. Since her work stems from conversations with clients about their frustrations with their natural hair, she hopes this installation will demonstrate how versatile and significant Black hair can be. Her recent works utilize synthetic hair—an industry increasingly sourced from Asian markets—to form the image and expand it beyond the limitations of a rectangular frame. With this new work for *TEXTURES*, the installation fosters an interactive experience with the viewers as they don the braided hairpiece and physically connect to Motaung's woven image. Even though a person's hair evokes aspects of their heritage or identity, the eponymous *Braided from the Roots* reminds us to avoid frameworks that flatten or essentialize those references. She encourages us to consider the split between how we use hair to project our sense of self, and how that differs from society's perception of us.

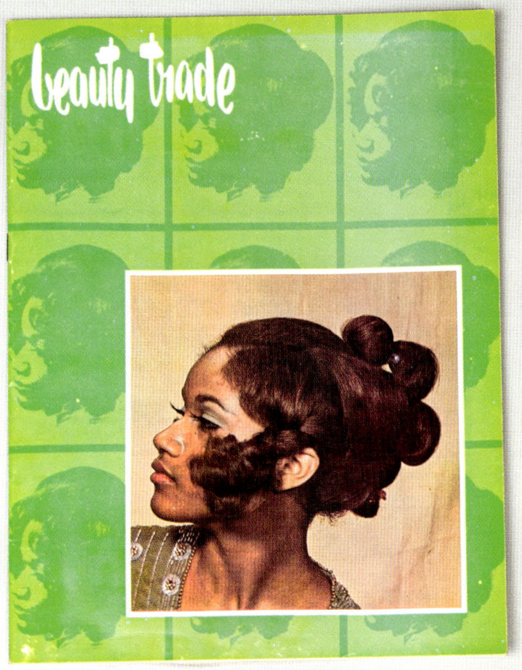

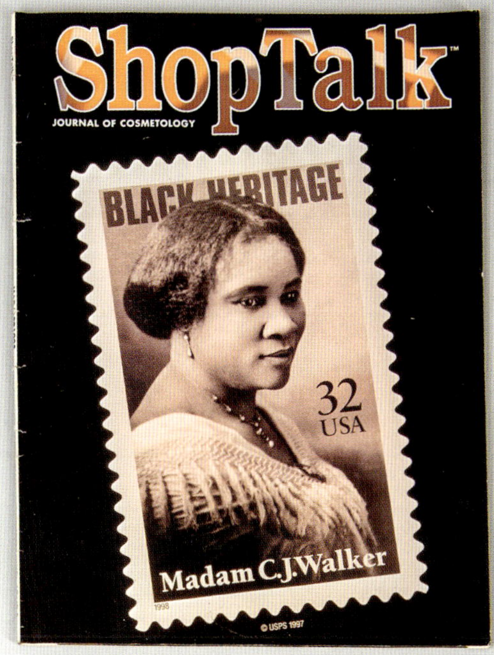

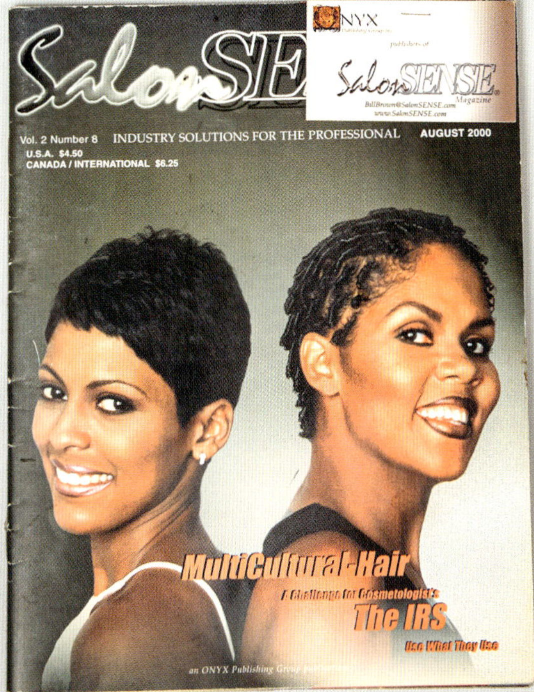

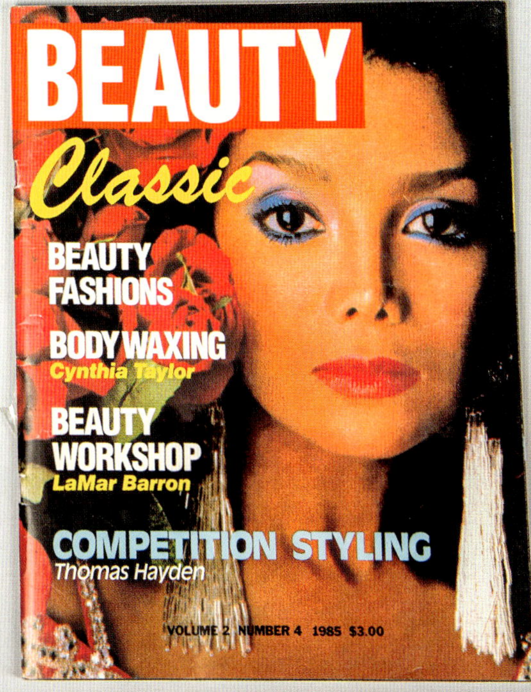

Beauty Trade, 1958
Shop Talk Journal of Cosmetology, 1988
Salon Sense (vol.2, no.8), 2000
Beauty (vol.2, no.4), 1985

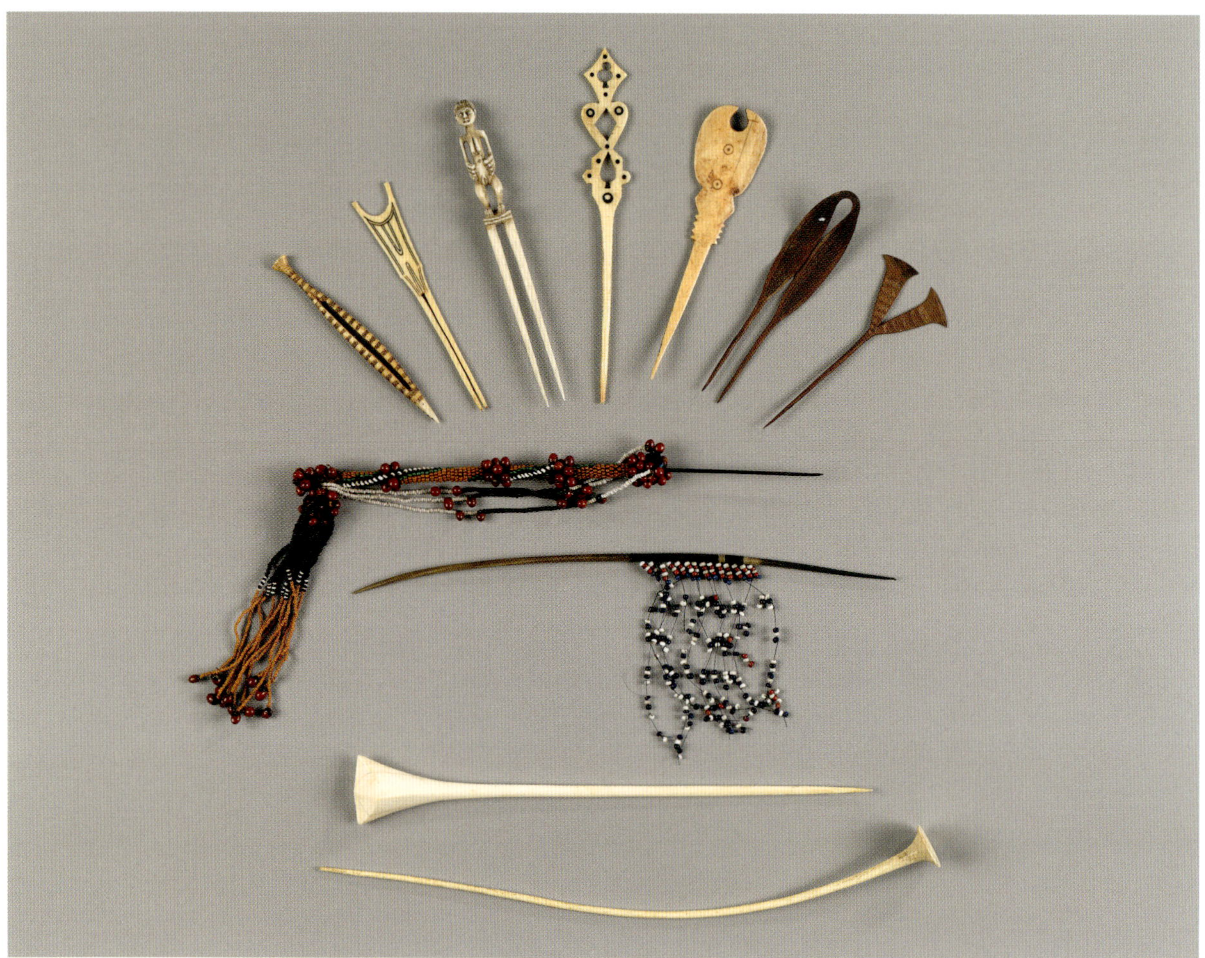

ASSORTMENT OF PINS

(top) Congolese, Congolese, Songye, African, Nigerian, Congolese, Tetela
(bottom) South African, South African, Zande, Mangbetu

Hairstyles have long been used to transmit information about a person's age, social status, and group affinity. As hair became one of the primary means to express an identity, the tools and instruments used to shape it also evolved in complexity. Hairpins have been used for thousands of years to hold the hair in place and provide ornamentation to the style. Only a few tools that humans invented have been so consistently functional and aesthetic at the same time. Some highlights include:

South African (Beads, steel)

Beadwork has been integrated into the arts of many cultures throughout Africa, hearkening back to their production in Ancient Egypt. While the British colonists increased the availability of glass beads to South Africa, ethnic groups like the Zulu already had a tradition of beadwork dating back to 1100 CE. For the Zulu people, beaded hairpins were worn in association with a woman's ancestral lineage.

Zande, Democratic Republic of the Congo (Ivory)

Zande men and women wore their hair in plaits, using ivory combs like these to separate their hair. Made from bone, these combs are long and narrow on one end—perfect for unweaving a matted plait. When not in use as a comb, these objects doubled as decorative hairpins.

Mangbetu, Democratic Republic of the Congo (Ivory)

The Mangbetu people have a long tradition of using the body as the vehicle for elaborate adornment. The classic hairstyle is created by weaving the braided hair into a vessel shape extending up from the back of the head. This hairstyle conveyed a woman's status as did the inclusion of simple, disk-topped hairpins within the coiffure, each carved from a single piece of ivory to reflect the sun.

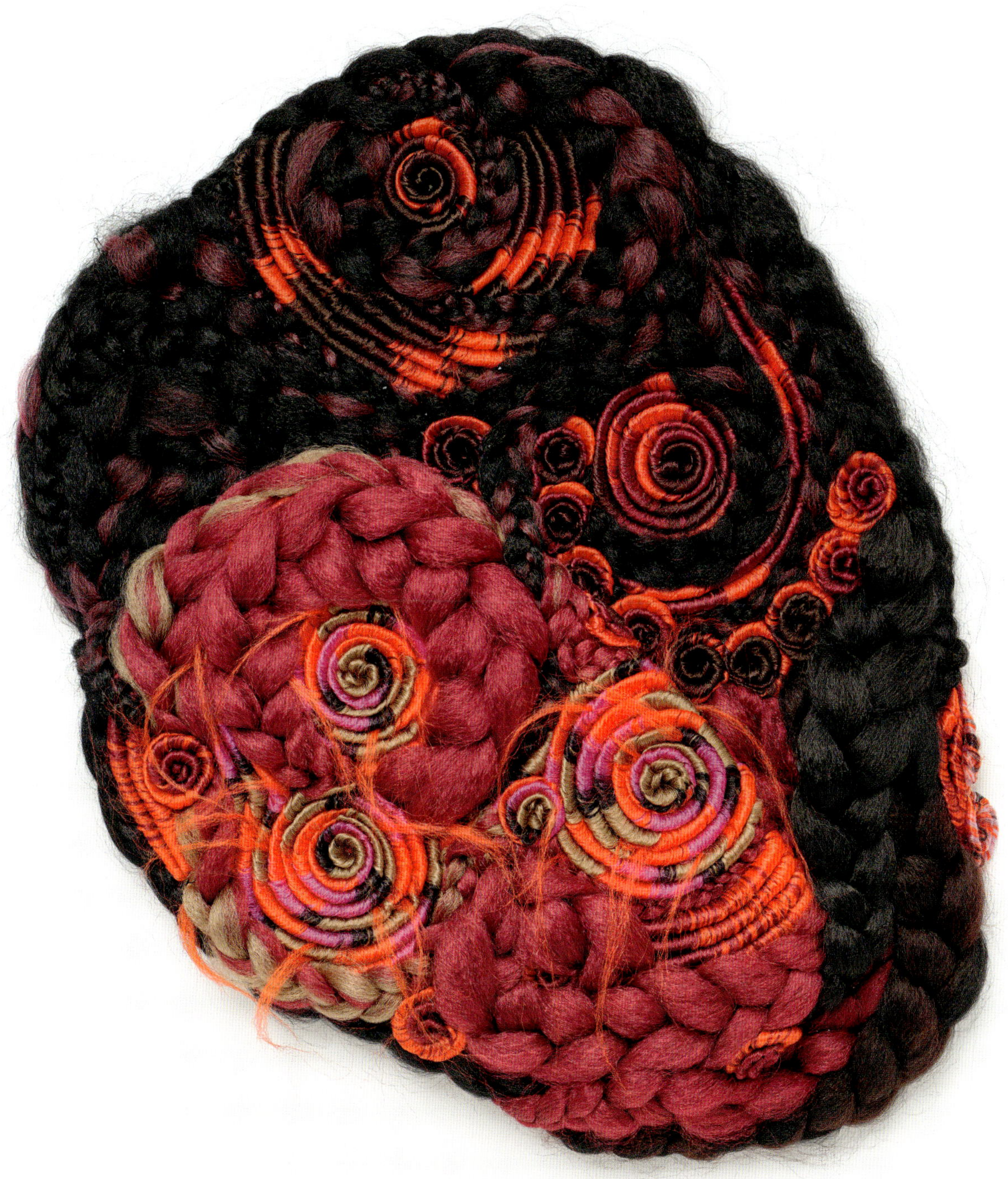

NAFIS M. WHITE

A Burst of Light, 2018

Multidisciplinary artist Nafis White creates from a sense of pride, specifically of Black women's innovation in the maintenance of hair. "My work is steeped in my identity, in my culture, and celebrates the inventiveness, care, and love that is shared between people, especially Black Women, through their fingertips, imbuing wisdom and insight, plaiting revolution and building community."

Ironically, she borrows heavily from complex braiding patterns that were popular among White women in Victorian England, recreating the knots with Black hair. A richly textured sculpture, the hair pieces, hair ties, and bobby pins in *A Burst of Light* are wrapped in exuberant colors, tints of red and black, and assembled with the pride and skill of a salon artist.

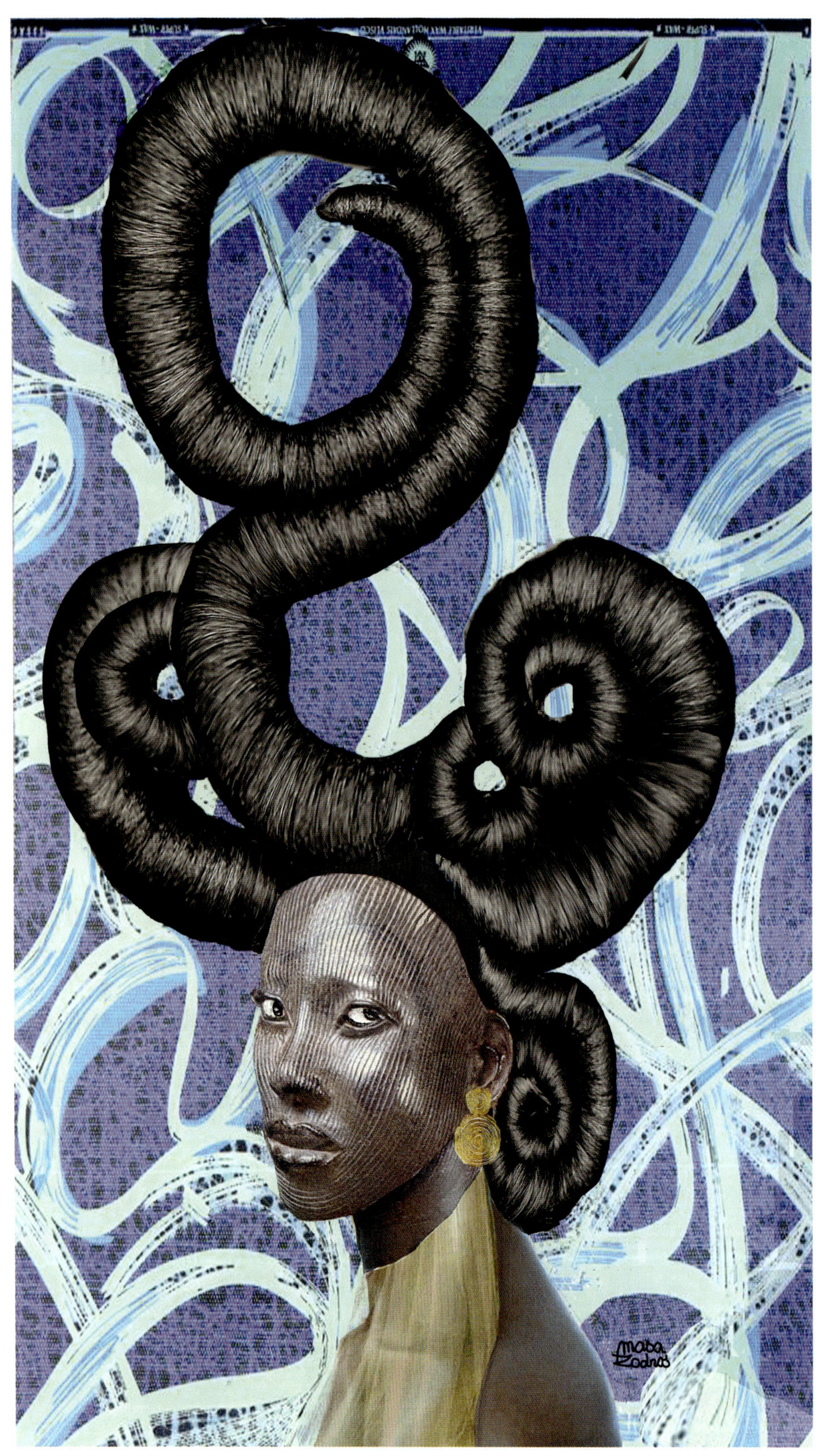

MASA ZODROS
Femme Totem Blue, 2018

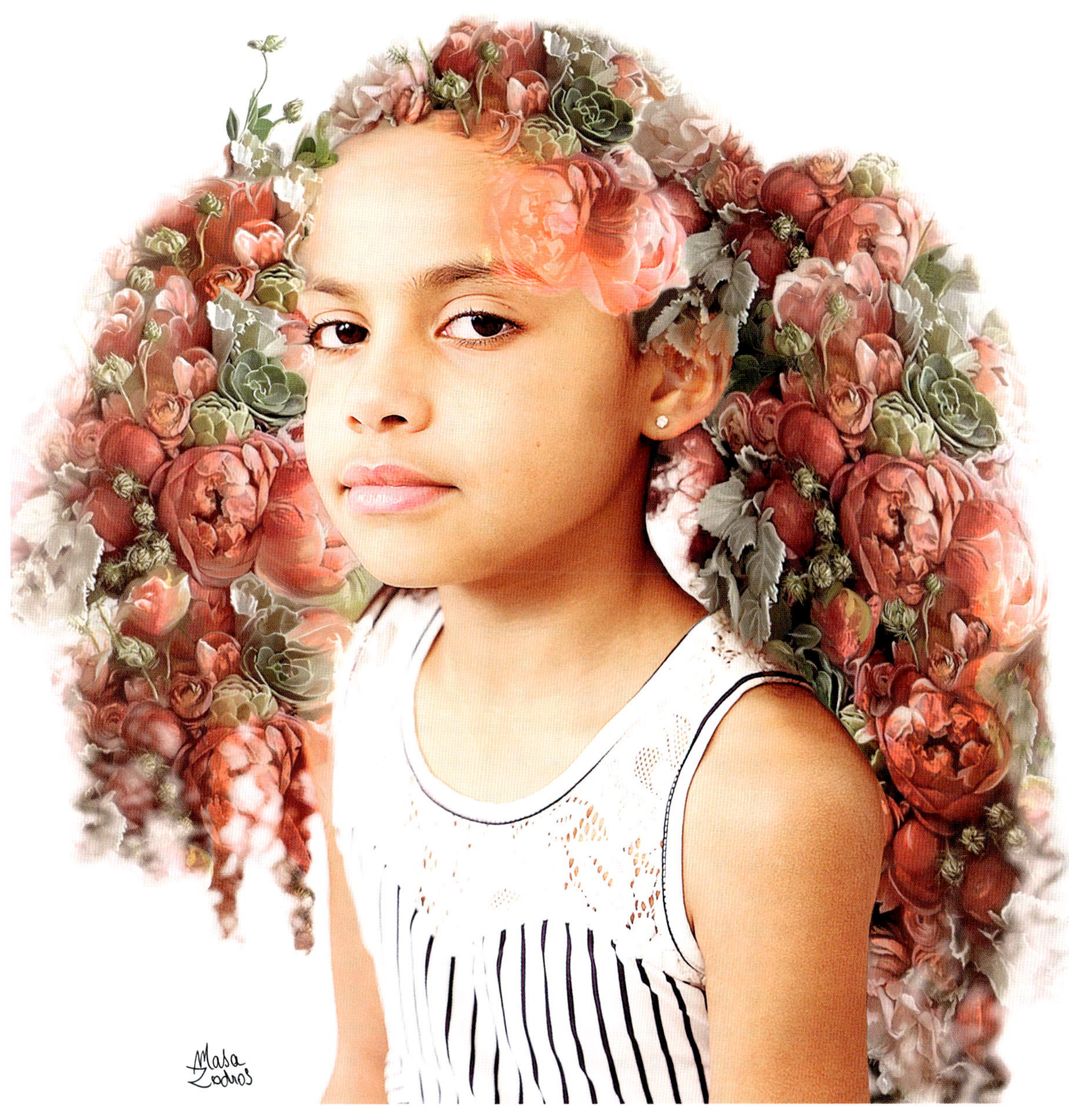

MASA ZODROS

Petite Lina, 2018

In *Petite Lina*, Zodros synthesizes traditional studio photography and digital manipulation techniques to create a striking portrait of her daughter. Given the nondescript attire and the stark white background, the viewer is immediately drawn to the girl's piercing expression and the cascade of flowers and succulents that replaced her hair. In Zodros' portraiture, hair is often intertwined with floral or plant motifs to connect the subject to traditional African spirituality practices. She emphasizes that the traits of botany in these practices are usually associated with the feminine, looking at the leadership women take in traditional African ritual and folklore. In establishing a triangle between hair, spirituality, and femininity in the contemporary, Zodros offers a portrait that is equal parts empowering and reflective.

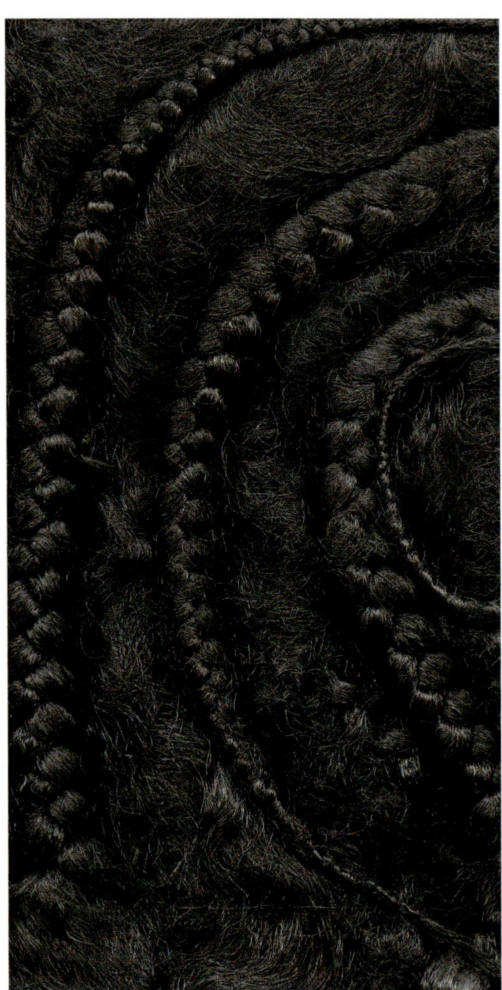

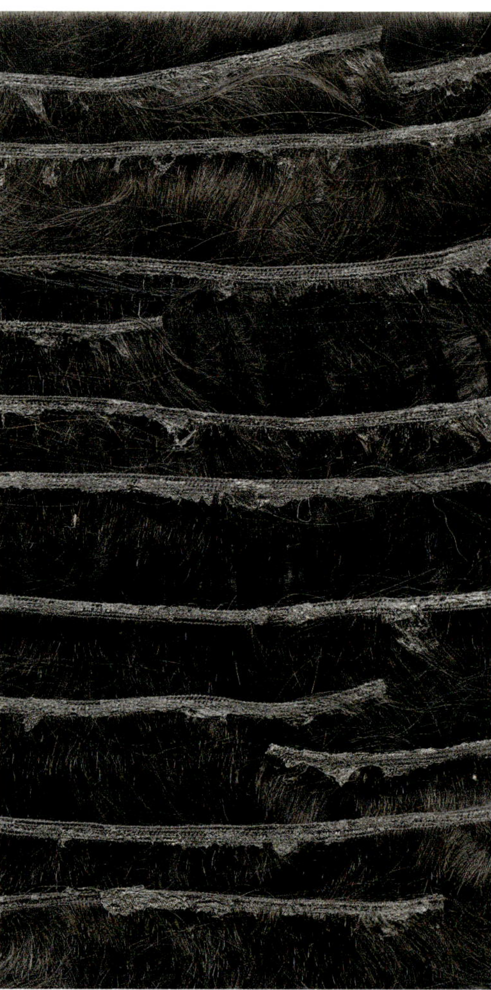

AMBER N. FORD
Feeders, 2019
Pronto, 2019

KEHINDE WILEY
Tanisha Crichlow (portrait of Henrietta Maria of France, Queen Consort of England, Scotland and Ireland), 2015

Since being commissioned to create Barack Obama's presidential portrait, Kehinde Wiley has become a household name. His larger-than-life portraits put contemporary Black men and women in the vistas, regalia, and manners that were reserved for elite sitters in paintings in the seventeenth, eighteenth, or nineteenth centuries. Always referring to canonical works from art history, Wiley invites friends and strangers to sit for his paintings and assume influential roles from history—a history that largely overlooked Black people.

Even set against a dazzling floral background that recalls plush oriental rugs or expensive wallpaper, the figure stands out for her regal costume. Her silver brocaded gown is adorned with emeralds and pearls, and the ensemble is completed by ornate jewelry. Despite the adoption of European court fashion, Wiley's model retains her individuality (see the "Tanisha" tattoo on her chest) and her Blackness (evidenced by the mass of curly hair extensions). The star of her outfit, however, is the hair. Historically, women of court had large sculptural hair that was built around wire, wool, and padding before being adored with feathers, caps, or jewels. Crichlow instead models weaves and braids, hairpieces ranging in hue from onyx and espresso, to auburn and jet black—no further ornaments necessary.

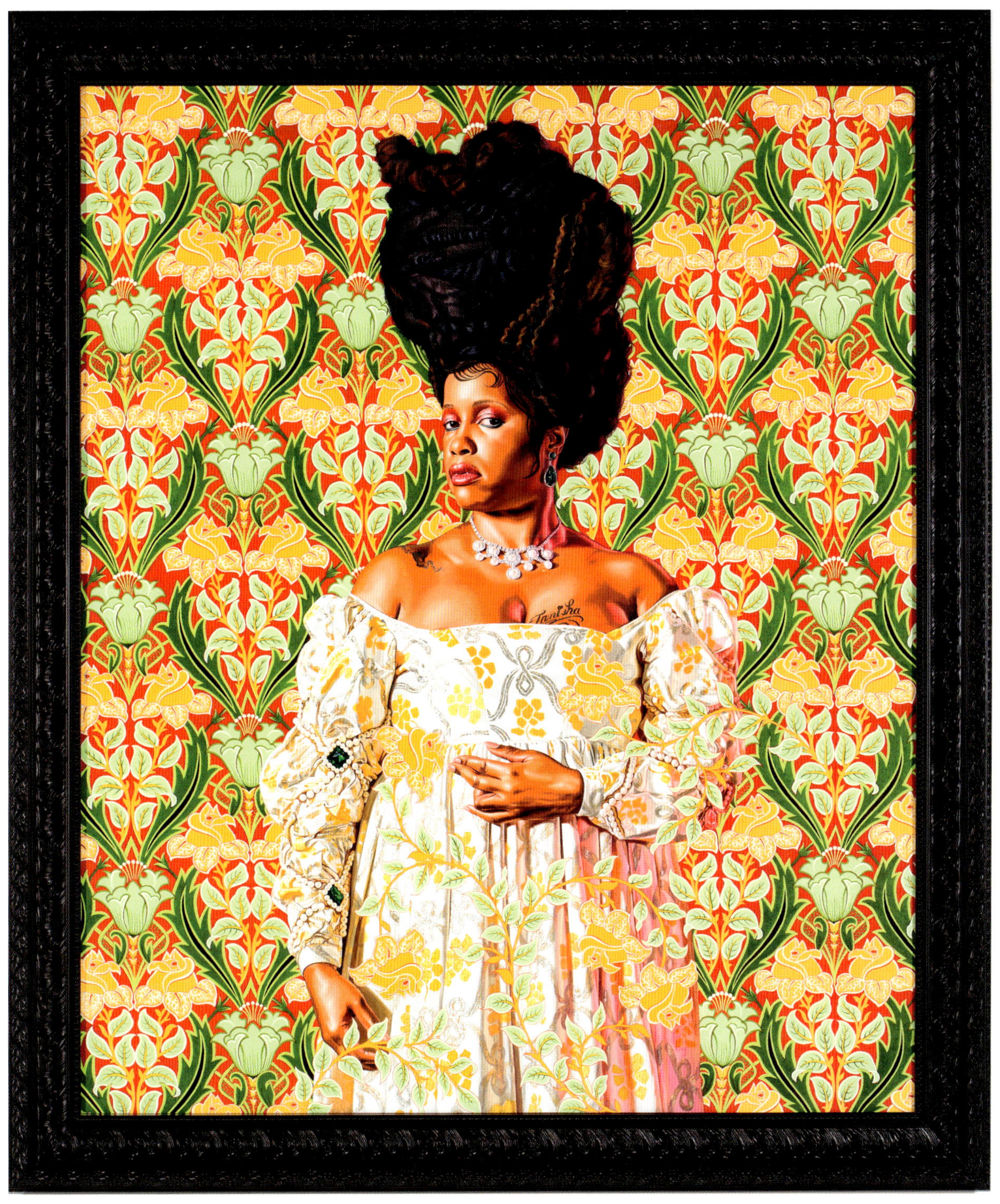

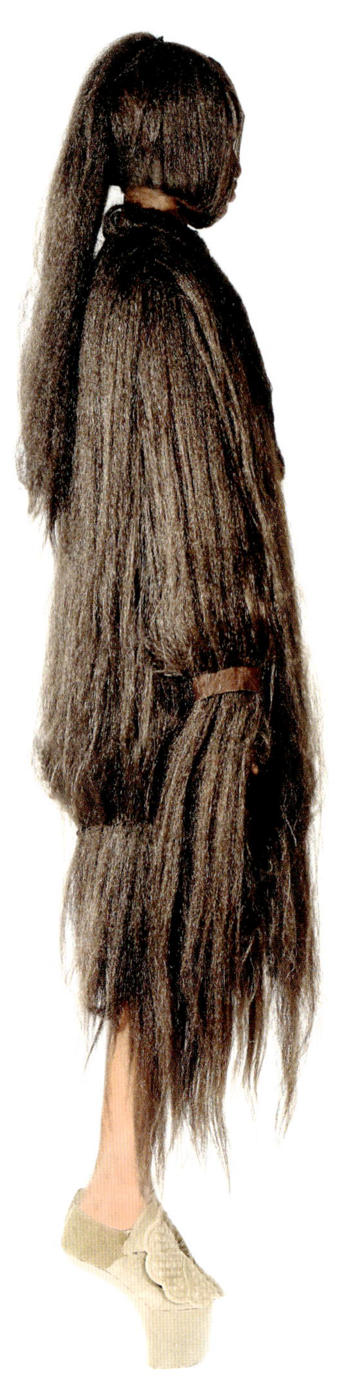

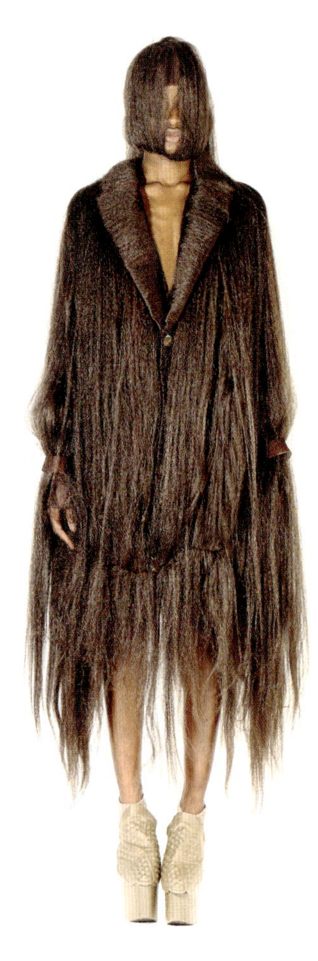

SARAH DUAH

La chevelure bleu: brown, 2012

Using artificial hair, Duah creates high-end fashion that explores how a non-traditional material, like hair, can be incorporated into clothing. This dress, from her series of the same title, is a garment designed for fashion shows. The use of hair extensions shows not only the versatility of Black hair as material, but also that its significance need not be limited to an adornment for the head. Duah's work poetically reflects on the evocation of a body, even when separated from a corporeal form: "Within my work, I am especially interested in the dialogue between art and fashion and how this dialogue is creating a dynamic system in which clothing can be perceived as a product of the fashion system and on the other hand can become material that is used to reference the human body when it is absent."

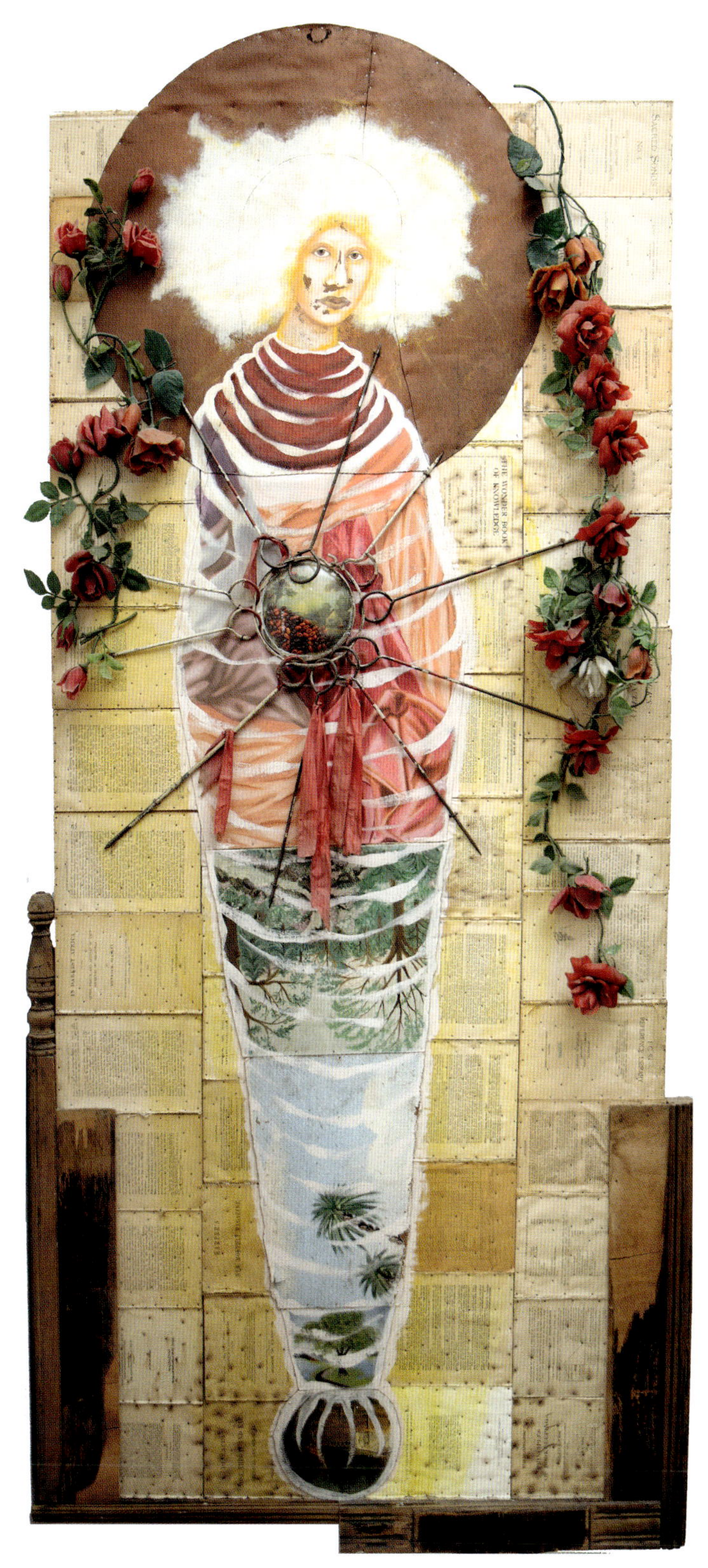

LEZLEY SAAR
Ascension of a Lily Skin, 1997

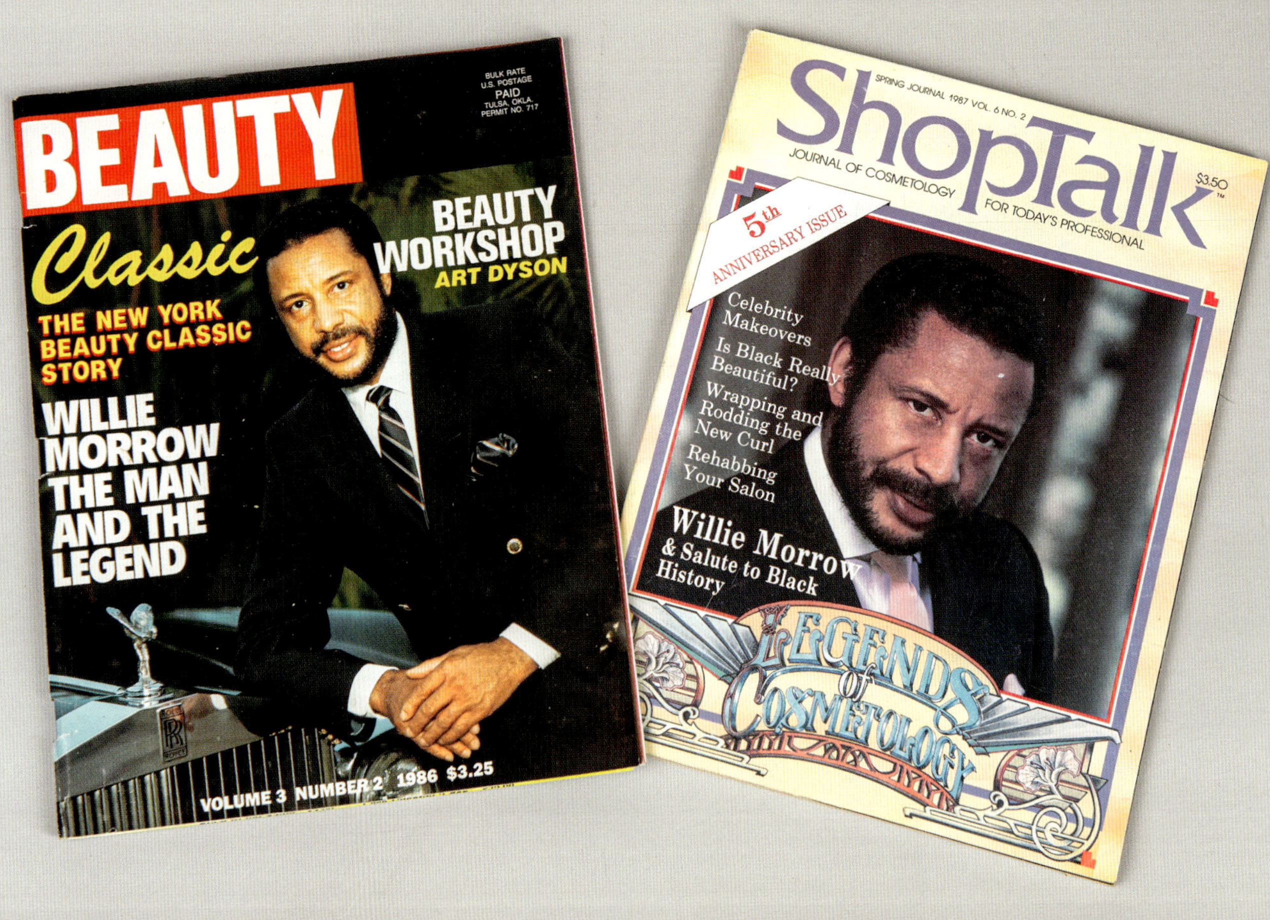

Beauty (vol. 3, no. 2), 1986
Shop Talk Journal of Cosmetology (vol. 6, no. 2), 1987

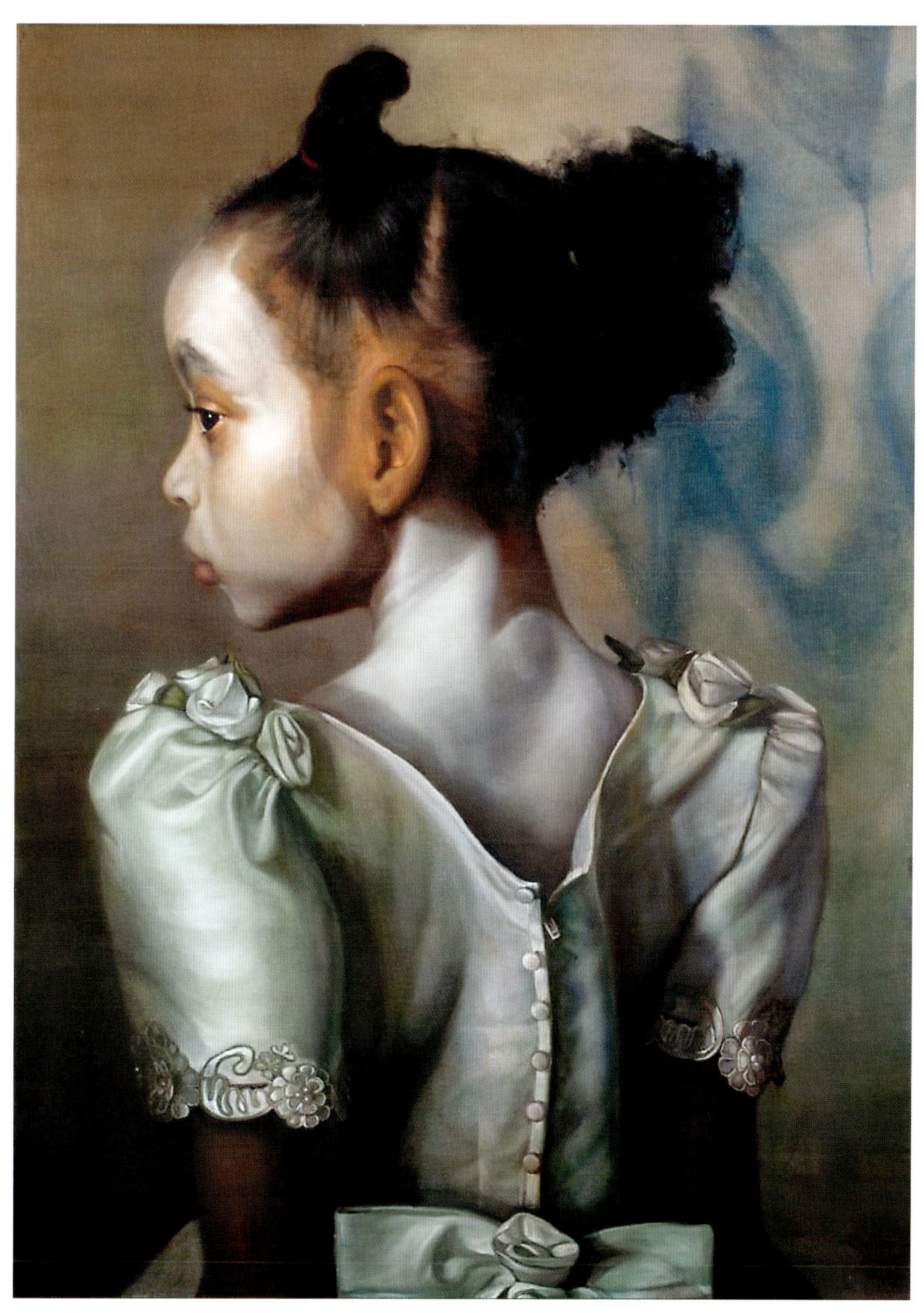

MARGARET BOWLAND
Isn't it Romantic?, 2011

NGOZI SCHOMMERS

Self-Portrait, 2019

As a Nigerian artist living between Germany and Ghana, Schommers reflects on images of herself to tease out nuances in identity, memory, and neo-colonial paradigms. Employing a breadth of media, ranging from sequins and confetti to charcoal and wood, the artist creates richly textured forms that integrate high and low art, as well as cultural references from various periods of history. In her recent exhibition, *The Way We Mask*, she studied pre-colonial Igbo hairstyles and integrated her findings with childhood memories to raise questions about her own hair and the hair care culture from which she descended. This self-portrait depicts her "hair day", a dedicated time to attune herself with her hair, a practice of self-care that she owes herself. In composing this portrait, she created a mirror of her own body. This mirror allows the visitor to share in this intimate moment; it is as if we are standing beside her and asked to reflect on her relationship with her hair and, in turn, our own.

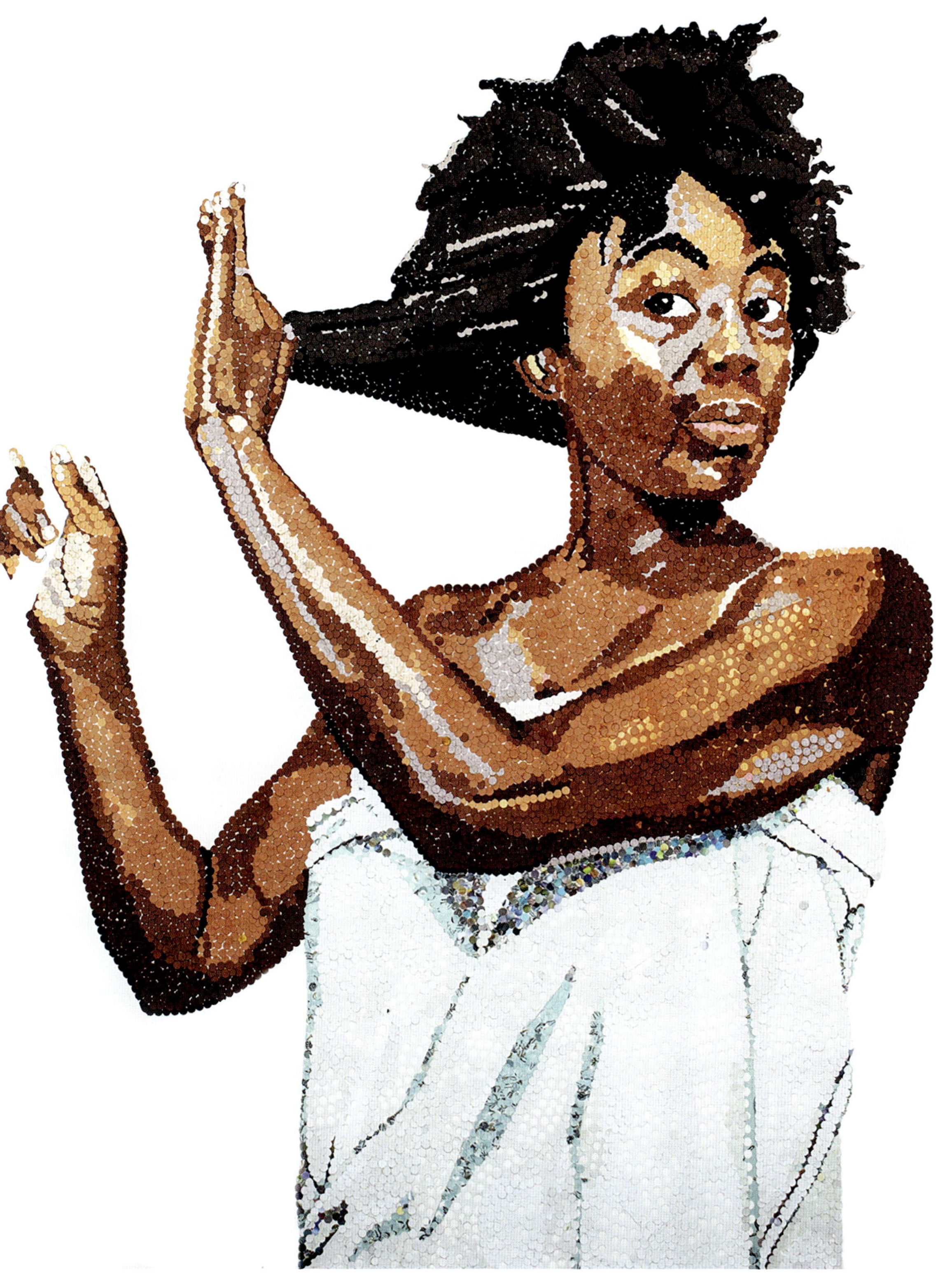

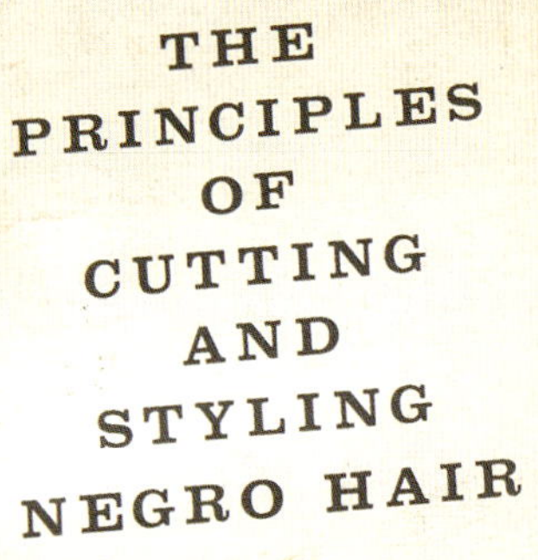

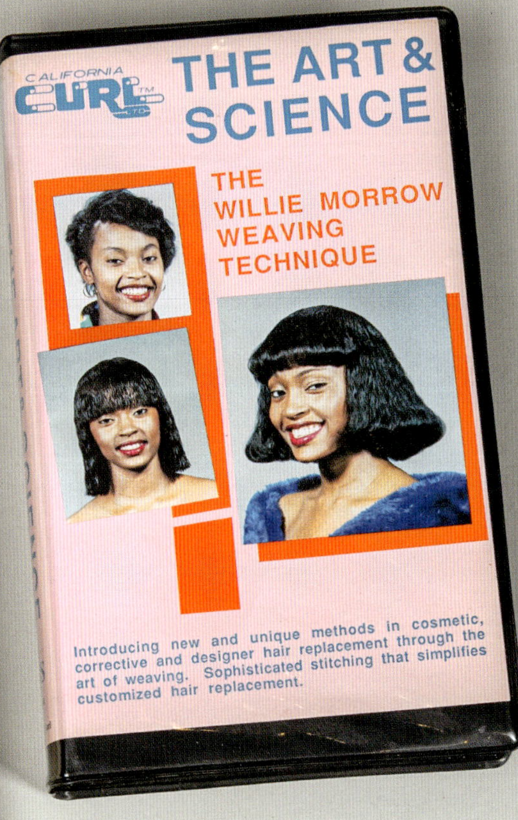

The Principles of Cutting and Styling Hair (First Edition), Willie Lee Morrow, 1966
The Art and Science: The Willie Morrow Weaving Technique, 1988
Willie Morrow's Unbreakable Thermo Blow Dry Nozzle, 1998

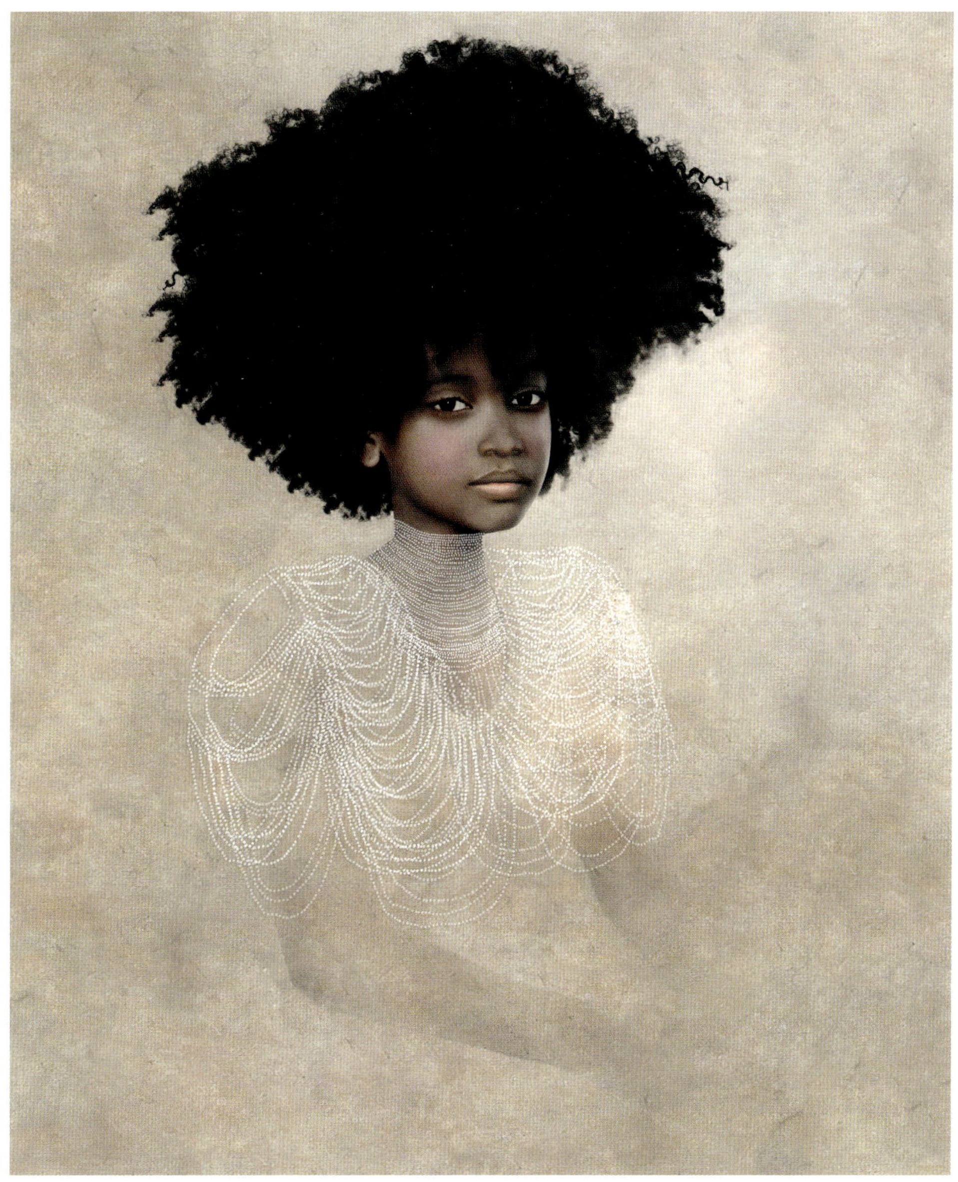

TAWNY CHATMON

Heir / A Present of God, 2017

Directly gazing at the viewer, the girl in this portrait expresses a gracious confidence. Her hands and body fade into the background, making her existence both physical and illusory. A photographer and multimedia artist, Chatmon creates portraits of Black children in an elevated and noble manner, echoing paintings from the Renaissance and Baroque that have been inspirations since childhood. Her work is fueled by frustration at the continued exclusion of Black women and children from school or work activities because of their decision to embrace natural hair or styles distinctive to Black communities. Chatmon uses her own children and family friends as subjects, subsequently manipulating the photos both digitally and physically. She often exaggerates the hair and substitutes the eyes with those of someone older to impart a sense of wisdom to the youthful sitters. The finished portraits are regal odes to Black children that encourage affirmation of self-expression.

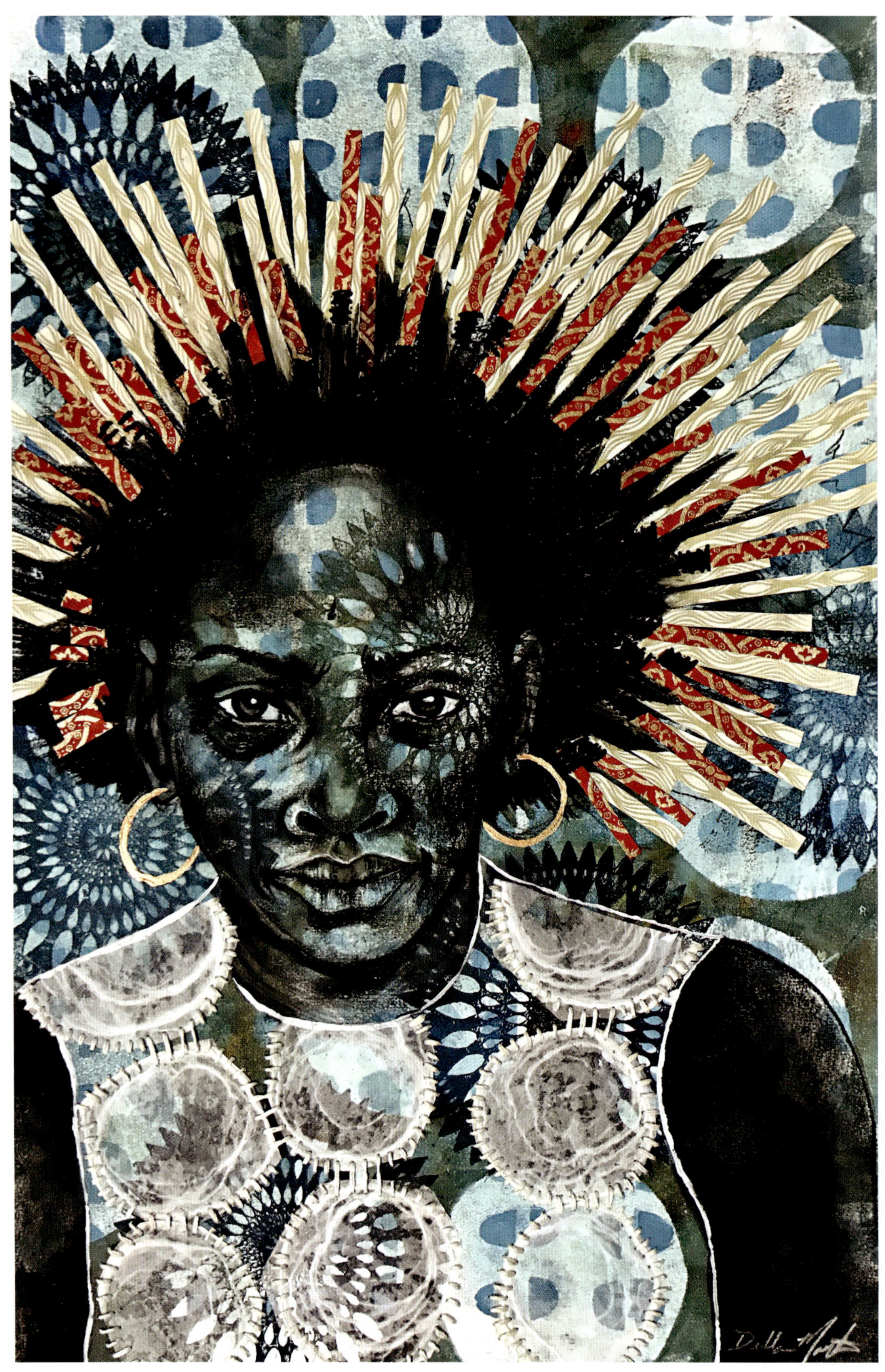

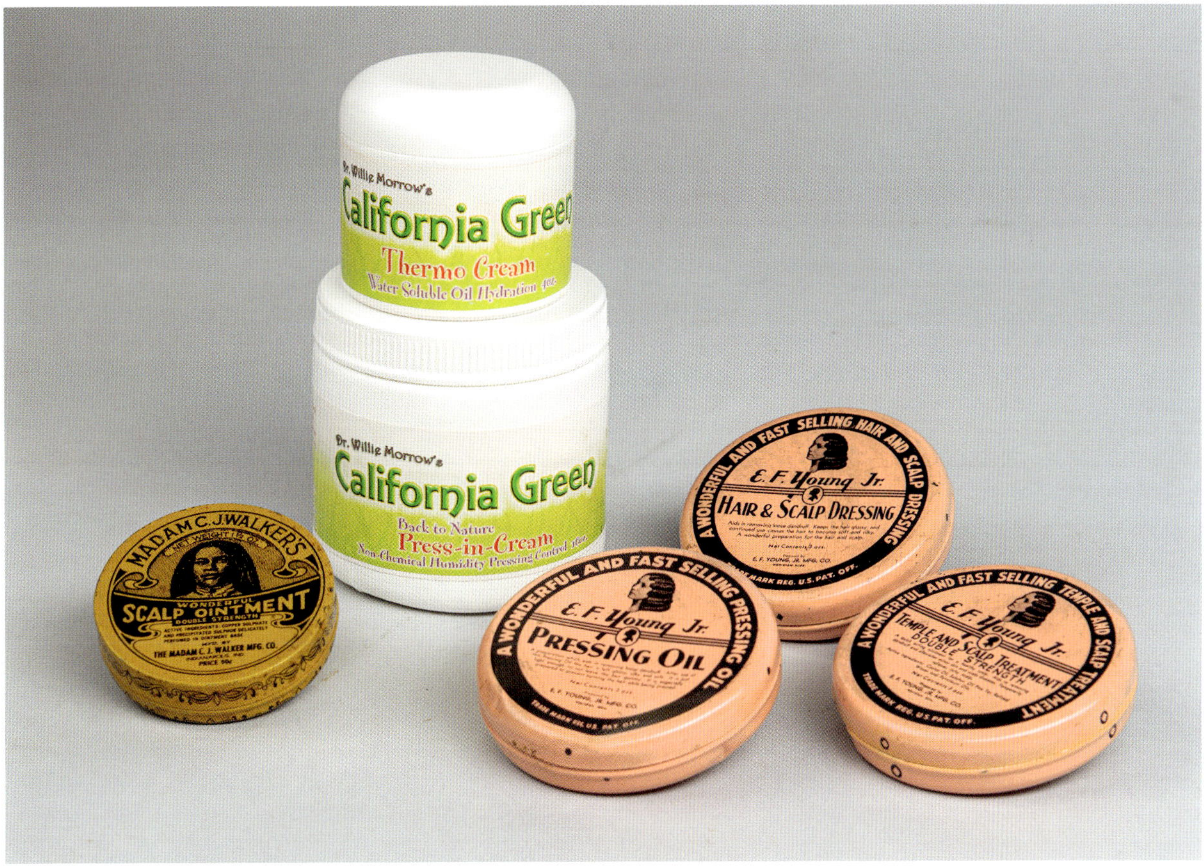

Madam C. J. Walker's Wonderful Scalp Ointment, *ca.* 1900
E. F. Young hair products, 1930s
Dr. Willie Morrow's California Green Press-in-Cream, 2010
Dr. Willie Morrow's Therma-Cream, 2010

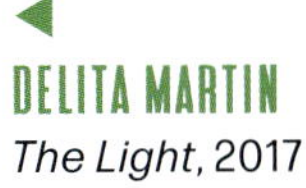

DELITA MARTIN

The Light, 2017

A master printmaker, Martin excels at seamlessly incorporating other processes like drawing, painting, and sewing in her work. In building her layers, she is able to suggest a sense of both psychological depth and an accumulated history. Facing us with calm determination, the figure in *The Light* is a dizzying fusion of textures, shapes, and patterns. Gold and crimson rays emanate from the roots of the woman's crown of natural hair as she stands before a printed backdrop of cobalt and aquamarine. The composition, like these bold color schemes, exudes dynamic—almost otherworldly—energy. This is typical of Martin's practice, as she constructs bold, flat scenes around a singular woman, a woman who is composed but fierce, complex but direct. *The Light* is dominated by circular forms, potentially for its resonance across cultures where the circle is a symbol for 'eternity,' 'woman,' or 'moon.' By building her ethereal images from everyday women who work as her models, Martin actively reconstructs the image of Black women by pitting their dynamism against the flat stereotypes that are common in mass media and pop culture.

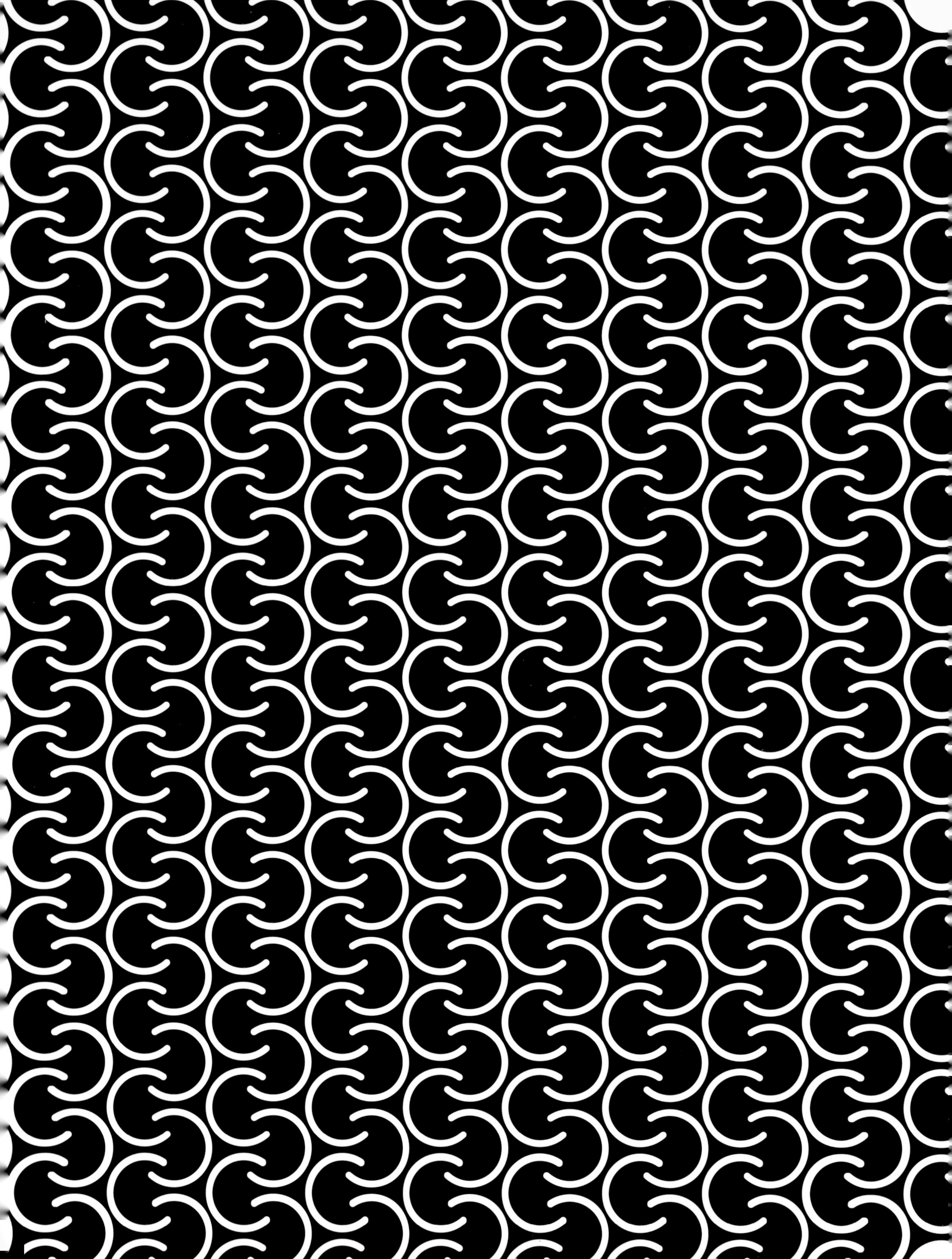

EXHIBITION CHECKLIST

ACEBES, HECTOR
Maasai Man, Tanzania, 1953 (printed 2003)
Silver gelatin print
16 × 20 in. (40.6 × 50.8 cm)
Courtesy of Hector Acebes Archive

ACEBES, HECTOR
Fulani (Foula) Woman, Guinea, 1953 (printed 2003)
Silver gelatin print (Edition of 5)
20 × 24 in. (50.8 × 61 cm)
Courtesy of Hector Acebes Archive

ADAMS, DERRICK
There's More Than One Beauty School, 2018
Fabric, acrylic, paint, wood, and mirror on wood panel
48 × 72 in. (121.9 × 182.9 cm)
Courtesy of the Artist, Luxembourg & Dayan, New York/London, and Salon 94, New York

AKPOKIERE, KARO
Annointed Cutz, 2015-2017
Digital mineral pigment ink print on matte paper
24 × 18 in. (70 × 45.7 cm)
Courtesy of the Artist

ANZINGER, DEBORAH
Growth index #3, 2019
Acrylic, afro kinky hair on paper
18.6 × 22.75 in. (47.2 × 57.8 cm), framed
Courtesy of the Artist

ANZINGER, DEBORAH
Growth index #4, 2019
Acrylic, afro kinky hair on paper
18.6 × 22.75 in. (47.2 × 57.8 cm), framed
Courtesy of the Artist

ANZINGER, DEBORAH
Growth index #5, 2019
Acrylic, afro kinky hair on paper
18.6 × 22.75 in. (47.2 × 57.8 cm), framed
Courtesy of the Artist

ARIEL, KETURAH
Internal Battle, 2013
Oil on wood
16 × 16 in. (40.6 × 40.6 cm)
Courtesy of Art by Keturah Ariel

BEY, APRIL
Creamy Chris, 2013
Silk screened hair relaxer over photo
27 × 17 in. (68.6 × 43.2 cm)
Courtesy of the Artist

BOHANNAH, CHARLES
Seated Woman, ca. 1940
Oil on canvas
24 × 14 in. (61 × 35.6 cm)
Courtesy Private Collection
Photo: Tyler Fine Art, The Melvin Holmes Collection of African American Art

BOWLAND, MARGARET
Isn't it Romantic? 2011
Oil on linen
70 × 50 in. (178 × 127 cm)
Collection of Susan and Dennis Sullivan

BROWN, NAKEYA
Hair Portrait #3 from the *Refutation of "Good" Hair* series, 2012
Archival inkjet print
19 × 19 in. (48.3 × 48.3 cm)
Courtesy of the Artist

CARPEAUX, JEAN-BAPTISTE
Woman of African Descent (or *La Négresse*), 1868 (recast 1979)
Bronze
23.75 × 16 × 13.1 in. (60.3 × 40.6 × 33.3 cm)
Collection of the University of Kentucky Art Museum, Gift of Mr. and Mrs. John R. Gaines in honor of President Otis A. Singletary, 1982.4

CHATMON, TAWNY
Heir / A Present of God, 2017
Print (open edition)
16 × 20 in. (40.6 × 50.8 cm)
Image courtesy artist Tawny Chatmon
On loan from the CCH Pounder-Koné Collection

CLARK, SONYA
Black Hair Flag, 2010
Paint, canvas, thread
51.25 × 26.1 × 1.1 in. (130.2 × 66.3 × 2.8 cm)
Collection of Pamela K. and William A. Royall, Jr.

DRISKELL, DAVID
Lady Day, 2014
Woodblock print
15 × 11.4 in. (38.1 × 29 cm)
Collection of Kent State University School of Art, 2017.034
Photo: Courtesy of the Artist and DC Moore Gallery, New York

DUAH, SARAH
La chevelure bleu: brown, 2012
Artificial hair - Super Braids color no. 2
57.75 × 22.75 × 26.1 in. (146.7 × 57.8 × 66.4 cm)
Courtesy of the Artist

ESIEBO, ANDREW
Nuance Mali from the *Pride* series, 2012
C-print (Edition of 3)
21.2 × 31.5 in. (53.8 × 80 cm)
Courtesy of the Artist

ESIEBO, ANDREW
Nuance Abidjan from the *Pride* series, 2012
C-print (Edition of 3)
21.2 × 31.5 in. (53.8 × 80 cm)
Courtesy of the Artist

EZE, JOSEPH
Stella Pomade #3, 2018
Acrylic and newspaper on canvas
36 × 36 in. (91.4 × 91.4 cm)
Courtesy of CCH Pounder-Koné

FORD, AMBER N.
Feeders, 2019
Silk print
84 × 44 in. (213.4 × 111.8 cm)
Courtesy of the Artist

FORD, AMBER N.
Pronto, 2019
Silk print
84 × 44 in. (213.4 × 111.8 cm)
Courtesy of the Artist

GABON, YRNEH
Cotton Head, 2016
Clay, cotton
16 × 15 × 15 in. (40.6 × 38.1 × 38.1 cm)
Courtesy of CCH Pounder-Koné

HAJEK, OLAF
Black Antoinette #001, 2017
Mixed media on canvas
48.75 × 37 in. (123.8 × 94 cm), framed
Courtesy of CCH Pounder-Koné
Photo: Courtesy of the Artist

HUTCHINSON, NAKAZZI
Humble Youth (Yute) from the *Roots Mask* series, 2017
Ceramic
4 × 12 in. (10.2 × 30.5 cm)
Courtesy of CCH Pounder-Koné

HUTCHINSON, NAKAZZI
Untitled, 2018
Ceramic
4 × 12 in. (10.2 × 30.5 cm)
Courtesy of CCH Pounder-Koné

JOHNSON, SHARA K.
Otjize, 2016
Photograph
24 × 17.5 in. (61 × 44.5 cm)
Courtesy of the Artist

JOHNSON, SHARA K.
Himba Hands, 2016
Photograph
24 × 16 in. (61 × 40.6 cm)
Courtesy of the Artist

LAFFORGUE, ERIC
Mr. Awol Mohammed, Afar Tribe Man with ghee on his hair, Mille, Ethiopia, 2014
Photograph
16.5 × 11.7 in. (42 × 29.7 cm)
Courtesy of the Artist

LAFFORGUE, ERIC
Miss Biremuda, Bana Tribe Girl, Key Afer, Ethiopia, 2012
Photograph
16.5 × 11.7 in. (42 × 29.7 cm)
Courtesy of the Artist

LEE, ANNIE
All That Glitters
Print (open edition)
21 × 17.5 in. (53.3 × 44.5 cm)
Purchase, Kent State University Museum
Photo: © Artist

MARTIN, DELITA
The Light, 2017
Mixed media
26 × 18 in. (66 × 45.7 cm), framed
Courtesy of CCH Pounder-Koné

MENSAH, CHARLOTTE
Hairstyle from the *Afrofuture* collection, 2017
Photograph
Dimensions variable
Courtesy of Mensah (stylist), Lan Nguyen (makeup artist), and John Rawson (photographer)
Photo: John Rawson (Rawson Partnership)

MENSAH, CHARLOTTE
Hairstyle from the *Afrofuture* collection, 2017
Photograph
Dimensions variable
Courtesy of Mensah (stylist), Lan Nguyen (makeup artist), and John Rawson (photographer)
Photo: John Rawson (Rawson Partnership)

MOTAUNG, LEBOHANG
Braided from the Roots, 2020
Synthetic hair and acrylic on canvas
Dimensions variable (3 × 3 ft., or 1 × 1 m)
Courtesy of the Artist

MUHOLI, ZANELE
Zinathi I, Johannesburg, 2015
Silver gelatin print (Edition 3 of 8)
30 × 20.5 in. (76.2 × 52.1 cm)
Private Collection
Photo: © Artist, courtesy of Stevenson, Cape Town/ Johannesburg and Yancey Richardson, New York

MUHOLI, ZANELE
Zibuyile I, Syracuse, 2015
Silver gelatin print (Edition 4 of 8)
26.75 × 20 in. (68 × 50.8 cm)
Private Collection
Photo: © Artist, courtesy of Stevenson, Cape Town/ Johannesburg and Yancey Richardson, New York

MURPHY-PRICE, ALTHEA
Barrettes no. 1, 2017
Screen print and collage
22 × 30 in. (55.9 × 76.2 cm)
Courtesy of the Artist

MURPHY-PRICE, ALTHEA
Barrettes no. 2, 2017
Screen print and collage
22 × 30 in. (55.9 × 76.2 cm)
Courtesy of the Artist

MUTITI, NONTSIKELELO
African Hair Braiding Salon Reader, 2014
Spiral bound booklet, laser print
5.5 × 8 in. (14 × 20.3 cm)
Courtesy of the Artist

MUTITI, NONTSIKELELO
Cassamance #2, 2020
Conceptual sketch for site-specific vinyl installation at KSU Museum
Dimensions variable
Courtesy of the Artist

NASH, WOODROW
Untitled, ca. 2010
Ceramic
26 × 21 in. (66 × 53.3 cm)
Collection of Larry and Donna James

NORWOOD, SHARON
The Root of the Matter XII, 2017
Digital collage on watercolor paper
13 × 19 in. (33 × 48.3 cm)
Courtesy of CCH Pounder-Koné

NUÑEZ, GLENFORD
The Coiffure Project: A portrait of Zaruta, 2011
Photograph, acrylic finish
50 × 40 in. (127 × 101.6 cm)
Collection of Brian Howell
Photo: © Artist

PALMER, CHARLY
Battleship 3, 2016
Acrylic on canvas
24 × 48 in. (61 × 122 cm)
Courtesy of the Artist and Hearne Fine Art

PARKS, GORDON
Muslim Women in Chicago, 1970
Silver gelatin print
20 × 29 in. (50.8 × 73.7 cm)
Courtesy of The Melvin Holmes Collection of African American Art
Photo: Tyler Fine Art, The Melvin Holmes Collection of African American Art

RINGGOLD, FAITH
Wynton's Tune, 2014
Screen print (Edition of 100)
30 × 22 in. (76.2 × 55.9 cm)
Collection of Kent State University School of Art, 2017.037
Photo: © 2020 Faith Ringgold/ Artists Rights Society (ARS), New York, Courtesy ACA Galleries, New York

SAAR, LEZLEY
Ascension of a Lily-Skin, 1997
Assemblage
86 × 40 in. (218.4 × 101.6 cm)
Courtesy of CCH Pounder-Koné

SAVAGE, AUGUSTA
Lift Every Voice and Sing, 1939
Silver oxide
11 × 9.5 × 4 in. (27.9 × 24.1 × 10.2 cm)
Courtesy of The Melvin Holmes Collection of African American Art
Photo: Tyler Fine Art, The Melvin Holmes Collection of African American Art

SCHOMMERS, NGOZI
Self-portrait, 2019
39.4 × 59 in (100 × 150 cm)
Perforated paper, confetti on watercolor paper
Courtesy of the Artist

SHIMOYAMA, DEVAN
Elijah, 2020
Oil, color pencil, jewelry, glitter, enamel, feathers, and rhinestones on canvas stretched over panel
40 × 30 in. (101.6 × 76.2 cm)
Private Collection (Los Angeles, CA)
Photo: Courtesy of the Artist and De Buck Gallery

SIBANDE, MARY
Sophie Velucia in conversation with Madam CJ Walker, 2009
Fiberglass, resin, cotton and synthetic hair embroidered on canvas
Dimensions variable
(19 × 19 ft., or 6 × 6 m)
Courtesy of Artist and SMAC Gallery
Photo: © Artist, courtesy of SMAC Gallery. Photographer: Eva Broekema

SIMPSON, LORNA
Square Deal, 1990
8 dye diffusion color Polaroid prints, 1 engraved plastic plaque (Edition 1 of 3)
Photos: 23.6 × 19.7 in. (60 × 50 cm), Plaque: 8 × 8 in. (20.3 × 20.3 cm)
Private Collection
Photo: © Artist, courtesy of the Artist and Hauser & Wirth

STEVENS, NELSON
Spirit Sister, 2013
Screen print (Edition of 75)
23 × 22.5 in. (58.4 × 57.2 cm)
Collection of Kent State University School of Art, 2017.01
Photo: © Artist, courtesy of Galerie Myrtis

THIAM, IBRAHIMA
Selection from the *Vintage Portrait* series, 2017
Photograph
23.6 × 15.75 in. (60 × 40 cm)
Courtesy of the Artist

UNIDENTIFIED AFRICAN ARTIST
Comb
Wood, wire
3.25 × 2.5 in. (8.3 × 6.4 cm)
Collection of Kent State University Museum, Gift of Howard E. and Jennie L. Hutchings & family, 2013.41.11

UNIDENTIFIED AFRICAN ARTIST
Comb
Wood, wire
3.3 × 2.5 in. (8.4 × 6.4 cm)
Collection of Kent State University Museum, Gift of Howard E. and Jennie L. Hutchings & family 2013.41.12

UNIDENTIFIED AFRICAN ARTIST
Hair pin, 19th century
Ivory
6.9 in. (17.5 cm)
Collection of the Fowler Museum at UCLA, Gift of the Wellcome Trust, X67.936
Photo: Don Cole, Fowler Museum at UCLA

UNIDENTIFIED AKAN ARTIST (GHANA)
Duafe (Comb)
Wood
8.1 × 3 × 0.3 in. (20.6 × 7.6 × 0.8 cm)
Collection of the Fowler Museum at UCLA, Gift of Dorothy M. Cordry in memory of Donald B. Cordry, X84.671
Photo: Don Cole, Fowler Museum at UCLA

UNIDENTIFIED AKAN ARTIST (GHANA)
Female Figure, 20th century
Wood
11.5 × 3.5 in. (29.2 × 8.9 cm)
Collection of Kent State University School of Art, 99.3.9

UNIDENTIFIED ASANTE ARTIST (GHANA)
Comb, *ca.* 1900
Wood
12.2 × 3.4 × 0.4 in. (31 × 8.6 × 1 cm)
Collection of the Fowler Museum at UCLA, Gift of Franklin D. and Judith H. Murphy, X96.8.31
Photo: Don Cole, Fowler Museum at UCLA

UNIDENTIFIED BAULE ARTIST (CÔTE D'IVOIRE)
Comb
Wood
5 × 2.6 × 0.5 in. (12.7 × 6.5 × 1.2 cm)
Collection of the Fowler Museum at UCLA, Gift of The Jerome L. Joss Collection, X87.1470
Photo: Don Cole, Fowler Museum at UCLA

UNIDENTIFIED BAULE ARTIST (CÔTE D'IVOIRE)
Male Figure, 20th century
Wood
15.5 × 3.5 in. (39.4 × 8.9 cm)
Collection of Kent State University School of Art, 84.2a

UNIDENTIFIED CHOKWE ARTIST (ANGOLA OR DEM. REP. OF THE CONGO)
Comb
Wood
9.8 × 4.1 in. (25 × 10.5 cm)
Collection of the Fowler Museum at UCLA, Museum Purchase, X87.1470
Photo: Don Cole, Fowler Museum at UCLA

UNIDENTIFIED CHOKWE ARTIST (ANGOLA OR DEM. REP. OF THE CONGO)
Female Figure, 20th century
Wood
11 × 2.75 × 2.5 in. (28 × 7 × 6.4 cm)
Collection of Kent State University School of Art, 99.5.29

UNIDENTIFIED CONGOLESE ARTIST (DEM. REP. OF THE CONGO)
Male Figure, 20th century
Wood
15 × 5 × 4.75 in. (38.1 × 12.7 × 12.1 cm)
Collection of Kent State University School of Art, 68.2

UNIDENTIFIED CONGOLESE ARTIST (DEM. REP. OF THE CONGO OR ANGOLA)
Comb
Wood
2 × 6.3 in. (5 × 16 cm)
Collection of the Fowler Museum at UCLA, Museum Purchase, X77.1323
Photo: Don Cole, Fowler Museum at UCLA

UNIDENTIFIED CONGOLESE ARTIST (DEM. REP. OF THE CONGO)
Comb
Wood
11.2 × 3.3 in. (28.3 × 8.4 cm)
Collection of the Fowler Museum at UCLA, Gift of the Wellcome Trust, X65.10033
Photo: Don Cole, Fowler Museum at UCLA

UNIDENTIFIED CONGOLESE ARTIST (KWANGO REGION, DEM. REP. OF THE CONGO)
Comb
Ivory
5.3 × 2 in. (13.4 × 5.1 cm)
Collection of the Fowler Museum at UCLA, Gift of the Wellcome Trust, X67.716
Photo: Don Cole, Fowler Museum at UCLA

UNIDENTIFIED CONGOLESE ARTIST (DEM. REP. OF THE CONGO)
Hair comb
Ivory
5.9 × 1.6 in. (15 × 4 cm)
Collection of the Fowler Museum at UCLA, Gift of the Wellcome Trust, X65.8507
Photo: Don Cole, Fowler Museum at UCLA

UNIDENTIFIED CONGOLESE ARTIST (DEM. REP. OF THE CONGO)
Hair pin
Copper alloy
4.75 × 1.1 in. (12.1 × 2.9 cm)
Collection of the Fowler Museum at UCLA, Gift of the Wellcome Trust, X65.8990
Photo: Don Cole, Fowler Museum at UCLA

UNIDENTIFIED CONGOLESE ARTIST (DEM. REP. OF THE CONGO)
Hair pin
Ivory
4.7 × 0.8 in. (12 × 2 cm)
Collection of the Fowler Museum at UCLA, Gift of the Wellcome Trust, X67.802
Photo: Don Cole, Fowler Museum at UCLA

UNIDENTIFIED CONGOLESE ARTIST (DEM. REP. OF THE CONGO)
Hair pin
Ivory
4.5 × 0.6 in. (11.5 × 1.5 cm)
Collection of the Fowler Museum at UCLA, Gift of the Wellcome Trust, X67.815
Photo: Don Cole, Fowler Museum at UCLA

UNIDENTIFIED CONGOLESE ARTIST (KWANGO REGION, DEM. REP. OF THE CONGO)
Hair pin
Copper alloy
13.5 in. (34.3 cm)
Collection of the Fowler Museum at UCLA, Gift of the Wellcome Trust, X65.9191
Photo: Don Cole, Fowler Museum at UCLA

UNIDENTIFIED DAN OR KRAN ARTIST (LIBERIA)
Go Ge or *Go Glih* Mask
Wood, animal skin and hair
11.5 × 5.5 × 6.5 in. (29.2 × 14 × 16.5 cm)
Collection of Kent State University School of Art, 2001.1.67

UNIDENTIFIED EGYPTIAN ARTIST
Statuette of Isis and Horus, 305–30 BCE
Egypt, Greco-Roman Period, probably Ptolemaic Dynasty
Bronze, solid cast
6.8 × 1.8 × 2.6 in. (17.3 × 4.6 × 6.5 cm)
Collection of the Cleveland Museum of Art, Bequest of John L. Severance, 1942.774

UNIDENTIFIED EGYPTIAN ARTIST
Stele of Djedatumiufankh, 664–525 BCE
Egypt, Late Period, Dynasty 26
Brown quartzite
10.8 × 9.8 in. (27.5 × 25 cm)
Collection of the Cleveland Museum of Art, Gift of the John Huntington Art and Polytechnic Trust, 1920.1977

UNIDENTIFIED EGYPTIAN ARTIST
Statuette of Khonsu, 664–525 BCE
Egypt, Late Period, Dynasty 26 or later
Bronze, solid cast
2.1 × 1.4 in. (5.4 × 3.7 cm)
Collection of the Cleveland Museum of Art, Gift of the John Huntington Art and Polytechnic Trust, 1914.572

UNIDENTIFIED EGYPTIAN ARTIST
Wig ornamentation elements (sidelocks, rosettes, and cylinders), 1980–1801 BCE
Egypt, Middle Kingdom, Dynasty 12
Silver
Between 0.5–1.0 in. (1.2–2.5 cm)
Collection of the Cleveland Museum of Art, Gift of the John Huntington Art and Polytechnic Trust, 1914.795

UNIDENTIFIED IVORIAN ARTIST
Comb
Wood
2.4 × 8 in. (6 × 20.3 cm)
Collection of the Fowler Museum at UCLA, Gift of Elaine Irell, X72.794
Photo: Don Cole, Fowler Museum at UCLA

UNIDENTIFIED LUBA ARTIST (DEM. REP. OF THE CONGO)
Comb
Wood, copper wire
6.5 × 3.5 in. (16.5 × 9 cm)
Collection of the Fowler Museum at UCLA, Museum Purchase, 382.176
Photo: Don Cole, Fowler Museum at UCLA

UNIDENTIFIED LUBA ARTIST (DEM. REP. OF THE CONGO)
Hair pin
Iron
5.7 × 1.6 × 0.2 in. (14.5 × 4 × 0.5 cm)
Collection of the Fowler Museum at UCLA, Museum Purchase, 382.41
Photo: Don Cole, Fowler Museum at UCLA

UNIDENTIFIED MANGBETU ARTIST (DEM. REP. OF THE CONGO)
Double comb
Bamboo, raffia
9.2 × 4.2 in. (23.4 × 10.6 cm)
Collection of the Fowler Museum at UCLA, Museum Purchase, 391.70
Photo: Don Cole, Fowler Museum at UCLA

UNIDENTIFIED MANGBETU ARTIST (DEM. REP. OF THE CONGO)
Hair pin
Ivory
12.2 in. (31 cm)
Collection of the Fowler Museum at UCLA, Museum Purchase, 391.40
Photo: Don Cole, Fowler Museum at UCLA

UNIDENTIFIED MENDE ARTIST (SIERRA LEONE)
Sowei (bundu) Helmet Mask, 20th century
Wood, aluminum strips, nails
15 × 9.25 in. (38.1 × 23.5 cm)
Collection of Kent State University School of Art, 92.6.1

UNIDENTIFIED MENDE ARTIST (SIERRA LEONE)
Sowei (bundu) Helmet Mask, 20th century
Wood, dark pigment
15 × 9.25 in. (38.1 × 23.5 cm)
Collection of Kent State University School of Art, 92.6.5

UNIDENTIFIED MENDE ARTIST (SIERRA LEONE)
Sowei (bundu) Helmet Mask, 20th century
Wood, dark pigment
13 × 9.25 in. (33 × 23.5 cm)
Collection of Kent State University School of Art, 94.5.1

UNIDENTIFIED NANDE ARTIST (DEM. REP. OF THE CONGO)
Comb
Wood
5.9 × 3.4 in. (15 × 8.5 cm)
Collection of the Fowler Museum at UCLA, Museum Purchase, 392.145
Photo: Don Cole, Fowler Museum at UCLA

UNIDENTIFIED NDYUKA (OR DJUKA) ARTIST (GODO OLO, SURINAME)
Comb
Wood
10.5 × 3.2 in. (26.6 × 8 cm)
Collection of the Fowler Museum at UCLA, Gift of William Lloyd Davis and the Rogers Family Foundation, X81.1332
Photo: Don Cole, Fowler Museum at UCLA

UNIDENTIFIED NDYUKA (OR DJUKA) ARTIST (UPPER TAPANAHONY RIVER, SURINAME)
Comb
Wood
12.5 × 2.25 in. (31.8 × 5.7 cm)
Collection of the Fowler Museum at UCLA, Gift of Mr. W. Thomas Davis, X73.431
Photo: Don Cole, Fowler Museum at UCLA

UNIDENTIFIED NIGERIAN ARTIST
Hair ornament, *ca.* 1932
Bone
5.5 × 1.4 in. (14 × 3.5 cm)
Collection of the Fowler Museum at UCLA, Gift of the Wellcome Trust, X65.9067
Photo: Don Cole, Fowler Museum at UCLA

UNIDENTIFIED SARAMAKA ARTIST (BOTOPASI, SURINAME)
Comb (*penti*)
Incised wood
7.5 × 1.5 in. (19.1 × 3.8 cm)
Collection of the Fowler Museum at UCLA, Museum Purchase, X70.40
Photo: Don Cole, Fowler Museum at UCLA

UNIDENTIFIED SONGYE ARTIST (DEM. REP. OF THE CONGO)
Figure, 20th century
Wood
6 × 3 in. (15.2 × 7.6 cm)
Collection of Kent State University School of Art, 99.3.14

UNIDENTIFIED SONGYE ARTIST (DEM. REP. OF THE CONGO)
Hair pin, before 1937
Ivory
6.1 in. (15.6 cm)
Collection of the Fowler Museum at UCLA, Gift of the Wellcome Trust, X65.9119
Photo: Don Cole, Fowler Museum at UCLA

UNIDENTIFIED SOUTH AFRICAN ARTIST
Hair pin
Bone, thread, beads, string
10.5 in. (26.7 cm)
Collection of the Fowler Museum at UCLA, Gift of the Wellcome Trust, X67.674
Photo: Don Cole, Fowler Museum at UCLA

UNIDENTIFIED SOUTH AFRICAN ARTIST
Hair pin
Beads, steel
10.5 × 0.75 in. (26.7 × 1.9 cm)
Collection of the Fowler Museum at UCLA, Gift of the Wellcome Trust, X67.923
Photo: Don Cole, Fowler Museum at UCLA

UNIDENTIFIED SURINAMESE ARTIST (POKIGRON, SURINAME)
Comb, early 20th century
Incised wood
7.75 × 1.5 in. (19.7 × 3.8 cm)
Collection of the Fowler Museum at UCLA, Museum Purchase, X70.41
Photo: Don Cole, Fowler Museum at UCLA

UNIDENTIFIED TETELA ARTIST (DEM. REP. OF THE CONGO)
Hair pin
Copper alloy
4.25 × 2 in. (10.8 × 5.1 cm)
Collection of the Fowler Museum at UCLA, Gift of the Wellcome Trust, X65.8988
Photo: Don Cole, Fowler Museum at UCLA

UNIDENTIFIED YAKA ARTIST (DEM. REP. OF THE CONGO)
Comb
Wood
6.5 × 1.3 in. (16.5 × 3.2 cm)
Collection of the Fowler Museum at UCLA, Gift of the Wellcome Trust, X67.702
Photo: Don Cole, Fowler Museum at UCLA

UNIDENTIFIED YAKA ARTIST (DEM. REP. OF THE CONGO)
Comb
Wood, metal
8.1 × 1.1 in. (20.6 × 2.9 cm)
Collection of the Fowler Museum at UCLA, Gift of the Wellcome Trust, X67.704
Photo: Don Cole, Fowler Museum at UCLA

UNIDENTIFIED YORUBA ARTIST (NIGERIA)
White beaded cap (*orikogbofo*), 1988
Glass beads, burlap, cloth, thread
7 × 7.4 × 9 in. (18 × 19 cm × 23 cm)
Collection of the Fowler Museum at UCLA, Museum Purchase with Manus Fund, X91.80
Photo: Don Cole, Fowler Museum at UCLA

UNIDENTIFIED ZANDE ARTIST (DEM. REP. OF THE CONGO)
Comb
Ivory
10.3 in. (26.1 cm)
Collection of the Fowler Museum at UCLA, Gift of the Wellcome Trust, X67.728
Photo: Don Cole, Fowler Museum at UCLA

VAN DER ZEE, JAMES
Portrait of a Black Girl in a Dance Outfit, 1936
Cyanotype
6.5 × 4.5 in. (16.5 × 11.4 cm)
Courtesy of Melvin Homes Collection of African American Art
Photo: Tyler Fine Art, Melvin Homes Collection of African American Art

VAN DER ZEE, JAMES
Harlem, ca. 1940
Silver gelatin print
8.5 × 6 in. (21.6 × 15.2 cm)
Courtesy of Melvin Homes Collection of African American Art
Photo: Tyler Fine Art, Melvin Homes Collection of African American Art

VIKTOR, LINA IRIS
The Massacre of the Innocents... No. XXIV from the *Dark Continent* series, 2017
24-karat gold, acrylic, ink, print on cotton rag paper
9.8 × 7.8 in. (24.9 × 19.8 cm)
Courtesy of CCH Pounder-Koné
Photo: © Artist, courtesy of Mariane Ibrahim Gallery

Wanted by the FBI: Angela Davis, 1970
Poster (reproduced from digital image)
16.1 × 10.6 in. (41 × 27 cm)
Courtesy of the Angela Y. Davis Papers, Schlesinger Library, Radcliffe institute, Harvard University

WHITE, NAFIS M.
A Burst of Light, 2018
Hair, embodied knowledge, ancestral recall, bobby pins
36 × 42 in. (91.4 × 106.7 cm)
Collection of RISD Museum, purchased with funds provided by the Perelman Family Foundation in support of the acquisition of artwork by graduates of the Rhode Island School of Design, 2018.38

WILEY, KEHINDE

Tanisha Crichlow (portrait of Henrietta Maria of France, Queen Consort of England, Scotland and Ireland), 2015
Oil on canvas
83 × 71 in. (210.8 × 180.3 cm), framed
Courtesy of the Mott-Warsh Collection, Flint, Michigan, 2015.867

ZODROS, MASA

Femme Totem Blue, 2018
Unique digital photograph
17.5 × 30 in. (44.5 × 76.2 cm)
Courtesy of the Artist

ZODROS, MASA

Petite Lina, 2018
Digital photograph (Edition of 30)
20 × 20 in. (50.8 × 50.8 cm)
Courtesy of the Artist

MADAM C. J. WALKER LOANS

Beauty and Success! Madam C. J. Walker advertisement, 1920s
Paper (reproduced from digital image)
24 × 18.1 in. (61 × 46 cm)
Courtesy of Beinecke Rare Book and Manuscript Library, Yale University

Walker Convention Badge
Ribbon, gold, metal (ribbon reproduced from digital image)
Approx. 4 × 1 in. (10.2 × 2.5 cm)
Courtesy of Madam C. J. Walker Supplemental Collection, Indiana Historical Society

The Madam C. J. Walker System of Beauty Culture, 1928
Ink on paper (reproduced from digital image)
Courtesy of Madam C. J. Walker Supplemental Collection, Indiana Historical Society

Hot Comb Demonstration, 1915
Acetate negative (reproduced from digital image)
4 × 5 in. (10.2 × 12.7 cm)
Courtesy of Madam C. J. Walker Supplemental Collection, Indiana Historical Society

Vanishing Cream Facial, *ca.* 1920
Photograph (reproduced from digital image)
8 × 10 in. (20.3 × 25.4 cm)
Courtesy of Madam C. J. Walker Supplemental Collection, Indiana Historical Society

Madam Walker Products Advertisement, *ca.* 1907
Photograph (reproduced from digital image)
5 × 7 in. (12.7 × 17.8 cm)
Courtesy of Madam C. J. Walker Supplemental Collection, Indiana Historical Society

Madam C. J. Walker's Gift Package, *ca.* 1925
Photograph (reproduced from digital image)
8 × 10 in. (20.3 × 25.4 cm)
Courtesy of Madam C. J. Walker Supplemental Collection, Indiana Historical Society

Photograph of Madam C. J. Walker, 1914–1915
4 × 6 in. (10.2 × 15.2 cm) (reproduced from digital image)
Courtesy of Madam C. J. Walker Supplemental Collection, Indiana Historical Society

Walker Special Outfit, 1930s
Ink on paper (reproduced from digital image)
Courtesy of Madam C. J. Walker Supplemental Collection, Indiana Historical Society

Walker Newsletter, vol. V, no. VII, October 1953
Ink on paper (reproduced from digital image)
Courtesy of Madam C. J. Walker Supplemental Collection, Indiana Historical Society

LOANS FROM THE COLLECTION OF DR. WILLIE MORROW

(Photos by Kent State University Communication and Marketing)

Marcel curlers, *ca.* 1890
Wood and iron

Marcel curlers, *ca.* 1890

Kerosene oven with curling iron, *ca.* 1890

Steam curling iron, *ca.* 1890

First generation hand clippers, *ca.* 1890
Stainless steel structure with oscillating blades

Second generation hand clippers, *ca.* 1900
Stainless steel structure with oscillating blades

Moore Electric Hair Cutter, *ca.* 1920
Iron case, electromagnetic motor, oscillating blades

Stove with hot comb and three-barrel Marcel curler, *ca.* 1920
Iron

Electric stove with removable Marcel curler, *ca.* 1920
Iron

Kerosene heater with pressing iron, *ca.* 1920

Electric pressing iron with curling implements, 1920s

Electric Marcel waver, *ca.* 1920
Iron and plastic

Electric Marcel waver, *ca.* 1920
Iron and plastic

Booklet from the 16th Annual Convention of the National Beauty Culturalist League, 1936
Ink on paper

Hand hairdryer, *ca.* 1920–1930
Steel and plastic

Hand hairdryer, *ca.* 1920–1930
Aluminum and plastic

Unknown photographer, *Hair being straightened with an iron*

White Rose Petroleum Jelly, *ca.* 1980
Scalp and hair grease
Approx. 2 × 3 in. (5.1 × 7.6 cm)

Posner's Special Gro hair conditioner, *ca.* 1960
Scalp and hair grease
Approx. 3 × 3 in. (7.6 × 7.6 cm)

Selection of African combs from the collection of Dr. Willie Morrow
Hand carved wood, 20th century

Barber pole from Dr. Willie Morrow's first barbershop, *ca.* 1950
Aluminum, wood, paper, vinyl, and glass
16 × 9 in. (40.6 × 22.9 cm)

Sally Beauty professional jumbo end wraps, *ca.* 1990
Paper squares for rolling hair
2.75 × 4.25 in (7 × 10.8 cm)

Lucky Brown Hair Dressing, 1937
Scalp and hair grease
1.75 × 3 in. (4.4 × 7.6 cm)

Corn shuck/grinder, *ca.* 1850
Cast iron
Approx. 10 × 8 × 16 in. (25.4 × 20.3 × 40.6 cm)

Selection of Picks from the collection of Dr. Willie Morrow, 1962-1974

Poro College Diploma signed by Annie M. Turnbo Malone, 1927
Ink on paper
Approx. 8.5 × 11 in. (21.6 × 27.9 cm)

Missouri State Board of Cosmetology Permanent License
Ink on paper

Drawing of Man with Dreadlocks, 1982
Graphite on paper

400 Years Without a Comb: The Inferior Seed, 1989
VHS

Sketches from *400 Years Without a Comb*, *ca.* 1971–73.
Graphite on paper
Approx. 11.75 × 36 in. (29.8 × 91.4 cm)

Photograph of Dr. Willie Morrow's Barbershop in San Diego, 1960s

Curly Cues booklets, 1974
Ink on paper

Beauty Trade, 1958
Approx. 8 × 10 in. (20.3 × 25.4 cm)

Shop Talk Journal of Cosmetology, 1998
Approx. 8 × 10 in. (20.3 × 25.4 cm)

Salon Sense (vol. 2 no. 8), 2000
Approx. 8 × 10 in. (20.3 × 25.4 cm)

Beauty (vol. 3 no. 2), 1985
8 × 10 in. (20.3 × 25.4 cm)

Beauty (vol. 2 no. 4), 1986
Approx. 8 × 10 in. (20.3 × 25.4 cm)

Shop Talk Journal of Cosmetology (vol. 6 no. 2), 1987
Approx. 8 × 10 in. (20.3 × 25.4 cm)

Dr. Willie Morrow
The Principles of Cutting and Styling Hair (First Edition), 1966
Ink on paper
Approx. 5 × 8 in (12.7 × 20.3 cm)

The Art and Science: The Willie Morrow Weaving Technique, 1988
VHS tape
Approx. 7 × 4 × 1 in. (17.8 × 10.2 × 2.5 cm)

Willie Morrow's Unbreakable Thermo Blow Dry Nozzle, 1998
Plastic and steel
Approx. 3 × 3 × 6 in. (7.6 × 7.6 × 17.8 cm)

Madam C. J. Walker's Wonderful Scalp Ointment, *ca.* 1900
Scalp and hair grease

E.F. Young hair products, *ca.* 1930s

Dr. Willie Morrow's California Green Press-in-Cream, 2010
Mineral cream for straightening curly hair

Dr. Willie Morrow's Therma-Cream, 2010
Mineral cream for straightening curly hair

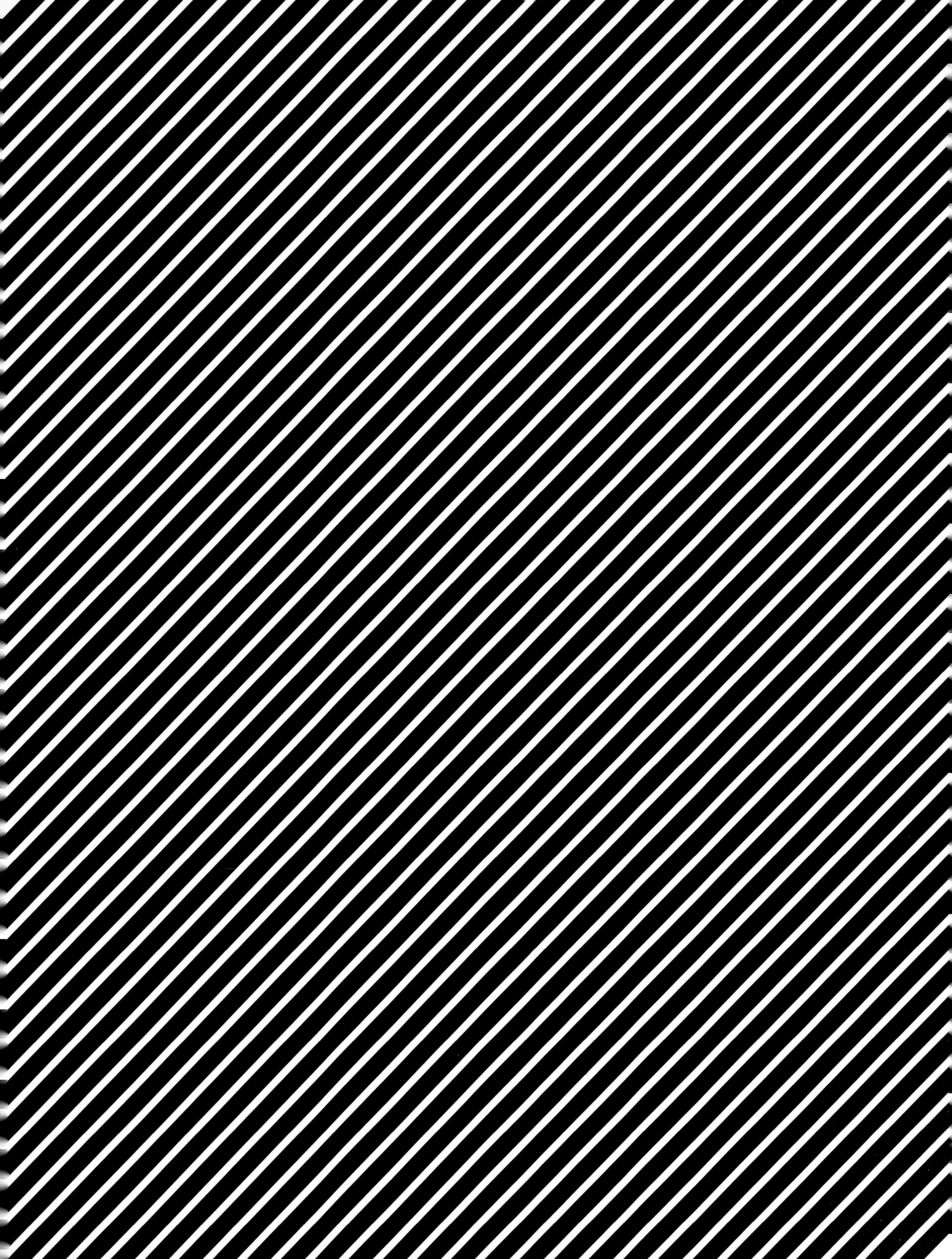

BIBLIOGRAPHY

Aju, A. I. Asiw. "Political Motivation and Oral Historical Traditions in Africa: The Case of Yoruba Crowns, 1900–1960." *Africa: Journal of the International African Institute* 46, no. 2 (1976): 113–27.

Alexander, Elizabeth. "Of the Black and Boisterous Hair." *Lorna Simpson Collages.* San Francisco: Chronical Books, 2018: 1–4.

Alexander, Shai. "A Point of View: Sometimes, I am my Hair – Untangling the Nuances of Coiffure in the Workplace." *The Inclusion Solution*, December 13, 2018. http://www.theinclusionsolution.me/point-view-sometimes-hair-untangling-nuances-coiffure-workplace-Black-women-natural-hair/.

Aptheker, Bettina. *The Morning Breaks: The Trial of Angela Davis.* New York: Cornell University Press, 1999.

Ashley, Wendy, and Jodi Constantine Brown. "Attachment THAIRapy: A Culturally Relevant Treatment Paradigm for African American Foster Youth." *Journal of Black Studies* 46, no. 6 (2015): 587–604.

Azoulay, Ariella Aïsha. *Potential History: Unlearning Imperialism.* London: Verso, 2019.

Baldwin, Davarian L., "Madam C. J. Walker and the 'recreation' of Race Womanhood." In *The Modern Girl Around the World: Consumption, Modernity, and Globalization*, edited by Alys Eve Weinbaum et al., 55–74. Duke University Press: Durham and London. 2008.

Bankhead, Teiahsha, and Tabora Johnson, "Self Esteem, Hair Esteem and Black Women with Natural Hair." *International Journal of Education and Social Science* 1, no. 4 (November 2014): 92–102.

Banks, Ingrid. *Hair Matters: Beauty, Power, and Black Women's Consciousness*. New York: New York University Press, 2000.

Barnwell, Andrea D., and Isolde Brielmaier. *Engaging the Camera: African Women, Portraits and the Photographs of Hector Acebes.* Atlanta: Spelman College Museum of Fine Art, 2004.

Beckwith, Carol, and Angela Fisher. *African Ceremonies*. Ann Arbor: Harry N. Abrams, 1999.

Belisle, Brooke. "Felt Surface, Visible Image: Lorna Simpson's Photography and the Embodiment of Appearance." *Photography and Culture* 4, no. 2 (July 2011): 157–178.

Bey, Jamila. "'Going Natural' Requires Lots of Help." *The New York Times*, June 8, 2011.

Bey, Sharif. "Augusta Savage: Sacrifice, Social Responsibility, and Early African American Art Education." *Studies in Art Education* 58, no. 2 (April 2017): 125–40.

Birt, Rodger C. "For the Record: James VanDerZee, Marcus Garvey, and the UNIA Photographs." *Exposure* 27, no. 4 (Fall 1990): 6.

Bothmer, Bernard V., Madeleine E. Cody, Paul Edmund Stanwick, and Marsha Hill. *Egyptian Art: Selected Writings of Bernard V. Bothmer.* Oxford University Press, 2004.

Brown, Nadia. "'It's More than Hair... That's Why You Should Care': The Politics of Appearance for Black Women State Legislators." *Politics, Groups, and Identities* 2, no. 3 (2014): 295–312.

Brooks, Wanda M., and Jonda C. McNair. "'Combing' Through Representations of Black Girls' Hair in African American Children's Literature." *Children's Literature in Education* 46, (September 2015): 296–307.

Byrd, Ayana D., and Lori L. Tharps. *Hair Story: Untangling the Roots of Black Hair in America*. 2nd ed. New York: St. Martin's Griffin, 2014.

Caldwell, Pamela. "A Hair Piece: Perspectives on the Intersections of Race and Gender." *Duke Law Journal* 2, no. 4 (1991): 365-396.

Capodilupo, Christina M. "One Size Does Not Fit All: Using Variables Other Than the Thin Ideal to Understand Black Women's Body Image." *Cultural Diversity & Ethnic Minority Psychology* 21, no. 2 (2015): 268-278.

Carrington, André M. "The Cultural Politics of Worldmaking Practice: Kehinde Wiley's Cosmopolitanism." *African & Black Diaspora* 8, no. 2 (July 2015): 245-57.

Clancy, Majella, and Louise Wallace. "Painting, Gender, and Space: Aspects of Contemporary Women's Painting Practice in Context." *Women's Studies* 41, no. 8 (December 2012): 959-975.

Copeland, Huey. "'Bye, Bye Black Girl': Lorna Simpson's Figurative Retreat." *Art Journal* 64, no. 2 (Summer 2005) 62-77.

Craig, Maxine, "The Decline and Fall of the Conk; or, How to Read a Process." *Fashion Theory: The Journal of Dress, Body & Culture* 1, no. 4 (1997): 339-419.

Crenshaw, Kimberlé Williams. "Whose Story is it Anyway?: Feminist and Antiracist Appropriations of Anita Hill." In *Race-ing Justice, En-gendering Power: Essays on Anita Hill, Clarence Thomas, and the Construction of Social Reality,* edited by Toni Morrison, 402-440. New York: Pantheon Books, 1992.

Cross, Lauren. "Mothers-For-Natural-Hair: The Afro-Cyberella's Social Media Guide to Afrocentric Hair." In *Mothering and Literacies*, edited by Linda Shuford Evans and Amanda B. Richey. Bradford: Demeter Press, 2013: 221-236.

Curry-Evans, Kim, and Neal A. Lester. *Hair Stories*. Scottsdale: Scottsdale Museum of Contemporary Art, 2004.

Cutler, Jody B. "A New Republic Kehinde Wiley." *Nka: Journal of Contemporary African Art* 2015, no. 38/39 (November 2016): 220-23.

Cutler, Jody B. "Kehinde Wiley: 3-D." *International Review of African American Art* 26, no. 2 (April 2016): 52-55.

Dallow, Jessica, Betye Saar, Lezley Saar, Alison Saar, Barbara C. Matilsky, and Tracye Saar-Cavanaugh. *Family Legacies: The Art of Betye, Lezley, and Alison Saar.* Chapel Hill: Ackland Art Museum, in association with Seattle and London: University of Washington, 2005.

Davis, Angela Y. "Afro Images: Politics, Fashion, and Nostalgia." *Critical Inquiry* 21, no. 1 (1994) 37-45.

Davis, Daniel, Afiya M. Mbilishaka, and Terrisia Templeton. "From 'About Me' to 'About We': Therapeutic Intentions of Black American Women's Natural Hair Blogs." *Journal of Social Media in Society* 8, no.1 (2019): 105-123.

Davis-Sivasothy, Angela. *The Science of Black Hair: A Comprehensive Guide to Textured Care*. Stafford: Saga Publishing Company LLC, 2011.

Dawson, Gail A., Katherine A. Karl, and Joy V. Peluchette. "Hair Matters: Toward Understanding Natural Black Hair Bias in the Workplace." *Journal of Leadership & Organizational Studies* 26, no. 3 (August 2019): 389-401.

Dodd, Alexandra. "Dressed to Thrill: The Victorian Postmodern and Counter-Archival Imaginings in the Work of Mary Sibande." *Critical Arts: A South-North Journal of Cultural & Media Studies* 24, no. 3 (November 2010): 467-74.

Donahoo, Saran. "Owning Black Hair: The Pursuit of Identity and Authenticity in Higher Education." In *Navigating Micro-Aggressions Toward Women in Higher Education,* edited by Ursula Thomas, 73-95. Hershey, PA: IGI Global, 2019.

Edqvist, Pia. "Materials of Construction and Use: African Hair Combs from the Museum of Archaeology and Anthropology, Cambridge." In *Origins of the Afro Comb, 6,000 Years of Culture, Politics and Identity*, edited by Sally Ann-Ashton, 24-29. Cambridge: Fitzwilliam Museum, 2013.

Ellington, Tameka N. "Social Networking Sites: A Support System for African-American Women Wearing Natural Hair." *International Journal of Fashion Design, Technology and Education* 8, no. 1 (2015): 21-29.

Ellington, Tameka N. "Bloggers, Vloggers, and a Virtual Sorority: A Means of Support for African American Women Wearing Natural Hair." *Journalism and Mass Communication* 4, no. 9 (September 2014): 552–564.

Ellington, Tameka N. "Natural Hair." In *Berg Encyclopedia of World Dress and Fashion*, edited by Joanne B. Eicher and Doran Ross, vol. 1. New York: Oxford University Press, 2010.

Ellis-Hervey, Nina, Ashley Doss, DeShae Davis, Robert Nicks, Perla Araiza. "African American Personal Presentation: Psychology of Hair and Self-Perception." *Journal of Black Studies* 47, no. 8 (November 2016): 869–882.

Ellsworth, Kirstin L. "Africobra and the Negotiation of Visual Afrocentrisms." *Civilisations* 58, no. 23 (2009): 21–38.

Enekwechi, Adaeze. "Children's Literature and the Politics of Hair in Books for African American Children." *Children's Literature Association Quarterly* 24, no. 4 (Winter 1999): 195–200.

Enwezor, Okwui, ed. *Events of the Self: Portraiture and Social Identity: Contemporary African Photography from the Walther Collection.* Göttingen: Steidl, 2010.

Faines, Ayesha K. "Did Natural Hair Kill the Black Hair Salon?" *Atlanta Black Star*, August 20, 2015. https://atlantaBlackstar.com/2015/08/20/natural-hair-kill-Black-hair-salon/.

Finley, Taryn. "Appeals Court Rules Employers Can Ban Dreadlocks at Work," *Huffington Post*, September 20, 2016. https://www.huffingtonpost.com/entry/appeals-court-rules-dreadlocks-work_us_57e0252ae4b0071a6e08a7c3.

Fitzpatrick, Orla. "Bristle: Hair and Hegemony." *Bristle: Hair and Hegemony, 8 July – 23 September 2017,* edited by Roisin Kennedy, Niamh McGuinne, Aoife Ruane. Drogheda, Ireland: Highlanes Municipal Art Gallery, 2017.

Fletcher, Joanne. *Ancient Egyptian Hair: A Study in Style, Form and Function*, Unpublished PhD thesis, University of Manchester, 1995.

Fletcher, Joanne. "Hair." In *Ancient Egyptian Materials and Technology*, edited by Paul T. Nicholson and Ian Shaw, 495–501. Cambridge: Cambridge University Press, 2000.

Gathers, Raechele Cochran, Michelle Jankowski, Melody Eide, Henry W. Lim. "Hair Grooming Practices and Central Centrifugal Cicatricial Alopecia," *Journal of the American Academy of Dermatology* 60, no. 4 (April 2009): 574–578.

Greene, Wendy D. "Black Women Can't Have Blonde Hair... in the Workplace," *Journal of Gender Race & Justice* 14, no. 2 (Spring 2011): 405–430.

Gill, Tiffany M. "#TeamNatural: Black Hair and The Politics of Community in Digital Media," *Nka Journal of Contemporary African Art* 2015, no. 37 (2015): 70–79.

Gill, Tiffany M. *Beauty Shop Politics: African American Women's Activism in the Beauty Industry.* Urbana: University of Illinois Press, 2010.

Griffin, Chanté. "How Natural Black Hair at Work Became a Civil Rights Issue." *JSTOR Daily*, July 3, 2019. https://daily.jstor.org/how-natural-Black-hair-at-work-became-a-civil-rights-issue/

Hafkin, Nancy J., and Sophia Huyer, eds. *Cinderella or Cyberella? Empowering Women in the Knowledge Society.* Bloomfield: Kumarian Press, Inc., 2006.

Hajek, Olaf, Robert Klanten, and Sonja Commentz. *Olaf Hajek: Flowerhead*. Berlin: Gestalten, 2009.

Hajek, Olaf, Robert Klanten, and Hendrik Hellige. *Black Antoinette: The Work of Olaf Hajek*. Berlin: Gestalten, 2012.

Hargo, Brina. "Hair Matters: African American Women and the Natural Hair Aesthetic." Thesis, Georgia State University, 2011.

Haxall, Daniel. "In the Spirit of Négritude: Kehinde Wiley in Africa." *Nka: Journal of Contemporary African Art*, no. 41 (November 2017): 126–39.

Helton, Laura, Justin Leroy, Max A. Mishler, Samantha Seeley, Shauna Sweeney. "The Question of Recovery: An Introduction," *Social Text* 33, no. 4 (2015): 1–18.

Herreman, Frank, and Roy Sieber, eds. *Hair in African Art and Culture*. New York: Museum for African Art, 2000.

Holton, Mark. "On the Geographies of Hair: Exploring the Entangled Margins of the Human Body." *Progress in Human Geography.* (March 2019). <https://doi.org/10.1177/0309132519838055>

hooks, bell. "From Black is a Woman's Color." *Callaloo*, no. 39 (Spring 1989): 382–388.

hooks, bell. "Straightening Our Hair." In *Tenderheaded: A Comb-Bending Collection of Hair Stories*, edited by Pamela Johnson and Juliette Harris, 111–115. New York: Washington Square Press, 2002.

Horton, Randal. *Margaret Bowland: Painting the Roses Red.* Raleigh: Contemporary Art Museum of Raleigh, 2018. Exhibition Guide.

Ibos, Caroline. "Subalterns Can Dream. Mary Sibande and the Resistance of South African Domestic Workers." *Sociétés & Représentations* 48, no. 2 (2019): 239–254.

Igor, Efeoghene. "Rethinking the Egalitarian Potential of Postapartheid South Africa: Zanele Muholi's Intervention." *Radical History Review* 2016, no. 126 (October 2016): 181–93.

Imperato, Gavin H., and Pascal James Imperato. *Bundu, Sowei Headpieces of the Sande Society of West Africa: The Imperato Family Collection*. Bayside: Queensborough Community College, 2012.

Jablonski, Nina G., and George Chaplin. "The Evolution of Skin Pigmentation and Hair Texture in People of African Ancestry." *Dermatologic Clinic* 32, no. 2 (2014): 113–121.

Jackson, Brian Keith, Krista A. Thompson, and Kehinde Wiley. *Black Light*. Brooklyn, NY: powerHouse Books, 2009.

Jackson, Tanisha. "Introducing Charly Palmer: Tar Baby and Culturally Responsive Teaching." *Art Education* 65, no. 6 (November 2012): 6–11.

Jacobs-Huey, Lanita. *From the Kitchen to the Parlor: Language and Becoming in African American Women's Hair Care*. New York: Oxford University Press, 2006.

Johnson, Angela Davis. "The Artist-Activist: History and Healing through Art." *Black History Bulletin* 79, no. 1 (2016): 27–33.

Johnson, Elizabeth. *Resistance and Empowerment in Black Women's Hair Styling*. Burlington: Ashgate Publishing, 2013.

Johnson, Tabora A., and Teiahsha Bankhead. "Hair It Is: Examining the Experiences of Black Women with Natural Hair." *Open Journal of Social Sciences* 2, no. 1 (2014): 86–100.

Keller, Candace M. "Framed and Hidden Histories: West African Photography from Local to Global Contexts." *African Arts* 47, no. 4 (2014): 36–47.

Kelley, Robin D. G. "Nap Time: Historicizing the Afro." *Fashion Theory* 1, no. 4 (1997): 339–51.

Kimbell, Regina, and Jay Bluemke, directors. *My Nappy Roots: A Journey Through Black Hair-itage*. Virgin Moon Entertainment, 2010. 90 min.

Labelle, Marie-Louise. "Beads of Life: Eastern and Southern African Adornments." *African Arts* 38, no. 1 (2005): 12–93.

Lafforgue, Eric. *Éthiopie*. Bordeaux: Elytis, 2018.

Lawal, Babatunde. "Àwòrán: Representing the Self and Its Metaphysical Other in Yoruba Art." *The Art Bulletin* 83, no. 3 (2001): 498–526.

LeBaron, Michelle, and Janie Sarra, eds. *Changing our Worlds: Art as Transformative Practice*. Stellenbosch, South Africa: African Sun Media, 2018.

Lester, Neal A. "Nappy Edges and Goldy Locks: African-American Daughters and the Politics of Hair." *The Lion and the Unicorn* 24, no. 2 (2000): 201–224.

Lewis, Marva L. "Hair Combing Interactions: A New Paradigm for Research With African American Mothers." *American Journal of Orthopsychiatry* 69, no. 4 (1999): 504–514.

Martin, Delita. *I Come from Women Who Could Fly: New Work from Delita Martin, May 29–August 31, 2014.* Pine Bluff, Ark: Arts & Science Center for Southeast Arkansas, 2014.

Martin, Delita Shante, Vicki Meek, Kheli R Willetts, Joshua Asante, and Garry Reece. *Shadows in the Garden*. Huffman, Texas: Black Box Press Studio, 2019.

Mbilishaka, Afiya M. "PsychoHairapy: Using Hair as an Entry Point into Black Women's Spiritual and Mental Health." *Meridians: Feminism, Race & Transnationalism* 16, no. 2 (2018): 382–392.

Mbilishaka, Afiya M. "Black Lives (and Stories) Matter: Race Narrative Therapy in Black Hair Care Spaces." *Community Psychology in Global Perspective* 4, no. 2 (2018): 22–33.

Mbilishaka, Afiya M. "Strands of Intimacy: Black Women's Narratives of Hair and Intimate Relationships with Men." *Journal of Black Sexuality and Relationships*, 5, no. 1 (2018): 43-61.

Mbilishaka, Afiya M., and Avery Lacey. "Don't Sweat Your Hair Out: The Frequency of Exercise for African American Women with Natural Hair" *Journal of Exercise and Nutrition* 2, no. 1 (2019): 4–11.

Mbilishaka, Afiya M., Wilson I.-P., Ray M., Hall J., Hall J. "'No toques mi pelo' (don't touch my hair): decoding Afro-Cuban identity politics through hair," *African and Black Diaspora* 13, no. 1 (2020): 114–126.

Mbilishaka, Afiya M. and Danielle Apugo. "Brushed aside: African American women's narratives of hair bias in school," *Race Ethnicity and Education* (2020): 1–20.

Mendelsohn, Meredith. "How an Artist Learned About Freedom From 'The Negro Motorist Green Book.'" *The New York Times*. January 19, 2018.

Mensah, Charlotte. *Good Hair: The Essential Guide to Afro, Textured and Curly Hair*. London: Penguin Life, 2020.

Mercer, Kobena. "Black Hair/Style Politics," In *Black British Culture and Society: A Text Reader*, edited by Kwesi Owusu, 117–128. New York: Routledge, 2005.

Morrow, Willie. *400 Years Without a Comb: The Untold Story*. San Diego: Black Publishers of San Diego, 1973.

Muholi, Zanele. *Zanele Muholi. Fotógrafas Africanas / African Women Photographers*. Madrid: La Fábrica, 2011.

Mussai, Renée Muholi and Zanele Muholi. *Zanele Muholi: Somnyama Ngonyama, Hail the Dark Lioness*. London: Autograph ABP, 2019.

Mutunhu, Sekai. Introduction to *Woodrow Nash, African Nouveau: A Collection of Sculptures and Vases*, 1–4. Madison: Creative Ceramics, 1997.

Naguib, Saphinaz-Amal. "Hair in Ancient Egypt." *Acta Orientalia* 51 (1990): 7–26.

National Gallery of Jamaica. *New Roots: 10 Emerging Artists, July 28–September 30, 2013*. Kingston: National Gallery of Jamaica, 2013.

Neil, Latisha, and Afiya M. Mbilishaka. "'Hey Curlfriends!': Hair Care and Self-Care Messaging on YouTube by Black Women Natural Hair Vloggers." *Journal of Black Studies* 50, no. 2 (March 2019): 156–177.

Nimocks, Joyce M. "The Natural Hair Movement as a Platform for Environmental Education," Thesis, Pomona College, 2015.

Norwood, Kimberly Jade. "'If You Is White, You's Alright. . . .' Stories About Colorism in America." *Washington University Global Studies Law Review* 14, no. 4 (2015): 584-607.

Opie, Tina R., and Katherine W. Phillips. "Hair Penalties: The Negative Influence of Afrocentric Hair on Ratings of Black Women's Dominance and Professionalism." *Frontiers in Psychology* 6 (August 31, 2015).

Omotoso, Sharon Adetutu. "Gender and Hair Politics: An African Philosophical Analysis." *Africology: The Journal of Pan African Studies* 12, no. 8 (December 2018): 5–19.

Patterson, Orlando. *Slavery and Social Death: A Comparative Study*. Cambridge: Harvard University Press, 1982.

Patton, Tracey Owens. "Hey Girl, Am I More than My Hair?: African American Women and Their Struggles with Beauty, Body Image, and Hair." *NWSA Journal* 18, no. 2 (2006): 24-51.

Phipps, Simone T. A. and Leon C. Prieto. "The Business of Black Beauty: Social Entrepreneurship or Social Injustice?" *Journal of Management History* 24, no. 1 (2018): 37–56.

Randle, Brenda A. "I Am Not My Hair: African American Women and Their Struggles with Embracing Natural Hair!" *Race, Gender & Class* 22, no. 1–2 (2015): 114–21.

Recent Histories: Contemporary African Photography and Video Art. Edited by Daniela Baumann and Oluremi Onabanjo. Neu-Ulm: Walther Collection, 2017.

Remington, Preston. "Jean-Baptiste Carpeaux." *The Metropolitan Museum of Art Bulletin* 21, no. 1 (1926): 8–10.

Reynolds, Gary A., Beryl J. Wright, and David C. Driskell. *Against the Odds: African-American Artists and the Harmon Foundation*. Newark: Newark Museum, 1989.

Riefstahl, Elizabeth. "An Ancient Egyptian Hairdresser." *Bulletin of the Brooklyn Museum* 13, no. 4 (1952): 7–16.

Riefstahl, Elizabeth. "Two Hairdressers of the Eleventh Dynasty", *Journal of Near Eastern Studies 15,* no. 1 (January 1956): 10–17.

Robins, Gay. "Hair and the Construction of Identity in Ancient Egypt, c. 1480–1350 B.C." *Journal of the American Research Center in Egypt* 36 (1999): 55–69.

Robinson, Cynthia L. "Hair as Race: Why 'Good Hair' May Be Bad for Black Females." *Howard Journal of Communications* 22, no. 4 (2011): 358–376.

Roethler, Jacque. "Reading in Color: Children's Book Illustrations and Identity Formation for Black Children in the United States." *African American Review* 32, no. 1 (1998): 95–105.

Rooks, Noliwe M. *Hair Raising: Beauty, Culture and African American Women*. New Brunswick: Rutgers University Press, 1996.

Rowell, Charles H. "An Interview with David C. Driskell." *Callaloo* 40, no. 5 (2017): 43–58.

Rowell, Charles H. "Sonia Clark." *Callaloo* 38, no. 4 (2015): 811–814.

Saitowitz, Sharma. "Towards a History of Glass Beads." In *Ezakwantu: Beadwork from the Eastern Cape*, edited by Emma Bedford, 35–45. Cape Town: South African National Gallery, 1993.

Schildkrout, Enid. "Les Parisiens d'Afrique: Mangbetu Women as Works of Art." In *Black Womanhood: Images, Icons, and Ideologies of the African* Body, edited by Barbara Thompson, 71–93. Hanover: Hood Museum of Art, Dartmouth College, 2008.

Shabazz, David. "Barbershops as Cultural Forums for African American Males." *Journal of Black Studies* 47, no. 4 (February 2016): 1–18.

Sheehan, Tanya. "Faith Ringgold: Forging Freedom and Declaring Independence." In *Declaration of Independence: Fifty Years of Art by Faith Ringgold,* 3–12. Rutgers: State University of New Jersey, 2009.

Sherrow, Victoria. *Encyclopedia of Hair: A Cultural History*. Westport: Greenwood Press, 2006.

Shimoyama, Devan, Jessica Beck, and Andy Warhol Museum. *Devan Shimoyama: Cry, Baby*. Pittsburgh: Andy Warhol Museum, 2018.

Sieber, Roy and Frank Herreman. "Hair in African Art and Culture." *African Arts* 33, no. 3 (Autumn 2000): 54–69, 96.

Silva, Bisi. *J. D. 'Okhai Ojeikere*. Lagos: Center for Contemporary Art, 2014.

Silva, Bisi and Abraaj Group. *Art Dubai 20–23.3.2013: In Partnership with The Abraaj Group*. Dubai: Art Dubai, 2013.

Sims, Lowery Stokes and National Gallery of Jamaica. *Curator's Eye I*. Kingston: National Gallery of Jamaica, 2004.

Smalls, James. "Sculpting African Nouveau: Primitivism, Ethnography, and Afro-Kitsch in the Works of Woodrow Nash." *The International Review of African American Art* 26, no 2 (2016): 28–43.

Snyder, Jeffrey B. *Printmakers Today*. Atglen, PA: Schiffer Pub, 2010.

Stevens, Ingrid, Anne Scheffer, and Amanda du Preez. "Hysterical Representation in the Art of Mary Sibande." *De Arte*, nos. 2-3 (2017): 4-28.

Stokes, Deborah. "Rediscovered Treasures: African Beadwork at the Field Museum, Chicago." *African Arts* 32, no. 3 (1999): 18-91.

Stange, Maren. *Bare Witness: Photographs by Gordon Parks.* Milan: Skira/Stanford University, 2006.

Tassie, Geoffrey John. *The Social and Ritual Contextualization of Ancient Egyptian Hair and Hairstyles from the Protodynastic to the End of the Old Kingdom.* London: Institute of Archaeology, University College. 2008.

Thomas, Tiffany. "'Hair' They Are: The Ideologies of Black Hair," *The York Review* 9, no. 1 (Spring 2013): 1-10.

Thompson, Cheryl. "Black Women, Beauty, and Hair as a Matter of *Being*." *Women's Studies* 38, no. 8 (2009): 831-856.

Thompson, Cheryl. "Black Women and Identity: What's Hair Got to Do with It?" *Michigan Feminist Studies* 22, no. 1 (Fall 2008-2009): 78-89.

Tsai, Eugenie, ed. *Kehinde Wiley: A New Republic*. Brooklyn Museum in association with DelMonico Books & Prestel, 2015.

Underwood, Joseph. *The View From Here: Contemporary Perspectives From Senegal.* Kent: Kent State University School of Art Collection & Galleries, 2018.

Underwood, Joseph. "ar•chi•pel•a•go: Trends in Contemporary Art from Africa and its Diaspora." In *Visual Arts of Africa: Gender, Power, and Life Cycle Rituals*, edited by Judith Perani and Fred Smith. London: Oxford University Press, 2021.

Versey, Shellae H. "Centering Perspectives on Black Women, Hair Politics, and Physical Activity." *American Journal of Public Health* 104, no. 5 (May 2014): 810-815.

Walker, Susannah. "Black Is Profitable: The Commodification of the Afro, 1960-1975." *Enterprise & Society* 1, no. 3 (2000): 536-564.

Walton, Nikki, and Ernessa T. Carter. *Better Than Good Hair: The Curly Girl Guide to Healthy, Gorgeous Natural Hair.* New York: Harper Collins, 2013.

White, Shauntae Brown. "Releasing the Pursuit of Bouncin' and Behavin' Hair: Natural Hair as An Afrocentric Feminist Aesthetic for Beauty." *International Journal of Media and Cultural Politics* 1, no. 3 (2005): 295-308.

Wilson, Ingrid-Penelope, Afiya M. Mbilishaka, and Marva L. Lewis. "'White Folks Ain't Got Hair like Us': African American Mother-Daughter Hair Stories and Racial Socialization." *Women, Gender, and Families of Color* 6, no. 2 (2018): 226-48.

Winfield-Thomas, Evelyn B. and Arthur L. Whaley. "Hair Stress: Physical and Mental Health Correlates of African American Women's Hair Care Practices." In *Women and Inequality in the 21st Century*, edited by Brittany C. Slatton and Carla D. Brailey, 159-176. New York: Routledge, 2019.

Wingfield, Adia Harvey. *Doing Business with Beauty: Black Women, Hair Salons, and the Racial Enclave Economy.* Lanham: Rowman & Littlefield, 2009.

Wright, George C. "Harlem Renaissance: Art of Black America." *The Journal of American History* 77, no. 1 (1990): 253-61.

Young, Allison K. and the New Orleans Museum of Art. *Lina Iris Viktor: A Haven, a Hell, a Dream Deferred*. Milano: Skira, 2019.

INDEX

IMPRINT

This book is published on the occasion of the exhibition **TEXTURES: THE HISTORY AND ART OF BLACK HAIR.**

Kent State University Museum
Kent, Ohio, USA
September 10, 2021 – August 14, 2022

EXHIBITION

CURATORS
Dr. Tameka N. Ellington
Dr. Joseph L. Underwood

EXHIBITION DESIGN
James Williams

COLLECTIONS MANAGER
Joanne Fenn

CURATORIAL ASSISTANTS
Sarah Hagglund, Maria Kuhn, Mark Libbey, Brianna Robinson, Christina Timmons, and Marissa Tiroly

BRAND DESIGN
Marshall Shorts, Artfluential

CATALOGUE

Published by
Hirmer Publishers
Bayerstraße 57-59
80335 Munich
Germany
www.hirmerpublishers.com

EDITORS
Joseph L. Underwood
and Tameka N. Ellington

COPYEDITING AND PROOF READING
Malcolm Imrie

DESIGN
Sophie Friederich

PROJECT MANAGER AT HIRMER PUBLISHERS
Rainer Arnold

SENIOR EDITOR AT HIRMER PUBLISHERS
Elisabeth Rochau-Shalem

LITHOGRAPHY AND PRE-PRESS
Reproline Mediateam, Unterföhring

PRINTING AND BINDING
Printer Trento s.r.l.

PAPER
Gardamatt Art 150 g/m2

Printed in Italy

COVER FRONT:
Chatmon, Tawny
Heir / A Present of God, 2017
(see p. 169)

COVER BACK:
Esiebo, Andrew
Detail of *Nuance Mali* from the *Pride* series, 2012
(see p. 79)

ISBN 978-3-7774-3554-1

KENT STATE UNIVERSITY MUSEUM

DIRECTOR
Sarah J. Rogers

CURATOR
Sara Hume

EXHIBITION DESIGNER AND PREPARATOR
James Williams

COLLECTIONS MANAGER
Joanne Fenn

SECURITY SUPERVISOR
John Puntel

ADMINISTRATIVE ASSISTANT
Bianka Hausknecht

Kent State University Museum
515 Hilltop
Kent, Ohio. 44242
www.kent.edu/museum
@ksumuseum

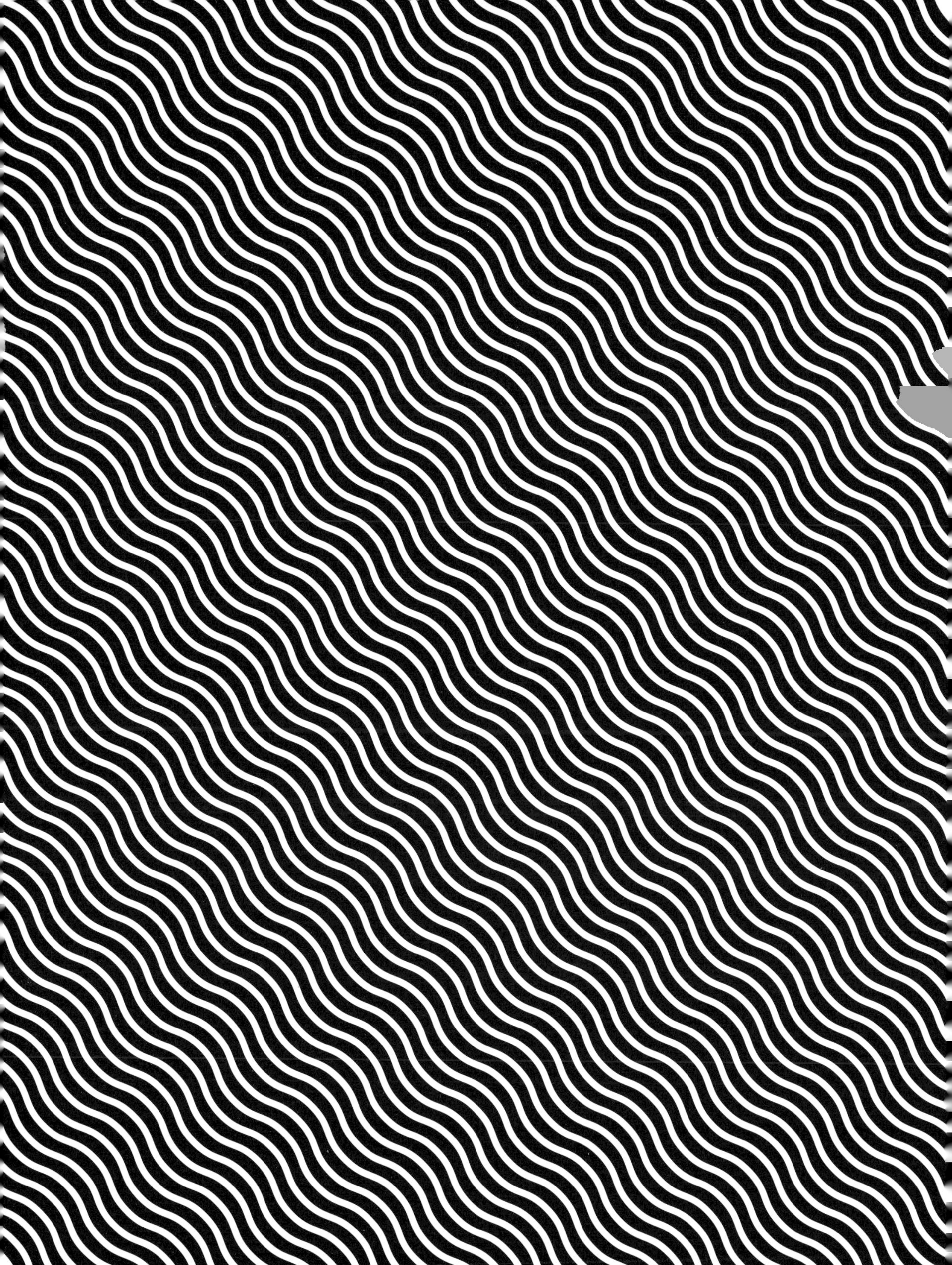

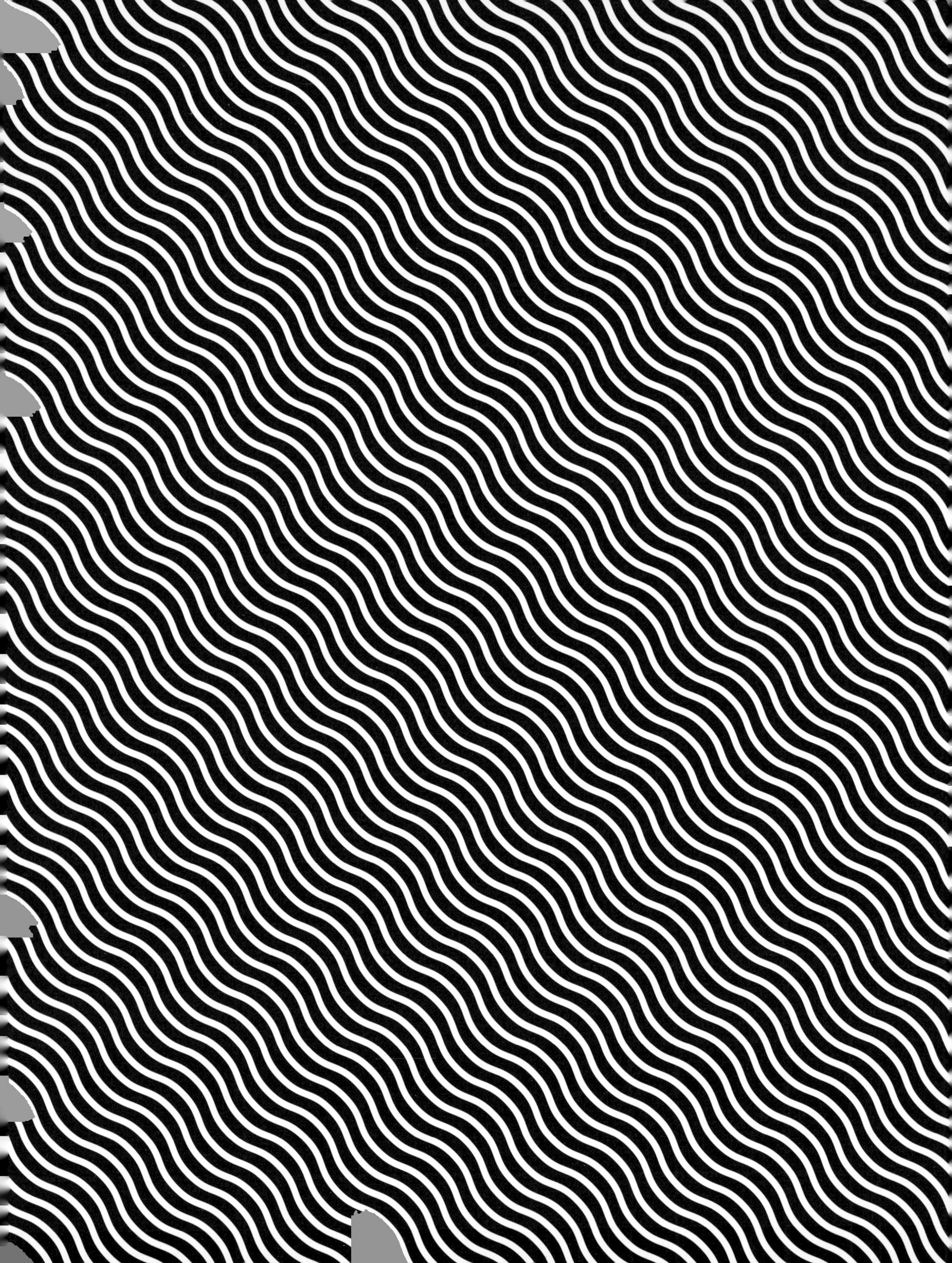